THE VIETNAM READER

THE VIETNAM READER

EDITED BY
WALTER CAPPS

ROUTLEDGE □ NEW YORK   LONDON

Published in 1991 by

Routledge
An imprint of Routledge, Chapman and Hall, Inc.
29 West 35 Street
New York, NY 10001

Published in Great Britain by

Routledge
11 New Fetter Lane
London EC4P 4EE

Library of Congress Cataloging in Publication Data

A Vietnam reader / Walter Capps.
    p. cm.
    Includes index.
    ISBN 0-415-90126-X.   ISBN 0-415-90127-8 (pbk.)
    1. Vietnamese Conflict, 1961–1975.   I. Capps, Walter H.
DS557.7.V5625   1991
959.704′3—dc20   91-23033
                                                    CIP

British Library Cataloguing in Publication also available.

for Don and Marilyn Gevirtz,
with affection and gratitude,
for bringing out the best in us

Table of Contents

Introduction   1

I. The Warrior's Testimony

  1. To Care Without Judging
    Davidson Loehr   15

  2. To Vietnam and Back
    Paul Sgroi   26

  3. It Don't Mean Nothin': The Vietnam Experience
    William P. Mahedy   33

  4. Living in Moral Pain
    Peter Marin   40

  5. Home From the War: The Psychology of Survival
    Robert Jay Lifton   54

  6. Why Men Love War
    William Broyles, Jr.   68

  7. The Vietnam War and the Erosion of
    Male Confidence
    Robert Bly   82

  8. The War That Won't End
    Frances FitzGerald   87

II. Lessons from the War

  9. What Are the Lessons of Vietnam?
    David Fromkin and James Chace   91

  10. Historiography: Vietnam Reconsidered
    Robert A. Divine   100

  11. Vietnam in Perspective
    William C. Westmoreland   116

12. An Interview with General Giap
    Stanley Karnow   125

13. The Legitimacy of the War
    Michael Walzer   136

14. Why We Did What We Did
    Clark Clifford   145

15.. Statement before the Senate Foreign Affairs
     Committee
     John Forbes Kerry   152

16. The Achievements of the War-protest Movement
    Todd Gitlin   157

17. After the War: The Emergence of Nihilism
    W. Richard Comstock   168

III. Diversities of Experience

18. Black Soldiers' Perspectives on the War
    Gerald Gill   173

19. Chicanos and Vietnam
    Douglas Martinez and Manuel Gomez   186

20. American Indian Veterans and the Vietnam War
    Thomas M. Holm   191

21. Life, Liberty, and the Right to Protest
    James Quay   205

22. What Did You Do in the Class War, Daddy?
    James Fallows   213

23. A Nurse's View
    Rose Sandecki   222

24. The Role of the Press
    Paul Dean   230

25. The Story of a Vietnamese Refugee in America
    Hien Duc Do   235

26. A World Turned Upside Down
    Le Ly Hayslip   240

IV. Symbolic Expressions, Ritual Healing

27. Remembering the Sacrifice
    Theodore H. Evans   249

28. Pilgrimage to the Wall
    John K. Simmons   253

29. The Father I Hardly Knew
    Roger Worthington   259

30. In Tribute to Bill
    Eleanor Wimbish   265

31. Reunion
    Wilson Hubbell   270

32. The Memorial as Symbol and Agent of Healing
    Lisa M. Capps   272

33. The Road to Hill 10
    William Broyles, Jr.   290

34. Marching Along Together at Last
    William P. Mahedy   301

35. Vietnam: My Enemy, My Brother
    Frederick Downs, Jr.   307

36. On Remembering the Vietnam War
    J. Robert Kerrey   313

Postscript   317

Introduction
Walter H. Capps

I once asked Senator Bob Kerrey of Nebraska if he could explain why there was much more discussion about the Vietnam War ten years after it ended then there had been during the first months and years following the fall of Saigon. He responded by citing an observation that the writer Elie Wiesel had made about the penetrating impact of the Holocaust: "when an event is unspeakable," he said, "it takes some time to learn the right words."

This is the way it has been with the Vietnam War. It has been with us so long, after occupying more years (from 1964 to 1975) than any in which the United States has been directly involved, that President George Bush even formally proposed that we end it, if not by proclamation then, perhaps, by earnest pleading. On January 20, 1989, in his Inaugural Address to the nation, President Bush inserted the following observation into his hopes for a "gentler, kinder America." "We need harmony," the President asserted. "We have a chorus of discordant voices. There's grown a certain divisiveness. We've seen the hard looks and heard the statements in which not only each other's ideas are challenged, but each other's motives . . ." Then, referring directly and unambiguously to the Vietnam War and its continuing impact on our collective consciousness, the President continued. "It's been this way since Vietnam," he observed. "That war cleaves us still." This was followed by the fervent request: "But, friends, that war began in earnest a quarter of a century ago. Surely the statute of limitations has been reached." And to make his point with even greater force and surer clarity, Bush proceeded to offer his considered summary generalization on the long-term meaning of the war. "This is a fact," he said, that "the final lesson of Vietnam is that no great nation can long afford to be sundered by a memory." And from this he returned to the overarching theme for his first address as President: "a new breeze is blowing . . ."

Sundered by a memory? Indeed, this is an accurate depiction of the post-Vietnam War mood of the nation. To be sure, the experience of the war was a profoundly negative experience for the American people, the most divisive event since the Civil War in our little more than two hundred year history. It was a negative experience for the nation, and a confusing and debilitating experience for many—perhaps the majority—of persons who were directly involved in the military undertaking. There can be no properly thorough acknowledgment of the pain, suffering, and heartache that the prolonged agony of the war created for millions of American citizens, not to mention its devastating effect on our national resolve and its keen ability to skew and scramble previously assumed bases of collective identity. More than 58,000 Americans died as a direct result of the military hostilities. Hundreds of thousands more were wounded. Approximately twenty percent of those who served have experienced deep and persistent emotional distress and psychological trauma. More than twice the number of those who lost lives there have taken their own lives since returning home. Huge percentages of America's homeless are veterans of the war. And when the Vietnamese people are included in these demographics, the statistics are even more alarming. Approximately 2 million Indochinese lost their lives from 1961 to 1975, and millions more were victims from the carnage that followed, principally, in Cambodia. The more we learn about the war, the heavier the burden becomes. Thus, the full impact of the pervasive physical, psychological, and moral devastation cannot be brought to cessation even by presidential declaration, no matter how timely, no matter how sincere, no matter how well intended. The enduring agony of the war experience will not go away simply because the leadership of the nation recognizes that it has been with us for a long, long time, and continues to have a manifestly preoccupying effect on our sense of who we are and how we should be exercising our place and purpose in the world.

Rather, the discussion continues, and the ambivalence haunts us, because the meaning of the event remains elusive. The conversation proceeds because the elongated and durable episode has more to teach us than has been learned so far. In truth, confusing, debilitating and divisive war experience cannot be understood or explained until we are confident that we know why it occurred, why it proved so stubbornly problematic for us, why it was so persistently difficult to dispose of even after the military hostilities ceased and the troops returned home, and why it continues to stand as the most significant historical event for millions of human beings whose lives were shaped by it and whose identities as Americans are reflected in it. The conversation—and accompanying confusion, consternation, and lack of clarity—continues on because there is much more in the event than can be reduced to any clear and simple explanation. There is simply no way to deal with the subject in quick, finished fashion, to dispose of it by reducing it to a clearly stated formula, for the mechanisms of closure are not yet present to surround it. Nor has it been possible for us to call "time out" or "recess," or to boldly sound the final buzzer to signal that no more time or attention can be obligated to it. On the contrary, the Vietnam War remains an unfinished war. We continue to remain troubled by it. We continue to be challenged by it.

The Vietnam Reader presents thoughtful, provocative responses to the war by writers who have tried to make the event intelligible and/or who have probed meaningful ways in which human beings might relate or respond to it. The essays in this collection vividly testify to the subject's unfinished character. But they also stand as testimony to the truth that a sundering memory can also be a teaching memory, that an event that "cleaves us still" can become an instrument through which we may learn profoundly, and that a devastating national tragedy can bring some of the essential ingredients of wisdom into closer reach. Because the event is unfinished, its permanent meaning lies, in large part, in what is made of it. And since the ingredients of closure are not yet apparent, the subject itself retains sufficient fluidity and malleability to carry some of the influences and repercussions that can be desired for it. In this respect, a new breeze can blow when the ramifications of a sundering memory are translated into a constructive key.

The essays included in this anthology are arranged according to four sub-headings. The first group focuses on veterans' testimony both during and following the war. Placed here are narrative accounts of what it was like to have gone through the war, and, in most instances, to have come home to something much less than a joyous welcome. Here too are the clinical descriptions of post-traumatic stress disorder, alongside fuller, more comprehensive psychological (and psychosocial) interpretations of how human beings face and respond to the activities required in war. Thus, this section of the anthology also contains essays on critical moral dimensions of the subject, as well as on motivating factors. William Broyles inquires as to "why men love war," and presents a captivating portrayal of how the human psyche responds to the excitement of prolonged high-risk adventure. Peter Marin raises probing philosophical questions about guilt, remorse, and what he prefers to call "moral pain," and places the war experience against a more comprehensive theoretical background within which there exists an ongoing intention to make such subjects intelligible. William Mahedy, who has been both chaplain and counselor to veterans, reflects on the meaning of the loss of meaning that many warriors experienced when they were no longer certain of the authority of proposed motivational factors. Robert Jay Lifton, a psychiatrist, outlines some of the terminology and interpretive categories that have been employed to approach the veterans' experiences. Frances FitzGerald, whose 1972 book *Fire in the Lake* explored the cultural dynamics of the situation in Vietnam, offers a brief comment on the veterans' penchant to write and tell "war stories." Two vets, Paul Sgroi and Davidson Loehr, provide compelling autobiographical accounts of what is required to wrestle with alternative and conflicting efforts to lend meaning to the event. And Robert Bly, a celebrated American poet, raises thoughtful questions about what the war experience did to "male confidence." In this respect, Bly is thinking not only of how male-warriors are effected by participating in a prolonged but failed military venture; he is also concerned about what happens to men psychologically when they exercise instinctive aggressive capacities to avoid confrontations through which, in previous sets of circumstances, they were expected to prove their manhood. Taken together, these essays summarize much that is already known on the subject while probing some areas that deserve further analysis. They tell us who the American veteran of the Vietnam War really is, and describe the motivational base from which this veteran influences the post-Vietnam War society.

The second section of the anthology concentrates on policy issues. The essays included here are directed toward understanding the larger meaning of the war, not simply from the perspectives of those who experienced it firsthand, but with references to our national life. Here we raise questions about lessons that were learned. With a nation so split over what was right and wrong (whether the war itself should have ended earlier, whether it should have been waged at all, whether it should have been brought to swift but dramatic conclusion, *et al.*), it is extremely difficult to achieve national consensus at any point. There were serious disagreements about the propriety of the war as it was being waged; there continue to be serious disagreements about the propriety of the war now that we can look back and assess it. Robert Divine surveys prominent interpretations and assessments of the event, identifies the dominant schools of interpretation, discusses the viewpoints they share as well as their major disagreements, and marks out some of the directions in which contemporary scholarship on the subject seem to be pointing, insisting all the while that this extended interpretive process is far from being finished. David Fromkin and James Chace survey the most frequently cited "lessons" of the war, try to distinguish the ones that seem most worthy of consideration, then ask whether we can be any clearer about that meaning now than we were when the event itself was occurring. Clark Clifford's testimony on the subject was offered to a special congressional hearing ten years after the fall of Saigon. General William C. Westmoreland, who was in command of U.S. military forces, also wonders what went wrong, who is to blame, why the fighting was made so difficult, and how such mistakes might have been avoided. During those war years, Westmoreland was plotting strategy against Ho Chi Minh's chief military strategist, General Vo Nguyen Giap. Thanks to a perceptive 1990 interview by Stanley Karnow, General Giap's views on the dynamics of the war are also available. Heretofore, there has been considerable guesswork on the part of Americans as to the way the war effort was envisioned and directed from "the other side." General Giap's responses to Karnow's questions fill in many missing blanks. Senator John Kerry (who fought in Vietnam) spells out the lessons of the war, as he learned them, in testimony (before he was elected Senator) to the Senate Foreign Affairs Committee. Todd Gitlin, who was instrumental in both the free-speech and the war-protest movements, draws lessons from these vantage points. Michael Walzer, a highly respected political philosopher, looks to the history of warfare for some appropriate rationale that may or may not apply to the U.S. involvement in Indochina. W. Richard Comstock considers the possibility that the Vietnam War contributed to a pervasive shift in worldview; he proposes that it stimulated a nihilistic attitude as well as atomistic social structures, and wonders how the debilitating implications of these related consequences will be assimilated or counteracted.

The third section of the book reflects diversities of experience. Here the intention is to illustrate that the war experience can be particularized beyond what individuals and the nation itself experienced. Much of the "dirty work" of the war, for example, was assigned to military units whose membership was selected primarily from minority populations. Combat fatality rates were much higher among such populations as were day-to-day degrees of risk. In addition, some American military units remained mostly racially segregated in Vietnam, while attempts were made, in some instances, to have minority and non-minority warriors fighting side by side. The matter is complicated by the fact that the Americans who served in Vietnam were understood to be allies of the South Vietnamese ARVN troops. But much of the time, such allegiances were more theoretical than emotional: American military personnel were often critical of both the technical skill and the individual dedication of ARVN soldiers. Then, there were native American combatants in Vietnam for whom the assumption of a warrior's role carried deep cultural and spiritual implications. Traditional native American mythology understands that becoming a warrior is a fundamental ingredient in the set of ritual acts by which one registers one's claim to manhood. But how are such claims to be registered when warriorship is being exercised on behalf of a white, Anglo population against a people with which the native American warriors feels some intrinsic and instinctive identification? Numerous native American warriors wondered if they were fighting for the right side, fearful that they have become unwitting instruments and agents of a military effort not unlike those by which their own people have been exploited and ravaged numerous times before. All of these examples simply illustrate that the racial tensions that characterized our national life in the 1960s and 1970s were also descriptive of relationships within military units fighting in Vietnam. And the fact that the fighting itself was occurring in Indochina, that is, on the mainland of Asia, only made those tensions the more complex.

We have included testimony within this section that reflects such diversity of experience. Gerald Gill summarizes elements of perspectives on the war that developed among American warriors. Douglas Martinez and Manuel Gomez write of the situation within the Chicano community. Thomas Holm, a political scientist, is involved in detailed study of how native Americans fared, both in Vietnam and subsequently. Rose Sandecki reflects the experience of women who served in Vietnam as Army nurses. Then we have included a series of parent-child conversations. James Fallows looks back on his successful effort to avoid the draft; being a white male who was attending Harvard University, he had been taught effective ways to fail the military admissions requirements, while those from lower economic classes, with less formal education, and representing minority populations, were quickly and rather routinely inducted. Fallows now wonders how he can explain this action to his children. James Quay, who was a conscientious objector during the war, and is currently a national public humanities leader, offers insight into the anti-war position he took during the Vietnam Era, and proposes that the fundamental dissatisfaction with the event stands in support of the compulsion to break the cycle of war. For Quay, it is not only the Vietnam War that is wrong, but war itself is no longer a viable option in a world like ours. Paul Dean, who viewed the war up-close as a reporter, describes the role of the press in alerting readers and viewers to the reality of this war and to the incomparable nature of war itself.

Until now the literature on the subject has been dominated by descriptions and analyses of what happened to Americans who served

in Vietnam. The subject that has received far too little attention concerns the experiences of Vietnamese people, in whose land the war
was fought. We have included two portrayals that touch on this subject. Hien Duc Do and Le Ly Hayslip recall what is was like to have
been born and raised in Vietnam, to have experienced the war there,
and then to have come to live in the United States, not, of course, as
immigrants, but as refugees.

In the fourth and final section of the anthology we have placed
essays that focus on ritual acts of healing. We refer to the specific
responses and reactions—the commemorative and ceremonial acts—
that have assisted individuals and the nation to come to terms with
the event. We recognize that responses to the war involve highly
symbolic expressions, which, at times, are manifestly ritualistic. Theoretical understanding and conceptual formulation are not sufficient.
Rather, participants have been prompted to write, to perform, and to
create some things, and even to travel to some places and pilgrimage
sites in order to exercise the ritual activity that is enjoined by what
they have learned about themselves and the world in which they live.
"When an event is unspeakable, it takes some time to learn the right
words." Words, yes, but it is also a matter of learning other processes
and pathways by which meaning can be discovered and significance
can be attributed. All such efforts require the interpreter to invoke
symbolic dimensions of human behavior. Thus, one finds former warriors seeking courage to march down the main streets of their communities in parades on patriotic holidays. One finds them wanting to
establish sacred memorials and monuments, dedicated to the memories of those among their number who did not return from the battlefield. One finds them journeying to pilgrimage locations, sometimes
alone, sometimes together, to explore previously unexplored dimensions of their experience. Such ritual action is dictated by the emotional texture of the event.

Included in this section of the anthology are three essays focusing on
the symbolic power of the Vietnam Veterans Memorial in Washington,
D.C. John Simmons, who was a conscientious objector during the war,
tells of making a pilgrimage to the Memorial in the company of several
returning combat veterans, none of whom had ever been there before.
Theodore Evans remembers the sacrifice of those who have given their
lives for the country. Lisa Capps writes of the extraordinary capacity
of the Memorial to serve as an effective symbol, not only as commemoration of the lives of those whose names are listed on the two black
granite slabs but also as the primary emotional vehicle for the nation's
response to the war. Wilson Hubbell recounts a chance encounter

with a brother-veteran at that same Memorial. Eleanor Wimbish reflects the sorrows of a mother's heart through letters she left at the Memorial for a son whose name is inscribed there.

The fourth section of the anthology also contains several essays that describe what Vietnam War veterans have done, and where they have traveled, to encourage healing to occur. William Broyles, author of "Why Men Love War," describes a journey he made back to Vietnam to reacquaint himself with scenes of battle that he left approximately twenty years ago. William Mahedy, in his second essay in this anthology, anticipates a pilgrimage that several American veterans of the war made to the Soviet Union to meet with Soviet veterans of the war in Afghanistan. Frederick Downs writes of the situation of making friends with warriors whom one once treated as the bitterest of enemies. Broyles's, Mahedy's, and Downs's essays illustrate dramatically that American vets have been willing to travel in both directions—both back to the scene of former battles and into the arena of real or perceived ideological conflict—in order to bring about reconciliation with those who were or are enemies and adversaries. Downs attests that wars do not end until the warrior is able to embrace the enemy. Appropriately, in the closing essay of the collection, Senator Bob Kerrey reflects on some of the positive and constructive aspects of the necessary and deliberate act of remembering the war.

To what does it all add up? The editor's easy answer to this question is that the essays stand on their own and have the ability to speak for themselves. It would violate their integrity to preview any conclusions before the interpretive process is given opportunity to chart its own course and readers have opportunity to come to their own considered judgments.

Nevertheless, there are some insights and observations that stand out clearly. The first is that the Vietnam War is so full of implication and rich with suggestion that it resists reduction to a single lesson, a single moral, or a single meaning. For all of the valid lessons that have already been drawn, and for all of the meaning that is being uncovered and proposed at the present time, the complicated war event continues to invite analysis and interpretation, no single example of which stands as the definitive statement or "last word" on the subject. The intellectual challenges that are embodied in the essays presented here can be counted upon to sustain interest for some time to come. Thus, in spite of the years of attention that have already been devoted to it, the subject is stubbornly resistant to satisfactory and comprehensive clarification. Wars can be more easily explained when the fighting is for an accepted purpose, and when the outcome of the military action is consonant with that purpose. When these elements are in place, we speak positively of successful outcomes: heroic deeds, correct strategy, appropriate consequences, righteous causes, and we praise warriors as necessary keepers of the boundaries. However, in the case of the Vietnam War, so many of these expectations were inverted, skewed, or made otherwise ambiguous and ambivalent that the implications are difficult to assess. So, too, is the fundamental point that was intended along the way. Differences between right and wrong were not always clear-cut. Distinctions between "good guys" and "bad guys" could not always be fixed with confidence. And the identification of whatever "noble cause" wars wish to claim for themselves could not be rendered with any assurance. Thus, since the war effort was not undergirded by any clear, shared moral consensus, so too it is impossible to appeal to any comprehensively acknowledged criteria to judge whether the objectives were met. If mistakes were made— and surely they were—it is not as easy as one might expect to pinpoint responsibility for them precisely, for even the line between failed strategy and misguided intention cannot be drawn with certainty. This is not to suggest that the opportunities for heroism were absent, or that the warriors themselves did not experience all of the elements of traditional warfare in their fullest intensity and authenticity. The point is simply that it remains difficult to write whatever overarching thesis about the subject is most appropriate. It is also impossible to file the incident away, as if all that is required now is to mark the event, learn, teach, and remember its lesson, and then continue on with whatever belongs next in the sequence.

The truth is that the Vietnam War will forever stand as a compelling morality play—a morality play belonging to the genre of tragedy. But who was the hero and who was the villain? Who is the protagonist, and who is the play's tragic figure? What lessons did the participants learn? What insights could the leadership draw in addition to being startled that the narrative they thought they had scripted did not stay within the bounds they thought they could assign to it? Francis FitzGerald has observed that the Vietnam War resists being "elevated to a mythic plane" or being "relegated to the cold storage of history." We have called it an unfinished war.

A second observation is that the truths the experience taught are much more fundamental than might have been expected. All wars are about the conditions under which it is appropriate to take life and give life, about situations under which it is appropriate to offer one's life as a sacrifice for a worthy cause or intention, and about the bonding that occurs between individuals who experience these realizations together and are made responsible for each other's fate. But most wars are clearly and deliberately about more particular concrete matters having to do with how specific disputes and disagreements between enemies or adversaries are to be resolved. In the Vietnam War, the American leadership saw the battle as the embodiment and focal point of the ongoing Cold War conflict between the two major competing world-systems—a conflict that was being fueled by diametrically opposite competing ideologies. Thus, the war, like all wars, was understood to be about contested territory: one group claimed that the other group had wrongfully sequestered territory, and was preparing to move from this position to seize even more territory illegitimately. The group registering this claim against the other was compelled to stop the sequestering action before any more momentum was gained. So it stepped in to quash the effort by interrupting the flow of arms into the region and by shoring up the local resisting government. The fundamental objective, as seen by the American side, was to prevent the errant (i.e., Communist) ideology from extending its influence further, blanketing even more territory, staking its claim over the rapidly diminishing and dwindling additional spaces on the globe.

The most compelling lessons the returning warriors brought back, however, pertained only secondarily to the official reasons and stated governmental warrants for the war. Indeed, they were directed much more to fundamental human philosophical concerns than to military competition between adversaries. Certainly at one level the Vietnam War was about American foreign policy and military strategy. Yes, the Vietnam War was also a key item in the continuing conflict and contest between competing worldviews. But, at a more basic moral and spiritual level, the Vietnam War became an eloquent, vivid text on how human beings are constituted, how human beings both respect and abuse life, how human beings set and modify priorities, and how human beings employ incentives to assist them in pursuing what they deem to be important.

When asked the meaning of the war, returning warriors offer commentaries that go far beyond mere descriptions of the particularities of the situation. Rather, they find themselves addressing subjects of a convictional status—subjects for which they were frequently ill-equipped in terms of formal educational training, but subjects whose inevitability they were compelled to confirm by virtue of the fact that they had been forced to address such matters via their own not always willful experience. That is, frequently without benefit of a cultivated and polished vocabulary, they speak philosophically. They tell about the insights they have acquired. They invoke the comprehensive moral issues. They testify to ways in which the war experience has effected their personal lives. "The political lessons learned from Vietnam are less important to me than the simple observations of those who fought there," Senator Kerrey has written. The war raised larger, more pervasive, and more fundamental moral, philosophical, and spiritual issues than the military events in and of themselves could resolve or clarify. This, of course, is another reason why the Vietnam War functions so effectively as an impetus to teaching. It possesses powerful pedagogical ingredients. It contains and exhibits indispensable lessons.

Thus, thirdly, if the war is the object and occasion for serious moral inquiry and acknowledged spiritual involvement, it is apparent that the wide range of human sensibilities are involved, and not only mental reasoning powers. "It is important to learn the right words," but these words are not only words of diplomacy, military strategy, and foreign policy. In addition, they implicate a vocabulary that belongs to therapeutic sciences, that probes the religious traditions for models and instruments of healing, and that attempts access to the experience, as veterans report, of "being scarred in the very deepest place." From the testimony we have offered, it is evident that the war experience is both psychological experience and religious experience. For, if the war became the context in which human life was experienced in its depth, vividness, and intensity, no one could participate in the event without confronting and engaging significant self-disclosures. No one back home—waiting for a son, husband, father, uncle, aunt, sister, brother, or friend to return from battle—could long endure such vicissitudes of soul without developing increased sensitivity concerning which causes are truly worth pursuing and which objectives ought to be accorded a lesser priority. When Eleanor Wimbish (whose son was killed in Vietnam) was asked about the meaning of the event, she spoke quietly of "the sacredness of every moment." Not all who have been deeply implicated phrase their responses in quite these words, but the fragility and miracle of life are frequently prominent foci in their evaluation and interpretation.

When the United States ended its military involvement in 1975, it took some time to learn the right psychological words, that is, to develop the vocabulary of delayed-stress disorders, and to identify some measures and mechanisms of effective treatment. But it has taken even longer to discover the appropriate religious concomitants and attach the right words to them. We have practice talking about wars religiously when war is an acknowledged just cause and when we have little difficulty associating God with this cause. Then we can sing the hymns that praise the union of God and country, piety and patriotism. But when those supporting conditions are lacking, the songs are more difficult to sing, let alone to identify, and the word "God" becomes problematic for us, alongside all those doctrinal schemes that presume that God and country have joined forces. It has taken some time to uncover a theology, if there is one, that applies to the "dark night of the soul," that is, to the situation within which personal experience has been so raw and debilitating that persons wonder if they'll ever be able to affirm anything again. This, for many, is what Vietnam means. This, for many, is what Vietnam will always mean.

The fourth observation is that the interpretive process still has some distance to go before it reaches closure. Indeed, the interpretation is unfinished because the event itself is unfinished. And, since the event is unfinished, and looks for completion and closure in how it is received and in the work that it inspires, the very acts of recollection, analysis, and interpretation can function as instruments through which the ingredients of completion and closure are placed within closer reach. And, since the war remains present to memory, it is available too to the constructive intelligence. Yes, it is there to be interpreted in such a way that it can be finished.

"My deepest thanks for your acknowledgments that Vietnam is not over, although some people say it is," said Oliver Stone after receiving the Best Director Academy Award in 1989 for his work on the film *Born on the Fourth of July*. Stone added, "Vietnam is a state of mind that continues all over the world."

"With charity for all, with firmness in the right as God gives us to see the right, let us finish the work we are in," President Abraham Lincoln enjoined, in 1855 in his Second Inaugural Address, referring to the devastations of the Civil War. The essays included in this anthology stand as witness to the fact that a similar reconstructive effort is at work within the society today, and, before it is finished, carries an ability to transform virtually everything that it touches.

I

THE WARRIOR'S
Testimony

1

To Care without Judging
Davidson Loehr

The Vietnam War is usually spoken of in that way—as "The Vietnam War." An entity, a thing, a single, massive phenomenon that stretched from perhaps 1954 to 1974, a beast which did no good but much harm, a debacle without redeeming value.

Or it is seen as a military fiasco, or a colonial endeavor, or a bad political dream.

Each of these views has in common the habit of viewing a twenty-one-year period which involved millions of people as though it were a single, monolithic thing. While political, military, and sociological analyses may demand that sort of reduction, the approach has at least one very unfortunate side effect—it promotes a sense of collective blame and guilt, tainting all alike who were involved in Vietnam, for whatever reasons. The war was bad, people who do bad things share the bad, and that's that.

The main point I hope to make you feel from this article is that that is *not* that. The different reductionisms which alone have created the illusion of unity have omitted at least one major dimension of that tragic era—the personal experiences of millions of individuals who lived through, not "The Vietnam War," but millions of wars, each one personal and each one different.

Davidson Loehr served in Vietnam for a year, then enrolled in the University of Michigan, where he earned a baccalaureate degree, before being admitted to the doctoral program in the Divinity School at the University of Chicago. This autobiographical statement was expressed first as a talk that Loehr gave to his fellow students at the University of Chicago, and then was published in *The University of Chicago Magazine*, in its Spring 1985 issue (pp. 28–33, 49). It is included in this anthology not only for its intrinsic power but to illustrate the point that there are varieties of ways of lending meaning to and finding meaning to an event. Loehr believes that it is virtually impossible to understand from the outside what veterans of the Vietnam War experience. Yet this statement of his creates resilient possibilities for outsiders to understand that they cannot fully understand, which, paradoxically, is the beginning of real understanding.

The historian Fernand Braudel has written that "no two men ever died for the same country." In much the same way, no two people ever experienced the same war.

Many of the veterans of that era are still having a very hard time shedding the role of scapegoat, in addition to whatever else from their years in Vietnam that may be giving them a hard time. And our society—perhaps especially the liberal sectors of it—has often cast them in that role. We can only create scapegoats, however, if we're very sure of what is right and wrong, and know a simple and sure way to tell which side we are on, and which side *they* are on.

I want you to be less sure. I want you to be so confused over what and who were right and wrong that you will have to suspend judgment— judgment which I have seen exclude and condemn a lot of human beings who were participants rather than spectators in the complex and regrettable era we call "The Vietnam War." And so I will try to speak of these things that are so hard to wrap words around.

And yet this is a hard thing to talk or write about, and I want to offer what may seem like a very strange analogy to illustrate how I feel about sharing these long-guarded memories. The analogy comes from a movie called *The Sandpiper*, made about twenty years ago. It stars Richard Burton as the very proper headmaster of an exclusive Episcopal boys' school, Eva Marie Saint as his saintly wife, and Elizabeth Taylor as Elizabeth Taylor. Burton and Taylor have an illicit affair, and Burton eventually tries to regain his sense of integrity by telling his wife of it. She leaves him. The he goes to see Liz Taylor, and tells her he has told his wife of their affair. Taylor is furious. "How could you! How could you tell her? It was too *private!*"

And that is how I feel about my experiences in Vietnam, that they too were an illicit affair, and that it too may be far too private to be sharing.

So I begin with an apology to the other Vietnam veterans reading this. I cannot do justice to your versions of the Vietnam era, and I hope that I will not, by talking about it, profane something which was—at least for me—in an illicit and dark way, sacred. . . .

I served in Vietnam from July 1966 to August 1967 as an army lieutenant. I had graduated from Artillery Officer Candidate School nine months earlier, and had been sent over to be a forward observer (FO) with the First Infantry Division.

I didn't want to go. I was afraid. I had read in the paper a week before leaving that the life expectancy of FOs with the First Division was thirty-three days. I couldn't read a military map to save my life, and it threatened to become more than just a figure of speech. Also, the job of hiding quietly in the middle of nowhere for ten hours a day looking for Viet Cong or NVA troops to call in artillery fire on was a damned boring prospect.

For at least these reasons, I contrived a "Catch-22" scheme to beat the game. And thanks to the nerve that can come from fear, I did beat the game, and in spades. Instead of becoming a forward observer, I became the Vietnam Entertainment Officer. They gave me a secretary and an air-conditioned office in Saigon, and my job consisted of meeting movie stars and professional entertainers at the airport, taking them out to dinner on an expense account, and keeping their refrigerator stocked with beer and soft drinks. After work, I stopped in at a steam bath on the way home for steam bath, massage, and sex; or, less often, spent the night with Thom, my favorite barmaid.

The celebrities I worked with included Martha Raye, Roy Rogers, and Dale Evans . . . Nancy Sinatra, Frank Sinatra, Jr., Arthur Godfrey, John Gavin, and Jennifer Jones (who danced divinely). At Christmas, I had a fourth-row seat for the Bob Hope show, three rows behind General Westmoreland. I would be running into him several more times during the coming year.

If the name of the game was survival, I had won.

And yet something wasn't right. What, deep down, was wrong? Why didn't I feel better about beating the game? Or *was* survival the name of the game?

Then one day a friend called, a man from my class at Officer Candidate School. Jim (I'll call him) said he was in town for the day, and I offered to take him out to dinner with one of the shows in town. Jim was mostly quiet, but Jim was almost always quiet. He just shook his head and flipped me the bird as we ate our fifty-dollar dinners at one of Saigon's best French restaurants.

A couple of weeks later, I went up with one of the shows to visit the First Division and to see my best friend Lou, who was a fire direction officer there. Lou asked if I had heard about Jim. I said I had seen him in Saigon a couple of weeks ago, and Lou said, "Oh, then you know."

Jim was in Saigon, it turned out, because he had just been released from the Third Field Hospital. The infantry company to which Jim was assigned had been hit by an early morning human wave assault, which means that about 600 Viet Cong rushed the camp, planning to lose hundreds of men, but to overrun the camp with those who could get through. It was like an infantry kamikaze mission. Jim's company commander, an infantry captain, was wounded in the shoulder and became hysterical, cringing in a corner and leaving his company without a leader. Jim was the only other officer present. He took command of the company, manned three radio networks, called in artillery fire, called the platoons to organize defenses, ordered point-blank artillery fire from their own guns when the attack neared, and shouted commands to organize the hand-to-hand fighting that ensued within the company perimeters.

When it was over Jim had a deep knife wound, hundreds of Viet Cong lay dead, no Americans were killed. He received a Purple Heart and a Silver Star, the third highest award for valor, for altruism under fire.

And something within me awoke.

Ten years later, in the movie *The Deer Hunter* Robert DeNiro says to a frightened young man, "You have to take one shot. You don't have to get hit, but you have to take a shot." A famous passage from a letter of Henry IV contains a similar insight: "Hang yourself, brave Crillon; we fought at Arques, and you were not there." And in the jargon of religion, we speak of a *kairos*, of that moment when the time is right and the time is ripe, when a decision must be made, a decision which will be a watershed for the rest of one's life. That's what awoke within me. It may not make any logical sense, but it has an existential force that cannot be denied or diluted. I knew that if I returned from that country without having experienced war, that in a deep and important way I would not be able to live with myself.

So I negotiated for a transfer to the field. Not to be a forward observer; I still couldn't read a map. I was not the stuff of which heroes are made, and I wanted a broader view of the war. I wanted to see and be in more aspects of it. So I negotiated a transfer to the field as a press officer and combat photographer for an armored cavalry regiment in Xuan Loc, about thirty-five kilometers east-north-east of Saigon, in the middle of dense woods and rubber trees. That was January 10, 1967, and I spent my remaining seven months in that job. I photographed the war, attended briefings from General Westmoreland and other major unit commanders, dealt briefly with Mike Wallace and Morley Safer at CBS, and tagged along with *LIFE* magazine photographer, Co Rentmeester after convincing him to do a feature story on our regiment.

A week after arriving in the field, we got a call to go to a nearby hamlet. The Viet Cong had had a recruiting drive the night before. They assembled the people in the center of the hamlet, where the head of the hamlet refused to help them. So they took his two daughters, aged about six and eight, raped them, then slit their throats, and threw their bodies into the well to pollute the drinking water. Our interpreter from the South Vietnamese Army, Captain Trang, was with us, and he became violently ill. "My two daughters," he said, "are the same ages, they are the same ages as my two girls, my girls are like that, they are like my little girls. . . ." He kept repeating it, over and over.

I never got to know Captain Trang very well, though we ate lunch together most of the time we were both in base camp. But half of what I ever knew about him I learned that morning.

The next story is about the first operation I went on, and it requires some background explanation. The armored unit I was attached to had three squadrons of about 2,000 men each. The first was commanded by a lieutenant colonel who was nicknamed "Tiger." He was a superb commander, and his men loved him. He volunteered them to be the lead element in every joint operation, and they were proud of being "the Tiger's guys." In their six months in the country, I don't think they had had a single man killed, though they had been involved in four or five major operations near Cambodia.

The second squadron remained a stranger to me until ten days before coming home, because Tiger's guys were always where the action was, and I needed action photos and stories to sell our little unit to the major news services. The third squadron was commanded by a man whose name I don't remember; he appeared to be a poor commander whose men followed his lead as Tiger's had followed his. The morale was so low in the third squadron that they couldn't be trusted to go out and fight, so they were left home to guard the base camp on every operation. In six months they had never seen a Viet Cong, never been in war. But they had had eight men killed while staying at home in base camp, in barracks fights, homosexual incidents, thefts, and all the other indicators of poor morale in a military unit.

Three days before a major operation we were to go with an infantry division, we were in a routine staff meeting when General Westmoreland walked in unannounced. General Westmoreland, it seemed, always came unannounced.

Unless you were in that man's presence over there, you just can't know the awesome look he had, the power of intimidation that he had, the unsettling ability he had to make everyone feel intensely uneasy at once. If he walked in here right now, I would probably salute him and still get that uneasy feeling we had all that day.

He stood at the side of the tent for awhile, then walked to the front to interrupt the meeting. He looked straight at the colonel without expression: "You have a morale problem in your third squadron, colonel," he said. "What do you intend to do about it?"

The colonel stammered. The colonel always stammered when Westmoreland was near.

"Do you know how many men have been killed because of the poor morale in your third squadron?"

The colonel did not.

"Eight," said the general. "Eight of your men, eight of *my* men, have died without purpose. What are you going to do about the morale problem?" The colonel stammered again. "This once," said Westmoreland, "I'll solve your leadership problem, colonel. The third squadron will be the lead element in the operation in three days. They need a fresh kill."

Among the things I'll never forget is the matter-of-fact way that General Westmoreland said that, the feel of the atmosphere in the tent after he said it, the silence in the officers' tent after the meeting, and the tension three days later as I went with the third squadron on their and my first operation, in search of the fresh kill.

We rode for two full days in the one-hundred-twenty to one-hundred-thirty degree temperatures without ever seeing a Viet Cong, and our young driver began showing signs of tension. Principally, he kept driving off the road to attack small trees with the vehicle, rolling up them until they bent over to the ground, then hooting like a hill-billy. Then he hit a four-inch tree that was too big to bend. When it snapped back at us, we were covered with inch-long fire ants. They bit everything they landed on, and by the time we had sprayed DDT down each other's backs and finally killed them, we were all burning from the bites and the DDT.

It was about then, I think, that we saw a large bunker by the road. Since a whole column of armored vehicles had just driven by it, there was little chance that anyone was inside. Nevertheless, it was the first real prop of war we had seen up close, so the column stopped and three of us got out to inspect: two men with guns and me with my camera. The bunker was empty, and the two other men said they should check the area out. I stood on the bunker to wait for them.

They spread out in a V and had walked about ten feet when both of them turned and opened fire on a clump of grass about fifteen feet directly in front of me.

The got their fresh kill. Two North Vietnamese officers lay dead. One held a rocket launcher, the other lay with a Russian AK-47 rifle. The two American soldiers began taking souvenirs—sandals and so on—and asked me if I wanted one. I wondered what the men were doing when they were killed. One, they said, was aiming his rocket launcher at our vehicle; the other was aiming his rifle at my head, and both were pulling the triggers when they were shot. The rifle was off safety; we snapped back the bolt, and a bullet popped out of the chamber. I have that bullet in a drawer, and it still has an eerie power, a reminder of the significance of perhaps a hundredth of a second and the fact that mere chance lets me stand here reminiscing rather than a North Vietnamese captain.

But I was not prepared for what happened next.

The word of the fresh kill was radioed through the column, and war whoops resounded. The two men with me put the bodies on the front carrier of our ACAV and drove through the column like deer hunters. Everyone wanted to see them, to take pictures, to pose by the trophies.

And their *eyes*—the eyes of the American soldiers were positively on fire as they swarmed around this irrefutable proof that they were, in fact, in the war; that they had, in fact, taken their shot. In that instant I understood Joseph Conrad's short story "The Heart of Darkness," and later understood why Francis Ford Coppola might base his movie *Apocalypse Now* on that story rather than directly on Vietnam.

The morale in the third squadron skyrocketed; they partied well into the night and ran on euphoria the next day. At last, something to write home about, at last they were off the bench and in the game, at last they were a part of this thing called the Vietnam War.

General Westmoreland had been right.

The final story comes from my last ten days in Vietnam—so I'm skipping six months. It serves as a paradigm for much of my understanding of that year and that war.

I had returned from my R & R (rest and recreation) in Tokyo just a week and a half earlier, and spent the last three weeks in Vietnam frankly terrified. I had seen civilization, a world outside without sand bags and taped windows. It had snapped the spell of adjustment, the suspension of disbelief in the war zone, and I couldn't readjust in the remaining twenty days. I heard every shot at night, every mortar round. Even though I had been through three mortar attacks during the past seven months, and knew the difference between the sound of an incoming and outgoing mortar round, I forgot it all and slept on alternate nights. One night I would awaken with every shot, every sound, and lie on the cot beneath the mosquito netting, soaked with sweat and scared to death and scared to die and sure that it would happen before morning. Then the next night, exhausted, I would fall asleep immediately and hear nothing until morning, when the two-day cycle would begin again.

Ten days before coming home, one of our companies was ambushed on the road with very heavy casualties, and I was sent out to cover it. The ambush had been bad. Thirteen men had been killed and fifty-nine wounded out of a company of about 250—very heavy casualties for an armored unit. Only one officer was left, so I helped him evacuate the wounded and find and collect the dead men and abandoned vehicles. I also did the enemy body count, and found ninety-eight Viet Cong in their trenches beside the road.

And I found something else. They had been dug in there for about three days, waiting for this company to come down this road. They were armed for an attack on an armored company, and we were the only armored unit in the south half of Vietnam. And we had never been down that road before.

There had been a leak. Someone had told the Viet Cong that we were coming, and the cost was 111 dead, fifty-nine wounded Americans, and an unknown number of wounded Vietnamese.

I was stunned and furious and incredulous. The other lieutenant and I thought maybe some GIs were talking about the travel route when they picked up their laundry, and the Vietnamese laundry people understood more English then they let on. Our desperate little theory of how it happened was accepted, and the two laundry people were fired.

A few days later I learned otherwise.

The colonel called me into his office to ask a favor. He wanted some big prints of about twenty of the war photographs I'd done to put on the walls of his office, and offered me a couple of paid days in Saigon to print the pictures. Then he said he had some good news and some bad news. The good news was that they had discovered who told the Viet Cong about the second squadron's company last week. The bad news was that it was Captain Trang.

Captain Trang, our interpreter, the man we had eaten lunch with, had purposely told the Viet Cong where we were going, knowing that they would ambush us.

Sometimes I can still feel the intensity of hatred and rage that hit me then. I wanted him dead. I didn't care how, but I wanted him dead, and immediately. If he had been near, I would have shot him without hesitation. But that had been taken care of. Captain Trang had been turned over to the South Vietnamese, who had tortured and executed him. It was small consolation, but it *was* consolation. I could still see the dead men, still smell and feel and taste that hot and humid day in the middle of nowhere, still hear Captain Trang's voice across the lunch table.

And I can still hear the colonel telling me the rest of the story. Captain Trang had leaked information to the Viet Cong because they had kidnapped his two daughters and threatened to kill them unless he cooperated.

It's a story with no exit. You can't know it without being in it and once you're in it you can't get out of it. Nothing that anyone did made any sense, unless you were they, and then it was the only thing there was to do. It was hard to know who to blame. It was even harder to accept finally the fact that there was no one to blame, no adequate or effective scapegoat to take away the sins of the world, to make it all harmonize as it had once seemed to when life was so much simpler, so much less powerful.

What was left was to come home—to a very poor GI Bill, to a radical University of Michigan campus with a categorical hatred for all veterans—"babykillers" we were called—and to a society that was beginning to find the scapegoat that it so desperately needed in the returning Vietnam veterans.

Yes, there is bitterness. Even after seventeen years, there is bitterness. And much of the reason I'm trying to talk about this now is to prevent or dilute the bitterness of future veterans at the hands of well-meaning folks back home who were not there.

We will all see more wars, we may each know someone in the future who serves in one. For their sakes, I hope it is a popular war, one the American people can have that same perverse fondness for that lets us still make and see innumerable movies about World War II. But if it is not a popular war, if the country once more makes an ass of itself by invading, meddling, or trying to colonize, and if it again needs a scapegoat to salve its own moral wounds, that collective scapegoat will probably be the soldiers, as it was after the Vietnam War.

When it happens, for it probably will, for God's sake *please* don't be among their accusers! The idea that soldiers know what they're fighting for, believing wholeheartedly in the causes involved, or that they even understand them, is just plain wrong and naive to boot. Soldiers are individuals, and they go and will continue to go to war for individuals reasons that range from indifference to patriotic fervor, from a pathological yen for mayhem to the naive idealism of a strong young buck going out to defend truth, goodness, and the American way. Some go "to take a shot," much as I did in transferring to the field; some go because they couldn't live with the alternatives, or don't think anything will happen to them, or just don't think.

But things happen in war to some of those individuals who were there that can change them forever. Perhaps those things are different for each person, but I think that there is a yearning within many of us for what might be called a sign of passage: A moment when something inescapable confronts us with an existential challenge that demands resources and strengths from the very depths of our being. The second-century Church Father Tertullian once wrote: "The Paradox: Faith keeps watch for that day . . . . and daily fears that for which she daily hopes." And the poet and preacher John Donne wrote "Lord, unless

Thou enslave me, I shall never be free. I shall never be chaste unless Thou ravish me." There is a yearning for a sense of wholeness, of participation in essential dimensions of reality, which may live in the hearts of all people. And there are rare experiences in life that seem to have the power of granting that sense of being united with one's depth. It is a sense of fundamental authenticity, of having "taken a shot," of "having been there," having "come through," of having reached down inside oneself for a strength, a feeling, a capacity, that had never been called forth before—and *finding it. That moment, wherever and whenever it happens, is one of the most profound and sacred moments in life.*

But a sacred moment is not restricted to polite parameters. It can happen anywhere—even in an illicit affair (as in the movie *The Sand-piper*) or an illicit war. In another place or time, it could have been embraced by one's community as a hierophany, a taste of that mythi-cal *mana*, a struggle with the forces which can grant an individual authentic life—like Jacob's wrestling match with his god at the river Jabbok, or Jesus' forty days in the wilderness, or even like a down-and-out boxer reaching into himself and finding a champion, as in the movie *Rocky*. But when those sacred moments happen in dark places and unpopular wars, the individual is imprisoned in a private story from which there may never be an exit.

And now I wonder, as I come to the end of these brief reflections, why I have done this, and what I can hope to expect. It's unrealistic to ask for understanding from those who were not there, for that is precisely the problem. To understand the experience of war you must be in war. Otherwise, it isn't war that you understand, but merely the intellectual and esthetic concept of the *idea* of war. And that's not what veterans lived through at all.

I harp on this partly because I know how dear to the heart of intellectuals is the dream of comprehending life with the same objec-tive certainty we claim in the study of rocks, bones, and stars. It is that vain hope of which "transcendental arguments" represent the pinnacle: the obscene idea that mere thinkers can, through mere thought, find structures which can let us understand—and judge—a life we have never lived. But when transcendental arguments become existential, they are no longer transcendental. No two people have the same combination of transcendental categories any more than they have the same experiences. No two men ever died for the same coun-try, and no two men were ever in the same war. Not even a veteran can really know what another veteran is going through, although we may trust each other to care without judging.

And that is what is so hard to trust others to do: to care without judging. A decade after the end of the Vietnam era, veterans are just beginning to wrap words and concepts around some of the rawest stuff of life, the experience of war. It's hard to do because experience goes so very far beyond mere words and concepts. It's hard to do because talking about it is also reliving it, pulling those video tapes out and watching and feeling as they begin to replay, sometimes painfully, on a wide and deep and vivid screen that only we can see. And then the brackets come off that year, and we're there again. Alone, and confused, and wanting to come home.

The way you can help, perhaps, is not by trying to understand at all, but by trying to care. Part of what does so much harm to veterans of the Vietnam era is precisely the effort to understand, to come to some sort of opinion, some moral judgment, by people who can never understand. That outsiders hope to understand is not only dangerous, but bad history as well. It is what historian Herbert Butterfield has called *The Whig Understanding of History*:

> The study of the past with one eye, so to speak, upon the present is the source of all sins and sophistries in history. . . . There is not an essence of history that can be got by evaporating the human and the personal factors, the incidental or momentary or local things, and the circumstantial elements, as though at the bottom of the well there were something absolute, some truth independent of time and circumstance. The historian must see principles caught amongst chance and accident; he must watch their logic being tricked and entangled in the events of a concrete world. . . . If history could be told in all its complexity and detail it would provide us with something as chaotic and baffling as life itself; but because it can be condensed there is nothing that cannot be made to seem simple, and the chaos acquires form by virtue of what we choose to omit. (Pp. 31, 66, 68, and 97)

"The chaos acquires form by virtue of what we choose to omit." In the cases of Vietnam era veterans, the chaos acquires form only by omitting the hearts and souls and lives of the veterans themselves.

So that's really my message and my hope: that you will not try to understand, not try to assign moral values to the stories of individuals in Vietnam, not try to come to an attitude of certainty about the right and wrong of it all. Rather, if you would try to be with us at all, be with us in the chaos and let yourself become confused and disoriented, all awash with feelings, hurts, and memories of both joys and regrets that will never be fully sorted out, never be fully assimilated, and never be gone.

Then, perhaps, we can begin to come home again.

2

To Vietnam and Back
Paul Sgroi

INTRODUCTION

It is difficult for me to explain why I decided to write this letter. In part it is an attempt towards catharsis on my part. It is something I have undertaken to bring my past into view for introspection and inspection. It is in part designed to be educational for those who have no knowledge of what the Vietnam experience is. It is in part an exercise which I hope will put events and my behavior in perspective for myself.

At times this letter is polemic, at times the grammar suffers, at times it will not make sense to everyone. This letter is personal as well as generic. At times the text is repetitive and rambles, I can't help that, I was schooled in political science and I presently am a bureaucrat.

I cannot and will not cover everything which I have experienced. That is not possible. Perhaps as time goes by I will add to this letter; perhaps I will throw it in the trash. Regardless of the outcome of this endeavor, it is tonight's assignment.

I am a seven year Army veteran who served with the First Cavalry Division Airmobile from October 1968 to October 1969 as a combat photographer. As such I was in a unique position to observe, participate, and record the events that occurred in Vietnam while I was

---

Paul Sgroi served seven years in the United States Army, and was stationed in Vietnam as a combat photographer with the First Cavalry Division Airmobile unit from October 1968 to October 1969. In 1985, he was an auditor in the University of California, Santa Barbara class on the impact of the Vietnam War, in which capacity he wrote this essay as, he said, "an open letter to myself, to those who know me, and to the students" in the class. Later the same year he accompanied the students on their annual pilgrimage to the Vietnam Veterans Memorial in Washington, D.C. He spoke at the ceremony, paying tribute to the many persons he knew who did not return from the war. In 1987, Mr. Sgroi died at his own hands in the Paradise area of the Santa Ynez River Valley.

there. I served as both a combat troop and a rear echelon troop. I have experienced Vietnam from many perspectives. What I will attempt to present is my personal interpretation of what the Vietnam experience is.

You will note that this letter is written in the present tense. For many of us who served in Vietnam the war continues. We are no longer faced with an actual enemy force who is out to kill us, but with enemies who lurk behind every door we open. The war continues within us and continues within the minds of people who continue to despise us.

Why are the veterans of Vietnam singled out as the tainted feather in the nation's cap?

The most common answer I have heard is that we lost. We used every weapon at our disposal short of our nuclear arsenal against a nation of rice farmers and fishermen, and we lost!

My own answer is that it is not possible to win a war of insurgency and guerrilla tactics, particularly if the guerrillas are well armed. Devotion to a cause, whether it be religious, political, economic, or philosophical, can and will defeat every obstacle placed in the way of the zealot. Hitler knew this. Ho Chi Minh knew this. The Ayatollah knew this. Would any of us be here today were it not for the devotion and perseverance of the nation's first army—the freedom fighters and minute men?

There are no words to describe the physical and mental reflex action of combat—the fear, desire to live, horror, instinct, willingness to save a friend, ability to ignore the dead, and relief when it is over. I think of a GI who had his arm shattered, who was lying on a stretcher with a smile on his face. He knew, at least for him, that the war was over. At that moment it did not matter that his arm would probably always be useless. All that mattered to him was that he didn't have to go back into the bush, and that he would soon be leaving Vietnam. The problem for many vets is that even when they left the country, they took Vietnam home with them. In their minds, they have continued to exist in the bush. Although they are physically on United States soil, they live in Vietnam.

The average college sophomore is about the same age as the average trooper was in Vietnam. Think about this in specific situations. The next time you go backpacking, think about the fact that we veterans went backpacking. Spend the next day you go backpacking imagining that someone is watching you, and that they have a weapon and are intent on using it against you. Imagine that you are walking point, and every disturbed piece of ground may be hiding a booby trap or mine. Every turn in the trail could lead to an ambush. Try going cross-country for a change of pace. Crawl under bushes. Cut down what is in your path. Keep track of where you are. That night, instead of sitting around a campfire, dig a hole a hundred yards from your tent and spend the night in that hole. The rules are simple. You sleep for two hours, then you wake up and listen for two hours. Repeat that cycle until daylight. This is how we went backpacking in Vietnam.

The day I turned twenty-one I carried approximately fifty pounds of gear all day. I was with an infantry company patrolling near a swamp area so we were in and out of water all day. In addition we had to stop every twenty minutes or so to inspect for leeches from our bodies and the backs of those around us. For my party I drank a warm can of beer and shared a joint with some of the guys. That night I woke to the revelry of gunfire. Our perimeter had detected movement, and set off a couple of claymores, fired aimlessly into the night, and waited for the response. It came in the form of a mortar barrage just before daylight. Some birthday celebration!

Other memories come to mind. I know a woman who takes at least two hot showers a day. During my entire year in Vietnam I had the opportunity to take no more than six hot showers. It isn't that I didn't shower. Where showers existed the water was fed by fifty-five gallon drums, Australian water bags or similar devices, heated by the sunlight. You used only as much water as was needed to soap up and rinse off. There was always someone waiting in line, so you didn't want to be the one to use the last of the lukewarm water.

Another thing we took for granted is the commode. You have a bowel movement, you push a little handle, and everything is gone. In Vietnam the standard-issue commode was half of a fifty-five gallon drum placed under a hole in a couple of wooden planks. Every morning someone was assigned to "shit duty." This person had to pull the drums from under the planks, pour paper and kerosene on the mess, and set it afire. After the contents were destroyed, the commode was replaced. In addition, on most landing zones and fire bases the showers and commodes were completely open. There was no privacy. To this day I can smell the burning shit.

And yet, in Saigon there was a branch of the Bank of America. There were television and radio stations, and some of the most modern mechanisms of warfare, just a few miles from tribes whose hunters used weapons no more advanced than the crossbow.

Vietnam was not knowing who your friend and enemy was. I never trusted a Vietnamese person while I was there. I wasn't sure that the interpreter or the others I worked with wouldn't shoot me in the back. To this day I have prejudice.

Vietnam was "beware of everything." Don't drink Vietnamese-bottled-coke; it could contain slivers of glass. Beware of the prostitutes; they either had venereal disease, had razor blades implanted in their vaginas, or might attack you in your sleep. Beware of the children; many were thieves. Every GI was aware of watches being snatched from wrists, pockets being sliced with razor blades, and wallets being stolen. Beware of the black market; you will get burned. Beware of everything except your own sanity, which, by now, didn't exist.

The tension that Vietnam caused for the average human being prompted some to react in unpredictable and sometimes violent ways. I once watched two engineers get into a fight one night and pull their weapons on each other. They sat for about four hours with their fingers on the triggers, prepared to shoot, before being talked out of this by observers. I also witnessed an officer pull his pistol and threaten to kill a chaplain who had invited the officer to attend religious services.

From my perspective, life in the United States has been only slightly better than my life was in Vietnam. The day I arrived home a woman of my own age walked up to me with several of her friends, while I was waiting for a bus, at the Newark, New Jersey Airport and asked me if I had been to Vietnam. When I responded that this was my first day home she spat in my face and the group let loose with a barrage of insults. I didn't know how to react or respond. The Airport Police ushered her and her friends away. I don't think that she knew then that her spit would forever stain my face. It is not possible to wipe that spittle clean. It is on my face today. I have been able to partially clean it off, but it will be a long time before I am able to clean all of it off. Welcome home.

I understand the conviction and feelings which the woman who assaulted me had. She was only doing what she felt was morally right. The problem is that she, and tens of thousands like her, misdirected their actions to the veterans themselves. We were mere pawns in a political and economic venture. The spit, the insults, and the permanent injury should have been directed towards corporate America and the government. Sure there were marches and demonstrations against the government. The problem is that for every organized demonstration there were hundreds of assaults on individual veterans. Airports and bus stations were the favorite targets for assaults on veterans. For many veterans those incidents were the first and last time they were welcomed home.

Welcome home. Those two words were never stated to me for fifteen years. A couple of simple words, but to the Vietnam Veteran they mean the difference between acceptance and rejection. The first time someone who was not a family member welcomed me home from

Vietnam was on October 11, 1984 when the veterans I marched with welcomed each other home. It took fifteen years and ten days for someone to acknowledge that I was home, and as has been the case with all other actions which have been undertaken to acknowledge the service of Vietnam Veterans, the action was initiated by Vietnam Veterans.

That is the legacy of the Vietnam Vet. The government and the citizens of this nation have done everything in their power to ignore the service of Vietnam Veterans. The memorials in Washington and Sacramento were constructed with funds donated by Vietnam Vets. Activities to welcome home and honor Vietnam Vets have traditionally been sponsored by Vietnam Vets. The best counseling services for Vietnam Vets are provided by other vets. In short, Vietnam Vets have had to take care of themselves. We took care of ourselves in the bush, we continue to take care of ourselves today.

The aspect of post-war life that haunts me most is my inability to get close to people. This is a direct consequence of the mechanisms I cultivated to deal with the deaths of others. After my best friend died, I was never able to develop a close friendship again. This is not to say that I have no friends. I do. The difference is that I am now able to walk away from friendships and feel nothing. Until just a few months ago, I had not written or attempted to contact anyone I have known for the past fifteen years unless that person tried to get in contact with me. I find it easier to get close to total strangers than to the ones I love. If you get close you run the risk of getting burned. There is no need to cry if someone dies or leaves if you haven't allowed yourself to get close to this person. I have former wives and children who know whereof I speak.

I also find myself being excessively ritualistic. Each night I "check the perimeter." That is, I inspect all doors and windows. I insure that all passageways are clear of any obstacles. I make certain that I know the exact location of everything near my bed. I rehearse what I will need in case of an emergency. I do this each night knowing that it will help me survive.

Once I do get to bed the fun begins. For the first seven years after the war I had nightmares. Sometimes I would wake up yelling. Sometimes I would wake up crying. The nightmares faded slowly, or I thought they had. My last wife tells me that right up through the past few years she would come to bed late and recognize that I was experiencing another nightmare.

I don't sleep well. I wake up at least once a night, and usually more frequently. Sometimes I wake up in the middle of the night and simply stay awake until morning. Often when I start off for work in the mornings, I am already exhausted.

I have not touched a rifle or pistol since my discharge. In the Army I had qualified as an expert on the rifle range. I had always been around guns. I was an avid hunter. My father and I went hunting each deer season. But now I'm mightily afraid of guns.

Loud noises bother me. This is especially true of anything that sounds like a gun. I don't hit the floor anymore. There was a time when a car's backfire would push me to the floor, or to the street, within the blinking of an eye. I don't like loud noises, including music. Loud noises distract me, and hamper my ability to distinguish all the sounds around me. Leaves rustling in the wind in my backyard is enough to get me out of bed to investigate.

Restlessness. When I first got out of the service, and my wife and I separated, I crossed the country five times, three times by hitchhiking. I have walked along the Appalachian trail numerous times. When I moved to this city, I had eleven different residences in the first three years, and held three different jobs the first seven months.

Alcohol became my best friend. I have survived by drinking. I drank from ten to twelve cans of beer per day in addition to whatever else I had. I did this for nearly fifteen years. I think the drinking has caused some brain damage.

I break down and begin crying for no apparent reason. An article in the paper or a movie on television can start the tears, but only if I am alone.

I don't like sitting with my back to windows or exposed to the public. I keep the shades down in my house. I don't like thinking that someone out there may be looking in on me.

There are times when I feel extremely volatile. For a while I could get into a fight at the drop of a name. I'm not as volatile as I once was; at least I don't get into as many fights. But, being a powder keg ready to go off at any time, I am trying to develop escape valves.

I have discovered that Vietnam Vets did not tell other people that they were Vietnam Vets. I lived thirty feet away from another Vietnam Vet, and for years neither of us would exchange this dark secret. It was six or seven years before we confessed it to each other.

It was my wife who recognized what was wrong with me. She knew I had delayed stress, and searched out a counseling program for me. I wasn't delighted with the idea, but marched off to the VA clinic for professional help. I spent two hours with a psychologist on my initial visit. The episode felt more like police interrogation than a counseling session. I thought he displayed a total lack of sensitivity. Eventually

I began seeing a psychiatrist on my own, who, after fifteen minutes, diagnosed me as suffering from depression.

Now I recognize that my wife saw it all clearly. But it was already too late for me. After ten years together we separated. I apologize to her because she was absolutely right: the Vietnam War had done something to me. The day they buried the unknown soldier from the Vietnam War, I cried uncontrollably for hours. Now I want to go to the wall, to see the names of those I know. I need to know that they have been remembered.

But aren't all of us Vietnam Vets, regardless of whether we participated in the war or not? It will be up to the next generation to see that this nation gets its act together. My only request is that non-vets remember that there is a lot going on in our heads. Please do not pity us. Please do not condemn us. And please do not categorize and classify us. All of us, whether we served or not, did what we felt was best for ourselves and for our nation.

Welcome Home, Paul.

3

It Don't Mean Nothin':
The Vietnam Experience
William P. Mahedy

"When I went to Vietnam, I believed in Jesus Christ and John Wayne. After Vietnam, both went down the tubes. It don't mean nothin'." Though I have heard other veterans say the same thing a thousand times in different ways, this statement made by a vet in a rap group is, for me, the most concise unmasking of American civil religion and its mythology of war. The loss of faith and meaning experienced by countless Vietnam veterans is now widely known, despite the best efforts of the religious and political right to incorporate Vietnam into the classical mythology of war. If the United States government is to rearm the country for the struggle against "godless communism"—including preparation for a protracted nuclear war— it must first encourage the remythologizing of America. Foreign policy must be consistent with our national myth: we are God's chosen people in all that we undertake. We believe America has a divine mandate to evangelize the world to its own political and economic systems. War is the sacred instrument, the great cultic activity, whereby this mission is achieved. Jesus Christ and John Wayne must again be linked after their brief separation by Vietnam.

William P. Mahedy is Episcopal campus minister at the University of California, San Diego, and in San Diego State University. A former Augustinian monk and United States Army Chaplain in Vietnam, Mahedy was a team leader in a Vet Center in San Diego, and was instrumental in writing and presenting legislation that authorized the establishment of more than 180 storefront Vet Centers throughout the nation.
Mahedy is author of the highly acclaimed book, *Out of the Night: The Spiritual Journey of Vietnam Vets* (New York: Ballantine, 1986), which approaches post-traumatic stress disorders via interpretive categories fashioned within the psychology of religion. Mahedy is responsible for viewing the post-war (and, primarily, post-combat) experience of the returning veterans as spiritual experience, and of connecting some of the ingredients of post-traumatic stress with what traditional Christian mystics, albeit of a previous time, referred to as "the dark night of the soul," which, of course, is the theoretical basis for the more colloquialized title of this essay, which first appeared in *The Christian Century*, January 26, 1983, pp. 65–68.

President Reagan has declared the Vietnam war a noble cause and the right wing has unleashed its fury against those who question the traditional mythology. The Reagan administration's attempt to dismantle the controversial Vietnam Veterans' Outreach Program shortly after taking office was consistent with this remythologizing: If the administration were to admit that the last war caused serious psychological, moral, and spiritual problems, then it would be more difficult to prepare the public for a similar conflict or for a much larger conflagration. The truth about the pain, anger, and disillusionment of the Vietnam veterans cannot be admitted if one espouses the traditional American civil religion. Having invested our political and cultural systems with religious characteristics, we must necessarily interpret our historical experience in terms of a sacred dimension. We must forever remain the chosen people, the "city on the hill" of our myth of origin. We cannot wage mere wars: we must 'fight crusades against the infidels.

It is, therefore, not surprising that the American people greeted with utter silence the anger and disillusionment of the Vietnam veterans. When at last some legitimacy was granted to their protest, it was only within the domesticated categories of psychotherapy. By now their rage, moral pain, and loss of faith have been almost completely contained within the psychiatric construct "post-traumatic stress disorder." Peter Marin believes that this containment is a misrepresentation of the condition and avoids the real issue. He writes of a "massive, unconscious cover-up in which those who fought and those who did not hide from themselves the true nature of the experience. . . ." ("Living in Moral Pain," *Psychology Today* [November 1981], p. 72). What was experienced was the harshness of war: brutality, death, and atrocity without a comprehensive rationale to "seal over" the reality. The Vietnam war provided no transcendent meaning by which the national purpose could be reinterpreted and transposed into a new key. War was, for the first time in American history, experienced by great numbers of its participants as sin. Psychotherapy is uneasy with the notion of sin, as are most Americans of the late 20th century. As a result, much of what the veterans have to say cannot even be articulated, much less understood. The language and the concepts they need no longer exist within the arena of public discourse.

A large segment of the American religious community (which does possess the linguistic and philosophical tools necessary to deal with the moral and religious questions raised by Vietnam) chooses not to see the war as sin. In *The Unfinished War: Vietnam and the American Conscience* (Beacon, 1982), Walter Capps argues that the "rise of Protestant conservatism . . . or the new religious right bears direct connection with individual and corporate wrestling over the ramifications of the Vietnam experience." Viewing the outcome of the war as a defeat of the forces of good at the hands of the powers of evil, the religious right has enshrouded itself within the American myth of origin. The Soviet Union is seen as a supernaturally evil entity which must be defeated by the United States—God's Kingdom—in an apocalyptic drama. But this false mythology, unmasked by the Vietnam experience, is certain to prove once again its utter moral and religious bankruptcy. Reflecting on Vietnam might provide some insights into the religious underpinnings which seem always to lock us into paths leading to disaster.

W. Taylor Stevenson diagnoses the nature of the Vietnam wound as "defilement"; i.e., coming into contact with an object which "has been culturally designated as being unclean" ("The Experience of Defilement," *Anglican Theological Review* [January 1982], p. 18). That there is a good bit of truth in this assessment is demonstrated by the curious fact that many Vietnam veterans describe themselves as unclean. They lament the absence (or, in the case of the recent Washington observance, the delay) of the cleansing rituals of return, such as parades or a hero's welcome, that a society usually grants to its warriors. The almost total inability both of veterans and of the American public to discuss Vietnam for so many years is a clear indication of defilement. Stevenson sees this defilement as resulting from the breaking of two prerational taboos. These two sacred beliefs are part of American civil religion: (1) America is innocent, and (2) America is powerful. Stevenson writes:

[handwritten margin note: America is ? Right]

> *America is innocent/powerful.* It is an implication of this innocency that America deserves to be peaceful and prosperous. A further implication here is that America's exercise of power is an innocent exercise of power necessary for our peace and prosperity. We were not "taught" this in any formal sense. It was not necessary to be taught this because this innocency is not a matter of idea or concept or doctrine; rather, it is a part of the texture of growing up in the United States. It is part of our story of how things *are*, how reality is structured, how life flows for us, and so on. Any violation of this asserted innocency is profoundly disturbing to our individual and social sense of structure and power. . . .
>
> What breaks this taboo and brings a sense of defilement? Any situation or event which challenges or defeats the taboo and all that the taboo protects. Did we go into Vietnam originally under the taboo "American is innocent"? The evidence is overwhelming that, for the

vast majority of Americans, we did (whatever reservations some had concerning Asian land wars).

Those on both sides of the Vietnam conflict were exposed to and participated in consciousness-altering, irreversible, massive evil. Atrocity, hatred, wholesale slaughter and barbarous acts of all kinds are the stuff of war. In the name of innocent America and its god, the GIs performed their duty in the great cultic act of war. But the myth was shattered. Neither they nor their country and its god were innocent. Perhaps, had the wages of sin been victory, a belief in our innocence could have been restored; but we were defeated. The other illusion, that of power, was also shattered. The warriors, their nation, and its god were shown to be powerless. The taboos had been broken. We had sinned, and the wages of sin was death. Only in this context can the pervasive loss of faith among the veterans be understood and discussed.

If, as John Wheeler writes, "God acting about us and through us redeems the brokenness of Vietnam" ("Theological Reflection Upon the Vietnam War," *Anglican Theological Review* [January 1982], p. 14), then this God can only be the God revealed to us in the Hebrew and Christian Scriptures. The veterans who told me that 500 years of life would not be sufficient to atone for what he did in Vietnam is quite correct, for those he killed would still be dead. Only death will erase the emotional and spiritual scars inflicted upon the widows and orphans of his victims. The veterans who asked me, "Where was God, that son-of-a-bitch, when the rounds were coming in at Khe Sanh?," asked the right question. The mystery of iniquity is too profound for the American tribal god. Religious conservatives who retreat from evil and identify religion with feeling good about Jesus, with the conversion experience and with the better life are not really prepared to grapple with the questions raised by war. Neither are the liberals who believe that personhood and human fulfillment are the end products of religion. The former construct religious and emotional defenses to insulate themselves from evil, and the latter often underestimate its power.

The only God who seems to make any sense is the one who refused to let Moses see his face, the God whose ways are not our ways. When confronted with the problem of Job, many vets ask the questions Job asked. The answer given to Job makes more religious sense than anything else: "Where were you when I laid the foundation of the earth?" (Job 38:4). All human words—even religious words—are frivolous in the face of evil and in the presence of the transcendent God. For veterans who have been seeking some vindication from the American people and its tribal god, it becomes clear that the only real vindication comes from the God of absolute holiness and mercy. Five hundred years may be insufficient for atonement in any human sense, but with the God to whom a thousand years are as a day, everything is possible. Having been expelled from the garden for tasting the forbidden fruit, we can find real hope only in the promise of redemption.

For post-Christian vets, those whose faith was destroyed by Vietnam, I believe the most powerful single utterance in Scripture is the utterance of Jesus on the cross: "My God, my God, why have you abandoned me?" Quite clearly, they too have walked the way of the cross, and the words of the psalmist are their words too. The tragedy is that no one has pointed out this connection. Nor has anyone dealt with the next and crucial step that must be taken by those who have experienced great evil and perceived its relationship to the cross. With Jesus, one must be able to say, "Father, into your hands I commend my spirit." All that has happened to the veterans in Vietnam and since Vietnam—their broken lives, broken bodies, and shattered dreams— must be placed in the hands of the Father. Experiential knowledge of the monstrous evil in the world and the recognition of humankind's utter inability to achieve any real shalom elicit the cry of agony. The next step requires the leap of faith, for the experience of evil is really the perception of God's absence from the world precisely in those situations which seem to demand a providential presence. To understand the apparent absence of God as one mode of his presence requires, first of all, the destruction of the American graven image, with its promise of innocence restored and power regained.

In more than ten years of working with Vietnam veterans, I have seen many discover the true nature of their wound. Although therapy, jobs, and benefits may be helpful in healing some of the hurt, the real source of the alienation and rage is gradually disclosed: it is the death of the national god. For many veterans this abyss is too deep. To survive they must rewrite the history of Vietnam in their own minds and hearts. Beating the drums of war again seems the only way to justify their own war. For others, a life of service to fellow veterans and to society is the way to overcome the evil they have experienced. The enormous dedication and selflessness shown by those in the self-help centers, in the outreach programs and in the political groups can be explained in terms of deliverance from evil. Some even articulate their ideals in religious terms: the Beatitudes and the prayer of St. Francis.

What is lacking for most veterans, however, is the willingness of Job to be silent, or the committing of one's own life and death and of all things to the Father as Jesus did. I have seen veterans break into tears of amazement and relief when they begin to understand, in the words of the anonymous author of *The Cloud of Unknowing,* that

> you . . . will feel nothing and know nothing except a naked intent toward God in the depths of your being. You will feel frustrated for your mind will be unable to grasp him and your heart will not relish the delight of his love. . . . If, in this life, you hope to see and feel God as he is in himself it must be within this darkness and this cloud. . . . God in his goodness will bring you to a deeper experience of himself. [quoted in W. H. Capps and W. M. Wright, *The Silent Fire* (Harper, 1978), p. 104]

The Vietnam experience has not yet been publicly connected with the dark night of the soul or with any theology of the cross. Yet I am aware of no other Christian point of reference adequate to it. Everything else "don't mean nothin'."

Unfortunately, veterans seldom find help from the clergy. Most pastors—of any denomination—do not articulate the Christian faith in these terms. A veteran has, I believe, a better chance of finding a competent guide in a contemplative monk or nun. A person who has spent years in prayer and solitude—however lacking he or she may be in the experience of war or of ministry or of the world—will be more able to relate to one who has undergone the shattering of culturally dominant images of God. The desolation of spirit so common in the life of solitude enters also into the lives of those who are touched by monstrous evil. A person who has encountered God in the darkness of unknowing is, I believe, the best guide for one who is groping in that darkness but who is unable to identify the cloud.

If the church wishes to learn to confront the evils which irrevocably alter consciousness (genocide, mass starvation, systemic injustice, nuclear war) then it must understand and be willing to live in the dark night of the soul and in the cloud of unknowing. If the church is to work actively in the world in behalf of justice and peace, it must not only do so in obedience to God but it must also be prepared to encounter God as present and active precisely in those situations where he seems most painfully absent. The idolatrous character of American civil religion is nowhere more clearly disclosed than in the variety of props it constructs to insulate its adherents from evil. In striking at the idol, however, American Christianity should be aware that its favorite images of God are also inadequate. The divine guarantor of success, personal healing, charismatic enthusiasm, social betterment, and psychological fulfillment also crumbles when confronted with monstrous evil. I think the Vietnam experience should teach us this if nothing else.

The only God who remains is the Totally Other, who commands us to empty ourselves in imitation of him who became obedient to the death on the cross. The neon lights of our idolatries fail in the darkness of evil that surrounds the cross. They "don't mean nothin'." To God alone belongs the power to redeem the broken world. Within the shadow of the cross all religious images are illusions and all religious discourse is cheap talk. The one remaining Christian possibility is to bend the knee and to confess that Jesus Christ is Lord, to the glory of God the Father.

4

Living in Moral Pain
Peter Marin

Two years ago I was asked by a magazine editor to write an essay on the Vietnam films that were then beginning to appear. Searching for a way to measure the quality and accuracy of the films, I began to talk to Vietnam veterans. What I found both astonished and moved me: a world of moral pain and seriousness that put to shame not only the films in question but also the way most Americans deal with their moral relation to the world around them. The films I was supposedly concerned with ceased to concern me; what became important, and what I eventually wrote about, was the vets themselves. They absorbed me not only in themselves but also for the questions their difficulties raised about the capacity of our society to deal with the psychological and ethical problems that beset them.

Those questions are not easily exhausted, and I have found them again on my mind these days as America's attention has turned back, grudgingly, to the vets. The veterans, still angered by the way they are treated, have grown increasingly vocal, increasingly visible, refusing to vanish into the past with the war.

Their public complaints are varied and familiar: the paucity of their benefits; the weakness in the programs designed for them, the ingratitude and indifference of their fellow citizens; the red tape and bureaucratic foul-ups in VA assistance; the unwillingness of the government to recognize its responsibility for many of their problems, including the effects of Agent Orange and what psychologists now label the "delayed-stress syndrome."

Peter Marin is a writer whose essays have been published in various magazines and journals, including *Harper's* and *Psychology Today*. Formerly with the Center for the Study of Democratic Institutions, and a visiting professor in numerous colleges and universities, Marin is well known and highly regarded for his analyses of the dynamics of alienation in contemporary American society. Often cited and quoted, "Living in Moral Pain" was originally published in *Psychology Today*, in November, 1981, pp. 71–80.

All of those complaints have validity. But something about them, and about the response being made to them, seems to me as inadequate as the films I was asked to review. *Time* magazine's cover story on the vets this past summer is typical of the response. It portrayed the vets as victims of the society that sent them to war, and said that the solution to their problems was increased acceptance and gratitude here at home. Left unsaid in such analyses are two crucial aspects of the vets' suffering that no one seems to want to confront. The first seems to me to be the unacknowledged source of much of the vets' pain and anger: profound moral distress, arising from the realization that one has committed acts with real and terrible consequences. And the second is the inadequacy of the prevailing cultural wisdom, models of human nature, and modes of therapy to explain moral pain or provide ways of dealing with it. Of course, many vets have problems directly traceable to other sources, and no doubt there are vets who are not disturbed in any way by their participation in the war.

Yet the fact remains that in private conversations with many disturbed vets, one begins to sense beneath the surface of their resentment the deep and unacknowledged roots of their anger. That is not only my experience. In the past several months a number of men and women who work with vets in clinics and rap groups have told me that both the war stories related by the vets and their explicit concerns have begun to change, revealing more and more clearly their moral distress.

Shad Meshad, western coordinator for the veterans' Outreach Program, put it this way: "We aren't just counselors; we're almost priests. They come to us for absolution as well as help."

A psychologist put it more explicitly: "Day in and day out, now, we hear stories about atrocities and slaughter, things we didn't hear before. Why men were silent before and now speak remains a mystery to me. But something has changed, and sometimes you hear almost more than you can stand. It is, I swear, like being in Germany after World War II."

It is no accident that the war in Vietnam, by far the most morally suspect war America has fought in modern times, has raised the most problems for those who fought it. Some of the problems can be ascribed to the vets' youthfulness, to the unfamiliar horrors of a guerrilla war, and to the fact that the ambiguity of American attitudes toward the war has indeed denied the vets gratitude and help they feel they deserve.

But none of these considerations should obscure the fact that what they now suffer is essentially the result of the bitter reality that caused the schisms here at home—the very nature of the war: what the veterans saw and did in Vietnam, the war's excessive brutality and cruelty, and the arbitrary violence with which we fought it. True, stories similar to those that have emerged from Vietnam occasionally surfaced after World War II and the Korean War. But one would probably have to go back to the American Indian wars to find something similar to the treatment of the civilian populations in Vietnam, and even then the extent of gratuitous violence might not be comparable.

There were two fundamental kinds of violence:

The first was programmatic, large-scale, widespread, and intentional—policies established at various levels of command. It included the conscious and wholesale slaughter of civilian populations, something that other nations (and war critics at home) perceived as genocide. The precedent for this kind of violence was set decades ago, during the World War II fire-bombing of Dresden, when civilian, not military sites became targets. In Vietnam, the policy was extended further; in the name of ending the war and protecting "innocent" soldiers, the administration punished "guilty" civilians, choosing as a conscious strategy the murder of noncombatants. Of course, that did not happen everywhere. Many of the U.S. commanders and troops attempted to distinguish between civilians and combatants—as difficult as such a task is in the midst of guerrilla warfare—and to observe the ordinary "rules" of war. But far more often than Americans like to realize those rules were broken, and the war literature indicates they were broken more often by the Americans than by the Vietnamese; as a nation, we were guilty of acts that would have appeared to most Americans, had they been committed by others, as barbaric.

The second kind of violence was more sporadic, and individualized, ranging from large-scale but apparently spontaneous massacres, such as those at My Lai, to the kinds of "recreational" violence in which a GI, just for the fun of it, might gun down a woman crossing a field or a child at the side of the road. How much of that went on is not clear, and we will probably never have an accurate picture of it, but stories abound. One cannot read through books like Gloria Emerson's *Winners and Losers* or the interviews in Mark Baker's *Nam* without coming upon several examples every few pages. Most veterans have stories of this sort. Few of them talk about their own actions, but there is always something they have seen, something a buddy described. What the stories reveal is that many of our soldiers acted as if they had been granted an implicit permission to act out at will, upon an entire population, gratuitous acts of violence.

One cannot tell how many soldiers were involved, nor how many now suffer psychological and emotional disturbances from their involvement. Even the number of Americans who served in Vietnam remains in doubt. Whereas the figure was once estimated as 2.5 million, it has now been revised upward to 4 million. Studies suggest that one out of five veterans has been severely affected by stress, which would put the figure at 800,000, and researchers and therapists seem to agree that perhaps 50,000 need immediate help. But whatever the figures, no one who speaks to many distressed vets can doubt that their involvement in the excessive violence of Vietnam is a fundamental source of their inner turmoil, and that it expresses not just psychological stress but moral pain.

It is here that our collective wisdom fails the vets, here that our dominant approaches to human nature and our prevailing modes of therapy prove inadequate. We seem as a society to have few useful ways to approach moral pain or guilt, it remains for us a form of neurosis or a pathological symptom, something to escape rather than something to learn from, a disease rather than—as it may well be for the vets—an appropriate if painful response to the past. As if he were reading my thoughts, a VA psychologist told me that he and his colleagues never dealt with problems of guilt. Nor did they raise the question of what the vets did in the war: "We treat the vets' difficulties as problems in adjustment."

That is true, I suspect, of most of the help the vets receive, save for what they and the therapists closest to them have begun to develop in their own rap groups and clinics, where they have been struggling for a decade to discover and describe the nature of their problems. Yet even within that struggle there are difficulties.

By now, a rather extensive body of written work pertaining to the vets exists: at least 15 new papers were presented just at the American Psychological Association convention last August. Most of the literature hinges on the notion of what is called the delayed-stress syndrome, a term whose widespread use arose in connection with the Vietnam veterans: the psychological and emotional disturbances that, well after the war's end, emerge in men who previously seemed unscathed. The concept is an important and useful one; no doubt there *is* a syndrome of symptoms and behaviors that appears several months or years after the war and that can be attributed, retrospectively, to its stresses. Such symptoms, all observers agree, include flashbacks, nightmares, uncontrollable anger, paranoia, anxiety, and depression.

But many researchers also extend the range of symptoms to include a variety of other emotional states—among them, feelings of guilt, perception of oneself as a scapegoat, alienation from one's feelings, an inability to trust or love. It is there that the trouble begins, for such symptoms are less persuasively attributable directly to the war, especially when they appear individually and not as a set of interrelated symptoms; one suspects that in many cases their classification as delayed stress obfuscate the real nature of the veterans' experience.

Let me give an example. Imagine (as is often the case) a particular vet who has seen close up not only the horrors of war but forms of human desperation, suffering, and tenacity that are altogether different from what he had seen before. He comes home sensing a relation between the nation's policies and the complex reality he has witnessed, between our privilege here and the suffering elsewhere in the world. Is it surprising that such a man, having seen his own comrades senselessly killed and reflecting upon the moral illegitimacy of the killing he himself has done, would find it increasingly difficult to come to terms with the "normal" life he left behind? How would the moral smugness and obliviousness of American life strike him? How would expensive restaurants strike him, the talk about interest rates, or even TV commercials?

No doubt such a man would be "irritable," would be angry, would find himself at odds with things, unable to resume his previous job, pursuits, or relationships. But to call all such problems delayed stress or to see them as explicable only in terms of the war would be to misstate the condition entirely; it would in effect avoid the real significance of the vet's condition, would *void* it in some way. Similarly, seemingly precise analytic terms for repressed guilt—"impacted grief," for one—and theories about psychological denial become systems of denial, a massive, unconscious cover-up in which both those who fought and those who did not hide from themselves the true nature of the experience the terms are supposedly identifying.

Reading through the literature on the vets, one notices again and again the ways in which various phrases and terms are used to empty the vets' experience of moral content, to defuse and bowdlerize it. Particularly in the early literature, one feels a kind of madness at work. Repugnance toward killing and the refusal to kill are routinely called "acute combat reaction," and the effects of slaughter and atrocity are called "stress," as if the clinicians describing the vets are talking about an executive's overwork or a hysterical housewife's blood pressure. Nowhere in the literature is one allowed to glimpse what is actually occurring: the real horror of the war and its effect on those who fought it. Much of this masking seems to have its root in the war itself, when the army psychiatrists charged with keeping the troops in the mood for killing treated as a pathology any rebellion against orders or the refusal to kill.

Such attitudes persist. Some VA therapists are now talking about the need to "deresponsibilize" their patients—that is, get the Vietnam vets to attribute their actions to external causes rather than moral choice. Those who mention guilt usually describe it as "survivor's" guilt—shame not for what was done, but for having outlived one's comrades—or hurriedly attribute guilt to "the expression of aggressive impulses," by which one can only assume they mean the slaughter of innocents. Even a sympathetic observer like John A. Wilson, a psychologist whose perceptive and sensitive work on stress was put into my hands by vets who found it important, manages to render the moral aspect of the war less important than it is. Wilson ascribes most of the vets' pain to the truncation of the "normal" development of the ego; drawing on the work of Erik Erikson, he uses a table that connects stressful experiences to "qualities of ego-development and personality integration," listing 11 stress-producing events. The eighth reads, in its entirety, "Death of Buddies and Atrocities." A single entry treats the death of one's friends and performing or witnessing atrocities as if they were all more or less the same thing or had the same moral or psychological impact.

There are, of course, several worthy authors who go beyond such thinking. Robert Jay Lifton's work comes first to mind, if only because his book _Home From the War_ (1974), published relatively early, has had a more powerful impact on other therapists than any other work. Lifton has been largely responsible for the idea of the vets as victims, and there is no doubt that he radically changed the way others saw the veterans' experiences.

There are others, too, who come to mind: Chaim Shatan, B. W. Gault, Arthur Egendorf, Arthur Blank, Bill Mahedy, Robert Laufer, and Jack Smith. These men have either written about the war or worked extensively with vets; often, they have done both. One can see in their work a moral deepening that seeks but has not yet found a completed form, a language and perception that will do justice to the realities of moral experience.

Why has most psychological thinking about Vietnam avoided the issue of judgment? There are several reasons. Much of the research on Vietnam veterans has been funded by government agencies or by veterans' organizations. Several psychiatrists who work with the vets have told me that in this area as in any other, researchers tend to look for results and frame findings that will keep their funding sources happy. Then, too, many of those writing about the vets are devoted to them; they want to see them get whatever they need from the government, and they feel that the best way to get such help is to portray the vets as victims, by locating the source of their troubles in the war itself. One also suspects that many shy away from the question of moral pain simply because it is likely to open up areas of pain for which there is really nothing like a "cure." As one therapist told me regarding the atrocities and attendant shame that were sometimes discussed in his rap group: "That, my friend, is the hardest thing to deal with. When somebody brings it up, we all fall silent. Nobody knows how in hell to handle it."

Beyond those reasons lies perhaps the most significant one of all: that of the limits of the discipline itself, the inadequacy of psychological categories and language in describing the nature and pain of human conscience. The truth is, much of our confusion in regard to therapy and moral pain stems from the therapeutic tradition itself.

A strain of moral sensibility and conscience was always present in the work of Freud. But it is also true that two elements combined in his work to separate considerations of psychological health from moral or social concerns. The first was the need to isolate the self in the therapeutic process from its complex familial or social connections in order to see it clearly and deal effectively with it. What began as a useful fiction gradually hardened into a central motif or approach: the self in therapy is characteristically seen as separate and discrete from what surrounds it—an isolated unit complete in itself, relatively unaffected by anything but inner or familial experience. Secondly, morality itself was often treated in Freud's work as a form of social intervention or outside imposition, something fundamentally alien to the individual ego. There were good reasons for his view, of course— most notably the heavy and oppressive German morality of the times and the obviously destructive dissonance between inner human life and the regulated social order established around it. Nonetheless, in its justifiable accent upon human need as opposed to social obligation, psychoanalysis established habits of thought that have now been honed in America into a morally vacuous view of human nature.

Our great therapeutic dream in America is that the past is escapable, that suffering can be avoided, that happiness is always possible, and that insight inevitably leads to joy. But life's lessons—so much more apparent in literature than in therapy—teach us something else again, something that is both true of, and applicable to, the experience of the vets. Try as they do to escape it, the past pursues them; the closer they come to the truth of their acts, the more troubled they are, the more apart they find themselves, and the more tragic becomes their view of life.

The veterans' situation is Oedipus' situation—not for the reasons Freud chose, but because it reveals to us the irreversibility of certain kinds of knowledge, the power of certain actions and perceptions to change an individual's life beyond any effort to change it back. Oedipus saw and was blinded, came close to the truth and lost the world of men, and once in exile he suffered not so much because of what he had done, but because of what he learned he had done: the terrible and tragic knowledge deprived him of the company both of men and of gods.

Such knowledge has come to many vets too. What they know is this: the world is real; the suffering of others is real; one's actions can sometimes irrevocably determine the destiny of others; the mistakes one makes are often transmuted directly into others' pain; there is sometimes no way to undo that pain—the dead remain dead, the maimed are forever maimed, and there is no way to deny one's responsibility or culpability, for those mistakes are written, forever and as if in fire, in others' flesh.

Though this is perhaps a terrible and demanding wisdom, it is no more and no less than what all men should know; it is the ethical lesson life teaches those who attend to the consequences of their actions. But because our age is what it is and because most Americans flee from such knowledge, this wisdom is especially hard for the vets to bear. Though it ought to bring them deeper into the human community, it isolates them instead, sets them irrevocably apart, locks them simultaneously into a seriousness and a silence that are as much a cause of pain as are their past actions. They become suffering pariahs not only because of what they have done but because of the questions it raises for them—questions that their countrymen do not want to confront, questions for which, as a society, we have no answers.

A few months ago, after I had talked about guilt and the war to a group of vets, professors, and students, a vet came up to me.

"I left in the middle of your talk," he said angrily. "What you were saying didn't make sense. I feel no guilt. There was no right or wrong over there. All of that is nonsense. It was a dream. That's how I leave it behind. I don't let it bother me. I couldn't understand what you were saying."

Yet he had returned to register his complaint, and as he spoke to me, his eyes filled with tears. There was a grief revealed by his gaze that he could not admit to me, nor perhaps even to himself, possibly because he had little hope of finding a useful way to deal with it. I suspect that its release, or at least its acknowledgment, would have radically changed him, radically changed his relation to the world; but it made itself felt instead as a refusal to consider the past in any moral way at all. I have now talked to enough vets to know that for many of them—though by no means for all—hopelessness lay behind the tears that neither one of us mentioned.

So, in responding, I chose to broaden the question of responsibility, arguing that, yes, the vets were guilty, but many of us had been guilty also, and that we were guilty not only for the war, but for countless public and private acts whose consequences had been pain or suffering for others. It was all of us, I tried to say, who ought to struggle to come to terms with human fallibility and culpability. The vets were not alone in that, or ought not to be alone in that. It was a struggle all men should share. At that, he relaxed. The tears were still there, but more obvious now, less masked. His voice was softer and less truculent.

"I see what you mean," he said. "But you didn't say that before. I can understand what you're saying now."

I *had* said it before, but I had said it in a way that made it impossible for him to listen, for in making the guilt his alone, or in making it sound as if it were his alone, I had deprived him of precisely the kind of community and good company that make it possible for people to see themselves clearly. What he needed, as do all the vets, was not only a way of thinking and speaking about his life, but the willingness of others to consider their lives *in the same way*.

This is precisely the point at which the failure of therapy becomes tragic, and it is at this point that the future task of therapy becomes clear: to see life once again in a context that includes the reality of moral experience and assigns a moral significance to human action. It may be that certain acts and certain kinds of guilt set men irrevocably apart from their fellows: Oedipus, after all, entered a realm in which the common wisdom was of no use to him. But one cannot help feeling that this is not the case with the vets, and that the isolation they feel has as much to do with our corrupt view of human nature as it does with their past actions. The moral anguish they feel, as intense as it gets, is in many cases simply an extreme form of certain painful experiences that would be entirely familiar to us if we paid as much attention to moral life in our therapies as we do to other forms of behavior.

What the problems of the vets ought to point toward are several categories of moral experience ignored in therapy but applicable to *all* men and women, and familiar to many of them. Those categories, if we could bring them to bear on the problems of the vets, would be of immense use in illuminating their torment. Beyond that, it would educate us all about the psychological consequences of the moral pain that their problems reveal.

The first category of moral pain is the common notion of "bad conscience," a person's reaction to past actions he or she finds inexcusable or inexplicable. Bad conscience causes the individual pain, shame, and guilt, and demands a way of setting right what has been done. But it goes beyond this reaction, approximating what Sartre, in *Being and Nothingness,* called "bad faith": the underlying and general sense of having betrayed what you feel you ought to have been.

We are familiar with that feeling in the emotional realm; we know how those who settle for emotional or sexual lives that do not satisfy them, or those who sacrifice desire to fear, can feel humiliated and depleted or experience an almost organic shame. In some way, at some level, they know their lives to be a lie. The same apprehension can be true in the moral realm; we can experience in the present a pain engendered by past actions that seem to us reprehensible, and to the extent that we merely try to outlive such events, forgetting or ignoring them, we may indeed feel ourselves to be guilty of a kind of bad faith—of breaking a covenant not only with others or with God, but with our own nature.

It seems to me that is the experience of many Americans who cannot help measuring in their minds their privileged condition and the way they choose to spend their lives against the varieties of need, deprivation, and pain they see around them. Many of us suffer a vague, inchoate sense of betrayal, of having somehow taken a wrong turning, of having somehow said yes or no at the wrong time and to the wrong things, of having somehow taken upon ourselves a peculiar and general kind of guilt, having two coats while others have none, or just having too much while others have too little—and yet proceeding, nonetheless, without lives as they are.

How much more painful, then, are such feelings for the vets, for in Vietnam, the consequences of their actions were irreversible and concrete suffering or death. Any response to those events save one that arises from an individual's deepest sense of debt or justice is likely to leave a person mired in bad faith.

The second category of moral pain has to do with what might be called "the world's pain"—the way we internalize and experience as our own the disorder, suffering, and brutality around us. Some people take on the pain of others as a personal burden; external suffering mixes with their own immediate emotional experience in a way that often makes it difficult to sort out what has been produced by one and what by the other. We can call it empathy if we want to, but it goes well beyond a specific response to a particular person's particular misfortune. It can take the form of a pervasive sense of suffering, injustice, and evil—a response to the world's condition that produces a feeling of despair, disgust, or even a sort of radical species-shame, in which one is simultaneously ashamed of oneself and one's kind.

Who can forget the images of John F. Kennedy falling in the open car or of the young female student at Kent State kneeling above her fallen comrade, her mouth open in a scream? And who cannot remember the televised images from Saigon of South Vietnamese soldiers crowding into the last planes to leave, the women and children clinging to them and falling through the air as they took off? The horror one feels in relation to such sights can be traumatic and perhaps permanent; it works in ways we do not understand, depriving us not of self-esteem but of something equally important to the ego's health: a sense of a habitable world and of trustworthy human connections.

Often this response to suffering is hidden away, repressed, or ignored; it eats at people from the inside out, but because they feel helpless in the face of what causes it, they try as best they can to ignore it or try to solve it in ways that have nothing to do with its causes. Much of the apparent "selfishness" at work in America, the tendency to turn toward self, is not a function of greed; it is instead an attempt to alleviate pain and guilt by turning away, by giving up the world—at least in terms of conscience.

Time and again one hears vets say about the war and its issues: "It don't mean nothin'." They struggle to empty the past of meaning—not because they are hardened to what happened or because it does not mean nothing, but because it is the only way they can preserve sanity in its shadow.

The veterans have seen in themselves and in their comrades behavior that visits upon them truths about human nature and human suffering that will (and should) remain with them for the rest of their lives, calling into question the thin surface of orderliness they see around them. They suffer now, in a bitter way for which we have no words, the brute condition of the human world, which is for them neither an abstraction nor an idea; it is, rather, what they know, how they feel, who they are. Their grief, akin to Oedipus', or to Buddha's at the sight of suffering, or to Christ's at human evil, is far more than a therapeutic problem; it raises instead, for each of them, the fundamental questions of how to live, who to be.

Here we come to the third category of moral pain: the way most of us suffer when we cannot act out in the world our response to the suffering we have seen in it.

In the past several decades, therapy has concentrated on analyzing individual pain or frustration in terms of loss and deprivation: how needs for warmth or love have gone unanswered. The therapeutic answer to that condition, which makes a certain sense, has been to teach us how to get what we want.

But in concentrating on that aspect of pain we have underestimated the ways in which we suffer when we cannot find how to express our love, to give back to the world in some generous way what it is we feel toward it. Morality, argued Kropotkin, is simply "an overflow of vitality." He meant that it is a natural and unconscious response to the world, a sort of natural gratitude engendered by the interplay of private energies and the surrounding reality. In such a view, there is no such thing as feeling separate from action; each response to the world naturally becomes and demands a gesture. But when the process is not fully completed, when it is truncated, we experience a sense of loss and humiliation, a sense of depletion akin to what we feel when rejected in love or frustrated in desire.

A few months ago, I attended a meeting of vets, academics, and therapists in which we were supposedly discussing "the healing process." The discussion had been rather dry and constrained until one vet began to speak. He had been in the war, he said, though not in combat. Coming back from it had been hard, and his feelings about it had grown stronger since its end; nothing had seemed right, he was unable to settle down or come to terms with life, but he seemed unable to explain why.

"I'm an artist," he said. "A sculptor. At least that's what I've been doing lately. Coming home from the war, I saw huge piles of shell-casings. And a couple of years ago I realized that I wanted to use them to make a gigantic sculpture. Something to commemorate the dead, to let people know what the war had been like. For years I tried to get those casings. But they wouldn't let me have them. They were being recycled, they said, to make new shells. . . ."

And suddenly he was shaking and weeping, unable to go on, crying, as vets will, at the impossibility of explaining to others what drives them.

Later he comes over to talk to me. "I don't know how to explain it," he said. "I keep thinking that if I could do this one thing, if I could just get it, if I could make this one thing, then somehow it would be all right, they'd see, they'd know, and then it wouldn't happen again."

This impulse, is, in essence, what one finds unacknowledged in many of the vets, and the inability to act upon it drives them deeper into distress than they were when they first emerged from the war. We know how imprisonment affects animals, how they are affected by the loss of space and freedom. Often they sicken and die. The same things happen to men and women, but we are far more complicated creatures, inhabiting history as well as nature. When we cannot act in history, when our response to the world around us cannot be spoken or acted on, we suffer inside—as do the vets—a set of experiences for which we have no psychological name.

Most good therapy, Paul Goodman once said, cutting pragmatically to the heart of the matter, is a combination of a whorehouse and an employment agency. What he meant is that if it did not teach people how to make lives for themselves embracing useful work and good loving, it did no one much good. The same thing can be said in relation to the vets. Somewhere along the line, therapy must enter those areas in which the therapist and patient become comrades, where what has been discovered about one's own experience and its related pain raises questions not only about psychological wholeness but also about moral responsibility: what to do, what to be, how to love? Though no one can solve these problems for another, it is safe to say that no one will be much use to the vets without taking these questions seriously and understanding that at the heart of each life and satisfaction lie fundamental moral questions about choice, responsibility, and the doing of good that must be answered with action that comes from one's deepest commitments.

There is one last point that must be made not only about the encounter between therapists and patients but also about any contemporary "helping" relationship (teacher and student, for example) that involves the shared redefinition of reality. For decades now, we have considered Buber's "I-thou" relationship the ideal model: a respectful intimacy in which the integrity of the other is not violated as the other's nature is fully perceived, understood, and embraced. No doubt all of that is morally insufficient. It is incomplete. For it does not fully take into account the inevitable presence of the invisible others, the distant witnesses: those who have suffered our past acts and those who may suffer them in the future.

The proper consideration for therapists and vets, for all therapists and all Americans, is "I-thou-they": the recognition that whatever we do or do not do in our encounters, whatever we forget or remember, whatever truths we keep alive or lies we fabricate will help form a world inhabited by others. Our actions will play a significant part in defining not only the social and moral life of our own people, but the future of countless and distant others as well, whose names we will not know and whose faces we will not see until perhaps, a decade from now, other American children view them through the sights of guns. The responsibility of the therapist, then, neither begins nor ends with the individual client; and the client's responsibility neither begins nor ends with himself or herself. Both extend far outward, from the past into the future, to countless other lives.

Whether a consideration of all these elements will make a difference to the vets is not at all clear. It may well be that many of them will be forced to live with certain kinds of pain and regret for the rest of their lives, though one can hope that they will be successful enough to turn the truths of the past to some use, becoming the keepers and bearers of those truths rather than the victims. What is clear is that their psychic well-being will depend in large part upon their capacity to resolve the issues of conscience that haunt them. Whatever skills or comfort they manage to salvage from traditional therapy, they will have to see through to the end, and largely on their own, the moral journey that they began in Vietnam.

One can hope that the rest of us will accompany them when we can and follow them when we should; and that perhaps out on the edges of acknowledged experience in those regions of the self into which the vets have been led and for which we have few words and little wisdom, therapy will regain a part of the seriousness that has so far eluded it and move a bit closer to coming of age.

5

Home From the War:
The Psychology of Survival
Robert Jay Lifton

SURVIVING

There is something special about Vietnam veterans. Everyone who has contact with them seems to agree that they are different from veterans of other wars. A favorite word to describe them is "alienated." Veterans Administration reports stress their sensitivity to issues of authority and autonomy. This group of veterans is seen as having "greater distrust of institutions and unwillingness to be awed by traditional authorities." so that "they are less willing to be passive recipients of our wisdom." The individual Vietnam veteran, it is said, "feels an intense positive identification with his own age group" and is part of "an unspoken 'pact of youth' which assures mutual safety from threats to his sense of individual identity."

Even when sufficiently incapacitated to require hospitalization in a VA psychiatric ward, Vietnam veterans tend to stress the issue of

---

Robert Jay Lifton, distinguished author, psychiatrist, and professor of psychiatry at Yale and City University of New York was the first to develop analytical and interpretive categories to help explain the experience of those who have encountered severe trauma at close range. In addition to working with veterans of the Vietnam War, Lifton has studied the survivors of the atomic bomb attack on Hiroshima (cf. his book, *Death in Life: Survivors of Hiroshima* [New York: Basic Books, 1982]) and the psychology of the Nazi movement (cf. his book, *The Nazi Doctors: Medical Killing and the Psychology of Genocide* [New York: Basic Books, 1986]). In all of these studies, Lifton displays the influence of Erik Erikson's work on "identity and the life cycle." Lifton's thesis is that traumatic events carry the power to reverse the desired psychological process, and to stimulate "identity crisis" instead of "ego-integrity." The subject addressed in this essay is explored in much greater detail in his book, *Home from the War: Vietnam Veterans: Neither Victims Nor Executioners* (New York: Basic Books, 1985). The attitude Lifton takes toward the subject is important for its own sake, but needs also to be understood as having fundamentally influenced the therapy that has been developed for post-traumatic stress disorders as well as the resocialization and adjustment techniques that are practiced in Vet Centers.

"generation gap" and larger social problems rather than merely their own "sickness." And there is evidence, confirmed by my own observations in a series of "rap groups" with returning Vietnam veterans, that large numbers of them feel themselves to be "hurting" and in need of psychological help, but avoid contact with the Veterans Administration—because they associate it with the war-military-government establishment, with the forces responsible for a hated ordeal, or because of their suspicion (whether on the basis of hearsay or personal experience) that VA doctors are likely to interpret their rage at everything connected with the war as no more than their own individual "problem." The result has been (again in the words of VA observers) "degrees of bitterness, distrust, and suspicion of those in positions of authority and responsibility."

To be sure, these patterns can occur in veterans of any war, along with restless shifting of jobs and living arrangements, and difficulty forming or maintaining intimate relationships. Precisely such tendencies in World War II veterans, men who had "lost a sense of personal sameness and historical continuity," led Erik Erikson to evolve his concepts of "identity crisis" and "loss of 'ego-identity.' "

But these men give the impression of something more. Murray *Murray* Polner, who interviewed more than two hundred Vietnam veterans of *Power* diverse views and backgrounds for his book *No Victory Parades: The Return of the Vietnam Veteran*, concluded that "not one of them— hawk, dove, or haunted—was entirely free of doubt about the nature of the war and the American role in it." As a group they retain the "gnawing suspicion that 'it was all for nothing.' " Polner concluded that "never before have so many questioned as much, as these veterans have, the essential rightness of what they were forced to do." Beyond just being young and having been asked to fight a war, these men have a sense of violated personal and social order, of fundamental break in human connection, which they relate to conditions imposed upon them by the war in Vietnam.

Some of the quality of that war experience is revealed in the following recollection of My Lai by a GI who was there, and whom I shall henceforth refer to as "the My Lai survivor":

> The landscape doesn't change much. For days and days you see just about nothing. It's unfamiliar—always unfamiliar. Even when you go back to the same place, it's unfamiliar. And it makes you feel as though, well, there's nothing left in the world but this. . . . You have the illusion of going great distances and traveling, like hundreds of miles . . . and you end up in the same place because you're only a couple of miles away . . . But you feel like it's not all real. It couldn't

possibly be. We couldn't still be in this country. We've been walking for days. . . . You're in Vietnam and they're using real bullets. . . . Here in Vietnam they're actually shooting people for no reason. . . . Any other time you think, it's such an extreme. Here you can go ahead and shoot them for nothing. . . . As a matter of fact it's even . . . smiled upon, you know. Good for you. Everything is backwards. That's part of the kind of unreality of the thing. To the grunt [infantryman] this isn't backwards. He doesn't understand. . . . But something [at My Lai] was missing. Something you thought was real that would accompany this. It wasn't there. . . . There was something missing in the whole business that made it seem it really wasn't happening. . . .

The predominant emotional tone here is all-encompassing absurdity and moral inversion. The absurdity has to do with a sense of being alien and profoundly lost, yet at the same time locked into a situation as meaningless and unreal as it is deadly. The moral inversion, eventuating in a sense of evil, has to do not only with the absolute reversal of ethical standards but with its occurrence in absurdity, without inner justification, so that the killing is rendered naked.

This overall emotional sense, which I came to view as one of *absurd evil*, is conveyed even more forcefully by something said in a rap group by a former "grunt." He had been talking about the horrors of combat, and told how, after a heavy air strike on an NLF unit, his company came upon a terrible scene of dismembered corpses. Many of the men then began a kind of wild victory dance, in the midst of which they mutilated the bodies still further. He recalled wondering to himself: "What am I doing here? We don't take any land. We don't give it back. We just mutilate bodies. What the fuck are we doing here?" Whatever the element of retrospective judgment in this kind of recollection, the wording was characteristic. During another rap-group discussion of how men felt about what they were doing in Vietnam, a man asked: "What the hell *was* going on? What the fuck *were* we doing?"

These questions express a sense of the war's total lack of order or structure, the feeling that there was no genuine purpose, that nothing could ever be secured or gained, and that there could be no measurable progress. We may say that there was no genuine "script" or "scenario" of war that could provide meaning or even sequence or progression, a script within which armies clash, battles are fought, won, or lost, and individual suffering, courage, cowardice, or honor can be evaluated. Nor could the patrols seeking out an elusive enemy, the ambushes in which Americans were likely to be the surprised victims, or the search-and-destroy missions lashing out blindly at noncombatants achieve the psychological status of meaningful combat ritual. Rather, these became part of the general absurdity, the antimeaning.

So did the "secret movements" on this alien terrain, since, as one man put it, "Little kids could tell us exactly where we would set up the next night." The men were adrift in an environment not only strange and hostile but offering no honorable encounter, no warrior grandeur.

Now there are mutilations, amidst absurdity and evil, in any war. Men who fight wars inevitably become aware of the terrible disparity between romantic views of heroism expressed "back home" and the reality of degradation and unspeakable suffering they have witnessed, experienced, and caused. One thinks of the answer given by Audie Murphy, much-decorated hero of World War II, to the question put to him about how long it takes a man to get over his war experiences. Murphy's reply, recorded in his obituary, was that one never does. What he meant was that residual inner conflicts—survivor conflicts— stay with one indefinitely. These conflicts have to do with anxiety in relationship to an indelible death imprint, death guilt inseparable from that imprint, various forms of prolonged psychic numbing and suppression of feeling, profound suspicion of the counterfeit (or of "counterfeit nurturance"), and an overall inability to give significant inner form—to "formulate"—one's war-linked death immersion. This was undoubtedly a factor in Murphy's repeated difficulties and disappointments after his return from his war, as it has been in the unrealized lives and premature deaths of many war heroes, and indeed in the paradox stated by Charles Omen about warriors during the Middle Ages being "the best of soldiers while the war lasted . . . [but] a most dangerous and unruly race in times of truce or peace."

Yet veterans have always come to some terms with their war experiences—some formulation of their survival permitting them to overcome much of their death anxiety and death guilt, their diffuse suspiciousness and numbing. Crucial even to this partial resolution of survivor conflict is the veteran's capacity to believe that his war had purpose and significance beyond the immediate horrors he witnessed. He can then connect his own actions with ultimately humane principles, and can come to feel that he performed a dirty but necessary job. He may even be able to experience renewed feelings of continuity or symbolic immortality around these larger principles, side by side with his residual survivor pain and conflict.

But the central fact of the Vietnam War is that no one really believes in it. The "larger purposes" put forth to explain the American presence—repelling "outside invaders," or giving the people of the South an opportunity "to choose their own form of government"—are directly contradicted by the overwhelming evidence a GI encounters that *he* is the outside invader, that the government he has come to defend is justly hated by the people he has come to "help," and that he, the American "helper," is hated by them most of all. Even those who seem to acquiesce to these claims do so, as Polner's work suggests, with profound inner doubt, and in response to tenuous and defensive "psychological work."

Nor do many actually fighting the war take seriously the quasi-religious impulse to "fight the Communists." Rather, their gut realization that something is wrong with this war is expressed in combat briefings (often by lieutenants or captains) as described to me by a number of former GI's: "*I* don't know why *I'm* here. *You* don't know why *you're* here. But since we're *both* here, we might as well try to do a good job and do our best to stay alive."

This is the very opposite of calling forth a heroic ideal or an immortalizing purpose. And while it is true that survival is the preoccupation of men in any war, this kind of briefing is not only a total disclaimer of any purpose beyond survival but a direct transmission of the absurdity and antimeaning pervading the Vietnam War. That transmission has a distinct psychological function. It inserts a modicum of outfront honesty into the situation's basic absurdity, so that the absurdity itself can become shared. And the way is paved for the intense cooperation, brotherhood, and mutual love characteristic of and necessary to military combat. In the end, however, everybody feels the absence of larger purpose. Hence the deadpan professional observation by a Veterans Administration psychiatrist, in response to a query from his chief medical director concerning the special characteristics and problems of the "Vietnam era veteran": "Vietnam combat veterans tend to see their experience as an exercise in survival rather than a defense of national values."

The distinction is important. Johan Huizinga, in discussing the connection between play and war, speaks of the concept of the "ordeal," its relationship to "the idea of glory" and ultimately to the warrior's quest for "a decision of holy validity." This theological vocabulary conveys well the immortalizing appeal battle holds for the warrior. But in Vietnam one has undergone the "ordeal" or test without the possibility of that "idea of glory" or "decision of holy validity." There is all of the pain but none of the glory. What we find instead is best understood as an *atrocity-producing situation.*

THE BODY COUNT

Many forms of desensitization and rage contributed to My Lai, some of them having to do with specifically American aberrations concerning race, class, and masculinity. But my assumption in speaking of an atrocity-producing situation is that, given the prevailing external conditions, men of very divergent backgrounds—indeed just about *anyone*—can enter into the "psychology of slaughter." This assumption is borne out by an examination of the step-by-step sequence by which the American men who actually went to My Lai came to internalize and then act upon an irresistible image of slaughter.

During Basic Training, the men encountered (as did most recruits) drill sergeants and other noncommissioned officers who were veterans of Vietnam and as such had a special aura of authority and demonic mystery. From these noncoms the recruit heard stories of Vietnam, of how tough and "dirty, rotten, and miserable" (as one remembered being told) it was there. He also heard descriptions of strange incidents in which it became clear that Vietnamese civilians were being indiscriminately killed—tales of Americans creeping up to village areas and tossing grenades into "hootches," of artillery strikes on inhabited areas, and of brutal treatment of Vietnamese picked up during patrols or combat sweeps. Sometimes pictures of badly mutilated Vietnamese corpses were shown to him to illustrate the tales.

Here and later on there is a striking contrast between the formal instruction (given by rote if at all) to kill only military adversaries, and the informal message (loud and clear) to kill just about everyone. That message, as the My Lai survivor put it, is that "it's OK to kill them," and in fact "that's what you're supposed to do"—or as a former marine received it: "You've gotta go to Vietnam, you've gotta kill the gooks." Similarly, American leaders have found it politically inexpedient and morally unacceptable (to themselves as well as to others) to state outright that all Vietnamese (or "gooks") are fair game; instead they have turned the other cheek and undergone their own psychic numbing, while permitting—indeed making inevitable—the message of slaughter. Sometimes the informal message of slaughter was conveyed by such crude symbolism as what the marines came to call the "rabbit lesson." On the last day before leaving for Vietnam, the staff NCO holds a rabbit as he lectures on escape, evasion, and survival in the jungle. The men become intrigued by the rabbit, fond of it, and then the NCO "cracks it in the neck, skins it, disembowels it . . . and then they throw the guts out into the audience." As one marine explained: "You can get anything out of that you want, but that's your last lesson you catch in the United States before you leave for Vietnam." The message reflected profound moral contradictions—something close to a counterfeit universe.

A key to understanding the psychology of My Lai, and of America in Vietnam, is the body count. Nothing else so well epitomizes the war's absurdity and evil. Recording the enemy's losses is a convention of war, but in the absence of any other goals or criteria for success, counting the "enemy" dead can become both malignant obsession and compulsive falsification. For the combat GI in Vietnam, killing Vietnamese was the entire mission, the number killed his and his unit's only standard of achievement, and the falsification of that count (on many levels) the only way to hold on to the Vietnam illusion of "noble battle." Killing *someone,* moreover, became necessary for overcoming one's own death anxiety. At My Lai, killing Vietnamese enabled men to cease feeling themselves guilty survivors and impotent targets, and to become instead omnipotent dispensers of death who had "realized" their "mission." Only killing, then, could affirm power, skill, and worth. . . .

I am convinced that the ethically sensitive historians of the future will select the phenomenon of the body count as the perfect symbol of America's descent into evil. The body count manages to distill the essence of the American numbing, brutalization, and illusion into a grotesque technicalization: there is something to count, a statistic for accomplishment. I know of no greater corruption than this phenomenon: the amount of killing—any killing—becomes the total measure of achievement. And concerning that measure, one lies, to others as well as to oneself, about why, who, what, and how many one kills.

OPENING UP

In earlier work, I found that survivors of the Hiroshima holocaust experienced what I described as "a vast breakdown of faith in the larger human matrix supporting each individual life, and therefore a loss of faith (or trust) in the structure of existence." The same is true not only for large numbers of Vietnam veterans but, perhaps in more indirect and muted ways, for Americans in general. This shattered existential faith has to do with remaining bound by the image of holocaust, of grotesque and absurd death and equally absurd survival. Even Americans who have not seen Vietnam feel something of a national descent into existential evil, a sense that the killing and dying done in their name cannot be placed within a meaningful system of symbols, cannot be convincingly "formulated." The result is a widespread if again vague feeling of lost integrity at times approaching moral-psychological disintegration.

What distinguishes Vietnam veterans from the rest of their countrymen is their awesome experience and knowledge of what others merely sense and resist knowing, their suffering on the basis of that knowledge and experience, and, in the case of antiwar veterans, their commitment to telling the tale. That commitment, especially for rap-group participants, meant asking a question very much like that of

Remarque's hero in *All Quiet on the Western Front:* "What would become of us if everything that happens out there were quite clear to us?" "Out there" means Vietnam, their own minds, and in the end, American society as well.

As part of their mission as survivors, antiwar veterans seek understanding of and liberation from the political and military agents of their own corruption. Their constant probing of these and other aspects of American society is less in the spirit of calm reflection than of anxious and pressured need. Amidst their confusions and touchiness, they have shared with one another a bond of brotherhood around their holocaust, their corruption, and their struggle against both. There is a sense in which they can fully trust only those who share their experience and their mission, though in each this trust may live side by side with suspicion of one another, related to suspicion of oneself.

They are loath to judge other veterans whose corruption has been much greater than their own. I recall a very tense moment during a psychiatric meeting at which a group of veterans described some of their experiences. When they had finished, a questioner from the floor asked them what they thought of a promise made by Lieutenant Calley (who was then still on trial) that, should he be acquitted, he would go on a speaking tour throughout the country on behalf of peace. The men visibly stiffened and answered in a series of terse phrases, such as "I can't judge him," "I have nothing to say about him," and "It could have been any of us." They knew too much about their own corruptibility and everyone else's within that specific atrocity-producing situation to be able to pass judgment upon a man in whom the disintegrative process had gone still further. They were trying to cope not only with their own guilt but with their overall formulation of their holocaust.

For they have taken on a very special survivor mission, one of extraordinary historical and psychological significance. They are flying in the face of the traditional pattern of coping with survivor emotions, which was to join organizations of veterans that not only justify their particular war but embrace war-making and militarism in general. Contemporary "antiwar warriors" are turning that pattern on its head, and finding significance in their survival by exposing precisely the meaninglessness—and the evil—of their war. They do so, not as individual poets or philosophers (like those who emerged, for instance, from World War I), but as an organized group of ordinary war veterans. The psychological rub in the process is the need to call forth and confront their own "warlike" selves, or, as they sometimes put it "the person in me that fought the war."

For a number of them, and at varying intervals, political activities become inseparable from psychological need. Telling their story to American society has been both a political act and a means of confronting psychologically an inauthentic experience and moving beyond it toward authenticity. For such people not only is protest necessary to psychological help—it *is* psychological help. At one moment one sees confused youngsters struggling to put together their shattered psychological selves—at another, young people with premature wisdom. As one of the expressed this uneasy combination to me, "I feel bitter because I'm a pretty young guy and the things I had to do and see I shouldn't have to in a normal lifetime." Still, they feel they have come to difficult truths that "adult" American society refuses to face. Indeed, in their eyes most of adult America lives in illusion. They describe others saying such things to them as "You're different from other people" or "You seem to know things that other people don't know." Since that knowledge has to do with death and pain, they have a double view of themselves in another way as well. They see themselves sometimes as a victimized group unrecognized and rejected by existing society, and sometimes as a special elite who alone can lay claim to a unique experience of considerable value in its very extremity and evil. . . .

There is a bitter paradox around the whole issue of wrongdoing that is neither lost on these men nor fully resolved by them. Sent as intruders in an Asian revolution, asked to fight a filthy and unfathomable war, they return as intruders in their own society, defiled by that war in the eyes of the very people who sent them as well as in their own. Images and feelings of guilt are generally associated with transgression—with having crossed boundaries that should not be crossed, with having gone beyond limits that should not be exceeded. Here the transgression has to do with two kinds of death, that which they witnessed and "survived" (deaths of buddies) and that which they inflicted on the Vietnamese. Though the two involve different experiences, they merge in the absurdity and evil of the entire project. Hence the men feel themselves to have been part of a "killing force" not only in the literal military sense but in a moral-psychological sense as well. Above all, they are survivors who cannot inwardly justify what they have seen and done—and are therefore caught in a vicious circle of death and guilt. Memories of deaths witnessed or inflicted, the *death imprint,* evoke disturbing feelings of guilt, which in turn activate that imprint. The resulting death guilt, at whatever level of consciousness, is the fundamental psychological legacy of this particular war.

Hence the touchiness of the veterans, revealed especially during early rap groups, about certain questions frequently asked them upon their return, especially by children: "Did you *kill* anyone over there? How *many* did you kill? How did you *feel* when you killed someone?" The veterans felt badly used by their questioners, saw them as deriving some kind of pleasure from hearing about killing, and interpreted these questions as proof that people in America, even children, are "programmed for violence." But they quickly came back to their own struggles about how much to condemn themselves for having killed or helped with killing, and for having remained alive. They explored the realization that they *could* kill, *did* kill, and only partly accepted the justification they themselves put forth, namely that it was *necessary to* kill in order to survive. Much of those early meetings was taken up with the men testing one another—and finding themselves wanting—by setting up virtually impossible moral choices: "If you had to kill someone again in order to survive, would you do it?" If you had to kill an innocent person in order to survive would you do *that?*" If you had to kill a *child* in order to survive, would you do *that?*"

In posing these dilemmas, they were groping for a moral and psychological "position" on what they had done. They were performing a kind of psychic *danse macabre* around their own death guilt, moving gingerly back and forth, toward and away from it. At times they seemed to pass judgments of total evil: on all men or on "human nature" (the idea that anyone would kill anyone to save his own life); on American society (its demand that everyone be violent); and ultimately on themselves (their willingness to kill, sometimes even with pleasure, having revealed them to be, at bottom, nothing but murderers). But one could also perceive a search for an alternative to total evil, for a better way to recognize and confront their own guilt. . . .

We see two general forms of guilt, that can be designated as *static* and *animating.* Static guilt is characterized by a closed universe of transgression and expected punishment in which one is unable to extricate oneself from a deathlike individual condition. One form we see it take is that of *numbed guilt,* in which one's "deadened state" seems to be a literal form of retribution for one's own act of killing: the punishment fits the crime.

Numbed guilt resembles what Freud called an unconscious sense of guilt—but I use the term to emphasize the extent to which the entire being is "frozen" or desensitized in order to avoid feeling the "wound" (or "death") one has caused (or thinks one has caused), leaving one anesthetized from much of life itself.

Numbed guilt includes a vague feeling of badness, of having transgressed, in the absence of a form or even a clear-cut emotional structure within which to articulate that guilt. Unable to confront what

Numbed Guilt

one has done, or even to feel clearly guilty, one is instead plagued by an unformed, free-floating discomfort with oneself, which is likely to be associated with touchiness, suspiciousness, and withdrawal.

"Self-lacerating" guilt is another form of static guilt, in which, rather than a sustained "deadening," one performs a perpetual "killing" of the self. That is, the *mea culpa* of self-condemnation takes the form of a repetition-compulsion, and the very insistence upon one's own unmitigated evil prevents actual "knowledge" of guilt. The "as if" situation here is that of continuous reenactment of the retribution, continuous killing of the self. Guilt accompanying clinical forms of depression, and what we speak of more generally as "neurotic guilt," tend to be of this self-lacerating variety.

In both of these forms of static guilt one is cut off from the life process—held in a state of separation and inner disintegration as well as stasis—that is, in a death-dominated condition.

Animating guilt, in contrast, is characterized by bringing oneself to life around one's guilt. This requires active imagery of possibility beyond the guilt itself. Animating guilt and image beyond the guilt are in a continuous dialectical relationship, the one requiring the other. Thus, animating guilt propels one toward connection, integrity, and movement. But for this self-propulsion to occur, one requires prior internal images of at least the possibility of these life-affirming patterns, imagery that can in turn relate to something in the external environment. In this sense, the imagery of possibility antedates the animating guilt, but it is also true that animating guilt can activate the individual to the point of virtually creating such imagery.

Above all, animating guilt is a source of self-knowledge—confirming Martin Buber's dictum that "man is the being who is capable of becoming guilty and is capable of illuminating his guilt." In illuminating one's guilt, one illuminates the self. Nor is animating guilt merely "restitutive," though it can certainly be that. Rather, it presses beyond existing arrangements, toward new images and possibilities, toward transformation. Above all, animating guilt is inseparable from the idea of being responsible for one's actions—so much so that we may define it as the anxiety of responsibility.

To be sure, these various forms of guilt do not separate out as precisely as this schema might suggest; they in fact overlap and probably never exist in pure form. But I have observed in a considerable number of veterans a relationship to guilt so animating as to be a form of personal liberation. The discovery of one's animating guilt can, for such men, be nothing less than rediscovery of oneself as a human being. One deserter, for instance, remembered his dramatic recognition that "I was somebody with feelings who had done something wrong and I—I was not an animal or some kind of killing machine."

RAGE AND VIOLENCE

Unresolved death guilt can also be expressed through feelings of rage and impulses toward violence. These are prominent in survivors of any war, but the binds, betrayals, and corruptions experienced by the Vietnam veteran fuel those tendencies to the point where they invade large zones of his psyche. Bursts of anger were very frequent during our rap sessions, and it was more or less taken for granted that rage close to the surface was the normal emotion of the Vietnam veteran. The important question was what one did with the rage. During individual and group sessions, three different patterns of rage and violence seemed to emerge.

There was first what could be called the habit of violence. In war, violence becomes a quick and absolute solution to whatever seems to threaten or intrude, all the more so when there is great confusion about where danger lies and who is the enemy. Beyond that, the veteran can become habituated to the survivor mission of "revenge" (for buddies killed and other forms of suffering) and extend it to the civilian environment. A number of veterans told how, when brushed by someone on the street—or simply annoyed by something another person had done—they would have an impulse to "throttle" or kill him. And they would directly associate this impulse with patterns of behavior cultivated in Vietnam: with "wasting" whoever passed for the enemy, with the numbing and brutalization underlying that behavior, but also with the rage beneath the numbing. As one man put it: "In Vietnam you're mad all the time—you wake up mad—you're mad when you eat, mad when you sleep, mad when you walk, mad when you sit—just mad all the time." He was undoubtedly overemphasizing the *awareness* of anger, but probably accurate about the extent of its inner existence, even if defended against. (His use of the word "mad" could also unwittingly imply "craziness.") In any case, an important segment of a generation of young American men built identities and life-styles around the rage and violence of a war environment as absorbing as it was corrupting. The guilt-linked sense of these inner zones of rage and violence is precisely what causes a man to retain the image of himself as a "monster". . . .

A second form of rage and potential violence centers around the theme of betrayal, the veterans' sense of having been victimized, badly used, or as they often put it, "fucked over," in having been sent to fight in Vietnam. They spoke about having been misled, put in a situation where they both slaughtered people and suffered for no reason, and were then abused or ignored on their return. There was sometimes talk of contemptuous treatment from employers or prospective employers, to whom "coming from Vietnam didn't mean a damn thing" (though they also realized that on many occasions, it was they, the veterans, who resisted the jobs). In this and other ways they expressed "victim's rage," which could extend to virtually every aspect of living.

At the same time the group was sensitive to, and would critically explore, tendencies to remain immobilized by extreme suspicion and a paranoid outlook, or by notions of "destroying everything"—American society, the people in it.

For just as the men rejected the imposed role of executioner, so they rejected that of "victim." It was always a matter of a particular person and his behavior, actions, or decisions—never a mere "victim"—however duped and badly treated by the all too real forces of victimization. These external forces (the government and military pursuing the war, the police and courts imposing absurd penalties for marihuana use as a way of suppressing a political militant, and so on) were taken seriously as part of the equation; there was never a reduction of all rage to childhood resentments, though these too were examined. Rage and indignation were too much respected for that: they were looked upon as significant, at times painful and self-destructive, but often appropriate and valuable emotions.

The rage could be directed toward any figures or symbols of authority, especially official authority—political leaders, the Veterans Administration, representatives of "the establishment" or ordinary middle-class society or the "older generation." Specific leaders and symbols were also discussed at length, so that psychological judgments could be informed by critical perspectives on "normal" social arrangements. But there was a special kind of rage reserved for the military.

The men expressed fantasies, old or current, of violent revenge toward those in the military who had abused them, especially toward "lifers" (regular army men), who seemed much more hated than anybody officially designated as "the enemy." These images could be relatively focused, or they could take on the diffuse, impotent quality of a recollection of one deserter: "I wanted to become a Communist. I wanted to assassinate the President. I wanted to organize some kind of uprising that would swoop down on the Pentagon—save the world from the imperialistic United States, et cetera, et cetera."

More frequently, the men would describe a gradually mounting bitterness at being "hassled" and ultimately betrayed by the military. That "betrayal" could take the form of a variety of small indignities, broken promises, bad assignments, lack of recognition, or brutalization by specific officers or noncoms—but always at the end of the road was the ultimate betrayal of Vietnam. Those most embittered toward the military were the ones who had initially believed in it and given themselves to it. Their resentful critique could extend far beyond the Vietnam War to corruptions throughout its structure, but they would always return to the war as both reflecting and furthering the poisoning of an institution they had admired, and within which they had for a time flourished. For them the betrayal was greatest.

These first two patterns—the habit of violence and the sense of having been betrayed—hearken back to the past, even if mostly the immediate past. But there is a third, more forward-looking pattern of rage and potential violence that seemed to dwarf the other two in intensity—or, more accurately, to combine with the other two patterns to give the rage a more immediate focus, I refer to the rage associated with a man telling his story of what he had experienced in Vietnam—to a considerable extent laying himself bare—and then being rebuffed. This rage was directed not so much toward war supporters or political opponents but toward those who "don't give a damn."

When the antiwar veterans hold their public hearings in various parts of the country and reveal details of brutality, murder, and atrocity, they are by no means simply beating their breasts to insist upon their own everlasting guilt. Rather, they are angrily exposing the atrocity-producing situation within which these acts were committed. Even the handful of veterans who "turned themselves in" to legal authorities at the time of the trial of Lieutenant Calley were saying something like: "Look, you bastards who are passing judgment—*I* did these things *too*—*everyone* did them." And when they flamboyantly cast away their medals near the Capitol building, they did so with the rage of "survivor-heroes" not only rejecting tainted awards but literally throwing them in the face of those who bestowed them. To be sure, there is guilt behind their actions. But there is also the bitter rage of men who have been betrayed, the angry insistence that the guilt be shared, and, above all, that the nature of the atrocity-producing situation be recognized. When they make this effort and are rebuffed, the antiwar veterans are left, so to speak, alone with their static guilt and impotent rage. What they seek and in some cases have partly achieved is a way of using their guilt and rage to transform themselves and their society.

6

Why Men Love War
William Broyles, Jr.

I last saw Hiers in a rice paddy in Vietnam. He was nineteen then—
my wonderfully skilled and maddeningly insubordinate radio opera-
tor. For months we were seldom more than three feet apart. Then one
day he went home, and fifteen years passed before we met by accident
last winter at the Vietnam Veterans Memorial in Washington. A few
months later I visited Hiers and his wife, Susan, in Vermont, where
they run a bed-and-breakfast place. The first morning we were up at
dawn trying to save five newborn rabbits. Hiers built a nest of rabbit
fur and straw in his barn and positioned a lamp to provide warmth
against the bitter cold.

"What people can't understand," Hiers said, gently picking up each
tiny rabbit and placing it in the nest, "is how much fun Vietnam was.
I loved it. I loved it, and I can't tell anybody."

Hiers loved war. And as I drove back from Vermont in a blizzard,
my children asleep in the back of the car, I had to admit that for all
these years I also had loved it, and more than I knew. I hated war,
too. Ask me, ask any man who has been to war about his experience,
and chances are we'll say we don't want to talk about it—implying
that we hated it so much, it was so terrible, that we would rather
leave it buried. And it is no mystery why men hate war. War is ugly,
horrible, evil, and it is reasonable for men to hate all that. But I believe
that most men who have been to war would have to admit, if they are
honest, that somewhere inside themselves they loved it too, loved it
as much as anything that has happened to them before or since. And

---

William Broyles, Jr. served as a Marine in Vietnam in 1969 and 1970. Subsequently, he
was editor-in-chief of *Newsweek* and of *Texas Monthly*. Following a journey to Vietnam in
1983, he wrote the book *Brothers in Arms* (New York: Alfred A. Knopf, 1986) document-
ing his experience. The essay that is being republished in this anthology first appeared
in *Esquire* magazine, November, 1984, pp. 55–65. It is nearly universally acknowledged
as the most perceptive statement on what motivates men to become soldiers, and why
the act of killing carries intense excitement in addition, at times, to remorse.

how do you explain that to your wife, your children, your parents, or your friends?

That's why men in their sixties and seventies sit in their dens and recreation rooms around America and know that nothing in their life will equal the day they parachuted into St. Lo or charged the bunker on Okinawa. That's why veterans' reunions are invariably filled with boozy awkwardness, forced camaraderie ending in sadness and tears: you are together again, these are the men who were your brothers, but it's not the same, can never be the same. That's why when we returned from Vietnam we moped around, listless, not interested in anything or anyone. Something had gone out of our lives forever, and our behavior on returning was inexplicable except as the behavior of men who had lost a great—perhaps the great—love of their lives, and had no way to tell anyone about it.

In part we couldn't describe our feelings because the language failed us: the civilian-issue adjectives and nouns, verbs, and adverbs, seemed made for a different universe. There were no metaphors that connected the war to everyday life. But we were also mute, I suspect, out of shame. Nothing in the way we are raised admits the possibility of loving war. It is at best a necessary evil, a patriotic duty to be discharged and then put behind us. To love war is to mock the very values we supposedly fight for. It is to be insensitive, reactionary, a brute.

But it may be more dangerous, both for men and nations, to suppress the reasons men love war than to admit them. In *Apocalypse Now* Robert Duvall, playing a brigade commander, surveys a particularly horrific combat scene and says, with great sadness, "You know, someday this war's gonna be over." He is clearly meant to be a psychopath, decorating enemy bodies with playing cards, riding to war with Wagner blaring. We laugh at him—Hey! nobody's like that! And last year in Grenada American boys charged into battle playing Wagner, a new generation aping the movies of Vietnam the way we aped the movies of World War II, learning nothing, remembering nothing.

Alfred Kazin wrote that war is the enduring condition of twentieth-century man. He was only partly right. War is the enduring condition of man, period. Men have gone to war over everything from Helen of Troy to Jenkin's ear. Two million Frenchmen and Englishmen died in muddy trenches in World War I because a student shot an archduke. The truth is, the reasons don't matter. There is a reason for every war and a war for every reason.

For centuries men have hoped that with history would come progress, and with progress, peace. But progress has simply given man the means to make war even more horrible; no wars in our savage past can begin to match the brutality of the wars spawned in this century, in the beautifully ordered, civilized landscape of Europe, where everyone is literate and classical music plays in every village café. War is not an aberration; it is part of the family, the crazy uncle we try—in vain—to keep locked in the basement.

Consider my own example. I am not a violent person. I have not been in a fight since grade school. Aside from being a fairly happy-go-lucky carnivore, I have no lust for blood, nor do I enjoy killing animals, fish, or even insects. My days are passed in reasonable contentment, filled with the details of work and everyday life. I am also a father now, and a man who has helped create life is war's natural enemy. I have seen what war does to children, makes them killers or victims, robs them of their parents, their homes, and their innocence—steals their childhood and leaves them marked in body, mind, and spirit.

I spent most of my combat tour in Vietnam trudging through its jungles and rice paddies without incident, but I have seen enough of war to know that I never want to fight again, and that I would do everything in my power to keep my son from fighting. Then why, at the oddest times—when I am in a meeting or running errands, or on beautiful summer evenings, with the light fading and children playing around me—do my thoughts turn back fifteen years to a war I didn't believe in and never wanted to fight? Why do I miss it?

I miss it because I loved it, loved it in strange and troubling ways. When I talk about loving war I don't mean the romantic notion of war that once mesmerized generations raised on Walter Scott. What little was left of that was ground into the mud at Verdun and Passchendaele; honor and glory do not survive the machine gun. And it's not the mindless bliss of martyrdom that sends Iranian teenagers armed with sticks against Iraqi tanks. Nor do I mean the sort of hysteria that can grip a whole country, the way during the Falklands war the English press inflamed the lust that lurks beneath the cool exterior of Britain. That is vicarious war, the thrill of participation without risk, the lust of the audience for blood. It is easily fanned, that lust; even the invasion of a tiny island like Grenada can do it. Like all lust, for as long as it lasts it dominates everything else; a nation's other problems are seared away, a phenomenon exploited by kings, dictators, and presidents since civilization began.

And I don't mean war as an addiction, the constant rush that war junkies get, the crazies mailing ears home to their girlfriends, the zoomies who couldn't get an erection unless they were cutting in the afterburners on their F-4s. And, finally, I'm not talking about how some men my age feel today, men who didn't go to war but now have a sort of nostalgic longing for something they missed, some classic male experience, the way some women who didn't have children worry they missed something basic about being a woman, something they didn't value when they could have done it.

I'm talking about why thoughtful, loving men can love war even while knowing and hating it. Like any love, the love of war is built on a complex of often contradictory reasons. Some of them are fairly painless to discuss; others go almost too deep, stir the caldron too much. I'll give the more respectable reasons first.

Part of the love of war stems from its being an experience of great intensity; its lure is the fundamental human passion to witness, to see things, what the Bible calls the lust of the eye and the Marines in Vietnam called eye fucking. War stops time, intensifies experience to the point of a terrible ecstasy. It is the dark opposite of that moment of passion caught in "Ode on a Grecian Urn": "For ever warm and still to be enjoy'd/ For ever panting, and for ever young." War offers endless exotic experiences, enough "I couldn't fucking believe it" 's to last a lifetime.

Most people fear freedom; war removes that fear. And like a stern father, it provides with its order and discipline both security and an irresistible urge to rebel against it, a constant yearning to fly over the cuckoo's nest. The midnight requisition is an honored example. I remember one elaborately planned and meticulously executed raid on our principal enemy—the U.S. Army, not the North Vietnamese— to get lightweight blankets and cleaning fluid for our rifles, repeated later in my tour, as a mark of my changed status, to obtain a refrigerator and an air-conditioner for our office. To escape the Vietnamese police we tied sheets together and let ourselves down from the top floor of whorehouses, and on one memorable occasion a friend who is now a respectable member of our diplomatic corps hid himself inside a rolled-up Oriental rug while the rest of us careered off in the truck, leaving him to make his way back stark naked to our base six miles away. War, since it steals our youth, offers a sanction to play boys' games.

War replaces the difficult gray areas of daily life with an eerie, serene clarity. In war you usually know who is your enemy and who is your friend, and are given means of dealing with both. (That was, incidentally, one of the great problems with Vietnam: it was hard to tell friend from foe—it was too much like ordinary life.)

War is an escape from the everyday into a special world where the bonds that hold us to our duties in daily life—the bonds of family, community, work—disappear. In war, all bets are off. It's the frontier beyond the last settlement, it's Las Vegas. The men who do well in peace do not necessarily do well at war, while those who were misfits and failures may find themselves touched with fire. U.S. Grant, selling firewood on the streets of St. Louis and then four years later commanding the Union armies, is the best example, although I knew many Marines who were great warriors but whose ability to adapt to civilian life was minimal.

I remember Kirby, a skinny kid with JUST YOU AND ME LORD tattooed on his shoulder. Kirby had extended his tour in Vietnam twice. He had long since ended his attachment to any known organization and lived alone out in the most dangerous areas, where he wandered about night and day, dressed only in his battered fatigue trousers with a .45 automatic tucked into the waistband, his skinny shoulders and arms as dark as a Montagnard's.

One day while out on patrol we found him on the floor of a hut, being tended by a girl in black pajamas, a bullet wound in his arm.

He asked me for a cigarette, then eyed me, deciding if I was worth telling his story to. "I stopped in for a mango, broad daylight, and there bigger'n hell were three NVA officers, real pretty tan uniforms. They got this map spread out on a table, just eyeballin' it, makin' themselves right at home. They looked at me. I looked at them. Then they went for their nine millimeters and I went for my .45."

"Yeah?" I answered. "So what happened?"

"I wasted 'em," he said, then puffed on his cigarette. Just another day at work, killing three men on the way to eat a mango.

"How are you ever going to go back to the world?" I asked him. (He didn't. A few months later a ten-year old Vietcong girl blew him up with a command-detonated booby trap.)

War is a brutal, deadly game, but a game, the best there is. And men love games. You can come back from war broken in mind or body, or not come back at all. But if you come back whole you bring with you the knowledge that you have explored regions of your soul that in most men will always remain uncharted. Nothing I had ever studied was as complex or as creative as the small-unit tactics of Vietnam. No sport I had ever played brought me to such deep awareness of my physical and emotional limits.

One night not long after I had arrived in Vietnam, one of my platoon's observation posts heard enemy movement. I immediately lost all saliva in my mouth. I could not talk; not a sound would pass my lips. My brain erased as if the plug had been pulled—I felt only a dull hum throughout my body, a low-grade current coursing through me like electricity through a power line. After a minute I could at least grunt, which I did as Hiers gave orders to the squad leaders, called in artillery and air support, and threw back the probe. I was terrified. I was ashamed and I couldn't wait for it to happen again.

The enduring emotion of war, when everything else has faded, is comradeship. A comrade in war is a man you can trust with anything, because you trust him with your life. "It is," Philip Caputo wrote in *A Rumor of War*, "unlike marriage, a bond that cannot be broken by a word, by boredom or divorce, or by anything other than death." Despite its extreme right-wing image, war is the only utopian experience most of us ever have. Individual possessions and advantage count for nothing; the group is everything. What you have is shared with your friends. It isn't a particularly selective process, but a love that needs no reasons, that transcends race and personality and education—all those things that would make a difference in peace. It is, simply, brotherly love.

What made this love so intense was that it had no limits, not even death. John Wheeler, in *Touched with Fire*, quotes the Congressional Medal of Honor citation of Hector Santiago-Colon: "Due to the heavy volume of enemy fire and exploding grenades around them, a North Vietnamese soldier was able to crawl, undetected, to their position. Suddenly, the enemy soldier lobbed a hand grenade into Sp4c. Santiago-Colon's foxhole. Realizing that there was no time to throw the grenade out of his position, Sp4c. Santiago-Colon retrieved the grenade, tucked it into his stomach, and, turning away from his comrades, absorbed the full impact of the blast." This is classic heroism, the final evidence of how much comrades can depend on each other. What went through Santiago-Colon's mind for that split second when he could just as easily have dived to safety? It had to be this: my comrades are more important to me than my most valuable possession—my own life.

Isolation is the greatest fear in war. The military historian S.L.A. Marshall conducted intensive studies of combat incidents during World War II and Korea and discovered that at most, only 25 percent of the men who were under fire actually fired their own weapons. The rest cowered behind cover, terrified and helpless—all systems off. Invariably, those men had felt alone, and to feel alone in combat is to cease to function; it is the terrifying prelude to the final loneliness of death. The only men who kept their heads felt connected to other men, a part of something, as if comradeship were some sort of collective life-force, the power to face death and stay conscious. But when those men came home from war, that fear of isolation stayed with many of them, a tiny mustard seed fallen on fertile soil.

When I came back from Vietnam I tried to keep up with my buddies. We wrote letters, made plans to meet, but something always came up and we never seemed to get together. For a few years we exchanged Christmas cards, then nothing. The special world that had sustained our intense comradeship was gone. Everyday life—our work, family, friends, reclaimed us, and we grew up.

But there was something not right about that. In Vietnam I had been closer to Hiers, for example, than to anyone before or since. We were connected by the radio; our lives depended on it, and on each other. We ate, slept, laughed, and were terrified together. When I first arrived in Vietnam I tried to get Hiers to salute me, but he simply wouldn't do it, mustering at most a "Howdy, Lieutenant, how's it hanging?" as we passed. For every time that he didn't salute I told him he would have to fill a hundred sandbags.

We'd reached several thousand sandbags when Hiers took me aside and said, "Look, Lieutenant, I'll be happy to salute you, really. But if I get in the habit back here in the rear I may salute you when we're out in the bush. And those gooks are just waiting for us to salute, tell 'em who the lieutenant is. You'd be the first one blown away." We forgot the sandbags—and the salutes. Months later, when Hiers left the platoon to go home, he turned to me as I stood on our hilltop position, and gave me the smartest salute I'd ever seen. I shot him the finger, and that was the last I saw of him for fifteen years. When we met by accident at the Vietnam memorial it was like a sign; enough time had passed—we were old enough to say goodbye to who we had been and become friends as who we had become.

For us and for thousands of veterans the memorial was special ground. War is theater, and Vietnam had been fought without a third act. It was a set that hadn't been struck; its characters were lost there, with no way to get off and no more lines to say. And so when we came to the Vietnam memorial in Washington we wrote our own endings as we stared at the names on the wall, reached out and touched them, washed them with our tears, said goodbye. We are older now, some of us grandfathers, some quite successful, but the memorial touched some part of us that is still out there, under fire, alone. When we came to that wall and met the memories of our buddies and gave them their due, pulled them up from their buried places and laid our love to rest, we were home at last.

For all these reasons, men love war. But these are the easy reasons, the first circle, the ones we can talk about without risk of disapproval, without plunging too far into the truth or ourselves. But there are other, more troubling reasons why men love war. The love of war stems from the union, deep in the core of our being, between sex and destruction, beauty and horror, love and death. War may be the only way in which most men touch the mythic domains in our soul. It is, for men, at some terrible level the closest thing to what childbirth is for women: the initiation into the power of life and death. It is like lifting off the corner of the universe and looking at what's underneath. To see war is to see into the dark heart of things, that no-man's-land between life and death, or even beyond.

And that explains a central fact about the stories men tell about war. Every good war story is, in at least some of its crucial elements, false. The better the war story, the less of it is likely to be true. Robert Graves wrote that his main legacy from World War I was "a difficulty in telling the truth." I have never once heard a grunt tell a reporter a war story that wasn't a lie, just as some of the stories that I tell about the war are lies. Not that even the lies aren't true, on a certain level. They have a moral, even a mythic, truth, rather than a literal one. They reach out and remind the tellers and listeners of their place in the world. They are the primitive stories told around the fire in smoky tepees after the pipe has been passed. They are all, at bottom, the same.

Some of the best war stories out of Vietnam are in Michael Herr's *Dispatches*. One of Herr's most quoted stories goes like this: "But what a story he told me, as one-pointed and resonant as any war story I ever heard, it took me a year to understand it:

" 'Patrol went up the mountain. One man came back. He died before he could tell us what happened.'

"I waited for the rest, but it seemed not to be that kind of story; when I asked him what had happened he just looked like he felt sorry for me, fucked if he'd waste time telling stories to anyone as dumb as I was."

It is a great story, a combat haiku, all negative space and darkness humming with portent. It seems rich, unique to Vietnam. But listen, now, to this:

"We all went up to Gettysburg, the summer of '63: and some of us came back from there: and that's all except the details." That is the account of Gettysburg by one Praxiteles Swan, onetime captain in the Confederate States Army. The language is different, but it is the same story. And it is a story that I would imagine has been told for as long as men have gone to war. Its purpose is not to enlighten but to exclude; its message is not its content but putting the listener in his place. I suffered. I was there. You were not. Only those facts matter. Everything else is beyond words to tell. As was said after the worst tragedies in Vietnam: "Don't mean nothin'." Which meant, "It means everything, it means too much." Language overload.

War stories inhabit the realm of myth because every war story is about death. And one of the most troubling reasons men love war is the love of destruction, the thrill of killing. In his superb book on World War II, *The Warriors*, J. Glenn Gray wrote that "thousands of youths who never suspected the presence of such an impulse in themselves have learned in military life the mad excitement of destroying." It's what Hemingway meant when he wrote, "Admit that you have liked to kill as all who are soldiers by choice have enjoyed it at some time whether they lie about it or not."

My platoon and I went through Vietnam burning hooches (note how language liberated us—we didn't burn houses and shoot people; we burned hooches and shot gooks), killing dogs and pigs and chickens, destroying, because, as my friend Hiers put it, "We thought it was fun at the time." As anyone who has fired a bazooka or an M-60 machine gun knows, there is something to that power in your finger, the soft, seductive touch of the trigger. It's like the magic sword, a grunt's Excalibur: all you do is move that finger so imperceptibly, just a wish flashing across your mind like a shadow, not even a full brain synapse, and *poof!* in a blast of sound and energy and light a truck or a house or even people disappear, everything flying and settling back into dust.

There is a connection between this thrill and the games we played as children, the endless games of cowboys and Indians and war, the games that ended with "Bang bang you're dead," and everyone who was "dead" got up and began another game. That's war as fantasy, and it's the same emotion that touches us in war movies and books, where death is something without consequence, and not something that ends with terrible finality as blood from our fatally fragile bodies flows out onto the mud. Boys aren't the only ones prone to this fantasy; it possesses the old men who have never been to war and who preside over our burials with the same tears they shed when soldiers die in the movies—tears of fantasy, cheap tears. The love of destruction and killing in war stems from that fantasy of war as a game, but it is the more seductive for being indulged at terrible risk. It is the game survivors play, after they have seen death up close and learned in their hearts how common, how ordinary, and how inescapable it is.

I don't know if I killed anyone in Vietnam, but I tried as hard as I could. I fired at muzzle flashes in the night, threw grenades during ambushes, ordered artillery and bombing where I thought the enemy was. Whenever another platoon got a higher body count, I was disappointed: it was like suiting up for the football game and then not getting to play. After one ambush my men brought back the body of a North Vietnamese soldier. I later found the dead man propped against some C-ration boxes. He had on sunglasses, and a *Playboy* magazine lay open in his lap; a cigarette dangled jauntily from his mouth, and on his head was perched a large and perfectly formed piece of shit.

I pretended to be outraged, since desecrating bodies was frowned on as un-American and counterproductive. But it wasn't outrage I felt. I kept my officer's face on, but inside I was . . . laughing. I laughed—I believe now—in part because of some subconscious appreciation of this obscene linkage of sex and excrement and death; and in part because of the exultant realization that he—whoever he had been— was dead and I—special, unique me—was alive. He was my brother, but I knew him not. In war the line between life and death is gossamer thin; there is joy, true joy, in being alive when so many around you are not. And from the joy of being alive in death's presence to the joy of causing death is, unfortunately, not that great a step.

A lieutenant colonel I knew, a true intellectual, was put in charge of civil affairs, the work we did helping the Vietnamese grow rice and otherwise improve their lives. He was a sensitive man who kept a journal and seemed far better equipped for winning hearts and minds than for a combat command. But he got one, and I remember flying out to visit his fire base the night after it had been attacked by an NVA sapper unit. Most of the combat troops had been out on an operation, so this colonel mustered a motley crew of clerks and cooks and drove the sappers off, chasing them across the rice paddies and killing dozens of these elite enemy troops by the light of flares. That morning, as they were surveying what they had done and loading the dead NVA—all naked and covered with grease and mud so they could penetrate the barbed wire—on mechanical mules like so much garbage, there was a look of beatific contentment on the colonel's face that I had not seen except in charismatic churches. It was the look of a person transported into ecstasy.

And I—what did I do, confronted with this beastly scene? I smiled back, as filled with bliss as he was. That was another of the times I stood on the edge of my humanity, looked into the pit, and loved what I saw there. I had surrendered to an aesthetic that was divorced from that crucial quality of empathy that lets us feel the sufferings of others. And I saw a terrible beauty there. War is not simply the spirit of ugliness, although it is certainly that, the devil's work. But to give the devil his due, it is also an affair of great and seductive beauty.

Art and war were for ages as linked as art and religion. Medieval and Renaissance artists gave us cathedrals, but they also gave us armor, sculptures of war, swords and muskets and cannons of great beauty, art offered to the god of war as reverently as the carved altars were offered to the god of love. War was a public ritual of the highest order, as the beautifully decorated cannons in the Invalides in Paris and the chariots with their depictions of the gods in the Metropolitan Museum of Art so eloquently attest. Men love their weapons, not simply for helping to keep them alive, but for a deeper reason. They love their rifles and their knives for the same reason that the medieval warriors loved their armor and their swords: they are instruments of beauty.

 War _is_ beautiful. There is something about a firefight at night, something about the mechanical elegance of an M-60 machine gun. They are everything they should be, perfect examples of their form. When you are firing out at night, the red tracers go out into the blackness as if you were drawing with a light pen. Then little dots of light start winking back, and green tracers from the AK-47s begin to weave in with the red to form brilliant patterns that seem, given their great speeds, oddly timeless, as if they had been etched on the night. And then perhaps the gunships called Spooky come in and fire their incredible guns like huge hoses washing down from the sky, like something God would do when He was really ticked off. And then the flares pop, casting eerie shadows as they float down on their little parachutes, swinging in the breeze, and anyone who moves in their light seems a ghost escaped from hell.

Daytime offers nothing so spectacular, but it also has its charms. Many men loved napalm, loved its silent power, the way it could make tree lines or houses explode as if by spontaneous combustion. But I always thought napalm was greatly overrated, unless you enjoy watching tires burn. I preferred white phosphorus, which exploded with a fulsome elegance, wreathing its target in intense and billowing white smoke, throwing out glowing red comets trailing brilliant white plumes. I loved it more—not less—because of its function: to destroy, to kill. The seduction of war is in its offering such intense beauty— divorced from all civilized values, but beauty still.

Most men who have been to war, and most women who have been around it, remember that never in their lives did they have so heightened a sexuality. War is, in short, a turn-on. War cloaks men in a costume that conceals the limits and inadequacies of their separate natures. It gives them an aura, a collective power, an almost animal force. They aren't just Billy or Johnny or Bobby, they are soldiers! But there's a price for all that: the agonizing loneliness of war, the way a soldier is cut off from everything that defines him as an individual—he is the true rootless man. The uniform did that, too, and all that heightened sexuality is not much solace late at night when the emptiness comes.

There were many men for whom this condition led to great decisions. I knew a Marine in Vietnam who was a great rarity, an Ivy League graduate. He also had an Ivy League wife, but he managed to fall in love with a Vietnamese bar girl who could barely speak English.

She was not particularly attractive, a peasant girl trying to support her family. He spent all his time with her, he fell in love with her— awkwardly, formally, but totally. At the end of his twelve months in Vietnam he went home, divorced his beautiful, intelligent, and socially correct wife, and then went back to Vietnam and proposed to the bar girl, who accepted. It was a marriage across a vast divide of language, culture, race, and class that could only have been made in war. I am not sure that it lasted, but it would not surprise me if, despite great difficulties, it did.

Of course, for every such story there are hundreds, thousands, of stories of passing contacts, a man and a woman holding each other tight for one moment, finding in sex some escape from the terrible reality of the war. The intensity that war brings to sex, the "let us love now because there may be no tomorrow," is based on death. No matter what our weapons on the battlefield, love is finally our only weapon against death. Sex is the weapon of life, the shooting sperm sent like an army of guerrillas to penetrate the egg's defenses—the only victory that really matters. War thrusts you into the well of loneliness, death breathing in your ear. Sex is a grappling hook that pulls you out, ends your isolation, makes you one with life again.

Not that such thoughts were anywhere near conscious. I remember going off to war with a copy of *War and Peace* and *The Charterhouse of Parma* stuffed into my pack. They were soon replaced with *The Story of O*. War heightens all appetites. I cannot describe the ache for candy, for taste; I wanted a Mars bar more than I had wanted anything in my life. And that hunger paled beside the force that pushed us toward women, any women; women we would not even have looked at in peace floated into our fantasies and lodged there. Too often we made our fantasies real, always to be disappointed, our hunger only greater. The ugliest prostitutes specialized in group affairs, passed among several men or even whole squads, in communion almost, a sharing more than sexual. In sex even more than in killing I could see the beast, crouched drooling on its haunches, could see it mocking me for my frailties, knowing I hated myself for them but that I could not get enough, that I would keep coming back again and again.

After I ended my tour in combat I came back to work at division headquarters and volunteered one night a week teaching English to Vietnamese adults. One of my students was a beautiful girl whose parents had been killed in Hué during the Tet Offensive of 1968. She had fallen in love with an American civilian who worked at the consulate in Da Nang. He had left for his next duty station and promised he would send for her. She never heard from him again. She had a seductive sadness about her. I found myself seeing her after class, then I was sneaking into the motor pool and commandeering a deuce-and-a-half truck and driving into Da Nang at night to visit her. She lived in a small house near the consulate with her grandparents and brothers and sisters. It had one room divided by a curtain. When I arrived, the rest of the family would retire behind the curtain. Amid their hushed voices and the smells of cooking oil and rotted fish we would talk and fumble toward each other, my need greater than hers.

I wanted her desperately. But her tenderness and vulnerability, the torn flower of her beauty, frustrated my death-obsessed lust. I didn't see her as one Vietnamese, I saw her as all Vietnamese. She was the suffering soul of war, and I was the soldier who had wounded it but would make it whole. My loneliness was pulling me into the same strong current that had swallowed my friend who married the bar girl. I could see it happening, but I seemed powerless to stop it. I wrote her long poems, made inquiries about staying on in Da Nang, built a fantasy future for the two of us. I wasn't going to betray her the way the other American had, the way all Americans had, the way all men betrayed the women who helped them through the war. I wasn't like that. But then I received orders sending me home two weeks early. I drove into Da Nang to talk to her, and to make definite plans. Halfway there, I turned back.

At the airport I threw the poems into a trash can. When the wheels of the plane lifted off the soil of Vietnam, I cheered like everyone else. And as I pressed my face against the window and watched Vietnam shrink to a distant green blur and finally disappear, I felt sad and guilty—for her, for my comrades who had been killed and wounded, for everything. But that feeling was overwhelmed by my vast sense of relief. I had survived. And I was going home. I would be myself again, or so I thought.

But some fifteen years later she and the war are still on my mind, all those memories, each with its secret passages and cutbacks, hundreds of labyrinths, all leading back to a truth not safe but essential. It is about why we can love and hate, why we can bring forth life and snuff it out, why each of us is a battleground where good and evil are always at war for our souls.

The power of war, like the power of love, springs from man's heart. The one yields death, the other life. But life without death has no meaning; nor, at its deepest level, does love without war. Without war we could not know from what depths love rises, or what power it must have to overcome such evil and redeem us. It is no accident that men love war, as love and war are at the core of man. It is not only that we must love one another or die. We must love one another *and* die. War, like death, is always with us, a constant companion, a secret sharer. To deny its seduction, to overcome death, our love for peace, for life itself, must be greater than we think possible, greater even than we can imagine.

Hiers and I were skiing down a mountain in Vermont, flying effortlessly over a world cloaked in white, beautiful, innocent, peaceful. On the ski lift up we had been talking about a different world, hot, green, smelling of decay and death, where each step out of the mud took all our strength. We stopped and looked back, the air pure and cold, our breath coming in puffs of vapor. Our children were following us down the hill, bent over, little balls of life racing on the edge of danger.

Hiers turned to me with a smile and said, "It's a long way from Nam, isn't it?"

Yes.

And no.

7

The Vietnam War and the
Erosion of Male Confidence
Robert Bly

Everywhere I go in the country I meet men roughly 20–40 years old
who live in considerable self-doubt. Many of them have few or no
close male friends. I meet young fathers who do not know what male
values they should attempt to teach their sons. These men, often
separated from their own remote fathers, and out of touch with their
grandfathers, do not feel they belong to a community of men. When
they reach out toward truly masculine values, they find nothing in
their hand when it closes.

The old anger against the father, so characteristic of the 19th Century and earlier centuries, has been replaced in many men by a kind
of passivity and remoteness, which spring from a feeling that the
father has abandoned or rejected them. In some cases, the father lost
his sons in divorce proceedings, and many sons interpret that event
to mean that men are untrustworthy. Still other sons have lived with
remote, over-worked, impassive, silent, controlling or condemnatory
fathers; and one feels in these men a longing for male values mingled
with a kind of helpless bitterness. Some men in recent years admire
only certain values which they associate with women—tenderness,
concern for the environment, nurturing, the sense of cooperation,
ability to stay in feeling. These men characteristically confide during
a crisis only in women. That is fine; what is missing is the confiding
in men. We could conclude by saying that women came out of the
Sixties and Seventies with considerable confidence in their values,
but men lack this clarity and belief. We all know many exceptions

Robert Bly is an American poet who hails from and lives in the State of Minnesota.
Among his best-known books of poetry are *Loving a Woman in Two Worlds* (New York:
Doubleday, 1985), *Talking All Morning* (Lansing: University of Michigan Press, 1980),
This Tree Will Be Here for a Thousand Years (New York: Harper and Row, 1979), and
The Eight Stages of Translation (Littleton, Colorado: Fred B. Rothman, 1986). The essay
included in this volume was transcribed from a speech that Bly gave in 1984, and was
first printed in the *Utne Reader*, October/November, 1984, pp. 74–81.

to this statement, and yet we sense a significant alteration in male confidence since, say, 1950 or 1960.

Because men of all social classes have lost confidence, it's clear that many forces affect this change. The Industrial Revolution has sent the father to work many miles from the home, and given him a work that he cannot teach his son. Male societies have disappeared, along with opportunities for older and younger men to meet each other and to do ordinary physical work together. The mythological layer, with all its models of adult male energy—Apollo, Dionysios, Hermes, Zeus— collapsed long ago, as have models of adult female energy for women. More recently the relatively humane or humanized male battle disappeared, destroyed by machine gun slaughter and bombing from the air. In old Irish and Greek stories we meet men who obey the rules of combat and honor their male enemy.

We all notice that suburban life gets along without male community. My parents brought me up on a Minnesota farm during years in which men lived in a community. My father ran a threshing rig, and all through the threshing season the men, young, old, and middle-aged, worked together, doggedly and humorously, in a kind of high-spirited cooperation at its best. I felt a confidence in the male community and I felt the goodness of it. But for men living in the suburbs all that is gone. We can all suggest many other forces and events that have contributed to the erosion of male confidence. I would say that a major recent cause for this erosion was the Vietnam War.

The Vietnam War had an enormous influence on men's confidence. A new situation evolved during the Vietnam War which amounts to older men lying to younger men. I enlisted in the Second World War when I was 17 and I, like most of the men I knew, did not feel that older men lied to me during that War. The older men, I felt, were aware of the younger ones, and though many younger men died, the older men died as well. There was a certain feeling of camaraderie and trust all up and down the line. (In Vietnam) the military and civilian leaders did not labor to awaken the sense of patriotism that gives battle labor some meaning. That sense of meaning bound old and young together in the Second World War.

As the Vietnam War went on, Walt Whitman Rostow, McGeorge Bundy, Dean Rusk, all lied. And I felt lied to by them. But at the time I didn't fully realize how the soldiers and officers in the battlefield would feel when, their lives at stake, they recognized the same lies.

I will tell you a story. I met recently in San Francisco a veteran who had been an ordinary draftee. I asked him how he felt now about the war. He said, "Well, I must tell you that I still feel tremendous anger." I said, "What about?" "Well," he said, "I've been thinking about it, and it had to do with my background. Being a young Catholic boy from Pennsylvania, I had taken in certain moral values, simply through living in that background. One was that killing was wrong. A second was respect for women. We even believed some of the moral declarations that racism was bad. All at once we were out in the jungle, and told to shoot at anything that moves. We couldn't tell if the people we were killing were men or women, let alone Communists or peasants. Moreover, everyone, officers included, called them "slopes" and "gooks." The older men never mentioned this nor told us what we were to do with the ideas we had taken in during Catholic grade school. After a month or so in the field suddenly I was shipped for R and R to a whorehouse in Thailand. Something was wrong with that. A lot of us still had feelings toward women. We had feelings about respect for women and what a woman means this way. Something got broken in me, and I'm still angry about that."

So the question we have to ask ourselves is, Who made that decision? I remember that during the Second World War the army supported the USO, where one went and danced a little with a woman, who was equally shy. It was very square, but nevertheless, the whole thing helped to preserve some continuity between civilian life and war life. Older men like Eisenhower supported such arrangements. The older men in the Vietnam War led the way to the whorehouses and made no attempt to preserve the continuity between civilian life and war life for these young males. It was a violation of trust. To repeat: when I came out of the Second World War there was a bond between younger men and older men and it helped all of us who served to move through our lives.

And then there were the body counts. The army didn't announce body counts of Germans during the Second World War, as we all know. We measured our progress in Vietnam not by land taken, but by lives taken. "Attrition" is the sugar-coated way of putting it. But the fact is that counting dead bodies is not a way for civilized human beings to behave, especially when your culture emphasizes the dignity of life. How can the same culture that prides itself on respecting the dignity of human life be in favor of body counts? The counting of bodies and the release of that information daily was approved by the Joint-Chiefs-of-Staff, and agreed on by the generals. You can't tell me that they didn't know the implications of this. Even worse, the generals and the Pentagon began to lie about the number of bodies. As we now know, the staff often doubled the count from the field.

Our subject here is the bad judgment of older men that resulted in damage to younger men or death of younger men. The generals decided to have a 365-day field term rotation. Such a plan broke with the traditional situation in which a company lives and dies together as a unit. The company learns to act as a unit; and each man learns to trust, or whom to trust. But the 365-day rotation breaks all that. Everyone is thinking about his own survival, and then suddenly the others can't depend on him, or he on them. I think the average age of the soldiers in Vietnam was around 18 years old; in the Second World War it was around 26. The average age of the company commanders in Vietnam was 22 years old; in the Second World War, 36. The decision for rotation was a bad one, and I think General Westmoreland made it; others here would know. General Westmoreland throughout made many unintelligent decisions and his advisors showed a specialist mentality, and a massive insensitivity to the needs of the younger men. The use of Agent Orange is a perfect example. Our first step in recovering from the war, I think, is simply to admit this.

Our feelings get damaged when we misuse our own language. All through the war, men like Rostow refused to use language in a clear and honest way. Words and phrases like "friendlies," "incursion," "Communist infrastructure," and "strategic hamlets" testify to a time in American history when language failed. And it was the older men who brought in that language, and led the movement toward failure of language. They had the responsibility to keep the language clear. The young men can't do that. They are helpless. They believe the older men when they called a dictatorship "democratic," or when they call a certain liquid "Agent Orange" rather than "Poison #465." Doesn't "Orange" imply nourishing?

We can say then that when the Vietnam veteran arrived home he found a large hole in himself where his values once were. What is the veteran going to do about that? Many veterans I meet say they still cannot find any values to put in there. The earlier values were blown out, the way acid blows out the brain. Harry Wilmer, a Jungian analyst, moved me tremendously when he talked about his experience of the dreams of Vietnam veterans. The dreams of certain veterans, he said, repeat events in exact detail, endlessly, meaninglessly. Only when the veteran is able to find a possibility of meaning—what a wonderful word that is—meaning, meaning, meaning—can his dreams begin to change. Then a veteran can begin to put something into this hole. But most veterans are not receiving help in moving toward meaning: they have not succeeded in finding a man like Harry Wilmer. They live in rage and in a sense of betrayal.

It's clear that this issue is a very serious issue, and the implications go far beyond the mistakes of the Vietnam War. When men lose their confidence in older men, what happens then? When older men betray younger men, and lie to them, in government and in the field, what happens then to male values? What happens to a society in which the males do not trust each other? What kind of a society is that? Do you feel it coming now? That mood in the country? Do you feel how the distrust erodes the confidence that males have in themselves? Did you know that the practice of "fragging," that is the killing by enlisted men of their own sergeants and lieutenants, was statistically not a factor until the Vietnam War? And I feel the poison of that distrust moving through the whole society now. The older men associated with the Vietnam War continue to lie to Vietnam veterans about chemical poisoning, and birth defects. Every man in the country knows that. It is no wonder that in Comtrex advertisements on television men are always presented as weak. What does the army's constant lying about Agent Orange do to our respect for men and for male values?

Our general subject is the Vietnam War and its effect on the erosion of male confidence. How can this nightmare end? What healing can take place? Harry Wilmer suggests, and I utterly agree, that no healing can take place until we decide to think actively about the dark side. Each of us has a dark side. If I shout at my small sons, I can say that I have a fatherly duty to discipline them, but we know that this shouting has a dark side. When so many whites moved to the suburbs during the Fifties, wasn't that a simple longing for open space? But it had a dark side. The dark side was that we let the centers of our cities disintegrate, in the same way that we let the center of our psyche disintegrate. When entertainment, in the form of television, floods our house every night, we are only sitting and listening. This is a simple thing surely, isn't it? But it has a dark side. It has a very strong dark side, in that we don't have to entertain others, or enter any larger sort of community to be entertained. Why don't we ever talk about that one? Well, when Johnson decided to raise troop levels sneakily, without public debate, that looked like a simple act, perfectly reasonable under the circumstances, as Dean Rusk says. But we know that it had a dark side. The decision to send 18-year-olds to whorehouses, whether they want to go or not, has a dark side, and the cool dryness with which McNamara and McGeorge Bundy and Dean Rusk discussed hideous realities has a dark side.

Did you notice how boyish McNamara looked in the PBS documentary on the Vietnam War? Probably he looked that way because he was a boy. What is a boy? A boy is a person who takes an act and does not think about the dark side of it. An adult is a person who takes an act and remains aware of its dark side. These boyish men—Reagan among them—so cheerful—are some of the most dangerous men on earth. One group of Americans carries the knowledge of their danger: the Vietnam veterans. They carry that knowledge for all of us.

8

The War that Won't End
Frances FitzGerald

The enduring images of the war come not from fiction, film, or print, but from the *cinéma vérité* of television. Most of the news media did not, it is true, grasp the significance of the fighting until 1968, but they did report on the experience of the American soldiers with a fair degree of realism. The proof is that none of the incidents the veterans report in [their] books—from acts of heroism to atrocities—would surprise anyone who had paid close attention to earlier coverage of the war. The veterans' stories are fresh, but they are in no way new.

The problem, then, is not that the war has been elevated to a mythic plane or relegated to the cold storage of history. To the contrary, the problem is that neither of these things has happened: the war has not yet been assimilated by Americans or integrated into American history. . . . The problem is that the war remains unresolved and the bodies unburied.

Of course, most of us can ignore this fact from day to day and block out our memories of the war. But the vets cannot, and that is the real poignancy of [their] books. Their stories are fresh precisely because they have not yet assimilated the war into their own histories. A decade or more after the fact, Vietnam vets remain capable of summoning up all the old impressions and all the old emotions—the grief, the pride, the despair, and the guilt—in the most precise and vivid detail. Not only are they capable of this, but they seem unable to do anything else. In telling [their] stories to each other and to the public at large, they seem to be calling not so much for sympathy as for some

Frances FitzGerald won the Pulitzer Prize, the Bancroft Prize for History, the National Book Award, and the National Institute of Arts and Letters Award, among other honors, for her book *Fire in the Lake*. She is also the author of *America Revised* and *Cities on a Hill*, and is a regular contributor to *The New Yorker*, *The New York Review of Books*, *Esquire*, *Vogue*, *Harper's*, and other periodicals. The essay presented here is a portion of a review article that was first published in *New Boston Review*, May/June, 1981, pp. 10–12, and is reprinted here with the permission of the editors.

conclusion, some transformation, some exit from this limbo of total recall.

Whether they will get it is not at all certain, for up until now they have been all too willing to take the whole burden of the war onto their own shoulders. Like the poor who think themselves wholly responsible for their poverty, the Vietnam vets have by and large no faith—and no real interest—in politics. They have fought in the most political of wars, where the acts of civilians on both sides almost outweighed the acts of the soldiers, and yet they remain political innocents. The vets [interviewed in some of the available books] rarely discuss the war's aims or legitimacy, though it is in just such discussion that they might resolve much of what troubles them. They wonder why the rest of the society does not seem to care about them, and they are right to wonder—except that they themselves are similarly careless: they feel no gratitude either to the peace movement or to the supporters of the war. The thought that they might have been victims does not lead them to conclude that those who sent them to the war—or those who opposed it—might have victimized them and should pay for it politically. Many vets have suffered—and continue to suffer—from a whole series of emotions and existential disorders which they call "post-Vietnam syndrome." The word "syndrome" of course suggests a pathology, and by accepting the term, they have in effect accepted their victimization. They have accepted the displacement of responsibility from the sphere of politics to the sphere of individual psychology. And from this solipsism there is no exit.

II

Lessons
FROM THE WAR

9

What Are the
Lessons of Vietnam?

David Fromkin and *James Chace*

Why did we intervene in Indochina?

For no evident reason, according to many. Roughly a decade ago [in 1975] a poll was taken of U.S. army generals that showed 70 percent of them believed that it was not clear what America had hoped to achieve in the Indochina war. The lesson, according to 91 percent of them, was that if the United States ever were to fight such a war again, it should begin by deciding what it wanted to accomplish. In fact, the United States did pursue defined objectives in Indochina; the trouble was that it kept changing its mind as to what they were. From first to last there was consistent agreement only about what our objective was not: we were not fighting to make South Vietnam into an American colony. Unfortunately, that is exactly what a great many people thought that we were doing.

John Foster Dulles was a strong opponent of British and French colonialism, which he viewed with considerable contempt, but he initiated an American policy in Indochina that was widely viewed as colonialist too. Indeed, some opponents of American policy believe that colonialism was a fatal flaw in that policy. Their view is that the Saigon regime could not draw upon ardor and devotion even from its

---

This was written as part of the tenth anniversary commemoration of the end of the war. The authors' task was to identify the lessons that had been learned in the war experience to assist the nation to meet its challenges and objectives with firmer dedication and clearer resolve. However, when the authors searched for lessons and truths, they found a wide variety of expert opinion but no educated consensus. Thus, their depiction of the lessons of the war takes the form of an ongoing conversation between respected authorities who hold conflicting opinions. The authors ask, how can a nation learn from its experience if the meaning of that experience remains inaccessible? David Fromkin, an international lawyer, is the author of *The Independence of Nations* (1981). James Chace, an editor of *The New York Times Book Review*, is the author of *Endless War* (1984), *Solvency: The Price of Survival* (1982), and other books and articles. The essay (from which our selection is taken) first appeared in *Foreign Affairs*, Vol. 63, Spring 1985, pp. 722–746.

own troops and supporters—so as to match the other side's—because the people of Vietnam believed the rulers of Saigon were America's representatives rather than their own.

By the middle of the 1960s, it began to appear to leaders of the Johnson Administration that we were fighting a war to impose a regime that even we found unsatisfactory upon a country of no clear importance to us. It then began to appear less evident why we were doing so.

On May 19, 1967, Secretary of Defense Robert McNamara drafted a memorandum redefining the goals worth fighting for in Vietnam. Since in his expressed view the goal of containing Chinese expansionism already had been attained, he no longer believed it vital that South Vietnam should remain independent or that it should remain non-communist. The only American goal left, he claimed, was to stop the application of force by North Vietnam such that "the people of the South" were denied "the ability to determine their own future." He admitted that "the line is hard to draw" as to the form and extent of North Vietnamese influence that we should deem acceptable. But surely in the conditions of 1967 in Vietnam it was illusory to believe that the great mass of the long-suffering illiterate peasantry, with no traditions of democracy, could express a free choice or would be allowed by their own government or any other to do so. It is difficult to read Secretary McNamara's memorandum without coming to believe that he thought there was no longer any compelling reason to go on fighting; at the end of 1984, breaking his long silence about Indochina policy, he confirmed that this was so.

When Clark Clifford replaced Mr. McNamara as Secretary of Defense, one of the questions he supposedly forced his associates to face was what purpose would be served by sending the reinforcements General Westmoreland requested in the wake of the Tet offensive. At that time—in the late winter of 1968—General Westmoreland still sought military victory; that, as Clark Clifford saw it, would result in an American-occupied Vietnam, something that we did not desire. What, then, *did* we desire? What vital national interest were we fighting in Vietnam to protect?

James Thomson, who served in the crucial years 1964–65 as an aide to the assistant secretary of state for Far Eastern affairs and as a staff member of the National Security Council, claims that while government officials frequently asserted that the preservation of Southeast Asia was a vital American national interest, they never thought matters through to examine whether and why that assertion was true.

Is it the case that we should intervene abroad militarily only in areas vital to our national interests? Arguably, but not necessarily; Indochina does not prove the case one way or another. It does not shed any light on the question of whether or not to intervene in situations the United States can dominate easily—in Grenada, to take an obvious example, or, in 1965, in the Dominican Republic. Vietnam only raised the question of whether the American people are prepared to take on a major fight—to undergo suffering, sacrifices, and casualties—if vital national interests are not at stake. And that question was raised because leading architects of America's Vietnam policy believed that we should intervene even if _national_ interests were not at stake.

Indeed, the American decision to intervene in Indochina was predicated on the view that the United States has a duty to look beyond its purely national interests. In this view, the United States has assumed global responsibilities that require it to serve the interests of mankind. That vision of America's destiny was particularly manifest during the Kennedy Administration, when British and other foreign observers remarked with admiration that while in London, Paris, and other capital cities, officials concerned themselves only with the parochial interests of their own countries, in Washington statesmen addressed the needs and aspirations of the human race. The decision to intervene against perceived communist aggression in Indochina was made in Washington in the name of the whole non-communist world's need for international security and world order.

The concept of international relations upon which that decision was based derived from the failure of the League of Nations—decades before—to carry into practice its theory of collective security against aggression. By the tenets of that theory, an aggressor would back down in the face of a league united against it, and a potential aggressor would be deterred from invading its neighbor by the certainty that such a league would confront it. In the 1930s the members of the League failed to stand together in the face of one aggressive challenge after another from Mussolini and Hitler. Countries allowed themselves to be picked off one at a time. The lesson of the 1930s, which political leaders carried with them into office in the 1950s and 1960s, was that the democracies ought to make a united stand against totalitarian aggression wherever and whenever it might occur.

As former Secretary of State Dean Rusk remarked in a recent interview, "I was part of a generation that had been given heavy responsibility during and after World War II. During the 1930s we had been led down the path to a war that could have been prevented. We came out of World War II thinking that the key to preventing World War III was collective security."

A parallel lesson of Munich was that certain political regimes—Nazi Germany being the prime example—are so constituted that it is a mistake to try to conciliate them. Their voracious appetite for conquest cannot be appeased; the more that is conceded to them, the more they are encouraged to demand.

This fit well with the theory of how to deal with Soviet conduct propounded by George Kennan, writing as "Mr. X," in his famous *Foreign Affairs* article which outlined the strategy of containment. William Bundy, deputy assistant and assistant Secretary of Defense for international security affairs (1961–64) and assistant secretary of state for East Asian and Pacific affairs (1964–69), said in an interview a few years ago that in the early 1960s, "the theory of containment was still the dominant way of thinking." He said that in Indochina "it was essentially what we were doing. We were seeking to prevent the Chinese version of communism from expanding into the area of East Asia."

In its military version (which Ambassador Kennan often has disavowed) containment came to be a misapplication of the lesson of Munich—a lesson to which American leaders often appealed. In the 1930s, up to the time of Munich, Hitler's Germany and Mussolini's Italy still were too weak to fight a war against the Allies; they were bluffing and would probably have backed down if their bluff had been called. But in the 1960s, the Soviet Union and China, though divided, were formidable powers. It was by no means certain that either would have backed down if confronted by an American expeditionary force, or that they would have been defeated if opposed. There were no powerful allies at our side whose strength, united to ours, necessarily would have intimidated or overwhelmed our adversaries. In these circumstances, for the United States unilaterally to send its armies into combat against communist aggression whenever and wherever it occurs was not collective and did not provide security.

It was on just such grounds that Walter Lippmann, in his book *The Cold War*, originally attacked Kennan's theory of containment. Lippmann's thesis was that the United States should select, in the light of its own interests and capabilities, the regions of the world in which it would engage itself. It should not extend itself by trying to act everywhere, and it should not allow its adversaries to dictate the time and place of confrontation.

There are those who believe that the United States *did* select Vietnam as Lippmann would have wished—as a region in which our interests were vital or as a battlefield particularly favorable to our side. If so, then those in our government who selected Vietnam on this basis were considerably wide of the mark in their judgment. Most policymakers, however, did not see us as choosing Vietnam but saw Vietnam as choosing us—we were drawn in because of communist aggression.

While opponents of the Vietnam War often assume that its outcome proved to the public that Lippmann was right—when the heaviness of the price was brought home to the American people, they refused to go on paying it because they did not deem Indochina *vitally* important—that view is still contested. Senator Robert Kasten (R-Wisc.), stressing the analogy between El Salvador and Vietnam in the spring of 1983, said:

> The Vietnam analogy is certainly popular with opponents of the administration. "No more Vietnams" is their battle cry. By this, they mean that the United States should remain inactive in the face of blatant acts of aggression by the Soviet Union or its Cuban and Nicaraguan surrogates. But what must be remembered is that in reality Vietnam represents a successful case of Soviet aggression and the imposition of a brutal tyranny over the people of Vietnam and Kampuchea. I agree that there should be "no more Vietnams" and that the United States must do what is necessary to prevent a repetition of that horror.

What Vietnam proved, in this view, is that the consequences of communist aggression are so terrible for the people who fall under communist rule as a result of it, that the United States always and everywhere must act to prevent blatant acts of aggression by the Soviet Union and its surrogates.

This view rests on the premise that we have a *moral* duty to act. The troubling aspect is that moral judgments are not always universally shared. They often are subjective matters of conscience. There are many who view it as immoral for one country, if unprovoked, to intervene in the affairs of another. There were many who judged America's Indochina war to be morally wrong. It is feasible for the United States to pursue a policy grounded in morality only if the moral issues in question are ones upon which Americans are agreed. The doctrine of global military containment—to the extent that it rests upon a moral duty—is vulnerable precisely because the moral values at issue are matters of dispute.

Closely allied with the theory of global containment is the so-called domino theory, according to which Southeast Asia was a region such that if one country fell to communism, the effect would be to knock down the countries around so that they would fall to communism too. C. L. Sulzberger of *The New York Times* employed a different metaphor and pictured America's Asian and Pacific allies as being caught in a giant nutcracker between Red China and radical Indonesia. Lyndon Johnson frequently told visitors to the White House that if we did not take our stand in Vietnam, one day we would have to make our stand in Hawaii. Opponents of the Vietnam War have assumed that this theory too—indeed, this theory above all—was fatally discredited by the results of the war. It is a decade since the war came to an end, and communist landing craft still have not been sighted off Honolulu.

Some of those most involved in sending American troops to Vietnam, however, argue that this is precisely because America won its anti-domino, anti-nutcracker victory two decades ago. Up until 1965, leaders of the domino countries—Malaysia, Singapore, Thailand, Australia, New Zealand, and even India—are said to have privately told the American government that it was vital for the United States to stay the course in Vietnam so as to save them from being crushed between China and Indonesia. In 1965–66 the arms of the nutcracker fell off: a new anti-communist government took power in Indonesia and destroyed the communist party in that country, while China withdrew from world affairs and concentrated her energies on the convulsions of the Cultural Revolution. In his 1967 memorandum, Secretary of Defense McNamara stated that, "To the extent that our original intervention and our existing actions in Vietnam were motivated by the perceived need to draw the line against Chinese expansionism in Asia, our objective has already been attained." His successor, Clark Clifford, toured Asia and found that the domino leaders were no longer vitally concerned about Vietnam, and he asked, "Was it possible that we were continuing to be guided by judgments that might once have had validity but were now obsolete?"

More recently, McGeorge Bundy, national security adviser to Presidents Kennedy and Johnson, has summarized the history of these events by stating that, while Vietnam may have seemed "vital" until 1965, "at least from the time of the anti-Communist revolution in Indonesia, late in 1965, that adjective was excessive, and so also was our effort." In this view, then, President Johnson's major military commitment to the Vietnam conflict was undertaken in the very year that it began to be unnecessary.

What, then, should the President have done? Having learned in 1966 that the enlarged war to which he had just committed the United States suddenly had become unnecessary, should he have recalled the American armies and brought them home? Would that not have inflicted a damaging blow to American prestige? Would it not have destroyed the world's belief in American reliability and steadiness? It is an axiom of statecraft that a great power trapped in a difficult or ultimately untenable position ought to persevere as long as possible in order to preserve the credibility of its other international commitments. That was the position adopted by the Johnson Administration and also by the incoming Nixon Administration in 1969.

Henry Kissinger writes in his memoirs,

> For nearly a generation the security and progress of free peoples had depended on confidence in America. We could not simply walk away from an enterprise involving two administrations, five allied countries, and thirty-one thousand dead as if we were switching a television channel. . . . As the leader of democratic alliances we had to remember that scores of countries and millions of people relied for their security on our willingness to stand by allies. . . . We could not revitalize the Atlantic Alliance. . . . We would not be able to move the Soviet Union toward the imperative of mutual restraint. . . . We might not achieve our opening to China. . . .

And, Mr. Kissinger added, we might not have succeeded in our Middle East diplomacy if world confidence in America's willingness to honor all of its international engagements were to be weakened or lost.

It is a strong case that Mr. Kissinger makes, but it is not a conclusive one. Was not confidence in American leadership deeply shaken by the spectacle of our persevering in the Vietnam War long after even the most pro-American foreigners agreed that the war was unpopular, unnecessary, and unwinnable? Does it increase confidence in the intelligence of our strategists if, when we perceive a trap starting to close around us, we manfully refuse to withdraw from it? Were 31,000 deaths made more meaningful by incurring 27,000 more?

In reflecting upon recent events in Lebanon, President Johnson's Undersecretary of State, George Ball, wrote in *The Washington Post* in the autumn of 1983:

> Our Vietnam experience also showed another reason for prudence: as a great power, we should avoid putting our troops in an untenable position, since we would then have to pay a political price to extricate them. Yet, as we learned to our sorrow in Vietnam, we should never let the prospect of that cost prevent us from closing out a hopeless situation. . . . Prestige, after all, is an elusive and evanescent abstraction that consists of many elements; other nations and peoples will respect us more if we demonstrate prudence, good sense, and realism than if we appear abstract and foolhardy.

Looking back a decade later, the American defeat in Vietnam seems not to have destroyed the world's confidence in the willingness of the United States to honor international commitments. This may be *because* the Nixon Administration persevered in the war for five more years (as Henry Kissinger believes) or *despite* the fact that it did— which is what the authors of this article believe.

In every respect the Indochina war was a profound experience, not only for the men and women who fought there but for all of us who lived through it. It was also an intensely personal, subjective experience. Not only are there diverse political and historical visions of what happened, but there are also diverse moral conclusions that persist.

President Reagan may have been right when he said, at the dedication of the Vietnam War Memorial in 1982, that the nation should "debate the lessons at some other time." But his use of force to back up his own foreign policy initiatives—the dispatch of marines to Lebanon, the widescale troop maneuvers in the Caribbean and Honduras, the invasion of Grenada, the sending of military advisers to the government of El Salvador—makes it all the more likely that the American people will not hold off from the debate. Indeed, if the foreign policy of the second Reagan Administration proves to be as assertive militarily as that of the first, the likelihood is that the debate over Vietnam will be renewed often and angrily in the years to come.

The passage of time has not helped, as yet, to resolve the debate over Vietnam. Richard Nixon still believes that the war was won, while seminars and symposia assemble to inquire why it was lost. In late 1984 Robert McNamara testified in a New York courtroom that he had disagreed with other Johnson Administration officials and with General Westmoreland about such basic questions as whether the war could be won. He indicated that in the intervening period neither he nor they had budged from their views. He did not believe that one could establish objectively which side was right. In describing his disagreement with his colleagues, he noted that "I say this without saying I was right and they were wrong."

The common theme running through most of the retrospective judgments about Indochina is the assumption that, once the lesson of Vietnam is pointed out, readers or listeners will see it for themselves. That basic assumption proves to be an illusion. The truth about Indochina is not self-evident; we all have our own views, but they are evident only to ourselves. The authors of this article also hold strong views about the Vietnam War, but no longer believe they can prove they are right to someone who holds contrary views. It is not because of any doubt as to the truth of the matter; it is for lack of objective evidence that cannot be controverted by the other side.

This leads to the conclusion that the Indochina experience is, at best, of limited use to the United States in building a contemporary consensus on the central issue—whether or not to intervene abroad with military force. The decision to send troops abroad is perhaps the most momentous decision a government can be called upon to make; whatever other value the Indochina experience may hold for us, it does not provide us with a point of departure for common discourse about how to face that challenge.

That robs us of something that could have been of great value. The Munich Pact was a disaster, but at least the Western world recognized it as such and learned that it would be a mistake to commit the same error again. The lesson of Munich can be misapplied—but the point is that it can also be *applied*. The lesson of Vietnam, if there is one, cannot be applied because we still do not agree about what happened. Far from helping to clarify policy issues in Central America or the Middle East, appeals to the lessons of Vietnam merely compound a conflict about current policy with an argument about history. Reference to Vietnam, therefore, is at this point divisive rather than unifying.

The Indochina war was surely the most tragic episode in the history of the United States in this century. If we could all look at that terrible experience through the same pair of eyes, it could teach us much. But we cannot, so it cannot. That may be the final tragedy of the Vietnam war.

10

Historiography:
Vietnam Reconsidered

Robert A. Divine

1988

Virtually all contemporary historical analysts of the Vietnam War shared a strong distaste for American intervention and a fervent belief that U.S. policy was seriously mistaken. Yet within this broad consensus, there were three distinct views of why the United States had become involved in such a hopeless situation. The first interpretation can be labeled the liberal internationalist perspective, and its chief advocate was the distinguished historian and adviser to President Kennedy, Arthur Schlesinger, Jr. Writing while the war was at its height, Schlesinger expressed the widely held view of American liberals that Vietnam was a quagmire. American leaders from Truman to Johnson had undertaken a series of incremental steps in Indochina which ended in disastrous U.S. involvement. This came about by chance, not design, and if any of the presidents had known where his policies were leading the nation, he never would have approved them. In a famous passage in his 1967 book, *Bitter Heritage*, Schlesinger observed that

> the policy of "one more step" lured the United States deeper and deeper into the morass. In retrospect, Vietnam is a triumph of the politics of inadvertence. We have achieved our present entanglement, not after due and deliberate consideration, but through a series of small decisions. It is not only idle but unfair to seek out guilty men.
> . . . Each step in the deepening of the American commitment was

This essay is a portion of a longer article, by the same title, that was published in *Diplomatic History*, Winter, 1988, and is here reprinted by permission of the editors. Robert Divine is professor of history at the University of Texas in Austin. His paper was originally presented at a conference in Yokohama in September 1986, sponsored by the Japan Association of International Relations. Divine is author of numerous books in American diplomatic history, including *Blowing on the Wind* (New York: Oxford University Press, 1978), and *Eisenhower and the Cold War* (New York: Oxford University Press, 1981).

reasonably regarded at the time as the last step that would be necessary. Yet, in retrospect, each step led only to the next, until we find
ourselves entrapped today in that nightmare of American strategists,
a land war in Asia—a war in which no President, including President
Johnson, desired or intended. The Vietnam story is a tragedy without
villains.[1]

Schlesinger's quagmire thesis, while condemning American involvement, nevertheless excused American leaders of any real responsibility. It was all an accident, a tragic series of mistakes, but not one
that called for a reconsideration of America's Cold War policies or for
a searching reappraisal of men and decisions. David Halberstam, in
a somewhat later account, *The Best and the Brightest*, took essentially
the same position. Although he stressed the arrogance of such presidential advisers as McGeorge Bundy, Robert McNamara, and Maxwell Taylor, he did not accuse them of deliberately leading the nation
astray. Instead, with the best intentions in the world, these paragons
had proved to be all too mortal, making mistakes like ordinary
humans.[2]

A second contemporary interpretation consciously rejected the
quagmire thesis as false, and instead offered a "stalemate" concept in
its place. According to this view, offered by civilian strategists involved in the compilation of the Pentagon Papers, American presidents had taken a series of steps with full knowledge that none was
likely to achieve the desired result. This view tends to excuse the
advisers, who supposedly gave sound advice, and blames the presidents, who decided on dubious actions for political reasons. The result
was a stalemate in Vietnam, but one deliberately achieved as a fore-
seeable consequence of American policy.

Leslie Gelb and Richard Betts offered the clearest statement of the
stalemate concept in their book *The Irony of Vietnam: The System
Worked*. The startling subtitle reflects their claim that "virtually all
important decisions were made without illusions about the odds of
success." The dominant consideration, according to this view, was the
perceived danger of losing Vietnam to communism. To prevent this
from happening American presidents were willing to take a series of
steps, none of which promised victory or peace. Lower ranking officials in the CIA and the State Department were fully aware of the
limitations of American policy but could not exert influence in the
White House, where advisers were willing to risk deeper entanglement
knowing full well that the outcome was likely to be failure. Thus
McGeorge Bundy, in recommending to LBJ the policy of reprisal
bombing of North Vietnam in February 1965, argued that "even if it

fails to turn the tide—as it may—the value of the effort seems to us to exceed its cost." This contention, according to Gelb and Betts, is the "good doctor" analogy: Even though the patient, South Vietnam, is likely to expire, the world would see the United States as the good doctor who did everything possible to prevent this calamity.[3]

The most provocative statement of the stalemate concept came from Daniel Ellsberg, the civilian Defense Department analyst who leaked the Pentagon Papers. In direct contrast to Schlesinger, Ellsberg blames the presidents, from Truman through Johnson, for allowing domestic political considerations to override the cautions and suggestions of their advisers. Thus Ellsberg accuses Kennedy in 1961 of suppressing Maxwell Taylor's recommendation for introducing combat troops, yet giving the public the impression that he was implementing Taylor's advice. This presidential deception, which reached its climax with Lyndon Johnson, but began with Eisenhower and Kennedy, leads Ellsberg to refute Schlesinger's claim that Vietnam was "a tragedy without villains," calling this "a process of immaculate deception" in which there are "war crimes without war criminals, lies without liars."[4]

The true explanation, according to Ellsberg, is the traumatic impact of the loss of China to communism in 1949 and the devastating effect of that event on the Democratic party. Neither Kennedy nor Johnson ever wanted to risk repeating that experience, and so anything was preferable to defeat in Vietnam, even a deliberate stalemate. Ellsberg describes the dilemma of American presidents in terms of the card game "Old Maid." Just as players did not want to be caught with the queen of spades in their hands, so no American president wanted to be held responsible for the loss of Vietnam to the Communists. But in observing rule one of this game, each president was in danger of violating rule two: "Do not commit U.S. ground troops to a land war in Asia." Truman, Eisenhower, and Kennedy all played the game successfully, undertaking limited measures to save South Vietnam while knowing that their policies had little chance of long-run success. It was Lyndon Johnson who got caught with the Old Maid—in order not to lose Vietnam to the Communists, he got involved in a land war in Asia that could not be won.[5]

The stalemate concept offers considerable insight into why American policy led only to deeper involvement, not victory, in Vietnam. But focusing on the political process and shifting blame to the presidents has the self-serving purpose of absolving civilian advisers such as Leslie Gelb and Daniel Ellsberg from any degree of responsibility for the Vietnam disaster. More importantly, this explanation ignores the question of why the United States placed such a high value on preserving Vietnam from the Communists.

A third contemporary explanation is more satisfactory in this regard. This view, expressed in several variations, claims not only that the system did not work, but that the system, defined as the entire postwar containment policy, was fatally flawed. This view thus makes George Kennan, not Lyndon Johnson, the scapegoat by portraying Vietnam as the logical culmination of the Cold War effort to contain communism.

Gabriel Kolko offered a radical version of the containment thesis in his 1969 book, *The Roots of American Foreign Policy*. He saw the intervention in Vietnam as revealing the bankruptcy of a policy that had been relentlessly pursued since the end of World War II:

> Ultimately, the United States has fought in Vietnam with increasing intensity to extend its hegemony over the world community and to stop every form of revolutionary movement which refuses to accept the predominant role of the United States in the direction of the affairs of its nation or region.[6]

Nearly twenty years later, in a much more detailed and more fully documented account of America's failure in Vietnam, Kolko restated the same basic explanation:

> The Vietnam War was for the United States the culmination of its frustrating postwar effort to merge its arms and politics to halt and reverse the emergence of states and social systems opposed to the international order Washington sought to establish. It was not the first serious trial of either its military power or its political strategy, only the most disastrous. Despite America's many real successes in imposing its hegemony elsewhere, Vietnam exposed the ultimate constraints on its power in the modern era.[7]

Other writers saw the fundamental mistake of American policy in less ideological terms. John Donovan, for example, blamed Vietnam on the American foreign-policy elite. Despite changes in administration, the same small band of lawyers, academics, and bankers, operating on the same shared assumptions, presided over American foreign policy throughout the Cold War. Never questioning the key belief that Vietnam was vital to American security until it was too late, these foreign-policy experts allowed the mandate of containment to lead them into disaster in Vietnam.[8]

The most balanced statement of the containment thesis comes from

George Herring, who wrote a concise history of American involvement in Vietnam in 1979. The containment policy which Truman had used so effectively in Europe in the 1940s, he wrote, was simply not applicable to Asia in the 1960s.

> The United States' involvement in Vietnam was not primarily a result of errors of judgment or of the personality quirks of the policymakers, although these things existed in abundance. It was a logical, if not inevitable outgrowth of a world view and a policy, the policy of containment, which Americans in and out of government accepted without serious question for more than two decades. The commitment in Vietnam expanded as the containment policy itself grew. In time, it outlived the conditions that had given rise to that policy. More than anything else, America's failure in Vietnam calls into question the basic premises of that policy and suggests the urgent need for a searching reappraisal of American attitudes toward the world and their place in it.[9]

Thus Herring, like Kolko and Donovan, thinks the system itself was at fault, not the presidents or their advisers. In his view, which was widely shared by the end of the 1970s, the lesson of Vietnam was clear. Containment was a bad policy which led to a global involvement that endangered rather than protected the best interests of the United States.

Vietnam revisionism, which began in the late 1970s and reached its peak in the early 1980s, reflected a growing conservative mood in the United States, symbolized by the election of Ronald Reagan in 1980, and a belated national effort to come to grips with the Vietnam experience, as indicated by the popularity of three remarkable motion pictures of the late 1970s—*Coming Home, The Deer Hunter,* and *Apocalypse Now.* Rejecting the prevailing view that the Vietnam War was an unmitigated evil, revisionists defended and justified American involvement. While few saw the Vietnam War as an unmixed blessing, they did feel compelled to correct what they considered a one-sided and unfair indictment of American policy. There is still considerable disagreement among these writers on many points, but they share a common desire to treat the American effort in Vietnam more sympathetically than earlier historians. The revisionists include academic political scientists, notably Guenter Lewy and Timothy Lomperis, military strategists such as Bruce Palmer and Harry Summers, and political advocates like journalist Norman Podhoretz and former president Richard Nixon.[10] Rather than discuss their work individually, I will focus on some of the common themes in the revisionist interpretation of the Vietnam experience.

A central point in revisionist accounts is the contention that the war could have been won. Richard Nixon goes even further, arguing that he had achieved victory by 1973 only to have Congress throw it away by refusing to aid South Vietnam two years later. "In the end, Vietnam was lost on the political front in the United States," he writes, "not on the battlefield in Southeast Asia."[11] Other revisionists, notably the military strategists, admit that the United States lost the war on the battlefield, but contend that defeat was not inevitable. Instead they argue that if the war had been fought differently, the United States could have prevailed.

Harry Summers offers two explanations for the American defeat. First, the United States tied its own hands by not making a maximum effort at victory. The nation did not declare war against North Vietnam, nor did it make the kind of sacrifices at home that had ensured victory in World War II. Instead, LBJ tried for guns and butter at the same time, and lost both. According to Summers, Johnson's "conscious political decision not to mobilize the American people for war" was a "fundamental mistake" that prevented the country from focusing its "full attention" on the war. He cites former Secretary of State Dean Rusk's admission that "we never made any effort to create a war psychology in the United States during the Vietnam affair. . . . We tried to do in cold blood perhaps what can only be done in hot blood." Summers blames not only Johnson for this "failure to invoke the national will" but also the Joint Chiefs of Staff, whom he thinks should have insisted on an all-out effort in Vietnam and then backed up their demands by threatening to resign if the president did not act.[12]

Summers's second contention is that the United States lost in Vietnam because the military waged a counterinsurgency campaign against the Viet Cong instead of a conventional war against North Vietnam's main forces. The search-and-destroy tactics employed by General William Westmoreland, according to Summers, were bound to fail. The real enemy was the invading army from North Vietnam, which he contends could have been defeated by the same tactics the United States used successfully in Korea and in World War II. Bruce Palmer agrees, offering a specific two-part strategy of concentrating American forces along the Demilitarized Zone to cut off North Vietnamese infiltration into the south and force fixed battles in which superior American firepower would prevail, together with a naval blockade of North Vietnam. "The U.S. resources were there—what was missing was a bold decision, admittedly involving some risk, and an imaginative concept that would have allowed the United States and its allies to turn the strategic tables on Hanoi." Such a conventional war, Palmer concedes, might not have produced outright victory, but could at least have provided "a better foundation for negotiations undertaken to end the war."[13]

Not all revisionists agree that the use of conventional military tactics could have avoided defeat in Vietnam. Guenter Lewy, for example, argues that the American military relied too heavily on traditional military concepts that were inappropriate for a guerrilla war that was essentially political in nature. Lewy believes that a greater effort on pacification, especially in the later stages of the conflict, might well have led to a stable and secure South Vietnam.[14]

There is one point in regard to military strategy on which all the revisionists agree. The Tet offensive of 1968, portrayed by the media and accepted by the American people as a great defeat, was in reality a major military victory. The Communists failed to take a single South Vietnamese city and they lost over 50,000 men in their futile attacks. Most important, they failed to achieve their main objective, which was to mobilize the population of South Vietnam in a true people's war. Timothy Lomperis stresses the failure of these revolutionary tactics in his provocative book, *The War Everyone Lost—and Won:*

> Tet was supposed to be the culmination of the people's war strategy, but the offensive was beaten back. More than just a military defeat, the Tet offensive shattered the revolutionary strategy. After some groping, the Communists thereafter essentially abandoned the people's war and took another road.

The ultimate irony, as Lomperis and other revisionists point out, is that the Communists achieved their final victory through conventional warfare. The successful North Vietnamese invasion and conquest of the South in 1975 was a traditional military action similar to those of World War II and Korea.[15]

In addition to claiming that the United States might have won in Vietnam with different tactics, revisionists also challenge the view that the American war effort was immoral. While they admit that the use of chemical defoliants, the free-fire zones, and the heavy air bombardments killed many civilians, they claim that this war was no worse in that respect than other twentieth-century conflicts. Guenter Lewy is particularly persuasive on this point. In his 1978 book, *America in Vietnam*, which was the first and in many ways the most impressive of the revisionist accounts, Lewy uses United Nations figures to rebut charges by antiwar activists that the United States engaged in acts of genocide in Vietnam. The civilian population of South Vietnam, far from being wiped out, increased from just over 16 million in 1965 to almost 20 million in 1973, while the population of

North Vietnam went from just under 19 million to over 22 million in the same period. "This fact," he comments, "makes the charge of genocide a bit grotesque." He also finds that the percentage of civilian deaths in the overall toll of the Vietnam War was 28 percent, lower than the 40 percent in World War II and much less than the 70 percent in the Korean War.[16]

Norman Podhoretz is much more strident on the moral issue. He claims that those who opposed the Vietnam War acted immorally by giving aid and encouragement to the enemy, ignoring the totalitarian nature of the North Vietnamese government, and exaggerating the damage done by American raids on North Vietnam. On this last point he notes that the American media compared the Christmas bombing of Hanoi in 1972 to Dresden and the 1945 incendiary raids on Tokyo, when in fact between 1,300 and 1,500 died in the Christmas bombings, compared to 35,000 at Dresden and over 80,000 in the Tokyo raids. More importantly, Podhoretz sees the American commitment to defend South Vietnam as a moral act. In contrast to Herring, Podhoretz believes in containment and thinks the United States was acting morally by trying to halt the expansion of communism. Thus he contends that

> the United States went into Vietnam for the sake not of its own direct interests in the ordinary sense but for the sake of an ideal. The intervention was the product of the Wilsonian side of the American character—the side that went to war in 1917 to "make the world safe for democracy." . . . Why, then, were we in Vietnam? To say it once again: because we were trying to save the Southern half of that country from the evils of Communism.[17]

The most striking difference between the revisionists and the earlier writers on Vietnam lies in the lessons they draw from this experience. Refusing to see American intervention as a tragic mistake, the revisionists are not willing to embrace the traditional conclusion that the United States should be very careful "never again" to become involved militarily in the Third World, a view best summed up by Earl Ravenal in his 1978 book, *Never Again*.[18] On the contrary, they warn against the danger of transforming Vietnam into a symbol like Munich. For thirty years after Chamberlain and Daladier gave in to Hitler at Munich in 1938, appeasement was viewed as the cardinal sin of diplomacy, giving any form of diplomatic negotiation a bad name. Instead of focusing on the weak performance of the negotiators at Munich, the revisionists point out, people tended to equate diplomacy with appeasement and thus opted for military measures instead. Thus one reason the United States ended up fighting in Vietnam was precisely because of this fear of another Munich. It would be equally mistaken, according to Podhoretz, to make "No More Vietnams" the guiding principle of American foreign policy for another generation.[19]

Timothy Lomperis makes the strongest case about being careful not to draw the wrong conclusions from the Vietnam experience. There was much that was contradictory in Vietnam, he argues, and little that has universal application:

> For most Americans, the memory of Viet Nam festers as a haunting nightmare of failure. Far from being a simple and abject failure, though, the American intervention in Viet Nam was one of rich variegation. As in the case of Mark Twain's cat drawing the wrong conclusion from sitting on a hot stove and therefore unquestioningly assuming that stoves are at all times and places hot, the burners of Viet Nam were hot and cold from time to time and place to place. ... Thus, in losing a people's war, the Communists went on to win the war itself. But in adopting a conventional war strategy, they won by a means they should have lost. The United States, on the other hand, won a war it thought it lost, and lost by default what it could have won.[20]

It is Harry Summers who draws the most surprising lesson from the Vietnam War. He sees the key difficulty as the artificial restraints that the United States placed on its war effort. When he says "never again," he means something very different from Earl Ravenal:

> Never again must the president commit American men to combat without first fully defining the nation's war aims and then rallying Congress and the nation for war. Otherwise, the courageous Americans who fought and died in the defense of South Vietnam will truly have done so in vain.[21]

Richard Nixon is even more outspoken in refuting what he calls the battle cry of the new isolationists, "No more Vietnams." Calling Vietnam only "a temporary setback," he continues, "it is vital that we learn the right lessons from that defeat. In Vietnam, we tried and failed in a just cause. 'No more Vietnams' can mean that we will not *try* again. It *should* mean that we will not *fail* again."[22]

This attempt to learn the lessons of Vietnam indicates once again the great difficulty in trying to draw a simple guide for future conduct from complex historical events. Throughout the twentieth century, Americans have kept making the same mistake. After World War I, Congress adopted the neutrality legislation on the theory that the sales of arms to England and France from 1914 to 1917 got us into war. Yet the first thing the nation did when World War II broke out in 1939 was to repeal the arms embargo so that the United States could become what Franklin Roosevelt described so aptly as "the arsenal of democracy." At the end of the Second World War the United States took the lead in founding the United Nations in the belief that American refusal to join the League of Nations had destroyed Wilson's dream of a lasting peace. But only nine days after the Senate ratified the United Nations Charter, the United States dropped the atomic bomb on Hiroshima, ushering in a nuclear age in which this global forum proved largely irrelevant. And in the ensuing Cold War, Americans took the lesson of Munich so much to heart that time after time the nation chose confrontation rather than negotiation, insuring a deepening of the conflict with the Soviet Union and the escalation of the nuclear arms race.

There are no simple lessons to be drawn from the Vietnam experience. But by challenging the superficial idea of "never again," the revisionists have provided a useful reminder of how complex the Vietnam War really was and the wide variety of possible guidelines for the future that can be drawn from this episode. If nothing else, the revisionists have forced scholars to do what American policymakers failed so conspicuously to do over Vietnam—reexamine basic premises and not take anything for granted.

The third phase of historical analysis, postrevisionism or synthesis, is just beginning for the Vietnam War. The early signs point to a view that is still highly critical of American intervention, but one which is more sympathetic, or at least understanding, of the dilemmas faced by American policymakers. The presidents and their advisers are no longer seen as villains, but as victims of ignorance and of circumstances beyond their control.

The first works of synthesis began to appear in the early 1980s and were marked by a much more dispassionate and scholarly tone than either the traditional or the revisionist books. Larry Berman began the trend with his careful analysis of Lyndon Johnson's 1965 decision to send American ground forces to Vietnam and Kathleen Turner added to it with her detached assessment of LBJ's credibility gap over the war. By far the most significant work of synthesis yet to appear is the 1986 study by George Kahin, *Intervention.* A political scientist who specializes in the governments of Southeast Asia, Kahin combined a comprehensive understanding of the culture and politics of South Vietnam with massive research in previously classified American government documents. The result is a richly detailed survey of U.S. policy in Vietnam from the end of World War II through the 1965 escalation, one which offers many new insights and interpretations. Finally, the 1985 book by radical historian Gabriel Kolko, while repeating his earlier critique of American policy and thus hardly qualifying as a work of synthesis, provides both a much fuller statement of Kolko's views and some surprising areas of agreement with Kahin's more balanced interpretation.[23]

Two issues stand out in the recent histories. The first is a revised assessment of the role of Lyndon Johnson. He no longer is portrayed as the thoughtless hawk who blundered into Vietnam; instead he is seen more sympathetically as a figure caught up in a difficult situation. Berman was the first to take a more neutral view of Johnson. As a political scientist concerned with the relationship between the president and his advisers, Berman used the extensive documentation at the LBJ Library to examine how Johnson arrived at his July 1965 decision to commit combat troops to Vietnam on a large scale. He concluded that Johnson carefully orchestrated the advisory process to "legitimize a previously selected option." Such manipulation by a politician with a legendary reputation for building a consensus was hardly surprising. But what Berman discovered was that Johnson used his considerable powers of persuasion to choose a middle road between the doves, notably George Ball, who urged disengagement, and his military advisers, who wanted to call up the reserves and go all out for victory in Vietnam. The result was disastrous. "The president committed the United States to fight a limited war against an enemy totally committed to revolutionary war."[24]

Berman's interpretation sustains the original stalemate concept pioneered by Gelb and Betts and by Ellsberg, portraying LBJ as ignoring the warnings of his advisers that the steps he is taking are not enough to bring about victory. But Berman offers a different explanation of why Johnson chose a cautious middle road. Rather than fear of the political consequences of losing Vietnam to the Communists, the author thinks LBJ was motivated by an intense desire to preserve his Great Society program, which was moving through Congress just when the situation in Vietnam became most critical. He insisted on limiting American military involvement in order to avoid asking Congress to put the nation on a war footing, which he feared would doom measures such as Medicare, federal aid to education, and civil rights legislation. As a consequence, he eventually lost both in Vietnam and at home, as the Great Society became overshadowed by the military venture abroad. "Lyndon Johnson's greatest fault as a leader," Berman concludes sympathetically, "was that *he chose* not to choose between the Great Society and the war in Vietnam."[25]

Kathleen Turner focuses on the consequences of Johnson's refusal to choose between reform at home and war abroad. He was caught in a "double bind—an inability to convince a large enough portion of the population that America was doing enough for Vietnam with an inability to convince another large element that America was not doing too much." The result was the credibility gap. Reporters thought the president was deliberately holding back on the extent of American involvement in Vietnam, when in fact he was trying to restrain public opinion to avoid a call for an all-out military effort. Vetoing a suggestion for a national television speech on the July 1965 troop decision, Johnson told his aides that he thought he could secure public support "without having to be too provocative and warlike." As Turner points out, this policy led only to confusion and dissent. "The United States was engaged in military conflict," she writes, "but hadn't declared war," a policy that "simply didn't make sense to a growing proportion of the population."[26]

This postrevisionist analysis offers an interesting contrast to the revisionist argument that Johnson should have declared war in Vietnam and rallied the nation behind him. Summers and other military strategists ignore the domestic scene and especially Johnson's genuine commitment to the cause of reform. And even though this refusal to make a choice between Vietnam and the Great Society would be his ultimate undoing, it offers a far more appealing portrait of LBJ as a leader caught in a genuine dilemma rather than as a political manipulator deceiving the American people.

George Kahin goes farthest in rehabilitating Johnson on Vietnam. In part he does so by putting more of the blame for the failure of American policy on his predecessors, especially on Eisenhower for committing the United States to the Diem regime in the mid-1950s and on Kennedy for deepening the commitment in 1961. But Kahin's most surprising point is to charge Johnson's advisers, not the president himself, with responsibility for the decision to escalate. Unlike writers of the stalemate school who blame the president and excuse the bureaucrats, Kahin sees LBJ as the last dove in the administration and accuses his advisers, especially McGeorge Bundy, Robert McNamara, and Maxwell Taylor, of misleading him. Despite Johnson's repeated requests, these men refused to present him with alternatives other than escalation or withdrawal, usually labeled as "bugging out." Kahin even accuses these advisers of deliberate deception, such as holding back the true facts of the Gulf of Tonkin incident and not giving the president George Ball's initial proposal for a negotiated withdrawal from Vietnam. He suggests that the advisers may well have confused what was best for the United States with what was best for their own careers. "It was usually not difficult for these men,"

Kahin notes, "to equate the U.S. national interest with their own reputations."[27]

Instead of the bloodthirsty hawk of legend, Johnson emerges as a prudent and cautious leader who has grave doubts about escalation. Told that it is necessary to bomb North Vietnam to save a tottering government in the South, Johnson objects, telling the chairman of the Joint Chiefs of Staff that he "did not wish to enter the patient in a 10-round bout, when he was in no shape to hold out for one round." And in the July 1965 debate over troop commitment, it was the president, not his advisers, who kept raising the critical questions, asking at one point, "Are we starting something that in two or three years we simply can't finish?"[28]

The second theme which runs through the postrevisionist books is the fatal American ignorance of the force and vitality of Vietnamese nationalism. In contrast to the revisionists, who keep wondering if the war could have been won, these scholars answer with a resounding "No!" Kahin is particularly effective on this point, stressing throughout the strength of nationalist sentiment in Vietnam and the folly of trying to create a separate state in the South. The Diem regime was doomed from the outset, he argues, because it owed its existence to a foreign power and was not an expression of indigenous nationalism.[29]

Gabriel Kolko agrees that the American cause was lost from the beginning, but he differs from Kahin by identifying the Communist Party in Vietnam as the dominant factor, rather than a vaguer form of nationalism. Where Kahin sees the National Liberation Front as a genuine expression of Vietnamese nationalism, Kolko is convinced that it is controlled by the leadership of the Communist Party in Hanoi all along. Thus Kolko refuses to accept Kahin's contention that the conflict began as a civil war rather than as a clear-cut case of aggression from the north, as the United States claimed. For Kolko, the fight was simply a continuation of the long struggle begun by Ho Chi Minh to deliver his nation from the grasp of foreign imperialists, whether French or American.[30]

Despite their differences, Kahin and Kolko reach similar conclusions. Whether perceived as a civil war or as a struggle against imperialism, the Vietnam conflict was bound to end in an American defeat. Nothing the United States might have done, short of nuclear destruction, would have altered the outcome. And both writers note the ultimate irony of the impact of massive American military intervention on the society and government of South Vietnam. The free-fire zones and search-and-destroy missions uprooted millions of people, destroyed the agricultural base of South Vietnam, and led to a massive influx of refugees into the cities. This social disruption eroded any chance a government in Saigon had of achieving legitimacy and popular support.[31] As a result, the harder the United States tried to determine the outcome in Vietnam, the more remote became the likelihood of victory. In that sense, the original Schlesinger analogy to a quagmire was even more apt than he realized.

It is still far too early to offer more than a tentative judgment on the American experience in Vietnam. But historians are already beginning to move beyond the early condemnation of a wicked policy to search for an understanding of how a great nation could go so wrong. And as they continue this quest, Vietnam is likely to be seen more and more as a national tragedy. The most striking finding so far is the degree of foreknowledge. The stalemate writers are correct in rejecting the original quagmire thesis—both the Pentagon Papers and recently opened government documents show that Johnson and his advisers had a realistic understanding of the difficulties they faced in Vietnam. They chose to escalate on a limited basis, knowing full well that the measures they took would not bring about a satisfactory conclusion. Domestic considerations, not just the political consequences of losing Vietnam to the Communists but the cost of all-out war in Southeast Asia to the Great Society program, placed very real limits on American policy. The result was, as Berman notes, that "President Johnson defined the situation in a way which severely constrained his military options and ultimately undid his political base."[32]

Thus the key to understanding American policy lies in domestic politics. At the present time Charles Chatfield is completing the late Charles DeBenedetti's study of the antiwar movement and its impact on the Johnson administration, while Terry Anderson is conducting research on student protests against the Vietnam War. And George Herring is studying the equally important issue of how Lyndon Johnson attempted to honor the commitment he had inherited in Southeast Asia without abandoning his reform program at home. When these books appear, we should have a much better understanding of the way in which political considerations shaped the course of American policy in Vietnam. Until then, we can at least be grateful that American historians have moved beyond the early, and often simplistic, analyses of the Vietnam War, to begin acquiring a more sophisticated and scholarly appreciation of the nature of this great national tragedy.

NOTES

1. Arthur M. Schlesinger, Jr., *The Bitter Heritage: Vietnam and American Democracy, 1941–1966* (Boston, 1967), 31–32.

① STALEMATE
② REVISIONIST
③ POST-REVISIONIST

2. David Halberstam, *The Best and the Brightest* (New York, 1972).

3. Leslie H. Gelb and Richard K. Betts, *The Irony of Vietnam: The System Worked* (Washington, D.C., 1979), 2, 25–26, 238–43.

4. Daniel Ellsberg, *Papers on the War* (New York, 1972), 64, 129.

5. Ibid., 80–82, 102–3.

6. Gabriel Kolko, *The Roots of American Foreign Policy: An Analysis of Power and Purpose* (Boston, 1969), 132.

7. Gabriel Kolko, *Anatomy of a War: Vietnam, the United States, and the Modern Historical Experience* (New York, 1985), 547.

8. John C. Donovan, *The Cold Warriors: A Policy-Making Elite* (Lexington, MA, 1974).

9. George C. Herring, *America's Longest War: The United States and Vietnam, 1950–1975* (New York, 1979), x.

10. Guenter Lewy, *America in Vietnam* (New York, 1978); Timothy J. Lomperis, *The War Everyone Lost—And Won: America's Intervention in Viet Nam's Twin Struggles* (Baton Rouge, LA, 1984); Bruce Palmer, Jr., *The 25-Year War: America's Military Role in Vietnam* (Lexington, KY, 1984); Harry G. Summers, Jr., *On Strategy: A Critical Analysis of the Vietnam War* (New York, 1984); Norman Podhoretz, *Why We Were in Vietnam* (New York, 1982); Richard Nixon, *No More Vietnams* (New York, 1985).

11. Nixon, *No More Vietnams*, 15.

12. Harry G. Summers, Jr., "Lessons: A Soldier's View," in *Vietnam as History: Ten Years after the Paris Peace Accords*, ed. Peter Braestrup (Washington, DC, 1984), 109, 111; Summers, *On Strategy*, 43, 168.

13. Summers, *On Strategy*, 122, 127–31; Palmer, *25-Year War*, 182–84, 187–88.

14. Lewy, *America in Vietnam*, 162–67.

15. Lomperis, *The War Everyone Lost*, 165; Summers, *On Strategy*, 157–61.

16. Lewy, *America in Vietnam*, 301, 451.

17. Podhoretz, *Why We Were in Vietnam*, 121–22, 197.

18. Earl C. Ravenal, *Never Again: Learning from America's Foreign Policy Failures* (Philadelphia, 1978).

19. Podhoretz, *Why We Were in Vietnam*, 11–13.

20. Lomperis, *The War Everyone Lost*, 176.

21. Summers, "Lessons," 114.

22. Nixon, *No More Vietnams*, 237.

23. Larry Berman, *Planning a Tragedy: The Americanization of the War in Vietnam* (New York, 1982); Kathleen J. Turner, *Lyndon Johnson's Dual War: Vietnam and the Press* (Chicago, 1985); George McT. Kahin, *Intervention: How America Became Involved in Vietnam* (New York, 1986); Kolko, *Anatomy*.

24. Berman, *Planning*, 93, 112.

25. Ibid., 145–50.

26. Turner, *Johnson's Dual War*, 6, 150, 164–65.

27. Kahin, *Intervention*, 66, 126, 191, 216, 245.

28. Ibid., 239, 383.
29. Ibid., 103, 323.
30. Ibid., 115–16; Kolko, *Anatomy*, 107, 460.
31. Kahin, *Intervention*, 403–12; Kolko, *Anatomy*, 238–46.
32. Berman, *Planning*, 143.

11

Vietnam in Perspective
William C. Westmoreland

Recent years have been traumatic in America. Vietnam and Watergate have been center stage. The Watergate episode has been dissected, plummeted, exploited. The blame for that messy affair has been firmly placed. Lessons have been learned and some heeded, but not so for the Vietnam disaster.

South Vietnam no longer exists; it has been gobbled up by North Vietnam following blatant aggression. The flicker of freedom there has been extinguished probably forever. Our erstwhile honorable country betrayed and deserted the Republic of Vietnam after it had enticed it to our bosom. It was a shabby performance by America, a blemish on our history and a possible blight on our future. Our creditability has been damaged. In our national interest, that unhappy experience should not be swept under the rug and forgotten. There are lessons to be learned and vulnerabilities in our national system that need careful examination.

As one who lived closely with the matter for many years, my observations and analyses may be of interest. I believe it was Josh Billings who said "It is not so much that we are ignorant, but we know so much that is not true." There is, however, one valid truth accepted by most: The handling of the Vietnam affair was a shameful national blunder.

Our interest in South Vietnam was born in the post-World War II period, motivated by a concern for unchecked Communist movement

---

General William C. Westmoreland, U.S. Army retired, is a graduate of the United States Military Academy, and was Chief of Staff of the Army from 1968 to 1972. Westmoreland was United States Commander in Vietnam from 1964 to 1968. In both capacities, he was the person most responsible for carrying out United States foreign policy, and for executing the military strategy that had been proposed. This essay, "Vietnam in Perspective," represents a summary of Westmoreland's analysis of both policy and strategy nearly five years after the war ended. It first appeared in *Military Review*, Vol. 50, 1979, pp. 34–43.

into insecure and unstable areas. In 1947, President Truman enunci- (+)TRUMAN
ated a national policy that pledged us to the unconditional support
of "free people who are resisting attempted subjugation by minorities
or by outside pressures." The Congress approved this doctrine by a
large majority. In 1950, we sent a military mission to Saigon. Presi- (?)EISENHOWER
dent Eisenhower emphasized the policy of "containment" in association with his massive retaliation strategy.

When Kennedy was elected president, he became interested in the
so-called "small war" concept, became concerned about the size and
readiness of the Army that he thought had been neglected under
Eisenhower, increased the size of the Army and personally sponsored
the Army's "Green Berets." He anticipated the advent of nuclear parity
between the United States and the Soviet Union. After his verbal
confrontation with Chairman Khrushchev in Vienna in 1961, Kennedy
reportedly told Scotty Reston of *The New York Times:* "We have a
problem in making our power credible, and Vietnam looks like the
place."

Kennedy set the tone of his administration in his inaugural address
when he pledged our nation "to bear any burden, meet any hardship,
support any friend, and oppose any foe to assure the survival and
success of liberty." Hence, he greatly increased our military effort in
Vietnam with advisers, Green Berets, American-manned helicopters,
and tactical aircraft.

The young president in his zeal made a grievous mistake in approv- (-)KENNEDY
ing our involvement in the overthrow of President Diem of South
Vietnam. This action morally locked us in Vietnam. Political chaos
prevailed for two years. If not for our involvement in the political
affairs of South Vietnam, and based on pragmatic considerations, we
could have gracefully withdrawn our support in view of a demonstrated lack of unity in South Vietnam. On the other hand, in the
wake of Kennedy's inaugural pronouncements, it is doubtful if his or
Johnson's administration would have risked the political repercussions. Kennedy's inaugural address was still ringing in the ears of
Americans.

Johnson inherited the problem and retained most of Kennedy's
advisers. He was obsessed with his "great society" program. In the (-)JOHNSON
hope that the war would go away, he made some decisions with the
endorsement of congressional leaders that were destined to drag the
war on indefinitely. He expanded our military effort to avoid inevitable defeat and increased the national debt to do so. His "guns and
butter" policy resulted in business as usual—in fact, a booming economy. No one "bore a burden, met a hardship" except those on the +!!
battlefield and their loved ones. In fact, if not for the sensational media

coverage piped for the first time into the homes of America, few would have appreciated that we were at war.

The president announced that we would not broaden the war. This set for us a defensive strategy on the ground and gave to the enemy great latitude for action. A force on the offensive is stronger than one on the defensive because it possesses the initiative and can mass its strength where and when it chooses without concern for the security of rear areas.

Johnson's administration formulated a strategy briefly described as: Hold the enemy, defeat him in the South, help build a nation, bomb war-related targets in the North on a gradually escalating basis until the enemy gets the message that he cannot win, and thus will negotiate or tacitly accept a divided Vietnam.

The trouble was the bombing was off and on—a thermometer of political pressure at home. Hanoi adjusted itself to every escalatory step. The enemy got a message, not of resolve and strength but of political insecurity and weakness, not only from official actions but from the vocal and emotional elements in our society who chose to resist actively national policy. From this syndrome came fallacies, and clichés, such as "illegal war" and "immoral war." The leaders in Hanoi foresaw that they could win the war politically in Washington as they had done against the French in Paris in 1954.

The control and prosecution of the war was not conducive to concluding it. Based on the success of Kennedy's tight personal control of tactical military action during the Cuban missile crisis, Kennedy's advisers, whom Johnson largely retained, saw such control as the modern way to confront an enemy.

The Gulf of Tonkin Resolution by the Congress in 1964, passed by a sizable majority, gave the president authority to commit military forces as he deemed necessary to achieve our objectives. As the war was allowed to drag on and on, the mood of the Congress, a reflection of public attitudes, in turn influenced profoundly by the media—particularly by daily television reports—grew further and further away from the policy of the executive branch. As the war became controversial, the president should have asked for affirmation each year of the Gulf of Tonkin Resolution. Indeed, the congressional leadership should have demanded it.

On the other hand, the policy of the Johnson administration was "low key." Both the president and the congressional leaders were afraid of an open national debate. They were unsure of the political repercussions and more concerned about the "hawks" than the "doves" on the convenient theory that Red China might be provoked to enter the war. They took counsel of their fears. The relevance of Vietnam to our security was not apparent, and the idealism implicit in Kennedy's words faded into obscurity.

Smoke screens were thrown up weekly by partisan politicians, intellectuals, the media, and "crusading" groups. As our prisoners of war attest to, the propaganda fed to them by their Communist captors was a repetition of statements by members of Congress and other public figures.

A decision of the president and the Congress to defer college students from military service was a cardinal mistake which had widespread repercussions. That unwise policy has been injurious to our society, degrading to our academic institutions and hindered our war effort. It was discriminatory, undemocratic, and resulted in the war being fought mainly by the poor man's son. I attribute the emotional anti-war sentiments on the campus to a guilt complex and the frustration of possibly having to participate in a war controlled by a no-win political policy.

The Reserve Officers' Training Corps (ROTC) on the campus became the symbolic "whipping boy," and that source of officers was crippled. In other wars, the military have logically drawn their officers from the college campuses. During the Vietnam War, that pool of young men with intelligence and leadership qualities was essentially denied the military. Therefore, the Army had to lower its standards for officers, and some marginal types were commissioned.

In the 1970 period, many college deferments ran out, and the Army received thousands of new soldiers in the rank of private with graduate and postgraduate degrees. Many came from emotionally charged campuses. An education inversion was created, with many privates being better educated than their sergeants and many of the lieutenants.

A communication problem evolved and had to be solved by unique methods. Underground newspaper and coffee houses sprang up, and a new lexicon emerged: A career man was a "lifer," a volunteer, a "paid killer." Leaflets were passed out as men left their military posts urging them to thwart military discipline. All of this was in the name of dissent.

Then came the Tet offensive by North Vietnam in 1968 which was the enemy's reaction to his major setbacks in South Vietnam during 1967. The enemy's objective was to inflict a military defeat on the South Vietnamese and the Americans and to generate a public uprising by the people of South Vietnam against the Saigon regime.

The enemy's military defeat was so severe that it took him four years to recover. There were no public uprisings. When the people fled from the North Vietnamese invaders, it was often described by the media as a movement to avoid our air and artillery. Most South Vietnamese units fought well, but it was not the "in thing" in media circles to say anything good about the South Vietnamese. The media misled the American people by their reporting of "Tet," and even a number of officials in Washington were taken in.

There is an old military axiom that "When the enemy is hurting, don't let up, increase the pressure on him." Despite military advice to the contrary, our political leaders decreased the pressure on the Hanoi regime and enticed the enemy to the conference table. There they sat in Paris for over four years and decided one thing only—the shape of the conference table. Our official and unofficial actions provided no incentive for Hanoi to do otherwise.

To demonstrate this principle, I remind you that in 1972 after Haiphong Harbor was mined, and *B52s* were used for the first time against important military targets in North Vietnam, Le Duc Tho and his colleagues came to the conference table and actually wept, saying that they could not take any more. We could have put that type of pressure on Hanoi after the defeat of the Tet offensive. The enemy would have been forced to negotiate on our terms, and thousands of lives would have been saved.

But that was not to be. The antiwar groups dedicated themselves to resisting national policy. They wanted to end the war. Who didn't? The sad thing was that those who were loudly dissenting were unwittingly encouraging the enemy to hang on. And hang on he did because every practical measure designed to encourage him to change his aggressive strategy was undercut by expressions and actions reflecting a lack of resolve, a naïve understanding of warfare, or blissful ignorance of the language that Communists understand—demonstrable resolve.

As our soldiers were fighting and dying for the principle of liberty and the right to dissent, what did we see at home? Burning the flag, abusing public officials, destroying ROTC buildings, extolling the Vietcong, lying and cheating by young men to disqualify themselves for military service, burning draft cards, draft resisters fleeing to Canada and Sweden—unconscionable conduct month after month. Some called it democracy at work. A better definition was anarchy. Call it what you will, it encouraged our enemies, prolonged the war and sadly cost lives.

In 1969, a withdrawal strategy was adopted without any quid pro quo from Hanoi. The North Vietnamese leadership persisted in promoting the fiction that the war was fundamentally a civil war—a people's revolution. The Tet offensive should have laid that myth to

? Nixon

rest. It should have been obvious that like the Korean War, it was a war of aggression by the Communist North.

Following the pressure that was finally put on the North Vietnamese by the invasion of their bases in Cambodia, the incursion into Laos, the mining of Haiphong Harbor, and the *B52* strikes into North Vietnam, the enemy decided for the first time to negotiate seriously. An agreement was reached in early 1973 which, although defective in many respects, was theoretically workable. But soon, any hope of success was dashed by the <u>Case-Church Amendment to the 1974 Ap-</u> propriation Act which prohibited any funds whatsoever.

Case-Church Amendment

> *. . . to finance directly or indirectly combat activities by U.S. military forces in or over or from off the shore of North Vietnam, South Vietnam, Laos, or Cambodia.*

This was recognized by Moscow and Hanoi as our instrument of surrender; they could break the Paris Peace Accord and get by with it. On top of that, the Congress cut military aid to South Vietnam by one-half and threatened to stop it entirely—all this following our presidents' many assurances by envoy and in writing to President Thieu that we would fully support his military forces after our withdrawal and would react if the enemy broke the Paris Agreement. As you know so well, in early 1975, the accord was flagrantly broken; Hanoi's gamble succeeded. The United States had paralyzed itself.

General Van Tien Dung, who commanded Hanoi's invading forces, in his account of his success in conquering South Vietnam tells the story. He has reported accurately that the reduction in US military aid ordered by Congress seriously impaired the ability of the South Vietnamese army to fight.

He estimates that the firepower by the South Vietnamese army was cut by 60 percent because of a shortage of bombs and communication, while its mobility was reduced by half because of inoperative aircraft and vehicles resulting from a shortage of spare parts and fuel. Thieu, he said, was forced "to fight a poor man's war." On the other hand, the North Vietnamese forces were fully equipped and supported by Russia and China. Dung gave no meaningful credit to the local Vietcong.

The leaders in Hanoi were students of our sensitive political system and the vulnerabilities of our open society. It was no accident that most of their initiatives were shrewdly coordinated with our national elections. They wished to encourage our political leaders to make decisions on the basis of political expediency rather than experienced sound judgment. They achieved considerable success.

Vietnam was both the most reported and the least reported war in history—if one considers both the coverage from Hanoi as well as Saigon. American families at home were able to see on "the tube" the bloodshed inevitably present on any battlefield. War was reported for the first time like crime on the police beat or a no-holds-barred political campaign.

Hanoi was able to cultivate the fiction that there were no North Vietnamese troops in the South, that the war was basically a people's revolution and that it was an illegal and immoral war. It is astonishing that numbers of our citizens, and some representatives of the news media, were taken in by Hanoi's propaganda.

Thieu became a favorite target for the press and was unfairly maligned while the conduct of the autocratic leaders in the North was not given equal time. Some of the news media suggested by their subjective reporting that the young country of South Vietnam with no experience in democracy or even self-government was expected to be as democratic and free of corruption as America with almost two centuries of experience. It was presumedly expected to demonstrate an advanced form of democracy while fighting for its survival.

By comparison, the enemy leaders appeared to be the "good guys." There were no television cameras behind the enemy lines. All news from North Vietnam was propaganda to serve their purposes. And serve it it did. I'm reminded of the expression: "If a mighty oak falls unobserved in a remote forest, it neither exists nor falls."

In a situation where our men's lives were put on the line, it is lamentable that so many did all possible to erode support for a policy associated with six presidents and endorsed by nine Congresses. Such evident disunity kept before the leaders in Hanoi the smell of victory. It is a sad commentary that our open society and our political systems were masterfully manipulated by Hanoi and Moscow to serve their interests.

My analyses would not be complete without mentioning those men in uniform and their civilian associates who tried zealously to make good the commitment our national leaders made to the people of South Vietnam. Those men and women performed admirably under circumstances unique in history. It is not easy to maintain morale on the battlefield if there are doubts about the support of the American people.

My thesis is simple. Our nation blundered in Vietnam and hence betrayed a chosen ally. One can learn more from failure than success. In our national interest, let us get about determining where we went wrong. I do not propose any more witch hunts, but I do urge that we not sweep the homemade mess under the rug.

I presume to conclude with several broad conclusions of my own.

We overextended ourselves in the post-World War II period econom- ically, militarily, psychologically, and politically. A day of reckoning was inevitable. Our foreign policy should be given a nonpartisan review at least every two years. We must develop a bipartisan foreign policy, free of politics as far as possible.

When there is a threat of war, our military leaders deserve a stronger voice in policymaking. When our political leaders commit us to war, the military voice should be given priority consideration.

It is unfair and fatal to send our troops to the battlefield if they are not going to be supported by the nation.

When we go to war, the burden and hardship must be shared by a cross section of our society.

We should heed an old Oriental saying: "It takes the full strength of a tiger to kill a rabbit," and we should use appropriate force to bring the war to an end.

When our national reputation and men's lives are at stake, the news media must show a more convincing sense of responsibility. We must be leery as a nation of our adversaries manipulating again the vulnera- bility of our political system and our open society.

The Vietnam episode is a travesty of the way America should func- tion. But those men and women who served honorably in the uniform of their country can be proud of their performance—and over 97 percent served honorably. During the period 1964–73, less than three percent of the over seven and a half million men who were discharged from the military received less than honorable discharges. This is not the picture some try to portray to the American people.

During the Vietnam War era, the US military—millions of patriotic American men and women—were:

- Loyal and responsive to their commander in chief, the president.
- Skillful and brave on the battlefield in the best American tra- dition.
- Humanitarian and compassionate (there were relatively few cases of misbehavior and disobedience, but these cases were given high visibility).
- Trustworthy in the performance of their duties—again with only a few exceptions.

Those men held as prisoners of war showed loyalty and pride in their country and the courage and stamina to resist intimidation. All but a few adhered to the Code of Conduct and are a great credit to our nation. Our fighting men kept their poise and did not waver as abuse was heaped upon them by misguided elements in our society.

But the burden and the wear and tear of a war allowed to drag on and on for seven long years took its toll on the individuals involved, military families and the military service organization. They passed the test. That sterling performance of the military has made a favorable impression on the vast majority of our countrymen. A recent poll taken by a reputable research organization (Potomac Associates) reports that the American people have greater confidence in the "military leadership" of our nation than any other segment of our society except themselves.

The military man has performed his role admirably throughout our history, and continues to do so. He has epitomized patriotism and loyalty to our ideals.

As the soldier prays for peace, he must be prepared to cope with the hardships of war and bear its scars.

12

An Interview with General Giap

Stanley Karnow

We met at the former French colonial governor's palace in Hanoi, an ornate mansion set in a spacious garden ablaze with hibiscus and bougainvillea, where senior Vietnamese officials receive guests. A short man with smooth skin, white hair, narrow eyes, and a spry gait, he wore a simple olive uniform, the four stars on its collar the only sign of his rank. Smiling broadly, he grasped me with soft, almost feminine hands and then, to my astonishment, bussed my cheeks in traditional French style.

Despite his Asian traits, this elfin figure might have been a courtly old Frenchman. But here was Gen. Vo Nguyen Giap, the Vietnamese Communist commander, the peer of Grant, Lee, Rommel, and MacArthur in the pantheon of military leaders.

A bold strategist, skilled logician, and tireless organizer, Giap fought for more than 30 years, building a handful of ragtag guerrillas into one of the world's most effective armies. He surmounted stupendous odds to crush the French, but his crowning achievement was to vanquish America's overwhelmingly superior forces in Vietnam—the only defeat the United States has sustained in its history.

I covered the two wars—which in may respects were phases of the same war—the first indirectly from Paris and the second as a correspondent in Vietnam. My reporting and subsequent research for a book brought me into contact with senior soldiers from the opposing sides. Giap was unique, having been both a policy maker and a field officer. I had studied his career, and sought to see him on an earlier

---

Stanley Karnow is the author of *Vietnam: A History* (New York: Viking, 1983), *Mao and China: Inside China's Cultural Revolution* (New York: Penguin, 1984), Vietnam: The War Nobody Won (Washington: Foreign Policy, 1983), and, more recently, *In Our Image: America's Empire in the Philippines* (New York: Viking, 1989), a winner of the Pulitzer Prize in history. The conversation with General Giap occurred early in 1990, and was first published in *The New York Times Magazine*, June 24, 1990.

trip to Hanoi. But only on this recent return did he grant me an interview.

The French once dubbed Giap the "snow-covered volcano"—a glacial exterior concealing a volatile temperament. Now approaching 80, he seems to have mellowed with age. But he still displays the intellectual vigor and fierce determination that propelled him to victory—and have made him a legend. Giap attributes his success to innate genius rather than to any formal training as a soldier. As he laughingly told me, "I was a self-taught general."

A day after our first encounter I drove to Giap's private residence, a handsome French colonial villa, its parlor lined with a polyglot assortment of volumes and decorated with busts and portraits of Marx, Lenin, and Ho Chi Minh, the deified leader of modern Vietnam. His wife, a buxom, cheerful woman, served fruit as he played the paterfamilias, proudly introducing his eldest daughter, an eminent nuclear physicist, and cuddling his grandchildren in his lap. He spoke flawless French slightly seasoned by a tonal Vietnamese inflection. Commenting on my fluency in French, he remarked, "I am glad to see that you are cosmopolitan"—as if he felt that we shared a bond as products of France's *grande mission civilisatrice*. Like many Vietnamese nationalists of his generation, Giap had embraced French culture while struggling against French colonialism.

But as he began to talk seriously, he exploded in a torrent of words. Endowed with a prodigious memory, he recalled the names of old comrades or detailed events dating back decades. He was often didactic, a vestige of his youth as a schoolteacher, and he lapsed into political bromides that evoked his revolutionary past. At times he sounded ironic—as he did when he cited Gen. William C. Westmoreland's "considerable military knowledge," then proceeded to list what he viewed as the American commander's blunders in Vietnam. And, like generals everywhere, he glossed over his setbacks. He admitted that, yes, "there were difficult moments when we wondered how we could go on." Yet, he thundered, "We were never pessimistic. Never! Never! Never!"

Giap's men did indeed show phenomenal tenacity during the war, confounding United States strategists who assumed that sheer might would crack their morale. Westmoreland, pointing to the grim "body count" of enemy dead, constantly claimed that the Communists were about to collapse. Following the war, still perplexed by his failure, Westmoreland said, "Any American commander who took the same vast losses as Giap would have been sacked overnight."

But Giap was not an American among strange people in a faraway land. His troops and their civilian supporters were fighting on their own soil, convinced that their sacrifices would erode the patience of their foes and, over time, bring Vietnam under Communist control. He had used this strategy against France, and he was confident that it would work against the United States.

"We were not strong enough to drive out a half-million American troops, but that wasn't our aim," he told me. "Our intention was to break the will of the American Government to continue the war. Westmoreland was wrong to expect that his superior firepower would grind us down. If we had focused on the balance of forces, we would have been defeated in two hours. We were waging a people's war— *a la manière vietnamienne.* America's sophisticated arms, electronic devices and all the rest were to no avail in the end. In war there are the two factors—human beings and weapons. Ultimately, though, human beings are the decisive factor. Human beings! Human beings!"

How long was he prepared to fight? "Another twenty years, even a hundred years, as long as it took to win, regardless of cost," Giap replied instantly. What, in fact, had been the cost? "We still don't know," he said, refusing, despite my persistence, to hazard a guess. But one of his aides confided to me that at least a million of their troops perished, the majority of them in the American war. As for the civilian toll, he said, "We haven't the faintest idea."

Listening to these horrendous statistics recalled to me the Americans who observed during the war that Asians have little regard for human life. But, judging from the carnage of two World Wars, the West is hardly a model of compassion. Moreover, Giap maintains, the Communists would have paid any price for victory because they were dedicated to a cause that reflects Vietnam's national heritage—a legacy that has also fueled its fierce martial spirit.

"Throughout our history," he intoned, "our profoundest ideology, the pervasive feeling of our people, has been patriotism." I knew what he meant. A battlefield for 4,000 years, Vietnam is awash in stories of real or mythical warriors who resisted foreign invaders, mainly Chinese. Its struggles forged a sense of national identity that is still alive in poetry and folk art, and in rural pagodas where children burn joss sticks before the statues of fabled heroes and heroines.

The French had conquered Vietnam by the early 20th century, but their authority was recurrently challenged by uprisings, which they often quelled brutally. Giap was nurtured in this climate of rebellion. The elder of two sons in a family of five children, he was born in 1911 in the Quang Binh Province village of An Xa, just above the line that would divide Vietnam 43 years later. The region of rice fields and jungles, set against a horizon of hazy mountains, had only been recently "pacified" by the French, and the exploits of its local partisans were still fresh memories.

At the village kindergarten Giap was taught elementary French, but at home his parents spoke only Vietnamese and, as he put it, "they ingrained patriotism in me." His father, a scholarly peasant, manifested his nationalism by teaching written Vietnamese in Chinese ideographs. From him Giap learned to read his first book, a child's history of Vietnam: "I discovered our forebears, our martyrs, our duty to expunge the disgrace of past humiliations."

His voice softened as he recalled the day he left home for primary school. "My mama and I were separating for the first time, and we both wept." In 1924, he went to the old imperial capital of Hue to attend the prestigious Quec Hoc academy, whose alumni included Ho Chi Minh and Ngo Din Diem, later the anti-Communist president of South Vietnam. There, barely 13, he began his political education.

Students met secretly to discuss anticolonial articles—particularly those by a mysterious expatriate, Nguyen A. Quoc, "Nguyen the Patriot," later known as Ho Chi Minh. But Giap was especially inspired by Phan Boi Chau, an early nationalist whom the French had put under house arrest in Hue. He imitated Chau's exhortations for me: "The cock is crowing! Arise, arise and prepare for action!"

Thus aroused, the youths protested openly against a French ban on nationalist activities. The protest fizzled, and Giap was expelled from school. "We now wondered what to do next," he recalled. "Nobody knew. We lacked direction."

He found his gospel after he was hired to assist a Vietnamese teacher who owned an illicit collection of Marx's works in French. "I spent my nights reading them, and my eyes opened," he said. "Marxism promised revolution, an end to oppression, the happiness of mankind. It echoed the appeals of Ho Chi Minh, who had written that downtrodden peoples should join the proletariat of all countries to gain their liberation. Nationalism made me a Marxist, as it did so many Vietnamese intellectuals and students."

Still he clung to the Confucian ethic of his father. "Marxism also seemed to me to coincide with the ideals of our ancient society," he added, "when the emperor and his subjects lived in harmony. It was a utopian dream."

By 1930, the global depression had hit Vietnam, and peasant unrest spread through the country, spurring radicals to rebel against the French, who summarily executed hundreds in reprisal. Foreseeing further revolts, Ho hastily founded the Indochinese Communist Party.

Now a professional agitator, Giap was arrested and sentenced to three years in prison, but a sympathetic French official released him earlier. He went to Hanoi, graduated from a French school, the Lycée Albert Sarraut, then obtained a law degree at the University of Hanoi, another French institution.

To earn a living, he taught at a private school, where his courses included Vietnamese history—"to imbue my students with patriotism," he told me. He also lectured on the French Revolution "to propagate the ideals of liberty, equality, and fraternity." When I asked him to name his French hero, he snapped, "Robespierre!" "But he was the architect of the Terror," I remonstrated. "Robespierre!" he repeated. "Robespierre fought to the end for the people." And Napoleon? "Bonaparte, yes. He was a revolutionary. Napoleon, no. He betrayed the people."

In 1936, Socialists and Communists formed a Popular Front government in Paris, and tensions in Vietnam eased. Giap had by then joined the Communist Party, which could now legally publish newspapers in French and Vietnamese, and he wrote articles in both languages. He married Minh Khai, a Communist militant, and they had a daughter. The physicist I met at his home in Hanoi was the child grown up.

Giap avidly read Ho's writings as they reached Vietnam. "I tried to imagine this man," he said. "I looked forward to meeting him some day." His chance came in early 1940.

Ho, then in China, decided to reinforce his movement in Vietnam, and he summoned Giap and Pham Van Dong, the future Vietnamese Prime Minister. Left behind, Giap's wife was arrested. She died in prison following the execution of her sister, also a Communist, by a French firing squad. Giap was distraught when he learned of their deaths three years afterward. He subsequently married Dang Bich Ha, his present wife, the daughter of a professor.

In Kunming, the Yunnan Province capital, Giap met Ho, a frail figure with a wispy beard, who then called himself Vuong. Giap was disappointed. "Here was this legend," he told me, "but he was just a man, like any other man."

He ordered him to Yenan, in north China, where the Chinese Communists conducted courses on guerrilla warfare. Balking, Giap said, "I wield a pen, not a sword." But he went nevertheless, wearing an oversized Chinese army uniform. En route, he received a telegram from Ho, countermanding the order. France had fallen to the Germans, and the situation in Vietnam was about to change completely. The moment had come, Ho said, to return to Vietnam.

Early in 1941, Ho set foot in his homeland for the first time in more than 30 years. He established his sanctuary in a cave near Pac Bo, a remote village nestled in an eerie landscape of limestone hills. There, joined by Giap and others, he founded the Vietnam Doc Lap Dong Minh, the Vietnam Independence League—Vietminh for short. From its name he borrowed his most famous alias, Ho Chi Minh—roughly Bringer of Light.

"Political action should precede military action," Ho asserted. Giap and his comrades started by recruiting the poor, alienated hill tribes of the region. They trekked through the mountains, creating cells of five men and women, who in turn converted other villagers to the cause. The cells multiplied swiftly—testimony to Giap's organizational skill.

Meanwhile, Giap began to form guerrilla bands to guard the political cadres. He assumed a *nom de guerre*, Van, but he had no military experience. Except for a dud Chinese shell, he had never handled a lethal device—not even a gun. His partisans possessed only knives and a few old flintlocks. Once they did acquire a grenade, but he could not figure out how to detonate it. He also tried in vain to polish his ragged ranks. Sounding like a drill sergeant as he told me the story, he said: "We didn't even know how to march in French—*un, deux, un, deux*. So I translated the numbers into Vietnamese—*mot, hai, mot, hai.*"

He recalls that time as harrowing. Hunted by French patrols, Giap's bands retreated into the jungle, where they suffered from diseases, and subsisted on bark and roots. Learning as he went along, Giap taught his soldiers to wade through streams or move during rainstorms to deter pursuit, to store supplies, to communicate secretly, and to ferret out informers. Despite his constant fear of failure, the movement grew.

Still he remained an intellectual, writing theoretical articles for his followers. Once, after scanning them, Ho sniffed, "No peasant will understand this stuff."

The Japanese had invaded Vietnam after entering World War II, and the Vietminh guerrillas resisted them as well as the French— thereby enhancing their nationalist image. By 1944 Ho was certain that America would win the war and back him. Not only had President Franklin D. Roosevelt denounced French colonialism, but the Office of Strategic Services, the precursor of the Central Intelligence Agency, was also then helping the Vietminh in exchange for information on Japanese troop deployments. Ho, calculating that a show of strength would boost his movement, ordered Giap to form larger "armed propaganda teams" and to attack isolated French garrisons.

Giap assembled a team of 34 guerrillas, among them three women. Resembling ordinary peasants in their conic hats and indigo pajamas, they attacked two tiny French posts on Christmas Eve, 1944, killing their French officers and seizing their arsenals. The skirmishes are commemorated to this day as the birth of the Vietnamese army. *1944* Beaming as he recalled these episodes, Giap said: "Recently I read an old French report on the engagements. It stated that our troops were brave and disciplined—and that their leader displayed a mastery of guerrilla tactics. *Quel compliment!*"

The victory swelled Ho's ranks. In September 1945, following Japan's surrender, he declared the independence of Vietnam. Named commander of the Vietminh armed forces, Giap assumed the rank of general. Ho also appointed him Minister of Interior, a position Giap reportedly used to liquidate a number of non-Communist nationalist parties—and, some sources allege, even his Communist rivals. Unlike Ho, who wore an ascetic cotton tunic and rubber-tire sandals, Giap affected a white suit, striped tie, and fedora, perhaps to advertise his Western tastes.

Ho offered to remain affiliated with France, but the French rebuffed his compromise, and war broke out in 1946. Giap preserved his teams and built up popular sympathy. By late 1949, the Chinese Communists had conquered China and begun to send him heavy weapons, which enabled him to enlarge his guerrilla bands into battalions, regiments, and ultimately divisions. Giap opened the path into Vietnam for Chinese arms shipments by destroying the French border posts in a series of lightning attacks.

Stunned, France sent out its most distinguished general: Jean de Lattre de Tassigny. Giap gallantly announced that the Vietminh now faced "an adversary worthy of its steel." But de Lattre died of cancer amid plans for an ambitious French offensive. Both sides sparred for the next three years as Gen. Henri Navarre, now the French commander, forecast victory in a statement that would be his unofficial epitaph: "We see it clearly—like light at the end of the tunnel."

By 1953 Ho was considering negotiations with France. But he knew he had to win on the battlefield to win at the conference table. The arena would be Dien Bien Phu, which was to equal Waterloo and Gettysburg among the great battles of history.

"At first I had no idea where—or even whether—the battle would take place," he recalled. Then, a veteran recounting his war, he reconstructed the scene by moving the cups and saucers around the coffee table in front of us.

Navarre, ordered to defend nearby Laos, chose the site by placing his best battalions at Dien Bien Phu, a distant valley not far from the Laotian border in northwest Vietnam—never imagining that Giap would fight there. He misjudged badly.

Giap brought a huge force into the area. His troops marched for weeks, carrying supplies on bicycles and their backs through jungles and over mountains. But no task was tougher than deploying the cannon that China had furnished them. Relying on sheer muscle, they dragged the howitzers up the hills above the French positions. "It was difficult, *n'est-ce pas*, very difficult," Giap recollected, adding that only truly "motivated" men could have performed such a feat.

He planned to launch his attack on Jan. 25, 1954, and at first heeded his Chinese military advisers, who proposed "human wave" assaults of the kind their forces had staged against the Americans in Korea. But, after a sleepless night, he concluded that it would be suicidal to hurl his troops against the deeply entrenched French, with their tanks and aircraft. His tone rose dramatically as he told me: "Suddenly I postponed the operation. My staff was confused, but no matter. I was in command, and I demanded absolute obedience—*sans discussion, sans explication!*"

Giap rescheduled the attack for March, and directed his men to creep toward the French through a maze of tunnels as his cannon pounded them from the heights above the valley. The battle dragged on for nearly two months and, one by one, the French positions fell.

At the time, President Dwight D. Eisenhower weighed and rejected the idea of United States air strikes. What if he had intervened? "We would have had problems," Giap allowed, "but the outcome would have been the same. The battlefield was too big for effective bombing."

The French surrendered on May 7, the day an international conference met in Geneva to seek an end to the war. The Vietminh failed to transform the battlefield victory into a full diplomatic victory. Under Soviet and Chinese pressure, its negotiators accepted a divided Vietnam pending a nationwide election to be held in 1956. Giap would only say that "we could have gained more." But Pham Van Dong, then the chief Vietminh delegate, had earlier told me: "We were betrayed."

With American approval, South Vietnam's President Diem reneged on the election and arrested thousands of southern Vietminh militants, executing many without trial. The Communist regime in Hanoi procrastinated. "Perhaps we should have acted sooner," Giap said, "but our people were tired after a long war, and they might not have responded to a call for yet another armed struggle. We would wait."

In 1957, however, Hanoi ordered its surviving southern activists to form armed teams, supplying them with weapons and cadres through the so-called Ho Chi Minh Trail. Soon, again under Hanoi's direction, the teams started to attack Diem's officials. Posing as a homegrown insurgency, the Vietcong surfaced in 1960, in the guise of the National Liberation Front of South Vietnam. But it too was invented by Hanoi.

I presumed that Giap must have been frustrated, after years of fighting the French, to be beginning another war against the Americans and their South Vietnamese clients. But, as he tells it, his zeal never waned as he resumed the same slow process of rebuilding the forces in the south.

Initially stumped after President John F. Kennedy sent aid and advisers to Vietnam, the Communists quickly regained their momentum and were soon routing Diem's army. Their strength also increased as numbers of peasants, alienated by Diem's rigidity, joined their camp.

Late in 1963, acting with American complicity, Diem's own generals staged a coup against him. His assassination dismayed the Hanoi regime. The new junta in Saigon promised reforms, prompting many Vietcong supporters to switch sides. Nor did it seem likely that President Lyndon B. Johnson, who had succeeded Kennedy, would withdraw from Vietnam. Giap, now seeing a protracted struggle ahead, concluded that he would eventually have to commit his own regular forces to the war. By the end of 1964, the first northern regiment was operating in the south.

The large Communist units gravely threatened the Saigon regime, which was now tottering amid internecine rivalries. Early in 1965, alarmed by the situation, Johnson unleashed air attacks against North Vietnam and sent United States combat troops to Vietnam. Surprisingly, Giap displayed a measure of sympathy for Johnson's predicament. "Of course he would have been wiser not to escalate the war," he mused. "But throughout history, even the most intelligent leaders have not always been masters of their fate."

By late 1967, however, Giap also faced a hard choice. The half-million United States troops then in Vietnam were chewing up his forces, and his hopes of an early victory seemed dim. But, as he wrote at the time, the Americans were stretched "as taut as a bowstring" and could not defend the entire country. He also detected growing antiwar feeling in the United States and rising unrest in South Vietnam's urban areas. Thus he gambled on a campaign that would break the deadlock. Later known as the Tet offensive of 1968, it would be a coordinated assault against South Vietnam's cities.

"For us, *vous savez*, there is never a single strategy," Giap explained. "Ours is always a synthesis, simultaneously military, political, and diplomatic—which is why, quite clearly, the offensive had multiple objectives. We foresaw uprisings in the cities. But above all, we wanted to show the Americans that we were not exhausted, that we could attack their arsenals, communications, elite units, even their headquarters, the brains behind the war. And we wanted to project the war into the homes of America's families, because we knew that most of them had nothing against us. In short, we sought a decisive victory that would persuade America to renounce the war."

Giap prefaced the drive in late 1967 with a diversion, striking a string of American garrisons in the Vietnamese highlands. Johnson, who viewed Giap's siege of Khe Sanh as a replay of his showdown against the French, pledged Westmoreland to hold the base—saying, "I don't want any damn Dinbinphoo." The Communist troops, bombed by B-52's, took ghastly losses. But Giap had lured the American forces away from the populated coast.

On the night of Jan. 31, 1968, the Lunar New Year, some 70,000 Communist soldiers attacked South Vietnam's cities. A suicide squad stormed into the United States Embassy compound in Saigon, and American troops fought for weeks to rescue Hue. The televised scenes shocked the American public, which was already souring on the war. His ratings plummeting as antiwar sentiment spread, Johnson abandoned the race for re-election. Vietnam, coupled with civil rights protests, threw America into turmoil.

Looking back, Giap maintains that Tet was a "victory" that showed "our discipline, strength, and ardor." But, he admits, it was not "decisive." Another seven years of war lay ahead and, he concedes, they were "difficult." Still, he added with typical bravado, "no obstacle, nothing the Americans could do, would stop us in the long run." This was a reality, he emphasized, that Westmoreland failed to perceive. "He was a cultivated soldier who had read many military texts," Giap said. "Yet he committed an error following the Tet offensive, when he requested another 206,000 troops. He could have put in 300,000, even 400,000 more men. It would have made no difference."

But the aftermath of Tet was bleak for the Communists. According to one of Giap's aides, their casualties during the drive had been "devastating." American bombing of the South Vietnamese countryside further crippled their forces as their peasant supporters fled to urban refugee camps. They were also ravaged by the Phoenix program, devised by the C.I.A. to destroy their rural sanctuaries. The Communist structure retreated to Cambodia, where it was again uprooted by President Richard M. Nixon's incursion in 1970.

As Nixon withdrew United States troops, however, Giap had only to wait until he faced the inept Saigon army. The climax, he figured, would involve big units. Early in 1972, he staged a massive offensive intended to improve Hanoi's hand for the final negotiations. It failed as American aircraft crushed his divisions. But Nixon, eager for peace before the United States Presidential election in November, compromised on a cease-fire. Signed in January 1973, it would gradually erode. The Communists rolled into Saigon two years later.

"I was delirious with joy," Giap said. "I flew there immediately, and inspected the South Vietnamese army's headquarters, with its modern American equipment. It had all been useless. The human factor had been decisive!"

A typical retired general, Giap now devotes much of his time to revisiting battlefields and addressing veterans. "If I had not become a soldier," he reflects, "I probably would have remained a teacher, maybe of philosophy or history. Someone recently asked me whether, when I first formed our army, I ever imagined I would fight the Americans. *Quelle question!* Did the Americans, back then, ever imagine that they would one day fight us?"

He gripped my hand as we parted, saying: "Remember, I am a general who fought for peace. I wanted peace—but not peace at any price." With that he walked off briskly, leaving me to contemplate the cemeteries, the war monuments, and the unhealed memories in France, America, and Vietnam, and the terrible price their peoples paid.

13

The Legitimacy of the War
Michael Walzer

WIDELY VIEWED AS MOST   ETHICIST   LEGITIMATE GOVERNMENT

BASED ON PREMISE - THAT VIETNAM WAS WAR OF AGGRESSION BASED ON LACK OF

I doubt that it is possible to tell the story of Vietnam in a way that
will command general agreement. The official American version—
that the struggle began with a North Vietnamese invasion of the
South, to which the United States responded in accordance with its
treaty obligations—follows the legalist paradigm closely, but is on its
surface unbelievable. Fortunately, it seems to be accepted by virtually
no one and need not detain us here. I want to pursue a more sophisticated version of the American defense, which concedes the existence
of a civil war and describes the U.S. role, first, as assistance to a
legitimate government, and secondly, as counter-intervention, a response to covert military moves by the North Vietnamese regime.[13]
The crucial terms here are "legitimate" and "response." The first suggests that the government on behalf of which our counter-intervention
was undertaken had a local status, a political presence independent
of ourselves, and hence that it could conceivably win the civil war if
no external force was brought to bear. The second suggests that our
own military operations followed upon and balanced those of another
power, in accordance with the argument I have put forward. Both
these suggestions are false, but they point to the peculiarly confined
character of counter-intervention and indicate what one has to say
(at least) when one joins in the civil wars of other states.

The Geneva Agreement of 1954, ending the first Vietnamese war,

---

Michael Walzer, a distinguished political scientist, is currently at the Institute for
Advanced Studies at Princeton. He is author of many books, articles, and essays including *Exodus and Revolution* (New York: Basic Books, 1985); *Obligations: Essays on
Disobedience, War, and Citizenship* (Cambridge: Harvard University Press, 1982); *Radical Principles: Reflections of an Unreconstructed Democrat* (New York: Basic Books,
1980); and *The Spheres of Justice* (New York: Basic Books, 1983). The essay included
here is a portion of Walzer's *Just and Unjust Wars* (New York: Basic Books, 1977),
reprinted by permission of the publishers.

JUST WAR THEORY

established a temporary frontier between the North and the South, and two temporary governments on either side of the line, pending elections scheduled for 1956.[14] When the South Vietnamese government refused to permit these elections, it clearly lost whatever legitimacy was conferred by the agreements. But I shall not dwell on this loss, nor on the fact that some sixty states nevertheless recognized the sovereignty of the new regime in the South and opened embassies in Saigon. I doubt that foreign states, whether they act independently or collectively, sign treaties or send ambassadors, can establish or disestablish the legitimacy of a government. What is crucial is the standing of that government with its own people. Had the new regime been able to rally support at home, Vietnam today would have joined the dual states of Germany and Korea, and Geneva 1954 would be remembered only as the setting for another cold war partition. But what is the test of popular support in a country where democracy is unknown and elections are routinely managed? The test, for governments as for insurgents, is self-help. That doesn't mean that foreign states cannot provide assistance. One assumes the legitimacy of new regimes; there is, so to speak, a period of grace, a time to build support. But that time was ill-used in South Vietnam, and the continuing dependence of the new regime on the U.S. is damning evidence against it. Its urgent call for military intervention in the early 1960's is more damning evidence still. One must ask of President Diem a question first posed by Montague Bernard: "How can he impersonate [represent] his people who is begging the assistance of a foreign power in order to reduce them to obedience?"[15] Indeed, it was never a successful impersonation.

The argument might be put more narrowly: a government that receives economic and technical aid, military supply, strategic and tactical advice, and is still unable to reduce its subjects to obedience, is clearly an illegitimate government. Whether legitimacy is defined sociologically or morally, such a government fails to meet the most minimal standards. One wonders how it survives at all. It must be the case that it survives because of the outside help it receives and for no other, no local reasons. The Saigon regime was so much an American creature that the U.S. government's claim to be committed to it and obligated to ensure its survival is hard to understand. It is as if our right hand were committed to our left. There is no independent moral or political agent on the other side of the bond and hence no genuine bond at all. Obligations to one's creatures (except insofar as they pertain to the personal safety of individuals) are as insignificant politically as obligations to oneself are insignificant morally. When the

U.S. did intervene militarily in Vietnam, then, it acted not to fulfill commitments to another state, but to pursue policies of its own contrivance.

Against all this, it is argued that the popular base of the South Vietnamese government was undermined by a systematic campaign of subversion, terrorism, and guerrilla war, largely directed and supplied from the North. That there was such a campaign, and that the North was involved in it, is clearly true, though the extent and timing of the involvement are very much in dispute. If one were writing a legal brief, these matters would be critically important, for the American claim is that the North Vietnamese were illegally supporting a local insurgency, with both men and material, at a time when the U.S. was still providing only economic assistance and military supply to a legitimate government. But that claim, whatever its legal force, somehow misses the moral reality of the Vietnamese case. It would be better to say that the U.S. was literally propping up a government— and shortly a series of governments—without a local political base, while the North Vietnamese were assisting an insurgent movement with deep roots in the countryside. We were far more vital to the government than they were to the insurgents. Indeed, it was the weakness of the government, its inability to help itself even against its internal enemies, that forced the steady escalation of American involvement. And that fact must raise the most serious questions about the American defense: for counter-intervention is morally possible only on behalf of a government (or a movement, party, or whatever) that has already passed the self-help test.

I can say very little here about the reasons for insurgent strength in the countryside. Why were the communists able, and the government unable, to "impersonate" Vietnamese nationalism? The character and scope of the American presence probably had a great deal to do with this. Nationalism is not easily represented by a regime as dependent as Saigon was on foreign support. It is also important that North Vietnamese moves did not similarly brand those they benefited as foreign agents. In nations divided as Vietnam was, infiltration across the dividing line is not necessarily regarded as outside interference by the men and women on the other side. The Korean War might look very different than it does if the Northerners had not marched in strength across the 38th parallel, but had made covert contact, instead, with a Southern rebellion. In contrast to Vietnam, however, there was no rebellion—and there was considerable support for the government—in South Korea.[16] These cold war dividing lines have the usual significance of an international border only insofar as they mark off, or come in time to mark off, two political communities within each of which individual citizens feel some local loyalty. Had South Vietnam taken shape in this way, American military activity, in the face of large-scale Northern connivance at terrorism and guerrilla war, might have qualified as counter-intervention. At least, the name would have been an arguable one. As it is, it is not.

It remains an issue whether the American counter-intervention, had it been such, could rightly have assumed the size and scope of the war we eventually fought. Some notion of symmetry is relevant here, though it cannot be fixed absolutely in arithmetic terms. When a state sets out to maintain or restore the integrity of a local struggle, its military activity should be roughly equivalent to that of the other intervening states. Counter-intervention is a balancing act. I have made this point before, but it is worth emphasizing, for it reflects a deep truth about the meaning of responsiveness: *the goal of counter-intervention is not to win the war.* That this is not an esoteric or obscure truth is suggested by President Kennedy's well-known description of the Vietnam War. "In the final analysis," Kennedy said, "it is their war. They are the ones who have to win it or lose it. We can help them, we can give them equipment, we can send our men out there as advisors, but they have to win it—the people of Vietnam against the Communists . . ."[17] Though this view was reiterated by later American leaders, it is not, unhappily, a definitive exposition of American policy. In fact, the United States failed in the most dramatic way to respect the character and dimensions of the Vietnamese civil war, and we failed because we could not win the war as long as it retained that character and was fought within those dimensions. Searching for a level of conflict at which our technological superiority could be brought to bear, we steadily escalated the struggle, until finally it was an American war, fought for American purposes, in someone else's country. . . .

If the previous argument is right, the American war in Vietnam was, first of all, an unjustified intervention, and it was, secondly, carried on in so brutal a manner that even had it initially been defensible, it would have to be condemned, not in this or that aspect but generally. I am not going to re-argue that description, but assume it, so that we can look closely at the responsibility of democratic citizens—and at a particular set of democratic citizens, namely, ourselves.[17]

Democracy is a way of distributing responsibility (just as monarchy is a way of refusing to distribute it). But that doesn't mean that all adult citizens share equally in the blame we assign for aggressive war. Our actual assignments will vary a great deal, depending on the precise nature of the democratic order, the place of a particular person in that order, and the pattern of his own political activities. Even in a perfect democracy, it cannot be said that every citizen is the author of every state policy, though every one of them can rightly be called to account. Imagine, for example, a small community where all the citizens are fully and accurately informed about public business, where all of them participate, argue, vote on matters of communal interest, and where they all take turns holding public office. Now this community, let us say, initiates and wages an unjust war against its neighbors—for the sake of some economic advantage, perhaps, or out of zeal to spread its (admirable) political system. There is no question of self-defense; no one has attacked it or is planning to do so. Who is responsible for this war? Surely all those men and women who voted for it and who cooperated in planning, initiating, and waging it. The soldiers who do the actual fighting are not responsible as soldiers; but as citizens, they are, assuming that they were old enough to have shared in the decision to fight.* All of them are guilty of the crime of aggressive war and of no lesser charge, and we would not hesitate in such a case to blame them publicly. Nor would it make any difference whether their motive was economic selfishness or a political zeal that appeared to them entirely disinterested. Either way, the blood of their victims would complain against them.

Those who voted against the war or who refused to cooperate in the waging of it could not be blamed. But what would we think of a group of citizens that didn't vote? Had they voted, let's say, the war might have been avoided, but they were lazy, didn't care, or were afraid to come down on one side or the other of a hotly disputed issue. The day of the crucial decision was a day off from work; they spent it in their gardens. I am inclined to say that they are blameworthy, though they are not guilty of aggressive war. Surely those of their fellow citizens who went to the assembly and opposed the war can blame them for

---

*Why aren't they responsible as soldiers? If they are morally bound to vote against the war, why aren't they also bound to refuse to fight? The answer is that they vote as individuals, each one deciding for himself, but they fight as members of the political community, the collective decision having already been made, subject to all the moral and material pressures that I described in chapter 3. They act very well if they refuse to fight, and we should honor those—they are likely to be few—who have the self-certainty and courage to stand against their fellows. I have argued elsewhere that democracies ought to respect such people and ought certainly to tolerate their refusals. (See the essay on "Conscientious Objection" in *Obligations*.) That doesn't mean, however, that the others can be called criminals. Patriotism may be the last refuge of scoundrels, but it is also the ordinary refuge of ordinary men and women, and it requires of us another sort of toleration. But we should expect opponents of the war to refuse to become officers or officials, even if they feel bound to share combat risks with their countrymen.

their indifference and inaction. This seems a clear counter-example to Gray's assertion that "No citizen of a free land can justly accuse his neighbor . . . of not having done as much as he should to prevent the state of war or the commission of this or that state crime. But each can . . . accuse himself . . ."[18] In a perfect democracy, we would know a great deal about one another's duties, and just accusations would not be impossible.

Imagine now that the minority of citizens that was defeated could have won (and prevented the war) if instead of merely voting, they had held meetings outside the assembly, marched and demonstrated, organized for a second vote. Let's assume that none of this would have been terribly dangerous to them, but they chose not to take these measures because their opposition to the war wasn't all that strong; they thought it unjust but were not horrified by the prospect; they hoped for a quick victory; and so on. Then they are blameworthy, too, though to a lesser degree than those slothful citizens who did not even bother to go to the assembly.

These last two examples resemble the good samaritan cases in domestic society, where we commonly say that if it is possible to do good, without risk or great cost, one ought to do good. But when the issue is war, the obligation is stronger, for it is not a question of doing good, but of preventing serious harm, and harm that will be done in the name of my own political community—hence, in some sense, in my own name. Here, assuming still that the community is a perfect democracy, it looks as if a citizen is blameless only if he takes back his name. I don't think this means that he must become a revolutionary or an exile, actually renouncing his citizenship or loyalty. But he must do all he can, short of accepting frightening risks, to prevent or stop the war. He must withdraw his name from this act (the war policy) though not necessarily from every communal action, for he may still value, as he probably should, the democracy he and his fellow citizens have achieved. This, then, is the meaning of Gray's maxim: the more one can do, the more one has to do.

We can now drop the myth of perfection and paint a more realistic picture. The state that goes to war is, like our own, an enormous state, governed at a great distance from its ordinary citizens by powerful and often arrogant officials. These officials, or at least the leading among them, are chosen through democratic elections, but at the time of the choice very little is known about their programs and commitments. Political participation is occasional, intermittent, limited in its effects, and it is mediated by a system for the distribution of news which is partially controlled by those distant officials and which in any case allows for considerable distortions. It may be that a politics of this sort is the best we can hope for (though I don't believe that) once the political community reaches a certain size. Anyway, it is no longer as easy to impose responsibility as it is in a perfect democracy. One doesn't want to regard those distant officials as if they were kings, but for certain sorts of state action, secretly prepared or suddenly launched, they bear a kind of regal responsibility.

When a state like this commits itself to a campaign of aggression, its citizens (or many of them) are likely to go along, as Americans did during the Vietnam war, arguing that the war may after all be just; that it is not possible for them to be sure whether it is just or not; that their leaders know best and tell them this or that, which sounds plausible enough; and that nothing they can do will make much difference anyway. These are not immoral arguments, though they reflect badly on the society within which they are made. And they can, no doubt, be made too quickly by citizens seeking to avoid the difficulties that might follow if they thought about the war for themselves. These people are or may be blameworthy, not for aggressive war, but for bad faith as citizens. But that is a hard charge to make, for citizenship plays such a small part in their everyday lives. "Free action in the communal sphere" is a possibility for men and women in such a state only in the formal sense that serious governmental restraint, actual repression, doesn't exist. Perhaps it should also be said that the "communal sphere" doesn't exist, for it is only the day-to-day assumption of responsibility that creates that sphere and gives it meaning. Even patriotic excitement, war fever, among such people is probably best understood as a reflex of distance, a desperate identification, stimulated, it may be, by a false account of what is going on. One might say of them what one says of soldiers in combat, that they are not to blame for the war, since it is not their war.*

But as an account of all the citizens, even in such a state, this is certainly exaggerated. For there exists a group of more knowledgeable men and women, members of what political scientists call the foreign policy elites, who are not so radically distanced from the national leadership; and some subset of these people, together with others in touch with them, is likely to form an "opposition" or perhaps even a movement of opposition to the war. It would seem possible to regard

---

*But see the note in Anne Frank's *Diary*: "I don't believe that only governments and capitalists are guilty of aggression. Oh no, the little man is just as keen on it, for otherwise the people of the world would have risen in revolt long ago." I'm sure she is right about the keenness, and I don't want to excuse it. But we don't, for all that, call the little men war criminals, and I am trying to explain why we don't. (*The Diary of a Young Girl*, trans. B. M. Mooyaart-Doubleday, New York, 1953, p. 201.)

the entire group of knowledgeable people as at least potentially blame-worthy if that war is aggressive and unless they join the opposition.[19] To say that is to presume upon the knowledge they have and their private sense of political possibility. But if we turn to an actual case of imperfect democracy, like the United States in the late 1960s and early 1970s, the presumption doesn't seem unwarranted. Surely there was knowledge and opportunity enough among the country's elites, the national and local leaders of its political parties, its religious establishments, its corporate hierarchies, and perhaps above all its intellectual teachers and spokesmen—the men and women whom Noam Chomsky has named, in tribute to the role they play in contemporary government, "the new mandarins."[20] Surely many of these people were morally complicitous in our Vietnam aggression. I suppose one can also say of them what many of them have said of themselves: that they were simply mistaken in their judgments of the war, failed to realize this or that, thought that was true when it was not, or hoped for this result which never came about. In moral life generally, one makes allowances for false beliefs, misinformation, and honest mistakes. But there comes a time in any tale of aggression and atrocity when such allowances can no longer be made. I cannot mark out that time here; nor am I interested in pointing at particular people or certain that I can do so. I only want to insist that there are responsible people even when, under the conditions of imperfect democracy, moral accounting is difficult and imprecise.

The real moral burden of the American war fell on that subset of men and women whose knowledge and sense of possibility was made manifest by their oppositional activity. They were the ones most likely to reproach themselves and one another, continually asking whether they were doing enough to stop the fighting, devoting enough time and energy, working hard enough, working as effectively as they could. For most of their fellow citizens, anxious, apathetic, and alienated, the war was merely an ugly or an exciting spectacle (until they were forced to join it). For the dissidents, it was a kind of moral torture—self-torture, as Gray describes it, though they also tortured one another, wastefully, in savage internecine conflicts over what was to be done. And this self-torture bred a kind of self-righteousness *vis-a-vis* the others, an endemic failing on the Left, though understandable enough under conditions of aggressive war and mass acquiescence. The expression of that self-righteousness, however, is not a useful way to get one's fellow citizens to think seriously about the war or to join the opposition: nor was it useful in this case. It is not easy to know what course of action might serve these purposes. Politics is difficult at such a time. But there is intellectual work to do that is less difficult:

one must describe as graphically as one can the moral reality of war, talk about what it means to force people to fight, analyze the nature of democratic responsibilities. These, at least, are encompassable tasks, and they are morally required of the men and women who are trained to perform them.

14

Why We Did What We Did
Clark Clifford

President Harry S. Truman used to remark, from time to time, that the man with hindsight had 20/20 vision.

I assume that this Committee wishes its witnesses to look back over the years in which we struggled with the Vietnam problem, and to search mainly for the vital lessons that we have learned, or should have learned, from this traumatic experience.

From the vantage point of ten years later certain stark factors of importance are clearly visible. We entered the conflict in Southeast Asia with the highest moral and ethical motives. We were coming to the aid of a poor, independent country which was resisting the efforts by powerful communist powers to subjugate the country and its people. With no hope of economic or territorial gain, we were engaged in the task of attempting to preserve the freedom of South Vietnam and preventing the spread of communism in Southeast Asia and the Pacific basin.

The overwhelming weight of opinion, in those early days, was that the forces of a monolithic communism were on the march and, if unimpeded, would engulf that part of the world and spread eastward. If there is any doubt as to the near unanimity of attitude toward the issue, one has only to consider the vote in the United States Congress in 1964 on the Gulf of Tonkin resolution. Only two Senators in the entire House and Senate voted against authorizing the President to use military force in Southeast Asia.

Despite the widespread opinion that prevailed at the time, it is clear

Clark Clifford, a Washington attorney and confidant to several U.S. Presidents, from Franklin D. Roosevelt to George H. W. Bush, became Secretary of Defense in the Johnson Administration, following the resignation of Robert McNamara in 1968. The address transcribed for publication in this volume was first given as testimony before the House Subcommittee on Asian and Pacific Affairs on the Subject of Vietnam, on April 29, 1985, ten years after the United States withdrawal from Saigon.

to me that our evaluation of the conditions that existed in Vietnam and Southeast Asia was in error. I have thought much about how we could have stumbled into such a costly miscalculation. I offer the following analysis as the basis for our entry into the Vietnam conflict.

I originally agreed with our country's policy. It appeared that there was a joint effort going on between the Soviet Union and Red China to spread communism throughout Southeast Asia. That is how it looked to us at the time. I was part of the generation that had gone through the experience of World War II and I was very conscious of the fact that World War II could have been prevented if the major nations of the world had understood the danger more clearly and more accurately.

When Hitler's army of the Third Reich, for instance, marched into the Rhineland he did so against the advice of the German general staff, and if France and England, supported by the United States, had objected at that time and moved, I believe the war could have been stopped. But they did not. Hitler then moved into Austria. Again there was an opportunity to stop him. He had marched again over the objections of the general staff. His next move was into Czechoslovakia, and then came the invasion of Poland. That triggered World War II.

Those of my generation who went through the war had this clear recognition that if we had moved earlier it could have been prevented. That is why they were predisposed to act the way they did when they saw signs of communist expansionism. You will remember that toward the end of World War II the Soviet Union embarked on a program of aggressive expansionism. They took over the countries on their western periphery, Latvia, Lithuania, Estonia, Bulgaria, Romania, Czechoslovakia, Yugoslavia, and later Hungary. We saw all that going on. We could have made the same mistake that we made before World War II, but fortunately we did not. Instead, we embarked upon a long and far-reaching and, I believe, masterfully planned defense against Soviet expansionism.

There was President Truman's speech to the Congress in March 1947, in which he enunciated what came to be known as the Truman Doctrine. That saved Greece and Turkey. He said that it should be the policy of the United States to come to the aid of countries which were the object of communist pressure.

After that came the formation of the North Atlantic Treaty Organization (NATO), which was a message to the Soviet Union that if they were to attack any of our allies in NATO it would be construed as an attack upon the United States. It is my opinion that NATO has kept the peace in Europe and in the adjoining areas for the last thirty-five years. Then came the Marshall Plan to resuscitate and recreate the economy of free nations in Europe. Here then was a planned opposition to aggression and it proved to be eminently successful under the shield and umbrella created by the United States. The nations of Western Europe, which were prostrate when World War II ended, had an opportunity of staging a comeback. They rebuilt their war-torn economies and flourished, and I consider this time one of the proudest periods of our country's history.

Thus we had two dramatic examples before us, one showing the results of a situation where free nations refused to face up to aggression, which is what happened when the world failed to recognize what Hitler and the Third Reich were doing. Then there was the example of recognizing and resisting aggression with the successes we enjoyed at the end of World War II when we halted Soviet expansionism.

This is an over-lengthy background but it helps explain what our attitude was when the contest in Southeast Asia began. Here again we placed the events within the framework of our past experience. We thought that we had the choice either to refuse to be involved which could have resulted in a new wave of communism sweeping over Southeast Asia—I am not telling you what the factual situation was, I am telling you about our perception of the situation—or, we could step in and oppose what we felt was a joint aggression at the time, by the Soviet Union and Red China, both of whom were providing military and economic assistance to North Vietnam. That is how we got engaged in the contest.

I recall, for instance, that there was overwhelming support for what we were doing when the Tonkin Gulf incident occurred and the North Vietnamese fired upon a United States naval vessel. The U.S. Congress met in solemn session and passed a resolution authorizing the President to use military force in Southeast Asia to prevent further encroachment upon what looked like an aggressive design upon neighboring countries. There were only two dissenting votes out of 530 members, a Senator from Oregon and the other a Senator from Alaska. All the rest voted for the resolution. The spirit of the country at the time was that we should resist aggression. I remember an occasion when the President said that we must face up to it then or we would have to confront it in the Philippines, in Australia, or in New Zealand. President Johnson said it was better to fight in Southeast Asia instead of fighting later on the west coast of California. That's the way it looked at the time.

President Eisenhower coined an expression, when he referred (in 1954) to the "domino theory"; unless we prevented the first domino from toppling, the others would all go down, after South Vietnam, Laos and Cambodia would fall, then Thailand, then Burma, and down into the sub-continent, pulling down Pakistan and India. It could then spread out in the Pacific through the Philippines and then go eastward. That was the feeling at the time and that was the basis of the so-called domino theory. President Eisenhower urged the incoming Kennedy Administration to face up to the challenge.

I had an interesting experience the day before President Kennedy took over. I accompanied President-elect Kennedy to the White House where he had an all-morning conference with President Eisenhower, who had his principal advisers with him. Eisenhower, while emphasizing the importance of Southeast Asia, went so far as to say that we must do everything in our power to get our allies to assist us in the defense of Southeast Asia, but if we could not persuade them to do so we must do it alone. That's the way it appeared to almost everyone at the time. I supported this policy because I believed it to be right. As time went on and the war continued to rage, we built up our troops from 50,000 to over 500,000 in Vietnam. I started having doubts about the policy, but deep down I still felt that we would come out all right.

President Johnson asked General Maxwell Taylor and me to go to Southeast Asia in the fall of 1967 and we visited all the so-called troop-contributing countries, including Korea, Australia, and New Zealand, to study the situation. I found that the heads of government and chiefs of state of those Pacific countries did not share our perception of the problem. That put some further doubts in my mind, but we appeared to be prevailing in Vietnam and it looked as though our efforts would, in the reasonably near future, lead to the establishment of peace.

At the beginning of 1968, President Johnson appointed me as Secretary of Defense and I went to the Pentagon. This was just after the Tet offensive had shattered the high hopes of an early victory. I was appointed the chairman of a group which was expected to analyze our entire participation in the war. My early weeks as Defense Secretary were devoted entirely to that problem, ten or twelve hours a day. It was in that process that my mind changed completely. I spent a number of days with our Joint Chiefs of Staff in their map room where all of the forces of the United States were designated; it was the nerve center of our entire military operations in the world. The answers that I was given by our Joint Chiefs of Staff were, to me, eminently unsatisfactory. They could not tell me when the war would end, nor how many more men it would take. They could not tell me whether the bombing of North Vietnam was proving effective. Finally, I asked for a plan of victory in Vietnam. They had none to offer. It was clear to me that our entire strategy was to maintain pressure until the attrition became unbearable for the enemy and he would be forced to capitulate. When would that point be reached? To that, too, they had no answer. I left those meetings with a growing sense of concern and a feeling that if we stayed in the conflict we would be courting disaster.

Some of President Johnson's advisers very much wanted to bring the war in Vietnam to an end by engaging in a land invasion of North Vietnam and occupying the country. For instance, there was a military plan to transport troops by naval vessels and make an Inchon-type landing, cutting North Vietnam in two. But there was this terrible problem that North Vietnam at the time had a mutual assistance pact with Red China. We were enemies with Red China at that stage. Every Far Eastern expert we had said, without equivocation, that the moment we started an invasion of North Vietnam it would trigger the mutual assistance pact between North Vietnam and Red China and the Chinese would enter the war. It was their opinion, with which I was in full agreement, that Red China would treat it as the opportunity of a lifetime to bleed the United States to death. Of all the alternatives I could think of, the worst was for our country to get involved in a land war some 10,000 miles away in an area bordering on China, which had a population of over 800 million at that time.

President Johnson declined to accede to the proposal to start an invasion. I believed that we had become involved in a war to which there was no end. It was after those early weeks of intense application to the problem that I became thoroughly convinced, beyond any reasonable doubt, that we should get out of Vietnam as soon as possible. That was the beginning of a lengthy and difficult period when it became our task to persuade President Johnson to change our country's policy in Vietnam. He didn't want to change the policy. He did it in the end, however, and bravely.

To a certain extent he had been troubled by the military asking him in March of that year (1968) to send 200,000 additional troops to Vietnam. He refused to do so. Now the people did not know and the world did not know, but I knew because of my intimate talks with President Johnson on a daily basis, that he had refused to send more troops to Vietnam because, in fact, he had decided to change our country's policy. For the first time he was willing to accept a negotiated settlement in Vietnam instead of an all-out military victory and that is the way we proceeded after that. We started negotiations with North Vietnam and they made some progress, though not as much as we had hoped. But the basic decision had been made and the incoming Nixon administration was left with a state of affairs in which we had already reached the decision not to try to gain a military victory in Vietnam.

In the letter of invitation of the Committee to testify on the subject of Vietnam, important questions are raised regarding the impact of the Vietnam experience on our country's foreign policy in the future. I shall address myself to the questions presented.

It is my belief that as a general principle we should not commit American combat forces unless the problem involves the national security of our country. If this had been our country's policy at the time of Vietnam, it would have been of immense importance in causing us to reach the decision to refrain from committing actual combat forces. We could have supported the South Vietnamese with advisers, with military equipment, with financial support, but stopped short of sending our troops.

As I have suggested above, we began in Vietnam because we proceeded upon the assumption that it represented the beginning of communist aggression that, unless stopped, would spread through all of Southeast Asia and into areas of strategic importance to us in the Pacific. As long as this theory prevailed, we continued to stay involved in Southeast Asia. It is my belief that gradually the American public reached the conclusion that this reasoning was incorrect and that we should withdraw our forces from that area. I believe strongly that the basis upon which we entered the war in Vietnam was a misevaluation of the circumstances that existed there. The lesson we learned is a bitter one, but if there were to be a repetition in the area of the conditions that existed back in the early sixties, I am comforted by the thought that we would not send combat forces to the area.

During the course of the war in Vietnam there were those who constantly urged that we engage in greater military activity in an all-out effort to win the war. It is my opinion that they were wrong. I believe that during most of the time we were there we were doing all that could be done within the limitations of the kind of war that we were fighting and the degree of public support that our policies had in this country. The kind of jungle warfare in which we were engaged did not lend itself either to the kind of training that our military had had or the vastly superior firepower we could marshal in the field. I reached the personal conclusion in early 1968 that we could not win the war, and as a result, we should withdraw as expeditiously as possible.

Some of our civilian and military advisers felt that the war could be brought to a conclusion by staging an Inchon-type landing midway in North Vietnam and moving our troops westward so as to cut North Vietnam in two. The argument had a certain surface appeal, but was rejected by President Johnson because of the fact that North Vietnam had a mutual assistance pact with Red China. It seemed clear at the time that if American combat troops were put into North Vietnam, that North Vietnam would call upon Red China for assistance, and the Chinese were all too ready, even anxious, to become involved at that time. It is difficult for me to imagine a more tragic posture for our country than to be involved in a land war in Southeast Asia with the Red Chinese, who at the time had a nation of some 800 million people.

One of the principal arguments in favor of our participation in the war was the existence of the so-called "domino" theory. General Eisenhower coined the expression and he clearly felt strongly that if South Vietnam and Laos were to fall, the rest of the nations in Southeast Asia would topple like dominoes. The theory seemed credible to me at the time, but as we learned more and more about the conditions that existed in that part of the world, I ultimately concluded that the theory was without foundation. We have only to look at Southeast Asia today to note that the dominoes have not toppled after North Vietnam occupied South Vietnam.

After President Johnson left office and President Nixon took over, we heard a great deal about the importance of our country continuing the struggle in Southeast Asia because our country's credibility was at stake. I rejected that position then and I reject it now. Our country does not have to concern itself constantly with this bugbear of credibility. We have demonstrated it over and over again, in the First World War, the Second World War, in Korea, and in our participation in world affairs in this century. In my contacts with officials of other countries of Western Europe, the question in their minds did not involve the credibility of our country, but involved the wisdom of our continuing to participate in the ever-deepening struggle in this faraway place in the world.

It is my hope that the basic lesson learned in Vietnam will stand us in good stead in the years that lie ahead. As we look at other troubled areas of the world and as we consider what our policy should be, it is my hope that we would not send our combat personnel to the area unless, after thorough consideration, we are convinced that our national security is at stake.

15

Statement before the
Senate Foreign Affairs Committee
John Forbes Kerry

Mr. Kerry: Thank you very much, Senator Fulbright, Senator Javits, Senator Symington, Senator Pell. I would like to say for the record, and also for the men behind me who are also wearing the uniform and their medals, that my sitting here is really symbolic. I am not here as John Kerry. I am here as one member of the group of 1,000, which is a small representation of a very much larger group of veterans in this country, and were it possible for all of them to sit at this table they would be here and have the same kind of testimony....

I would like to talk to you a little bit about what the result is of the feelings these men carry with them after coming back from Vietnam. The country doesn't know it yet but it has created a monster, a monster in the form of millions of men who have been taught to deal and to trade in violence and who are given the chance to die for the biggest nothing in history; men who have returned with a sense of anger and a sense of betrayal which no one has yet grasped.

As a veteran and one who feels this anger I would like to talk about it. We are angry because we feel we have been used in the worst fashion by the administration of this country.

In 1970 at West Point Vice President Agnew said "some glamorize the criminal misfits of society while our best men die in Asian rice paddies to preserve the freedom which most of those misfits abuse," and this was used as a rallying point for our effort in Vietnam.

But for us, as boys in Asia whom the country was supposed to

John Kerry won the Silver Star, Bronze Star, and three Purple Hearts during his year as a naval officer in Vietnam. Following the war he became a national coordinator of an antiwar group, Vietnam Veterans Against the War. In this capacity, he was invited to address the Senate Committee on Foreign Relations, on April 22, 1971. Subsequently he ran for elected office in the State of Massachusetts, serving as the state's lieutenant governor before winning a seat in the United States Senate in 1984. The essay included here is the famous speech, "Where Are the Leaders of Our Country?," presented to the Senate Committee in 1971. It was published in the *Congressional Record.*

support, his statement is a terrible distortion from which we can only draw a very deep sense of revulsion, and hence the anger of some of the men who are here in Washington today. It is a distortion because we in no way consider ourselves the best men of this country; because those he calls misfits were standing up for us in a way that nobody else in this country dared to; because so many who have died would have returned to this country to join the misfits in their efforts to ask for an immediate withdrawal from South Vietnam; because so many of those best men have returned as quadruplegics and amputees— and they lie forgotten in Veterans Administration Hospitals in this country which fly the flag which so many have chosen as their own personal symbol—and we cannot consider ourselves America's best men when we are ashamed of and hated for what we were called on to do in Southeast Asia.

In our opinion, and from our experience, there is nothing in South Vietnam which could happen that realistically threatens the United States of America. And to attempt to justify the loss of one American life in Vietnam, Cambodia, or Laos by linking such loss to the preservation of freedom, which those misfits supposedly abuse, is to us the height of criminal hypocrisy, and it is that kind of hypocrisy which we feel has torn this country apart. . . .

We are probably angriest about all that we were told about Vietnam and about the mythical war against communism. We found that not only was it a civil war, an effort by a people who had for years been seeking their liberation from any colonial influence whatsoever, but also we found that the Vietnamese whom we had enthusiastically molded after our own image were hard put to take up the fight against the threat we were supposedly saving them from.

We found most people didn't even know the difference between communism and democracy. They only wanted to work in rice paddies without helicopters strafing them and bombs with napalm burning their villages and tearing their country apart. They wanted everything to do with the war, particularly with this foreign presence of the United States of America, to leave them alone in peace, and they practiced the art of survival by siding with whichever military force was present at a particular time, be it Viet Cong, North Vietnamese, or American.

We found also that all too often American men were dying in those rice paddies for want of support from their allies. We saw firsthand how monies from American taxes were used for a corrupt dictatorial regime. We saw that many people in this country had a one-sided idea of who was kept free by our flag, and blacks provided the highest percentage of casualties. We saw Vietnam ravaged equally by American bombs and search and destroy missions, as well as by Viet Cong terrorism, and yet we listened while this country tried to blame all of the havoc on the Viet Cong.

We rationalized destroying villages in order to save them. We saw America lose her sense of morality as she accepted very cooly a My Lai and refused to give up the image of American soldiers who hand out chocolate bars and chewing gum.

We learned the meaning of free fire zones, shooting anything that moves, and we watched while America placed a cheapness on the lives of Orientals.

We watched the United States' falsification of body counts. We listened while month after month we were told the back of the enemy was about to break. We fought using weapons against "oriental human beings." We fought using weapons against those people which I do not believe this country would dream of using were we fighting in the European theater. We watched while men charged up hills because a general said that hill had to be taken, and after losing one platoon or two platoons they marched away to leave the hill for reoccupation by the North Vietnamese. We watched pride allow the most unimportant battles to be blown into extravaganzas, because we couldn't lose, and we couldn't retreat, and because it didn't matter how many American bodies were lost to prove that point, and so there were Hamburger Hills and Khe Sahns and Hill 81s and Fire Base 6s, and so many others.

Now we are told that the men who fought there must watch quietly while American lives are lost so that we can exercise the incredible arrogance of Vietnamizing the Vietnamese. Each day to facilitate the process by which the United States washes her hands of Vietnam someone has to give up his life so that the United States doesn't have to admit something that the entire world already knows, so that we can't say that we have made a mistake. Someone has to die so that President Nixon won't be, and these are his words, "the first President to lose a war."

We are asking Americans to think about that because how do you ask a man to be the last man to die in Vietnam? How do you ask a man to be the last man to die for a mistake? But we are trying to do that, and we are doing it with thousands of rationalizations, and if you read carefully the President's last speech to the people of this country, you can see that he says, and says clearly, "but the issue, gentlemen, the issue, is communism, and the question is whether or not we will leave that country to the communists or whether or not we will try to give it hope to be a free people." But the point is they are not a free people now under us. They are not a free people, and we cannot fight communism all over the world. I think we should have learned that lesson by now. . . .

Suddenly we are faced with a very sickening situation in this country, because there is no moral indignation and, if there is, it comes from people who are almost exhausted by their past indignations. . . . The country seems to have lain down and shrugged off something as serious as Laos, just as we calmly shrugged off the loss of 700,000 lives in Pakistan, the so-called greatest disaster of all times.

But we are here as veterans to say we think we are in the midst of the greatest disaster of all times now, because they are still dying over there—not just Americans, but Vietnamese—and we are rationalizing leaving that country so that those people can go on killing each other for years to come.

Americans seem to have accepted the idea that the war is winding down, at least for Americans, and they have also allowed the bodies which were once used by a President for statistics to prove that we were winning that war, to be used as evidence against a man who followed orders and who interpreted those orders no differently than hundreds of other men in Vietnam.

We veterans can only look with amazement on the fact that this country has been unable to see there is absolutely no difference between ground troops and a helicopter crew, and yet people have accepted a differentiation fed them by the administration.

No ground troops are in Laos so it is all right to kill Laotians by remote control. But believe me the helicopter crews fill the same body bags and they wreak the same kind of damage on the Vietnamese and Laotian countryside as anybody else, and the President is talking about allowing that to go on for many years to come. One can only ask if we will really be satisfied only when the troops march into Hanoi.

We are asking here in Washington for some action; action from the Congress of the United States of America which has the power to raise and maintain armies, and which by the Constitution also has the power to declare war. We have come here, not to the President, because we believe that this body can be responsive to the will of the people, and we believe that the will of the people says that we should be out of Vietnam now.

We are here in Washington also to say that the problem of this war is not just a question of war and diplomacy. It is part and parcel of everything that we are trying as human beings to communicate to people in this country—the question of racism, which is rampant in the military, and so many other questions such as the use of weapons; the hypocrisy in our taking umbrage in the Geneva Conventions and using that as justification for a continuation of this war when we are more guilty than any other body of violations of those Geneva Conventions; in the use of free fire zones, harassment interdiction fire, search and destroy missions, the bombings, the torture of prisoners, the killing of prisoners, all accepted policy by many units in South Vietnam. That is what we are trying to say. . . .

We are also here to ask, and we are here to ask vehemently, where are the leaders of our country? Where is the leadership? We are here to ask where are McNamara, Rostow, Bundy, Gilpatric, and so many others? Where are they now that we, the men whom they sent off to war, have returned? These are commanders who have deserted their troops, and there is no more serious crime in the law of war. The Army says they never leave their wounded. The Marines say they never leave even their dead. These men have left all the casualties and retreated behind a pious shield of public rectitude. They have left the real stuff of their reputations bleaching behind them in the sun in this country.

Finally, this administration has done us the ultimate dishonor. They have attempted to disown us and the sacrifices we made for this country. In their blindness and fear they have tried to deny that we are veterans or that we served in Nam. We do not need their testimony. Our own scars and stumps of limbs are witness enough for others and for ourselves.

We wish that a merciful God could wipe away our own memories of that service as easily as this administration has wiped away their memories of us. But all that they have done, all that they can do by this denial is to make more clear than ever our own determination to undertake one last mission—to search out and destroy the last vestige of this barbaric war, to pacify our own hearts, to conquer the hate and the fear that have driven this country these last ten years and more, so when 30 years from now our brothers go down the street without a leg, without an arm, or a face, and small boys ask why, we will be able to say "Vietnam" and not mean a desert, nor a filthy obscene memory, but mean instead the place where America finally turned and where soldiers like us helped it in the turning.

Thank you.

16

The Achievements of the War-protest Movement

Todd Gitlin

ι9ȣ3

As my generation teeters uneasily between late youth and early middle age, and American expeditionary forces are launched toward new wars in the Third World, a good number of my old political buddies are wondering whether the antiwar passions of the 1960s were worth the effort. The Vietnam War dragged on and on, after all, and in the end, didn't Khmer Rouge genocide and Vietnamese authoritarianism discredit our hopes? Prompted by once-over-lightly media treatments of the era, today's campus inactivists also seem to believe that the '60s demonstrated conclusively that you can't change history to match your ideals. So why go to the trouble of letting tainted politics interfere with the rigors of preparing for the law boards?

Meanwhile, it's the so-called conservatives, neo- and paleo-, who give the antiwar movement credit. They firmly believe that the country was seized during the '60s by a "new class" of overeducated left intellectuals, tantrum-throwing students, media liberals, uppity minorities, feminists, hedonists, homosexuals, and assorted bleeding hearts, who not only succeeded in trashing tradition, standards, the family, and all natural hierarchy, but also broke the back of national security, leveling America's just position in the world and costing us an achievable and noble victory in Vietnam. They have spent the past ten years trying to figure out how to recapture lost terrain from the barbarians. And they are haunted by the specter of revived antiwar activity—for good reason. For despite their paranoid exaggerations

---

Todd Gitlin is professor of sociology at the University of California, Berkeley, and is the author of several books, among which are The *Whole World is Watching* (Berkeley: University of California Press, 1980), *Inside Prime Time* (New York: Pantheon, 1983), and *Watching Television* (New York: Pantheon, 1987). This essay originated as an address to the conference on "Vietnam Reconsidered" that was sponsored by the University of Southern California in 1983. It was published in *Mother Jones*, Vol. VIII, No. IX, November, 1983, pp. 31–38, 48.

and their self-serving refusal to acknowledge just how much ideological ground they have already reconquered, they know in their bones
what many veterans of the '60s don't know or have forgotten: that the
movement against the Vietnam War was history's most successful
movement against a shooting war.

Not that there's much reason for unqualified self-congratulation.
The napalm no longer falls on Vietnam, but the country still lives
under dictatorship, on a perpetual war footing. Moreover, while the
movement counted heavily in American politics, much of the leadership, eventually, wasn't satisfied simply to be against the war. Feeling
either futile or giddy, they finally wanted a revolution, and came to
define success accordingly. Those who persisted in that course made
themselves irrelevant to the politics of the '70s and '80s. If the movement was effective, a less insular and more sophisticated movement
might have been all the more so. To understand both the achievement
and the limits, to learn lessons apropos impending wars, we have to
look carefully at the movement's effects on the war and, with equal
care, at the war's effects on the movement.

Already, the passing of time shrouds the '60s; the end is confounded
with the beginning, the consequences with the causes; the all-impor-
tant sequence of events is obscured. Our collective memory, such as
it is, rests on a few disjointed images snatched out of order. For
example, I was shocked in 1975 when the most sophisticated student
in a class I was teaching at the University of California, Santa Cruz,
said to me one day, "You were in SDS, right?" Right, I said. "That
was the Weathermen, right?" How could I explain easily that the
Weathermen were one of the factions that *ended* Students for a Democratic Society, exploded its ten-year history? (As an early leader of
SDS I had fervently opposed them, in fact.)

The media and popular lore have dwelt on the lurid, easily pigeon-
holed images of 1968–71, as if they encompassed and defined the
whole of "The '60s" in living color once and for all: the flags of the
National Liberation Front of South Vietnam flying at antiwar demonstrations, singled out by TV cameras however outnumbered they were
by American flags; window-trashers and rock-throwers, however outnumbered they were by peaceful marchers; the bombings and torch-
ings of ROTC buildings; and the lethal explosions of the Weather
Underground townhouse and the University of Wisconsin Army Math-
ematics Research Center in 1970.

To fathom the antiwar movement, though, we have to go back to
1964–65, when the Johnson administration committed itself to the
war. In September 1964, while Lyndon Johnson was campaigning
for peace votes with the slogan "We seek no wider war," American

gunboats just offshore North Vietnam provoked an attack by the North Vietnamese, and a gullible Senate gave Johnson a carte blanche resolution that was to supply the questionable legal basis for years of subsequent escalation. The political climate of that moment is measured by the fact that the dissenting votes numbered a grand total of two—Wayne Morse and Ernest Gruening. That Christmas, Students for a Democratic Society, with all of a few hundred active members, presumptuously called for a demonstration against the war, to be held in Washington, D.C., in April. In February, Johnson began the systematic bombing of North Vietnam. In March came the first campus teach-ins against the war, and in April more than 25,000 marched in Washington—the majority dressed in jackets, ties, skirts. During the fall of 1965 there were the first coordinated demonstrations across the country, some of them more militant (a few symbolic attempts to block troop trains); there were a few widely publicized draft card burnings and a national media hysteria about a nonexistent SDS plan to disrupt the draft. Within the next 18 months, some leaders of the civil rights movement began denouncing the war—first the militants of the Student Nonviolent Coordinating Committee, then the Reverend Dr. Martin Luther King, Jr. There were attempts to get antiwar measures onto local ballots and to carry the war issue into professional associations.

With the number of American troops steadily swelling to almost the half-million mark and the bombing continuing mercilessly, antiwar militancy—still nonviolent—grew apace. In October 1967 there were vast mobilizations at the Pentagon and in Oakland, California, where, for the first time, armed troops and riot-control police wreaked havoc on active nonviolence. Only in 1968, after the assassinations of Martin Luther King and Robert F. Kennedy, did significant numbers of antiwar people murmur about the need for violence to raise the political cost of the war at home. There were also the first activities by government *agents provocateurs.*

We don't know nearly enough, and are not collectively curious enough, about government provocation. But one item may suggest how tantalizing this subject should be for a new generation of researchers. In August 1968, a few thousand demonstrators went out into the streets of Chicago. The tear-gas clouds and media spotlights during the Democratic convention polarized public opinion and established a new threshold for militancy while fatally discrediting the Democrats. Who were these protesters? According to army intelligence documents pried loose by CBS News ten years later, "About one demonstrator in six was an undercover agent." As flag-burning and cop-provoking increased, the movement became open territory for

[margin note: infiltrators in Anti-War Movement]

tough-talking infiltrators. With glacial slowness, information seeps into the light; but our famous investigative press—busy now uncovering the startling news that the KGB tries to influence antinuclear politics in Europe—is largely uninterested in this ancient history.

In any event, to gauge the effects of the movements as a whole, we might begin by asking what would have happened if the war had gone on without any material public opposition. Suppose, in other words, that without a movement in the streets there had been only a passive and ambiguous dissent in the polls as the American body-count mounted. Suppose also a numbed and passive Congress. Suppose, that is, a war very much like the Korean War.

What would have kept the war from escalating even more intensely than it actually did, with more ordnance and more troops producing more devastation, more refugees, more death? There were, of course, other forces working against the war: the economic drain; the breakdown of military discipline (inspired in a curious way by the movement); and the political mainstream's sense of the war's futility. But the North Vietnamese and the NLF were prepared to suffer huge casualties indefinitely rather than surrender. And once "Vietnamization" had changed the color of the corpses, the United States could have withdrawn its combat troops and still continued the air war for years without producing massive disgruntlement, for the bomber missions cost relatively few American lives. Support would likely have grown for the military's designs to press the war to the screaming limits of military technology in order to maintain an anti-Communist South Vietnam, indefinitely, at all costs.

Concrete evidence of the movement's influence was hard to come by. So much so, in fact, that, day to day, many movement people felt we were accomplishing next to nothing. After all, although the worst escalations *might* be averted or postponed at any given moment, this was abstract surmise; concretely, the bombs kept falling, and successive administrations weren't handing out public prizes for tying their hands.

Meanwhile, public opinion after the Tet offensive of early 1968 was ambiguous. It registered the growing conviction that the war was a mistake and a futility, coupled with the desire to "get it all over with" by any means possible, including bombing. This was the combination that Nixon brilliantly exploited to win the presidency in 1968, with vague references to a secret plan to end the war. So emerged the movement's desperate cycle of trying to raise the stakes, double or nothing—more fury and more violence—especially when the media dutifully played their part by amplifying the most flamboyant gestures of antiwar theater.

Nonetheless, evidence is coming to light that the movement had a direct veto power over war escalations at a number of points. David Halberstam tells us in *The Best and the Brightest*, for example, that in late 1966 the military was already urging President Johnson to bomb Hanoi and Haiphong, to block the harbor and, in Halberstam's words, to "[take] apart the industrial capacity of both cities." "How long [will] it take," Johnson lamented, "[for] five hundred thousand angry Americans to climb that White House wall . . . and lynch their president if he does something like that?" "Which ended for a time," Halberstam writes, "the plan to bomb Hanoi and Haiphong."

Despite their denials at the time, Nixon administration officials were no less sensitive to the actual and potential political threat of movement protest. Early in the first Nixon administration, for example, during a lull in demonstrations—so writes Henry Kissinger in *White House Years*—Secretary of Defense Melvin Laird argued against the secret bombing of Cambodia for fear of "[waking] the dormant beast of public protest." At another point, Kissinger refers to "the hammer of antiwar pressure" as a factor that he and Nixon could never ignore.

The denials were, at times, actually a backhanded index of the movement's real influence. Unbeknownst to the movement, its greatest impact was exerted just when it felt most desperate. In the summer of 1969, while withdrawing some ground troops, amidst great fanfare, Nixon and Kissinger decided on a "November ultimatum" to Hanoi. Either Hanoi would accommodate to Nixon's bargaining terms by November 1, or Nixon would launch an unprecedented new assault, including, as Seymour Hersh writes in *The Price of Power*, "the massive bombing of Hanoi, Haiphong, and other key areas in North Vietnam; the mining of harbors and rivers; the bombing of the dike system; a ground invasion of North Vietnam; the destruction—possibly with nuclear devices—of the main north-south passes along the Ho Chi Minh Trail; and the bombing of North Vietnam's main railroad links with China." For a full month, in utter secrecy, Nixon kept American B-52s, on full nuclear alert—the first such alert since the Cuban missile crisis.

Some White House staff members objected to the November ultimatum plans on military grounds, but by Nixon's own account, antiwar demonstrations were central to his decision not to go ahead with this blockbuster escalation. The massive October 15 Moratorium, and the promise of more of the same on November 15, convinced Nixon (as he wrote later) that "after all the protests and the Moratorium, American public opinion would be seriously divided by any military escalation of the war."

For public consumption, Nixon made a show of ignoring the demonstrations and claiming they were of no avail. The movement, for its part, had no way of knowing what catastrophe it was averting, and thus felt helpless. Nixon, meanwhile, moved to split militants from moderates. He combined stepped-up repression, surveillance, and press manipulation with a calming strategy that included markedly lower draft calls and, eventually, a draft lottery system that defused opposition by pitting the unlucky few against the lucky. Within the movement, the minority who faulted the Moratorium for its relative moderation began arguing that a new level of militancy was required: first came trashing, then sideline cheerleading for the newly organized splinter group, the Weathermen. The result was a general demoralization on the Left.

At the moment of its maximum veto power, much of the movement's hard core fell victim to all-or-nothing thinking. White House secrecy was one reason the movement misunderstood its own force; the intrinsic difficulty of gauging political results was a second; the third was the movement's own bitter-end mentality. Much of the movement succumbed to a politics of rage. Relatively privileged youth had been raised in child-centered families and conditioned by a consumer culture to expect quick results. An excess of impatience made it easy for them to resort to terrorism. Thus, the movement drove itself toward self-isolating militancy and, by 1971, away from most activity altogether. A desperately revolutionary self-image drove the hard core to disdain alliance with moderates, which, of course, was just what the White House wanted.

When Nixon ordered the invasion of Cambodia in the spring of 1970, hundreds of thousands poured into the streets in protest. But the old movement leadership had burned out or burrowed into underground fantasies, and the new activists lacked leadership. This new round of protest flared and disappeared quickly, especially as shrinking draft calls eliminated the immediate threat to many college students. At the same time the killings at Kent State stripped students of their feeling of safety. With their sense of exemption gone, results invisible, and leadership lacking, it wasn't long before they subsided into inactivity. And yet, even then, the demonstrations convinced Nixon to limit the invasion's scope and cut it short. "Nixon's decision to limit the Cambodia offensive," Seymour Hersh concludes, "demonstrated anew the ultimate power of the antiwar movement." Even though the frequency and size of demonstrations declined over the next two years, their threat restrained Nixon's hand.

By this time, the movement's influence on the war was mostly indirect: a nudging of the elites whose children were in revolt, which paved the way for Establishment skepticism. Although radicals didn't want to think of themselves as "mere" reformists, they amounted to a small engine that turned the more potent engines that could, in fact, retard the war.

The movement continued to stimulate moderate antiwar sentiment in Congress, the media, and churches even in later years, when demonstrations had become only a ghostly echo. As early as 1968, political, corporate, and media elites grew disillusioned with the war. It wasn't "working." Although they accepted little of the antiwar movement's analysis, the elites capitalized on the movement's initiative and sometimes—as in the case of the McCarthy and Kennedy campaigns for the Democratic nomination in 1968—recruited troops as well.

The pivotal movement came just after the Tet offensive, when Johnson's top advisors decided that the war was costing too much in political, economic, and military terms. Clark Clifford, Johnson's new secretary of defense, lost faith in the war effort and set out to mobilize influential opposition among the political elite that had represented foreign policy consensus since 1945. At the same time that the Joint Chiefs of Staff were requesting 206,000 new troops for Vietnam, Clifford was persuading Johnson to meet with the informal advisory group later known as the Wise Men: Dean Acheson, McGeorge Bundy, George Ball, C. Douglas Dillon, Cyrus Vance, General Maxwell Taylor, and others, men who had occupied top positions in the Truman and Kennedy as well as Johnson administrations. If there was an Establishment, this was it.

Cyrus Vance said later, "We were weighing not only what was happening in Vietnam, but the social and political effects in the United States, the impact on the U.S. economy, the attitudes of other nations. The divisiveness in the country was growing with such acuteness that it was threatening to tear the United States apart." As guardians of America's world position, the Wise Men were sensitive to European doubts and frightened by the war's economic consequences—deficit financing, incipient inflation, a negative balance of payments, and gold outflow. Some of them were also aware that American troops were becoming unreliable in the field and that, in an unanticipated echo of the antiwar movement, some soldiers were wearing peace symbols on their helmets.

"The meeting with the Wise Men served the purpose that I hoped it would," Clifford exulted later. "It really shook the president." Three days later, Johnson refused the Joint Chiefs' troop request, announced a partial bombing halt—and took himself out of the presidential race. Major new shipments of American troops became politically taboo for the duration of the war.

Nevertheless, the war went on for years, leaving hundreds of thousands of corpses as testimony to the movement's failure to achieve the peace it longed for. If it had been more astute, had cultivated more allies, it might have been able to cut the war shorter and reduce the general destruction. The largely middle-class antiwar movement could have broadened in several directions. If it had supported the growing GI antiwar faction more concertedly, had gotten over its squeamishness toward soldiers, the combination might have succeeded in frightening Johnson and Nixon earlier. A more serious alliance with antiwar veterans and working-class draftees might have broken the movement out of its middle-class ghetto, might have established before a hostile public and a cynical administration that the movement was more than a rabble of middle-class kids trying to preserve their privilege of avoiding combat.

If the largely white movement had paid more attention to broad-based interracial alliances (as with the 1970 Chicano National Moratorium) and less to the glamor of revolutionary showmanship, it might have capitalized on high-level governmental fears of what Air Force Undersecretary Townsend Hoopes in his memoirs called "the fateful merging of antiwar and racial dissension." As we now know, the White House was terrified of black protest even into the Nixon years. A full year after Martin Luther King was assassinated, J. Edgar Hoover was sending memos on King's sex life to Henry Kissinger, who kept them on file, one National Security Council staff member said, "to blunt the black antiwar movement."

If anything, the movement should be faulted for not being effective, ecumenical, persistent enough. It is even conceivable (history affords no certitudes) that a stronger movement might have kept the ferocious U.S. bombing from driving Cambodian peasants into the arms of the increasingly fanatical Khmer Rouge. All civilized people who are revolted by the Khmer Rouge mass atrocities should also remember that it was the Nixon administration, not the movement, that encouraged the overthrow of Prince Sihanouk and weakened opposition to this regime of mass murderers. Moreover, whatever the movement's willingness to overlook authoritarianism in North Vietnam, a shorter, less destructive war might also have made postwar reconciliation easier in a unified Vietnam. And if the movement had survived to demand that the U.S. keep up its end of the 1973 Paris peace agreement, the promised American postwar aid might have overcome some of the austerity that later served Hanoi as a rationale for repression.

The movement left a mixed legacy. Even with most of its force spent, after the McGovern catastrophe of 1972, the phantom movement, coupled with the belated resolve of congressional doves, succeeded in keeping Nixon from a wholehearted new assault on Vietnam. Watergate was the decisive turn, though, that distracted Nixon from keeping his secret promises to Nguyen Van Thieu and short-circuiting the Paris agreements with a resurgence of American bombing. By the cunning of reason, Nixon's paranoia about the antiwar movement, among other bêtes noire, led him to such grossly illegal measures that he was ultimately prevented from continuing the war itself. And, of course, the antiwar feeling outlasted Nixon. As late as 1975, Congress was able to stop American intervention in Angola.

Even today, the memory of the movement against the Vietnam War works against maximum direct military intervention in Central America. Again, there's no cause for pure and simple jubilation: the doves failed to anticipate how easy it would be for later administrations to substitute heavy military aid and troop maneuvers for direct combat forces. The movement also failed to persuade enough of the country that democratic revolutionary change is often the superior alternative to hunger and massacre in the Third World, and that American support (what the New Left used to call "critical support") might soften the most repressive features of revolutionary regimes. The result of simplistic Cold War thinking is hardened revolutions and Third World dependency on the Soviet Union—which after the fact seems to confirm the Cold War notion that revolutions are nothing more than props for Soviet expansion. American troops en masse are not at this moment being sacrificed to unwinnable wars, but the same bitter-end purpose is supporting Somocista guerrillas in Nicaragua, genocidal killers in Guatemala, death squads in El Salvador, a seemingly permanent U.S. base in Honduras—at a relatively cut-rate cost to American society.

The movement against the Vietnam War can be counted a real if incomplete success, even despite itself. But what happened to the movement in the process?

The movement sloppily squandered much of its moral authority. Too much of the leadership, and some of the rank and file, slid into a romance with the other side. If napalm was evil, then the other side was endowed with nobility. If the American flag was dirty, the NLF flag was clean. If the deluded make-Vietnam-safe-for-democracy barbarism of the war could be glibly equated with the deliberate slaughter of millions in Nazi gas chambers—if the American Christ turned out to look like the Antichrist—then by this cramped, left-wing logic, the Communist Antichrist must really have been Christ. Ironically, some of the movement anticipated the Great Communicator's jubilant proclamation that Vietnam was a "noble enterprise," but with the sides reversed. This helped discredit the movement in the eyes of moderate potential supporters—who were, in turn, too quick to find reasons to write it off. For too long the movement swallowed North Vietnamese claims that it had no troops in South Vietnam, even though, by the logic of the movement's argument that Vietnam was one country, artificially kept divided by American intervention, it should not have been surprising that northern troops would be in the south.

Romanticism and rage dictated that North Vietnamese and National Liberation Front heroism be transmuted into the image of a good society that *had* to exist out there somewhere. American activists who thought they were making a revolution, not a mere antiwar movement, borrowed their prepackaged imagery—their slogans and mystique—from Vietnamese cadres whose suffering and courage were undeniable but who had little to teach us about how to conduct a modern democratic society. In 1969, when zealots chanting "Ho, Ho, Ho Chi Minh" confronted other zealots chanting "Mao, Mao, Mao Tse Tung" and tore up SDS between them, both sides were surrendering political reason and curling up to father figures.

This kind of moral corrosion has become all too familiar in the 20th century: the know-it-alls explain away revolutionary abominations, try to corner the market in utopian futures and, in the process, become mirror-images of the absolutist authority they detest. In the end, the revolutionists have helped return moral title to conservatives.

Even today, we hear voices on the left conjuring rationalizations for crimes committed by left-wing guerrillas. A curious partial freedom is parceled out to state-sponsored socialism, as if revolutions are responsible for their accomplishments, while their brutality, if acknowledged at all, is credited to American imperialism. Why is it necessary to keep silent about the shutting down of newspapers in Managua in order to oppose American intervention on behalf of death squads?

There is no simple explanation why much of the antiwar movement leadership found it hard to criticize authoritarian socialism. Partly there was the fear of putting ammunition in the hands of the Right— as though if the Right were right about anything, it might be right about everything. Then, too, dressing up for revolution was easier than reckoning with the strangeness of being a radical movement, based on youth, spunk, marginality, and educated arrogance, in a society that not only permitted dissent but made it possible to act in history without wholesale bloodshed. The heavily middle-class revolutionists tried to bull past their own isolation: they made themselves Leninists of the will. Others went the Yippie route, with toy machine guns and glib youth-cult gestures. The publicity loop boosted the most flamboyant leaders into celebrity and helped limit the movement's reach.

Caught in a maelstrom of images, the rest of the movement became massively demoralized by 1970. This vast, unorganized, indeed silent majority was appalled to watch SDS decompose into warring sects speaking in Marxist-Leninist tongues. They didn't think revolutionary Vietnam was the promised land. They hated illegitimate authority in all forms. If they were understandably sentimental about peasants shooting at fighter bombers with rifles from alongside their water buffalo, they also knew that by far the greatest bloodbath going on in the world came from American firepower—and that no halfway desirable objective could be worth it. And they were right. From their impulses, on top of the civil rights movement, came a more general refusal of unjust authority, which led, most profoundly, to the movement for the liberation of women. To choose political passivity today on the spurious ground that the antiwar movement of the '60s "failed" is to succumb to all-or-nothing petulance, to insist that history promise to bear out all one's dreams before one tries to stop a slaughter. We'll travel lighter now without the burden of revolutionary myths.

A final legacy of the antiwar movement is that it battered the unreflective anticommunism of the 1950s and made it possible to open new doors. Now it also becomes possible to think past the kneejerk anti-*anti*-communism of the '60s, and to oppose American interventionism on the ground that it violates the elementary rights of human beings, not that it obstructs the Third World's revolutionary emergence into the highest stage of social existence. Anyway, movements are compost for later movements. The Vietnam War bred succeeding wars, and so, in a sense, the meaning of the movement against the war is still up for grabs. The meaning depends on what happens as we try to stop sequels in Central America and elsewhere. After throwing weight against a juggernaut once, and slowing it, the right lesson to learn is: Do it better and smarter next time. I like what William Morris wrote: "Men fight and lose the battle, and the thing that they fought for comes about in spite of their defeat, and when it comes, turns out not to be what they meant, and other men have to fight for what they meant under another name."

17

After the War:
The Emergence of Nihilism

W. Richard Comstock

1977

Through the Vietnam experience, we have witnessed and, indeed, have participated in a dissolution of the synthesis of religious and political values that has characterized America. All great civilizations have such a synthesis, whereby that which is religious, or transcendent, is combined with, gives force to, transforms, and lends moral direction to the political order. The Vietnam War did not cause the dissolution of this synthesis, but it did bring it to the surface.

I view this dissolution with sadness. On the one hand, the American ideology supported a humanistic individualism. The self-sufficient individual is a heritage of the Enlightenment, but it is practically an axiom, an *a priori* assumption of every American.

On the other hand, what is intriguing is that this individualistic value system was connected to a political commonwealth. We were not only individuals, we were also citizens. In religious terms, we sought private salvation and also the Kingdom of God on earth. These were not contradictory; somehow each would reinforce the other.

Now, through the Vietnam experience, we are beginning to lack confidence in the value and integrity of the commonwealth ideal. We lack confidence in government. We know the government lied. We always felt that while there might be some duplicity in government, still on the fundamental issues we all participated in the decision-making process. Now we know we were lied to, and that is carrying over to other things. Take the nuclear accident at Three Mile Island. We had been absolutely assured there was no danger. Then, when

W. Richard Comstock is professor of religious studies at the University of California, Santa Barbara, and former Chair of the Department of Religious Studies. He is an accomplished author and a distinguished teacher. This paper was originally given in a conference sponsored by the Center for the Study of Democratic Institutions in Santa Barbara, in 1977, on "The Impact of the Vietnam War on American Culture," that is, less than two years after the end of the war.

danger emerged, we were told we had misunderstood the authorities, that, of course, there is some danger, but that danger is part of life. If you fly in an airplane, you might crash. If you live near an atomic plant, there are risks.

But all of us now feel that some of us are being made sacrificial goats for the rest of us. That leads to a lack of confidence, a lack of faith, a lack of trust in our government. That is the disintegration of the commonwealth ideal.

Many have tried to justify the war on legal grounds, but this is irrelevant. The issue is not whether the Vietnam war was waged according to some international standard of what a just war should be. I am quite ready to entertain the hypothesis that other wars may have been more unjust and that in many ways the American military in Vietnam conformed generally to international law. That doesn't matter. What matters is the devastated land, the deaths, the repugnance for war itself. The Vietnam experience brought all that to a head. Values have a deep emotional layer. If you witness an atrocity like an ax murder you don't want someone to try to mitigate that with a detailed explanation of why it really is not as bad as it seems. You are appalled. That is what happened to many Americans because of Vietnam. . . .

We are falling back, more and more, on the individualistic norm. That can reflect personal integrity, but perhaps more often it means a hedonistic and narcissistic repudiation of all values. We are seeing the emergence of a nihilism which is leading to the dissolution of all values. That may have been going on before Vietnam, but we still treasured the American ideal of God and country. Now that is disappearing. So we fall back on ethnic values and familial kinship systems. If those go, then, of course, we fall back on the individual himself. But who or what is the individual? A nihilistic nothing? Or a source of new values?

Consider but two of the many movies on the Vietnam experience: *Who Will Stop the Rain?* and *The Deer Hunter. Who Will Stop the Rain?* used the metaphor of heroin. The hero, a Vietnam soldier about to return to the States, becomes obsessed with a sense of nihilism. He had heard that the government had ordered the soldiers to strafe elephants because of their transportation value. It suddenly came to him that a world in which one must strafe elephants is a world without meaning. He then decides to become a heroin carrier, a symbol of the loss and dissolution of values.

The Deer Hunter has an even more powerful metaphor—Russian roulette. Life is reduced to that level, and there seems to be no way out. It is significant that in the first hour of *The Deer Hunter*, the stress is on an ethnic community. That is to say if there is any value left, it is in ethnic values. But what you do not see in the film is anything of the political order, the American values that transcend the ethnic or melting-pot idea. You are reduced to either ethnic values or the nihilism of Russian roulette.

Vietnam has caused us to lose confidence in the integrity of our way of life. It is hard to predict the future. We may proceed further into nihilism. We do see many evidences of the growth of individualistic religion, religion that no longer connects with the political order, but simply seeks to give the individual private salvation. For many this has become a source of meaning.

On the other hand, there could be a renaissance of the commonwealth or kingdom ideal. One of the things I have lost in recent years is my belief in irresistible trends. I no longer believe that we are necessarily moving toward either utopia or the final holocaust. Things can be reversed. The people in the Renaissance complained of nihilism. Martin Luther could not imagine the world becoming more corrupt than it was during his day. Luther expected the end of the world in a few years. But there are always reversals, new opportunities.

Vietnam was the symptom of a crisis. In a crisis, the patient may die, but he may return to health. It is not yet clear how this crisis will end.

III

DIVERSITIES OF *Experience*

18

Black Soldiers' Perspectives on the War
Gerald Gill

1984

> *Perhaps a more tragic recognition of reality took place when it became clear to me that the war was doing far more than devastating the hopes of the poor at home. It was sending their sons and their brothers and their husbands to fight and to die and in extraordinarily higher proportions relative to the rest of the population. We were taking the black young men who had been crippled by our society and sending them eight thousand miles away to guarantee liberties in Southeast Asia which they had not found in southwest Georgia and East Harlem. And so we have been repeatedly faced with the cruel irony of watching Negro and white boys on TV screens as they kill and die together for a nation that has been unable to seat them together in the same schools. We watch them in brutal solidarity burning the huts of a poor village, but we realize that they would never live on the same block in Detroit. I could not be silent in the face of such cruel manipulation of the poor.*
> —Martin Luther King, 1967

In a letter to the editor of the black monthly magazine *Sepia*, army private James Brown described his current experiences in and reactions to the American military involvement in Vietnam. Concluding his letter on a somber note, Brown wrote: "We, the unwilling, led by the unqualified, doing the unnecessary, for the ungrateful."[1] In a sense, Brown's observations reflected the increasingly negative attitudes that more and more troops stationed in Vietnam were voicing and expressing against their and the nation's participation in a war that many had come to view as "unnecessary." Although his comments

---

Gerald Gill is professor of history in Tufts University. His essay was one of the first published portrayals of the experience of Black Americans in the war, and afterwards. It is an essential topic, for the statistics are staggering. Throughout the war period, blacks were more than twice as vulnerable to draft-board calls as whites, and by 1965 had accounted for 25% of American combat deaths. Of the 16,000 persons who served on draft boards, blacks constituted less than 2% of the total and were not represented at all on draft boards in Alabama, Arkansas, Louisiana, and Mississippi. In many combat units, over 50% of the group was composed of blacks, Puerto Ricans, Chicano/Latino Americans, Nisei, and Guamanians. Among blacks serving in Vietnam, barely half had a high school education. 12.5% of the names on the Vietnam Memorial are of Black Americans. This essay first appeared in *Indochina Newsletter*, Jan/Feb 1984, Issue #25.

against the war and the military hierarchy were similar to those expressed by many combat "grunts," Brown's terse observations more readily applied to the dissatisfaction being expressed by his fellow black troops. By 1970, most black troops were in agreement that the war, individually and/or collectively, had been and was mistakenly entered, hypocritical in intent, and racist and imperialist by design.

EARLY SUPPORT FOR THE WAR

Yet, the sentiments and thoughts of black soldiers in 1970 were far different from those voiced by black military personnel stationed in Southeast Asia in the mid-1960's. Then, black soldiers had reacted more positively to both the military as a career choice and the increasing American military presence and combat role in South Vietnam. At the time of Congress' enactment of the Gulf of Tonkin Resolution in mid-summer of 1964, the United States armed forces had been *fully* integrated for just over a decade. With the ending of officially sanctioned discrimination and segregation in the armed services, many black military personnel and civilians alike viewed the armed forces favorably. Military service, they argued, offered young black males more opportunities for social mobility and occupational advancement than did the more racially stratified civilian sector. In the mid-1960's, black soldiers repeatedly stressed that military service provided "a chance to improve yourself professionally" and that the armed forces was one of the few institutions in the United States where one's race was not an apparent barrier.[2]

Such positive assessments of military service, particularly those voiced by career soldiers, helped to shape the early responses and reactions of many black soldiers to the growing American military involvement in Southeast Asia from 1965 through late 1968. In letters and in comments to journalists, many proudly defended their presence in and the American military commitment to South Vietnam. Whether they voiced their true feelings or whether they told visiting journalists what they wanted to hear, black soldiers expressed support of the Johnson administration's decision to intervene militarily in Southeast Asia. Communist aggression, many agreed, had to be stopped. Without the American military presence, one black private stationed in Vietnam wrote, "the 'commies' would take over." Many black troops supported a complete and total American victory on the battlefield. Foreseeing an early end to the American combat role in Southeast Asia, one black enlisted man prematurely quipped: "We've got them [the National Liberation Front armies] whipped only they don't have sense enough to know it. The Viet Cong efforts are fruitless and stupid. All they're doing now is dying and not gaining anything."[3]

BLACKS AND THE PEACE MOVEMENT

In addition to their expressed support for an American military victory in the early years of the war, many black servicemen stationed in Vietnam opposed the activities and argument of stateside critics of the war. Some denounced those individuals who burned their draft cards; others called for more public expressions of support for the war. Particularly galling to many black servicemen during the years 1966 and 1967 were the arguments and activities of blacks opposed to the war. "What disturbs me even more," one black enlisted man wrote, "is the fact that some Negroes say this isn't their war." However, black servicemen were less inclined to criticize the moral and political arguments raised against the war by Dr. Martin Luther King, Jr. Instead their anger was directed against the younger, more militant critics and opponents of the war—heavyweight champion Muhammad Ali and the then head of the Student Nonviolent Coordinating Committee, Stokely Carmichael. To one soldier, the source of a 1967 *Time* magazine cover story on the Negro soldier in Vietnam, Ali "gave up being a man when he decided against getting inducted and I don't want him as no Negro either."[4]

TIDE BEGINS TO CHANGE

During the years 1965 to 1967, few black soldiers expressed negative comments about the American combat role in Vietnam. However, in the course of their combat tours during these years, the views and attitudes of many black soldiers towards the war began to change markedly. Individual soldiers who had been supportive initially of the American effort to preserve "freedom" and "democracy" in South Vietnam began to alter or to revise their prior views. In his book *GI Diary*, an account based upon his year-long stint in South Vietnam during 1967, former infantryman David Parks depicts his growing ambivalence towards the war. In one entry, Parks wrote:

> . . . I hate being in this place, but there is a job to be done. It's our job, so they tell us, but I don't know the whole story—and nobody seems to be explaining it to us, at least so it makes sense. I sometimes wonder if we are helping or hurting these poor people.

Early in his tour, Parks had been unclear morally and militarily as to why American troops were fighting in South Vietnam. He was further jolted by the news of the urban disturbances during the summer of 1967. Describing his reactions to the rebellions in Newark and in Detroit, Parks wrote: "They leave me confused, the police brutality and all. It makes me wonder whether we're fighting the right war."[5]

BLACKS AND THE DRAFT

Parks' early doubts and ambivalence and later questioning of the war were not the isolated views of one disillusioned and disenchanted black soldier. Increasingly more and more black troops were starting to express first their ambivalence towards and later their opposition and their resistance to the war. Several factors help to explain the changing attitudes and perceptions of black soldiers about the war.

1. Due to increased manpower needs after 1966–1967, many of the troop sent to Vietnam were conscripts, not enlistees or career soldiers.

2. Once inducted, many black soldiers became more conscious of and more critical of why they were fighting and dying in Vietnam.

In the early years of the American buildup, a large percentage of military personnel sent to South Vietnam were enlistees and career soldiers from the elite combat units. With rising and persistently high draft calls from 1966 through 1970, a much larger percentage of the American combat troops stationed in Vietnam were conscriptees. Many of these black draftees were the intended "beneficiaries" of the Defense Department's Project 100,000 (the Pentagon's deliberate effort to induct a higher number of poor black youths as a means of combatting the "pathology of the Negro family"). Many of these youths inducted no longer saw military service, particularly if it entailed duty in Vietnam, as being reflective of the "great society in uniform."

By early 1967 an increasing number of black troops were starting to view the war as a "mistake." In letters to stateside publications, black troops described the war as both inane and costly. "I have been here about ten months," wrote one black marine to the editor of *Sepia*, "and have yet to see a good reason for being here." With increasing frequency, black troops saw the war as not being "worth the lives being lost."[6]

"NOTHING LESS THAN A WASTE"

Conscious of the mounting casualties and keenly aware of the disproportionate numbers of black troops being killed in the war, many black GI's saw it as "nothing less than a waste—a real hang-up." Others were or came to be more suspicious of the war's intent. Throughout the war more politically conscious black troops remarked upon the class and racial aspects of the war. The United States, testified one black veteran before the 1967 Bertrand Russell International War Crimes Tribunal, "uses its minorities to do its dirty work up front in Vietnam—Negroes, Puerto Ricans, and hillbillies." Others argued that the war was one of racial genocide. Whereas many white troops were assigned to support duties in the rear, black troops disproportionately were given combat assignments. In the minds of many black troops the draft and the awarding of combat assignments were implemented directly "to get rid of us—eliminate the black male."[7]

From early 1968 onward, an increasing number of black troops vocally questioned why they were fighting in Vietnam. If black troops had held such views earlier in the war, many had been less willing to voice their dissenting views. However, black troops, in arguments similar to those voiced by individuals such as Rev. Dr. Martin Luther King, Jr., and by earlier critics from SNCC, argued "why should we go thousands of miles to help people of another country gain their freedom when we don't have freedom in our own country?" In their responses and comments to news reporters and in their letters to the editor of *Sepia*, more and more black troops argued that the country's commitment to campaigns for civil rights and social justice should take precedence over the waging of the war. Instead of spending billions yearly to finance the war, black soldiers maintained the nation should ensure civil and political rights to all its citizens and should redirect its resources to addressing domestic concerns.[8]

KING'S ASSASSINATION EXPLODES IN VIETNAM

Increasingly, black troops voiced resentment and bitterness at continuing discrimination and oppression at home. The killing of two black college students at South Carolina State College in 1968 for attempting to use a local white-owned bowling alley provoked "bitterness" among black troops. The assassination of Martin Luther King, according to Michael Herr, "intruded on the war in a way that no other outside event had ever done." Career soldiers who disagreed with King's views on Vietnam were enraged by news of the civil rights leader's death. More militant draftees saw King's death as further proof of American hypocrisy. Black troops in his unit, according to the recollections of one veteran, thought "If they kill a preacher, what are they going to do to us, even though we're over here fighting for them?"[9]

By early 1970, due in part to the growing unpopularity of the war at home but due in large measure to their growing racial and political consciousness of the era, most black servicemen then stationed in Vietnam expressed opposition to the war. According to an extensive 1970 poll by Wallace Terry, former *Time* war correspondent, "many black enlisted men are fed up with fighting and dying for a racist America." Nearly two-thirds of 392 black enlisted men polled answered no to the question "Should black people fight in Vietnam?" Whether in response to Terry or in their letters, a majority of black troops argued that their "war" was at home.[10]

BLACK TROOPS RADICALIZED

Black troops in 1970–1971 were also supportive of the domestic protests against the war. Many now expressed support for demonstrations against the war. Others praised those individuals and organizations opposed to the war. Whereas Muhammad Ali had earlier been vilified for his refusal to be inducted into the army, he was now revered. Praising Ali's stance, one soldier wrote:

> [he] refuses to be bullied or tricked into this war and treated like two cents. Also, he's showing the white man that he doesn't have to jump everytime he moves his finger. If he doesn't want to come into this Army, that is his prerogative.[11]

Black troops also expressed admiration for the Black Panther Party. To many, the Black Panther Party's philosophy of self-defense was appealing; others strongly considered joining the Black Panthers upon their return to the United States.

By the late 1960's–1970 a clear majority of black troops stationed in Vietnam had come to recognize the hypocrisy inherent in American military participation in Vietnam. While many voiced or expressed both their opposition to and discontent with their participation in the war, others chose to express more demonstratively and/or collectively their opposition and their resistance to the war. In one of the first publicized instances of GI opposition to the war, army private Ronald Lockman refused to obey his 1967 orders to report to Vietnam. At his court-martial Lockman proclaimed "I could not subject myself to the atrocities being committed by our soldiers in Vietnam." Lockman was sentenced to 1½ years at hard labor and given a dishonorable discharge from the army, but his refusal to report for duty in Vietnam was one of the first public protests by black soldiers against the war and the military.[12]

From 1967 up until the end of the war, protests, either individual or group, continued. Some, such as the highly publicized protest by the Fort Hood 43, stemmed from the refusal of black troops to participate in quelling possible urban rebellions. Other protests were more directly related to the war. In 1967, two black marines were court-martialed for "encouraging" dissent. In conversations with other marines, the two had described the war as a "white man's war" and had counseled other marines to resist being sent and serving in Vietnam. Other troops, particularly those known collectively as the Fort Jackson 8, were part of the beginning GI movement against the war.[13]

RESISTANCE IN VIETNAM

Military protests against the war were not limited solely to stateside opposition and resistance. Throughout the war there were recurrent episodes of black soldiers refusing to go out on patrols or to participate in missions that they perceived as overly dangerous or suicidal. While many of these acts of resistance were never publicized, others, particularly those occurring late in the war, did come to the public's attention. In the spring of 1970, a small group of black soldiers refused to report for patrol duty. In the fall of 1970, seven soldiers from 176th Regiment refused to report for patrol duty, arguing that their lives would be endangered by racist commanding officers. Based upon his conversations with black grunts, one black doctor stationed in South Vietnam sympathetically wrote "They would do anything to remain out of the war."[14]

Refusal to report for patrol duty was but one form of black GI resistance to the war. Many black troops willingly chose imprisonment, short-term and long-term, in South Vietnam's infamous Long Binh Jail rather than to report for patrol duty. "The black soldier," according to the jail's black commanding officer, "is anti-establishment and anti-war." Yet much of the black soldiers' "anti-establishment and anti-war" posture was attributable to the rising black consciousness movement in the military in the late 1960's. Not only were black soldiers opposing and resisting the war, but many more saw the need for black soldiers to unite. Racial solidarity was necessary, many maintained, so that they could fight against racism in the military as well as protect and look after each other. Reflective of the solidarity

DAP of black soldiers was the "DAP," a ritual performance in which black soldiers professed their allegiance to look out for and to protect each other.[15]

Rising resentment against the war and against the military led to the increased desertions from the armed forces. Conscious protest against the war, according to one federal report, may not have been the most common explanation given by those individuals who went "over the hill." However, for more than an isolated few, black and white, desertion was a conscious act of political opposition to the war. Although data is imprecise, it is estimated that ten percent of those deserters seeking refuge overseas were black. Like their white counterparts, black deserters largely came from working-class backgrounds and had shown little political consciousness prior to their entering the military. Many had been radicalized politically and racially by their participation in the war. For one black soldier stationed in South Vietnam in 1968, his decision to desert was prompted by his participation in an "immoral" war. In explaining his decision, Terry Whitmore has written: "It was disgusting and I'm none too proud that I was once a part of killing women and their children when my country was supposed to be there to help them. No more of that shit for me, Jack."[16]

BLACK TROOPS AND THE VIETNAMESE

Although a small but undetermined number of black troops deserted and sought refuge in either Canada or Sweden, none, as can be determined deserted to the armies of the National Liberation Front or North Vietnam. Yet, throughout the war leaflets circulated by both the National Liberation Front and the North Vietnamese encouraged American troops first to defect and, secondly, to take part in the GI anti-war movement. Concerted efforts were made by NLF pamphleteers and by North Vietnam broadcasters to influence black soldiers. Conscious of the stateside discrimination faced by blacks and aware of the grievances voiced by blacks against discrimination in the military, the NLF appealed to the discontent of black troops. "The slayers of negroes [sic] in America," one leaflet read, "are the very same as those who force black GI's to go and die needlessly in South Vietnam." Black troops were encouraged to "DEMAND IMMEDIATE RETURN HOME TO FIGHT FOR THE VITAL RIGHTS OF THE AMERICAN BLACK PEOPLE."[17]

Many black troops rejected the NLF and North Vietnamese messages. Others, after picking up and reading the leaflets, thought deeply about the discrimination they faced at home and in the military.

According to the recollections of one former infantryman, such pamphlets "would make us wonder why we were there." Other individuals came to accept parts of the North Vietnamese argument over the nature of the war. As more and more black troops began to question and to disagree with the aims and purposes of the war, more became "sympathetic with Ho Chi Minh." By 1970, approximately forty percent of the black soldiers polled by Wallace Terry described the war as a civil war or as an Asian war.[18]

THE NLF'S ATTITUDE TOWARD BLACK GI'S

Such sympathy and sentiment, often based upon respect and racial considerations, occasionally entered into the combatant phase of the war. In the early years of the war, NLF soldiers did not attack areas of Saigon heavily frequented by black troops. According to black troops, there was an "unwritten understanding" between Afro-American and NLF soldiers in non-combat situations. Stories also abound of personal encounters between individual black soldiers and individual NLF troops. Recounting his chance encounter with an armed NLF soldier in Saigon, one black airman recalled that the NLF soldier "pulled a hand grenade on me. I pulled out my .38 [revolver], but he told me 'this is not for you brother, it's for charlie' [whites]." In another instance a black soldier and a NLF soldier, erstwhile suitors of the same Vietnamese woman, declared a "cease-fire" during one such visit. Even in the midst of combat, according to black veterans, NLF soldiers sometimes would try to avoid shooting or killing black troops. Some black troops do recall that North Vietnamese soldiers would occasionally fire away from black soldiers. Others recall instances in which either NVA or NLF troops would not kill injured black troops.[19]

Whatever their individual and collective responses and reactions to the war, black troops longed to be "back in the world." Increasingly black troops expressed their support for efforts to wind down or to end the war. Indeed, singer Freda Payne's 1971 hit "Bring the Boys Home" was quite popular among black troops stationed in South Vietnam. Others urged individuals to continue to pressure the Nixon administration to end the war. Writing in 1971, one black private urged: "You citizens back in the U.S. can have it done. So please, for the sake of the next generation, do all you can to stop the war."[20]

COMING HOME

The majority of returning black troops were decidedly anti-war. However, the vast majority of returning black veterans did not affiliate or associate themselves with the newly formed Vietnam Veterans Against the War. Many black veterans were more concerned with the immediate problems confronting black people and black neighborhoods. "Why march for peace in Vietnam," a black veteran stated, "when you haven't got peace here?" Racial antipathies also precluded contact between black veterans and VVAW. As the war and tensions wrought by the war led to a worsening of race relations in Vietnam, fewer black veterans were willing to cooperate with white veterans. Still, some black veterans were impressed with VVAW. For one black veteran, the 1971 VVAW demonstrations in Washington, D.C. were eye-opening. Watching the demonstrations and the tossing away of medals, he recalled thinking that "why aren't blacks taking part since we are treated worse than whites in the military?"[21]

While vast numbers of black veterans did not vent publicly their opposition and anger over the war and the continuation of the war, upon their return they were among the most bitter about all aspects of the war. Commenting upon the 1975 defeat of South Vietnam, one black veteran remarked: "I feel like it was a total waste of time . . . All the people got killed over there for what?" To one former Marine, "the United States had no business over there." Regretting the loss of lives for an ignoble cause, he added

> None of those brothers who died over there should have. We should not have been there fighting somebody else's war, risking our lives for oppression and capitalism.
>
> All we were doing was being mercenaries for capitalist regimes. We were trying to help a capitalist regime get started in South Vietnam.[22]

THE PLIGHT OF THE BLACK VETERAN

The war in Vietnam deeply affected all of those who participated. However, the war and its aftermath have been painfully traumatic for many of those black soldiers. Studies conducted in the early-to-mid-1970's found that a "large minority of black veterans [were] returning to civilian life alienated." Such alienation was more pronounced among younger, combat-experienced draftees who had entered the service after 1968. Describing their findings of alienation among black veterans, social scientists James M. Fendrich and Michael A. Pearson have contended that "the experiences in the military en-inforced [sic] rather than diminished levels of alienation of both combat and non-combat veterans."[23]

Such attitudes towards military service and towards the larger society were substantiated by a 1977 published study by psychologist John P. Wilson. Making use of a sample of 333 veterans, black and white, Wilson found that white veterans, combat and non-combat alike, were more supportive of the war, the American political process, and the motives of political leaders than were their black counterparts. In near total agreement, over 90 percent of black and white combat veterans sampled answered negatively when asked about their participation in a future war similar to Vietnam. However, black combat veterans were inclined not to support their sons' participation in future wars.[24]

SILENT ANGER

It is still too early to present the full range of experiences of black troops who fought and served in Vietnam. Many are still too hesitant and too embittered to talk about what they saw, what they did, and how they felt. However, what is apparent is that the present attitudes of many black Vietnam veterans are far different from what their views were when they entered the military. Many have rejected the "John Wayne mentality" and have become more overtly skeptical and critical of aspects of current foreign policy. Many others, citing their reception and treatment by an insensitive government bureaucracy and an often indifferent and hostile citizenry, vow that they and their relatives will not make the same mistakes in judgment. Reflecting on his tour in Vietnam, one black veteran has stated, "nobody gives a shit. If I have a son, I won't let him go. I'll send him to Canada first."[25]

NOTES

1. *Sepia*, August 1970, p. 38.

2. Gene Grove, "The Army and the Negro," *New York Times Magazine*, 24 July 1966, pp. 48–49.

3. Donald Kirk, *Tell It to the Dead: Memories of a War* (Chicago: Nelson-Hall, 1975), pp. 36–50; Wallace Terry and Janice Terry, "The War and Race," in *The Wounded Generation: America after Vietnam*, ed. A.D. Horne (Englewood Cliffs, New Jersey; Prentice-Hall, Inc., 1981), pp. 167–182. *Pittsburgh Courier*, 22 April 1967; Samuel Vance, *The Courageous and the Proud* (New York: W.W. Norton and Company, Inc., 1970); Whitney M. Young, Jr. "When the Negroes in Vietnam Come Home," *Harper's*, June 1967, pp. 63–69; Edward Co. Briscoe, *Diary of a Short-Timer in Vietnam* (New York: Vantage Press, 1970), *Sepia*, February 1968 letters, September 1968 letters, November 1968 letters.

4. Kirk, *Tell It to the Dead*, p. 40; *Sepia*, January 1968 letters, February 1968 letters; March 1968 letters, Pittsburgh Courier, 22 April 1967; *Time*.

5. David Parks, *GI Diary* (New York: Harper and Row, Publishers, 1968), pp. 85, 129.

6. See letters in *Sepia*, January 1958, June 1968, April 1969, June 1969.

7. Sol Stern, "When the Black G.I. Comes Back from Vietnam," *New York Times Magazine*, 20 March 1968, pp. 27, 37; Stanley Goff, Robert Sanders with Clark Smith, *Brothers: Black Soldiers in the Nam* (Novato, California: Presidio Press, 1982), p. 11.

8. Vance, *The Courageous and the Proud*, pp. 23, 60; *New York Times*, 29 July 1968, pp. 1, 14; *Sepia*, letters, September 1968, November 1968, August 1969, September 1964, June 1970, August 1970, September 1970; Goff, Sanders, Smith, *Brothers*, pp. 24–30.

9. Jack Nelson and Jack Bass, *The Orangeburg Massacre* (New York: The World Publishing Company, 1970), pp. 236–237; Michael Herz, *Dispatches* (New York: Avon Books, 1978), pp. 158–159; Goff, Sanders, Smith, *Brothers*, pp. 132–133; Eldson McGhee, "From Vietnam to Prison: The Education of Eldson McGhee," *Black World-View* 1 (Number 5):14.

10. Wallace Terry II, "Bringing the War Home" in *Vietnam and Black America: An Anthology of Protest and Resistance*, ed., Clyde Taylor (Garden City, New York: Anchor Books, 1973), pp. 200–219; *Sepia*, February 1971 letters.

11. *Sepia*, May 1971; Terry, "Bringing the War Home," p. 207.

12. *Washington Post*, 14 November 1967; *New York Amsterdam News*, 18 November 1967.

13. *Time*, 13 September 1968, pp. 22–23, Murray Polner, "18-Minute Verdict: Military Justice and Constitutional Rights" in *When Can I Come Home! A Debate on Amnesty for Exiles, Anti-War Prisoners and Others* (Garden City, New York: Anchor Books, 1972), pp. 248–250; Fred Halstead, *GIs Speaks Out Against the War: The Case of the Ft. Jackson 8* (New York: Pathfinder Press, 1970); Matthew Rinaldi, "The Olive-Drab Rebels: Military Organizing During the Vietnam Era," *Radical America* 8 (May–June 1974): 17–52.

14. Kirk, *Tell It to the Dead*, p. 201; *Pittsburgh Courier*, 9 June 1979, p. 1; David Cortright, *Soldiers in Revolt: The American Military Today* (Garden City, New York: Anchor Press/Doubleday, 1975), pp. 39–42, 210–211; Fenton A. Williams, *Just Before the Dawn: A Doctor's Experiences in Vietnam* (New York: Exposition Press, 1971), pp. 57, 114–115.

15. *New York Amsterdam News*, 18 July 1970, pp. 1, 33; Charles C. Moskos, "The American Dilemma in Uniform: Race in the Armed Forces," *Annals of the American Academy of Political Social Science* 406 (March 1973): 94–106; Jack White, "The Angry Black Soldiers," *Progressive*, March 1970, pp. 22–26; Kirk, *Tell It to the Dead*, p. 55; Terry, "Bring It Home," pp. 210–216.

16. D. Bruce Bell and Beverly W. Bell, "Desertion and Antiwar Protest," *Armed Forces and Society* 3 (May 1977): 433–443; John Cooney and Dana Spitzer, "Hell, No, We Won't Go," in *The American Military*, ed., Martin Oppenheimer (Chicago: Aldine Publishing Co., 1971), pp. 124–125; Thomas Lee Hayes, *American Deserters in Sweden: The Men and Their Challenge* (New York: Association Press, 1971), pp. 51, 76–77; Terry Whitmore, *Memphis-Nam-Sweden: The Autobiography of a Black American Exile* (Garden City, New York: Doubleday and Company, Inc., 1971), pp. 135–135, 169.

17. *Time*, 19 January 1968, pp. 20–21; John Helmer, *Bringing the War Home: The American Soldier in Vietnam and After* (New York: The Free Press, 1974), p. 101;

Martin F. Herz, "VC/NVA Propaganda Leaflets Addressed to U.S. Troops: Some Reflections," *Orbis* 21 (Winter 1978): 913–926.

18. Personal interviews with black veterans, February 1980; Goff, Sanders with Smith, *Brothers*, pp. 131–132; Terry, "Bringing the War Home," p. 205.

19. *Pittsburgh Courier*, 18 February 1967, p. 2; *New York Amsterdam News*, 13 February 1971, p. 32, 20 February 1971, p. 42; Peter Goldman and Tony Fuller, *Charlie Company: What Vietnam Did to Us* (New York: William Morrow and Company, Inc., 1983), pp. 116–117; Vance, *The Courageous and the Proud*, pp. 132–133; Helmer, *Bringing the War Home*, p. 101; personal interview with a black veteran, April 1980.

20. Terry, "Bringing the War Home," pp. 204–205; *Sepia*, October 1971 letters.

21. Stern, "When the Black G.I. Comes Back," p. 42; Kirk, *Tell It to the Dead*, p. 203; interviews with black veterans, February, April 1980.

22. *Jet*, 22 May 1975, pp. 52–53.

23. "The Returning GI: What Does He Do Now?" *Black Enterprise*, February 1971, pp. 23–27, 30; James Fendrich and Michael Pearson, "Black Veterans Return," *Translation* 7 (March 1970): 32–37; James M. Fendrich and Michael A. Pearson, "Alienation and Its Correlates Among Black Veterans," *Sociological Symposium* Number Four (Spring 1970): 55–85.

24. John P. Wilson, "Identity, Ideology and Crisis: The Vietnam Veteran in Transition, Part I" (Cleveland: Cleveland State University, 1977), pp. 70–76.

25. *Washington Post*, 15 March 1981, 14 November 1982; Goff, Sanders, with Smith, *Brothers*, p. 179; Goldman and Fuller, *Charlie Company*, pp. 276–277.

19

Chicanos and Vietnam

1978

Douglas Martinez and *Manuel Gomez*

"Chicanos saw that Americans loved patriots and it was a fantastic opportunity for them to prove their right to be in this country. Chicanos tried harder and those who did try harder died in greater numbers . . ."
—Dr. Ralph Guzmán, University of California at Santa Cruz.

Douglas Martinez

Of the 37 Hispanic men who received the nation's highest military decoration, the Congressional Medal of Honor, more than half, 19, did not live to see it.

"I think it is very significant," said Gerard White, one of the nation's experts on the history of the medal and its recipients. "As an individual [ethnic] group, they are receiving the highest number being awarded posthumously. Something that is characteristic of Spanish-Americans is how they will die for their flag."

Raúl Morin, who chronicled the Hispanic contributions to World War II and Korea in his book, *Among the Valiant,* described it in somewhat more dramatic terms.

Detailing the exploits of Congressional Medal of Honor winner Luciano Adams, who sliced through fire and explosions to destroy a German machine-gun emplacement in World War II, Morin said that "Adams . . . proud of the Aztec blood that flowed through his veins, used to the life of the underdog and of uphill struggles, knowing very little fear . . . [knew] that a duty had to be done and he wasn't going to wait around for someone else to do it."

It is clear that the nation's three most recent wars have been taking their toll in Hispanic communities. Vietnam, in particular, seems to have had a disastrous impact on young Hispanic men.

Douglas R. Martinez describes the overall situation with respect to Hispanic, Latino, Chicano, and Mexican-American involvement in the war. His survey was first published under the title "Hispanics on the Battlefield," in *The Nation.* September/October, 1978, pp. 12–13. Manuel Gomez testifies why he decided not to get involved in the fighting. Gomez' essay was originally published as "I Am My Brother" in a series of statements on "Chicanos and the War," in *La Raza Magazine,* Vol. I, No. 3 (no date), p. 16. Testimonials from Chicanos who fought in Vietnam are included in Charley Trujillo, editor, *Soldados: Chicanos in Viet Nam* (San Jose: Chusma House Publications, 1990).

But this may be so because the statistics of minority casualties in that undeclared war have been studied more thoroughly than in previous wars.

A study by University of California Professor Ralph Guzmán done in 1970–71 showed that more than 19 percent of the Vietnam war dead from the five Southwestern states of Arizona, Colorado, California, New Mexico, and Texas were Chicanos and Spanish-origin persons. At the time of the study, the Hispanic population of those states was no more than 11 percent. Guzmán, who says the Hispanic deaths in World War II and Korea have not been researched and recorded believes nonetheless that the same pattern of high, disproportionate Hispanic deaths and casualties, prevailed.

"There's no question at all that there was a very substantial contribution, if you want to call it that, to the Vietnam war," Guzmán said in an interview from his home in California. "And I can prove it. I can bring out my reams of data and prove it. What I reported, I reported very deliberately in a conservative way."

Guzmán performed the study by selecting the Spanish-surnamed from official Defense Department casualty lists for the Southwest. He said that Hispanos simply gave more during their wartime service because of their concentration in infantry ranks and dangerous combat assignments.

"More than the deaths and the casualties, it was the kind of military service that Chicanos gave," Guzmán explained. "Qualitatively, we fear that they were the point men in Vietnam, that they were the scouts, that they volunteered in excessive numbers."

Guzmán added, "I saw a lot of that in World War II, but they didn't live to enjoy that recognition. They were in all these high-risk areas, and apparently with the Vietnam War, this same thing happened again. Chicanos tried harder and the Chicanos who did try harder died in greater numbers."

Guzmán is a sociologist who teamed with other scholars during the 1960's to produce the monumental, Ford Foundation-financed Mexican American Study Project of the University of California, Los Angeles. It was the first major research study of Chicanos funded by a foundation.

Guzmán says there are very logical reasons for the pattern of high Chicano involvement in wars. "There has been a drive among Chicanos for acceptance in this society, and the military has been a channel in American society for most different groups," he said. "Both World War II and the Korean War offered very special opportunities for

Chicanos to validate themselves socially. Chicanos saw that Americans loved patriots and it was a fantastic opportunity for them to prove their right to be in this country."

He added, however, that this feeling on the part of Chicanos was often misplaced, and in many cases the expected and hoped for respect and recognition did not come.

In fact, American G.I. Forum, a national Hispanic veterans' organization, was formed after World War II partly because of several incidents in which highly decorated servicemen were denied entrance to bars and restaurants because of their Hispanic heritage.

Guzmán said that Vietnam was a tragic turn for the worse for Hispanics. "Chicanos in Vietnam went in part because they wanted to prove their patriotism, but in many cases they didn't know how to avoid going," he said. "They were working-class people. They had language problems. They were drafted because they weren't going to college and because they didn't have parents to finagle for them. The bottom line is that there were many Chicanos that didn't want to go to the damn war. There were many that went AWOL (Absent Without Leave) and wound up in military prisons and we don't know how large (a number) that is."

Moreover, said Guzmán, "the Vietnam veterans have not received anywhere near the kind of reward that veterans of my generation got. And if this is so, Chicanos who were limited in the first place when they went in got even less. Among the group of veterans who were badly short-changed—and came out with all the ills and hurts of the Vietnam veterans—drugs, crime, broken homes—Chicanos came out the worst. They were in the lowest of the low ranks: Infantry and Marines. If I got on a soapbox, the government owes Chicanos enormous debts for contributions in agriculture and industry, but it owes the Chicano veteran of Vietnam more."

Hispanic Medal of Honor winners won their awards in the following wars and numbers: World War II, 13; Korea, 9; Vietnam, 9; other, pre-World War I conflicts, 7.

One of those who believes that the Vietnam war has not yet ended for Hispanics is Rolando Mora, who was until recently the highest-ranking Hispanic in the Labor Department. Mora is a former Marine Captain who served as intelligence chief among the first United States troops to hit the beaches of Vietnam in 1965. He is prominently mentioned in the best-selling book by Philip Caputo, *A Rumor of War*, which chronicles American involvement in the Vietnam venture.

At his swearing-in ceremony in September, 1977, Mora eloquently talked about the Hispanic veteran: "For the most part, they were drafted or enlisted under the threat of conscription. Many were poor or disadvantaged. These men were not eligible for college deferments. These men came home with the same lack of skills, education, and training they left with. They came home bearing the stigma of drug dependency and the stigma of somehow having performed less than honorably."

But as Deputy Assistant Secretary for Veterans' Employment, whose job it was to advise the Secretary of Labor in all areas of concern to veterans, Mora said he saw firsthand the administration's lack of concern for Vietnam veterans as evidenced by the lackluster programs conceived to aid veterans.

"Vietnam caused a lot of problems for our country," he explained. "The country doesn't like to be identified with a loser. The Vietnam veteran lost the war. If you forget the veterans, you forget the war."

Furthermore, Mora charges, the traditional veterans' organizations have failed to help Hispanic veterans. "They didn't understand the role of the minority disabled veteran," Mora said. "They didn't understand the war. They bought the big lie of the Vietnam war—that it was a just and necessary war—and many are still selling it."

He continued. "I hold them [veterans' groups] responsible for the devastation of lives the damn war caused. They won't own up to it; they'd rather forget about it and the problems of Vietnam veterans in Harlem or San Juan, Puerto Rico."

Mora adds that the loss of lives he is referring to were the Hispanics and other minorities who he feels were overrepresented in the military ranks. "Hispanics were the disproportionate number of the fighting forces and the casualties in Vietnam," he said. "The statistics bear that out."

Manuel Gomez

Today, December 8, 1969, I must refuse induction into the Armed Services of the United States. Please understand it is difficult for me to communicate my feelings through writing, but nevertheless, I will try to let you see through my window.

In my veins runs the blood of all the people of the world. I am a son of La Raza, the universal children, and cannot be trained and ordered to kill my brother. When the first man was killed, too many had died. For my people, I refuse to respect your induction papers.

It is well known that Mexicans were among the first victims of your empire. The memory of the United States-Mexico war is still an open wound in the souls of my people. The Treaty of Guadalupe Hidalgo is a lie, similar to all the treaties signed with our indian brothers. The war did not end. It has continued in the minds and hearts of the people of the Southwest. Strife and bloodshed has never stopped between us.

This society with its Texas Rangers and Green Berets has never allowed our people to live in peace. The blood is still moist on the land. Too many of my brothers have been killed fighting for a lie called "American freedom," both in our streets and in foreign lands.

My people have known nothing but racist tyranny and brutal oppression from this society. Your educational system has butchered our minds, stung our hearts, and poisoned our souls. You bit our tongue, and castrated our culture making us strangers in our own land. The sweat of my people watered the fields and their aching bones harvested your food. Today we continue to do your sweatwork for you, with our hands and backs. Though you occupy the land, you have not conquered us. I am a free man. I choose my own battles. My fight is here.

In the short time that you've held the land we have felt the pain of seeing beautiful lands turn into parking lots and freeways, of seeing the birds disappear, the fish die, and the waters become undrinkable. Seeing the sign "Private Property" hung on a fence surrounding lands once held in common, and having our mountains become but vague shadows behind a veil of choking smog.

Your judges armed with the cold sword called law, held in the diseased arm of justice, have frozen the life of my brothers in your barbaric prisons, scarring them deeply. A man steals to live and you call him a criminal and lock him up worse than an animal. A soldier massacres and pillages a village and he's made a hero, awarded a medal. I believe that if it is wrong to kill within society, then it must also be wrong to kill outside of the society. I am of a peace-loving people.

I see rabid leaders of this land live in luxury and comfort while they send my poor brothers to kill in a war no one wants or understands. The helpless and the innocent have lost on both sides as has been the case in all wars. My ears hear the screams of the fatherless children, my heart hurts with the tears of mothers moaning for their sons, my soul shrinks from the knowledge of the unspeakable horrors of Song My and the rest to come. For the Vietnamese people, I refuse to respect your induction papers.

I cannot betray the blood of my brothers. We are all branches of the same tree, flowers of the same garden, waves of the same sea. The Vietnamese people are not my enemy but brothers involved in the same struggle for justice against a common enemy. We are all under the same sky. East and West are one.

My heart is dedicated to seeking justice and peace in this world. My eyes see a new sun, with a far more beautiful horizon, where all the trees can see the sky and share the same water from the one river. I cannot fight for the enemy of the spirit of life. For my soul, I refuse to obey your induction orders. Peace and Justice.

20

American Indian Veterans and the Vietnam War

Thomas M. Holm

Over the past 15 years, a large body of literature has developed on the subject of posttraumatic stress disorders in Vietnam veterans.[1] In large part the disorder is viewed as originating from the shock of combat and/or the feeling of being rejected by society for participating in the conflict. Generally, the symptoms of PTSD are frequent inexplicable headaches, flashbacks, depression, severe alienation, sleep intrusions, extreme nervousness, and a heightened startle response. The problems are often manifested in antisocial behavior, chemical abuse, chronic unemployment, or the inability to maintain close personal relationships with friends or family members.[2]

Despite the interest in this problem, only a few studies have focused on Hispanics, blacks, and women, and *none* on American Indians, except for a brief mention of an intertribal ceremony held in honor of Vietnam veterans (described by the author) in *Four Winds* magazine.[3] The present study, based on extensive interviews with 35 American Indian Vietnam veterans and on direct observations in Indian communities, intends partially to correct this gap in the literature and place some of what we know about PTSD within a cultural context.

The sample is admittedly small. There were over 42,000 American Indians who served in Vietnam between 1964 and 1973.[4] However, this study group was extremely responsive and the interviews insightful. In terms of culture, it was a very diverse group, representing 25 tribes or combinations of tribes: Kiowas and Comanches from the southern plains; Caddoes, Cherokees, and Creeks, originally from the

Professor Thomas M. Holm teaches in the political science department at the University of Arizona in Tucson. Shocked by the fact that there is so little published information on the experience of native Americans in the Vietnam War, Holm began conducting interviews in Indian communities throughout the Southwest. His initial findings are summarized in this essay, which he has written as the first in a projected series of ongoing studies that he is conducting. This essay was originally published in *Armed Forces and Society*, Vol. 12, No. 2, Winter 1986, pp. 237–251.

southern woodlands culture area; Sioux from the northern plains; Chippewas, Sae and Fox, and Menominees from the Great Lakes; Navajos from the Southwest; and Colville and Shoshone from the northwest plateau. Most were born between 1944 and 1952, and all entered the military between the ages of 17 and 21. Nearly half of the 35 now live in urban areas, but only 8 actually grew up in large population centers. In other words, they were fairly representative of the demographic trends of Indians of their age group.[5] On the whole, their educational levels were quite high, but most admitted that these levels were attained after their military service.[6]

PTSD IN AMERICAN INDIAN VETERANS

There are strong indications that minority veterans display stress symptoms to a greater degree than other veterans. According to a 1981 study commissioned by the Veterans Administration (VA),

> Vietnam veterans as a group were three times as likely to be stressed as Vietnam era veterans [those who served in the military in the period but did not go to Vietnam] and the latter were twice as stressed as men who did not enter the military [during the war]. Blacks and Chicanos, at every point of stressful experience, evidenced somewhat higher levels than whites. Just being in Vietnam for black respondents was as stressful as being in heavy combat for white veterans.[7]

These higher levels of stress in minority veterans are usually seen in terms of class rather than race. Members of the lower economic strata were twice as likely to be assigned to nontechnical military occupations and see combat in Vietnam as members of the upper classes.[8] Minority men, because of their generally lower economic and educational levels, were more apt to see duty in Vietnam and to participate in combat. Already alienated from mainstream, middle-class society, they returned from the war to find that their service gained them neither social nor economic status.[9]

Given the foregoing, it is reasonable to assume that American Indians should display a great many stress symptoms. Historically, Indians were crushed by U.S. military might, forced to abandon many of their religious ceremonies, stripped of numerous tribal institutions, and left as one of the poorest economic groups in the nation. Low economic and educational levels (some reservations have reported unemployment rates as high as 80 percent and education averaging at the eighth-grade level) virtually assured that most Indians would be assigned to nontechnical duties upon entering the military. Thus, they were very likely to become infantrymen and experience combat in Vietnam.[10]

On another level, it seems that because of white-held stereotypes of Indians, native Americans tended to draw some very hazardous duties in Southeast Asia. That Indians are tenacious fighters, good scouts, and obedient and knowledgeable warriors has long been held. In 1799, Col. James Smith, who had been in the Revolutionary Army fighting the British and Indians, wrote,

> The business of the private [Indian] warriors is to be under command, or punctually to obey orders; to learn to march abreast in scattered order, so as to be in readiness to surround the enemy, or to prevent being surrounded; to be good marksmen, and active in the use of arms; to practice running; to learn to endure hunger or hardships with patience and fortitude; to tell the truth at all times to their officers, but more especially when sent out to spy the enemy.[11]

Nearly 150 years later, high-ranking Washington officials were echoing Smith's views. Harold Ickes, Secretary of the Interior, wrote during World War II that the Indian was "uniquely valuable" to the war effort because he possessed

> endurance, rhythm, a feeling for timing, co-ordination, sense percep- tion, an uncanny ability to get over any sort of terrain at night, and better than all else, an enthusiasm for fighting. He takes a rough job and makes a game of it. Rigors of combat hold no terrors for him; severe discipline and hard duties do not deter him.[12]

These kinds of stereotypes followed Indian soldiers in Vietnam. Well over half of those interviewed mentioned they had endured some form of discrimination based on white stereotypes of Indians. A number reported they were typically referred to as "blanketasses" or "red- skins," and almost all had been called "chief" at one time or another during their tours. Perhaps their most common complaint was that company and platoon commanders habitually assigned them to walk "point" on patrols and large-scale troop movements. (In Vietnam, because of booby traps, ambushes, and snipers, point was extremely perilous duty.) A Menominee from Wisconsin related that his platoon commander thought that since Indians "grew up in the woods," they should know how to track and generally "feel" when something in the immediate environment was disturbed or out of place. Therefore, the officer reasoned, Indians should make good point men or scouts. One Navajo veteran concurred about the false labeling. He said he was stereotyped by the cowboys and Indian movies. Nicknamed "Chief" right away. Non-Indians claimed Indians could see through trees and hear the unhearable. Bullshit, they even believed Indians could walk on water.

Because of their assignments and apparently high rate of infantry service, American Indians garnered a number of awards and also suffered considerable casualties. Of the 35 veterans, 13 had been wounded in Vietnam. The most decorated Indian soldier of the war, Billy Walkabout, a Cherokee, won the Distinguished Service Cross, five Silver Stars, five Bronze Stars, and was wounded on six occasions.[13]

There can be no doubt both that Indians made sacrifices in the war and (apparent from the interviews) that they suffer from PTSD. For some the problem in Vietnam was severe:

> I saw faces, you know, looking at me. Their hands up like they were telling secrets. I had a rage. . . . Sometimes I thought that the top of my head would just blow off.

Said another,

> I couldn't get the war out of my head. So, I stuck my head in a bottle. I hated everybody except when I was drunk. It took me five years, five years, man, to get straight, and now I've been sober for quite a while. Other guys still are drinking.

One veteran engaged in daredevil activities to relieve the pressure:

> I rode bulls, I drove stock cars, I piled up my own cars and a couple of motorcycles. I drank all the time. . . . Goddamn war put me in a world of shit. I think now that I had some sort of death wish.

For another, the trauma of combat was exacerbated because his own tribal conditions "forbade" what he saw and did in Vietnam:

> We went into a ville [village] one day after an air strike. The first body I saw in Nam was a little kid. He was burnt up—napalm—and his arms were kind of curled up. He was on his back but his arms were curled but sticking up in the air, stiff. Made me sick. It turned me around. See, in our way we're not supposed to kill women and children in battle. The old people say that it's bad medicine and killing women and children doesn't prove that you're brave. It's just the opposite.

Other Indian veterans had grave doubts about Indians participating in the war in the first place:

> We went into their [the Vietnamese] country and killed them and took land that wasn't ours. Just like what the whites did to us. I helped load up ville and ville and pack it off to a resettlement area. Just like when they moved us to the rez [reservation]. We shouldn't have done that. Browns against browns. That screwed me up, you know.

For several veterans, the return to the United States was not exactly what they expected. It seemed as if American society, of which they were only a peripheral part, had sent them to war and then rejected them for actually serving. Several stated that they were called "baby-killers" and "warmongers." One man described his arrival back in the "world" with a great deal of bitterness:

> We fought a white man's war, you know, and the first thing that happens when I get back is that some white kid, a girl, at the L.A. airport, spits on me.

American society angered another Indian veteran in a different way:

> The white dudes stayed in school, you know, and we fought the war. They don't know nothing about anything except what they get out of a book. But they get the jobs. . . .

The veterans' stressful combat and readjustment experiences were also compounded by a more general dissatisfaction with U.S. Indian policies. A number of them joined Indian political organizations and participated in protests against federal policies and local racism directed at Indians. For the most part, they also agreed in principle with the ideas underlying the occupation by American Indians of Alcatraz Island in 1969; the Bureau of Indian Affairs building in Washington, D.C., in 1972; and the hamlet of Wounded Knee, S. Dak., in 1973. (Although several Indian Vietnam veterans were actually involved in the Wounded Knee takeover, none figured in this study.) A few men out of the 35 interviewed stated they had been active in the American Indian Movement and/or the National Indian Youth Council, the two principal Indian youth-activist groups of the period.

TRIBAL CULTURES AND VIETNAM VETERANS

A 1981 VA study pointed out that most Vietnam veterans still felt that their sacrifices, and those of their comrades, were meaningless

within the context of the larger American society. In the words of the
report,

> Many combat veterans continue to dwell on the belief that they were
> sent to fight a war they were not intended to win. . . . They often
> emphasize public antipathy to the war and feel that their sacrifice
> was not appreciated. . . . More important, perhaps, is the fact that
> American society has created an environment in which men who
> were exposed to combat continue to define the experience in a nega-
> tive way.[14]

During the interviews it became increasingly clear, however, that
despite their combat experiences, general dissatisfaction with American Indian policy, and society's attitudes toward Vietnam veterans,
some of the Indian veterans had relatively healthy feelings about their
duty in Southeast Asia. According to one, "I wouldn't trade that time
for anything. Being in the war taught me how to survive." A few
others, including those who had seen heavy combat, felt their wartime
experiences had given them knowledge and abilities over and above
those of their nonveteran peers. In short, they seemed reasonably
satisfied that their sacrifices had meaning—an attitude that appears
to have eluded most of the other veterans. One Cheyenne veteran
summed it up in a revealing statement: "I'm proud of our warrior
status."

The reasons underlying this positive outlook are somewhat complex
but basically rooted in individual tribal cultures. Several respondents
stated they had taken part in tribal ceremonies designed either to
purify or honor returning warriors. Information gleaned from elders
of various tribes suggests that in the past many Indian groups in this
country engaged in distinct, separate rituals to celebrate the activities
of war and peace. Some tribes lived under the constant threat of attack
by enemies; basically, they felt that unless the military dimension of
life were placed in a ritualistic context, it might well permanently
dominate all other considerations. Other tribes viewed warfare as a
severe disruption in the divinely created natural scheme of things.
The Papagos, for example, defined war as a form of insanity.[15] In either
case, the line between war and peace was well circumscribed.

In fact, the line was so rigid that many tribes even categorized their
leadership in those terms. Among the Sioux, the Comanches, the Sac
and Fox, the Creeks, and numerous other tribes, there were "war
chiefs" and "peace," or civil, leaders. Although the civil leaders usually
had good war records in their tribes, their duties involved attempts

to prevent younger men from rashly courting conflict.[16] The Creeks and Cherokees determined clan identification along the lines of "white" (peace) and "red" (war) categories.[17] Even the Pueblos, whose ancient traditions strongly opposed violence in any form, had war priests and warrior sodalities.[18]

As a consequence of this rigid distinction between war and peace, most tribes developed special ceremonies to aid individuals—and, indeed, entire societies—in making the transition from peace to war and back again. Warriors were ritually prepared for war and offered protective medicine to assure their safe return to the community. In addition to the rituals for war, many tribes devised purification ceremonies to restore individual warriors, as well as the rest of the community, to a harmonious state. Unless the returning warriors were purged of the trauma of battle, it was felt they might bring back memories of conflict to the tribe and seek to perpetuate patterns of behavior unacceptable to the community in its ordinary functioning. All these ceremonies were thought necessary to maintain a tribe's continued harmonious existence with its environment.

Despite bureaucratic complaints and government prohibitions against war-related performances throughout the nineteenth and early twentieth centuries, many tribes maintained a wide variety of such ceremonies. In 1919, Commissioner of Indian Affairs Cato Sells expressed his irritation at the fact that dances and ceremonies were being conducted among a number of tribes for the Indian soldiers who had just returned from the trenches in France.[19] Honoring and purification ceremonies for Indian veterans also followed the Second World War,[20] despite the widespread (and erroneous) idea in the United States that Indian soldiers would refuse to take part in "yesterday's culture."[21] The Sioux held victory ceremonies; Kiowas took part in soldier dances; Cherokees were ritually cleansed of the taint of battle by medicine men; and Navajos went through elaborate "Enemy Way" ceremonies to restore returning veterans to a harmonious place in the community.[22]

It is significant to note that following World War II, several plains tribes, including the Kiowas, Cheyennes, and the Pawnees, rejuvenated some of their old warrior societies and corresponding ceremonials. The Kiowa Tiah-piah, or Gourd society, has become especially important. After going into a decline because of federal policies, it was rejuvenated after World War II.[23] Since the 1950s, the society's ceremonial dance has been instituted by members of other tribes. Gourd dances are now held regularly during intertribal gatherings in Arizona, New Mexico, Colorado, Kansas, and Nebraska, as well as in

Oklahoma, home of the Kiowas. The society was originally a warrior's group and, in many instances, a police force. The Gourd dance itself is now seen as a veterans' ceremony.

A number (22) of the 35 Indian veterans interviewed said they had taken part in one or more honoring or purification ceremonies—either before they were inducted or assigned or upon their return from Southeast Asia. The ceremonies ranged from the relatively simple to the highly elaborate. A Cherokee informant said that on the last day of his leave prior to being sent overseas an elderly uncle awoke him before dawn in order to watch the sunrise and smoke a pipe of tobacco. His uncle said a few prayers and gave the informant some protective medicine. A Navajo veteran was given a "Blessing Way" ceremony prior to his overseas tour. This ceremony, which lasts for several days, is a highly formalized narrative of the Navajo creation legend; it is also a curing ritual intended to make sure an individual is in harmony with his or her surroundings. It was utilized in this particular case as protective medicine.

Several veterans also mentioned carrying protective charms given to them by tribal elders and close relatives. For the most part, these Indians took part in honoring or cleansing ceremonies after their return. The Navajo veteran (mentioned above) was given a "squaw dance" upon his return from Vietnam. The squaw dance, or Enemy Way, is a four-day ritual in which the medicine man narrates the story of the Hero Twins who killed the monsters of the world in order to make a safe place for human beings. As the story goes,

> The Twins were successful in their attempts to kill all the Monsters. However, in the process of destroying the Monsters the Twins abused their special powers and weapons and disrupted the harmony in nature by killing some people. As a consequence the Twins became ill and misfortunes set in upon them. Another Holy Being recognized that the Twins had put themselves out of harmony with nature by killing, and thus needed a special ceremony to restore them to harmony. Thus was born the first "Enemy Way."[24]

In effect, the ritual removes the stigma of death and the disharmony caused by war. Other Indian Vietnam veterans were honored with special dances, peyote ceremonies, and prayer meetings. All of the individuals who took part in these ceremonies had the strong support of their extended family groups. In fact, few if any of these ceremonials could have been arranged without the intercession of certain family members.

There can be no doubt that at least some of the veterans were helped psychologically by the tribal events. According to one Navajo,

> When I got back I had a lot of trouble. My mother even called in one
> of our medicine men. It cost them but my folks had an "Enemy Way"
> done for me. It's a pretty big thing. . . . It snapped me out of it.

In the same vein, a Kiowa veteran related,

> My people honored me as a warrior. We had a feast and my parents
> and grandparents thanked everyone who prayed for my safe return.
> We had a "special" and I remembered as we circled the drum I got
> a feeling of pride. I felt good inside because that's the way the Kiowa
> people tell you that you've done well.

Several veterans no longer living in their home communities were
honored or purified by ceremonies in other areas. One Cherokee veteran living in Oklahoma City went—at his wife's insistence—to see a
Cherokee doctor over 100 miles away. The Cherokee medicine man
purified him in a ceremony called "going to the water." A Menominee
veteran in Wisconsin told of how he presented an eagle feather to
another veteran at an intertribal powwow. The recipient, a Sioux
from South Dakota, in effect, was paid one of the highest honors a
Menominee can bestow on a person. (According to Menominee tradition, eagle feathers are given away only by medicine people and warriors.)

Perhaps of equal psychological value is the fact that many of these
men received a certain amount of prestige within their communities
as a result of their wartime service. Although the idea of gaining status
in an Indian tribe by entering the armed forces and "fighting a white
man's war" seems incongruous—after all, the tribes were subdued by
the U.S. Army, and militarily enforced Indian policies prohibited
tribal ceremonies in many cases—it is nevertheless understandable.

The veterans, simply by taking part in these time-honored ceremonials, essentially demonstrated a commitment to their cultural continuity. In addition, they created a rapprochement with the tribal elders
who conduct and/or sponsor the rituals.[25] Several tribes in the United
States—the Kiowas and Comanches, the Cheyennes, and to a certain
extent the Winnebagos, the Sioux, and the Chippewas—have syncre-
tized service in the American armed forces with their own tribal
customs.[26] For these tribes there are certain functions that can only
be performed by veterans. At powwows, for example, if a dancer
drops an eagle feather, it can only be retrieved by a warrior who is
accompanied by a chorus singing an appropriate honor song. At some
tribal gatherings, veterans are still asked to "count coup," or tell a
war story, before any ceremonies can begin.

Tribes apparently recognize a psychological condition known as "age acceleration" and treat it in a positive light. In combat, a person is exposed to the deaths of others who are of a similar age. They are, in effect, experiencing the kinds of emotions that many individuals undergo toward the end of their lives.[27] Seeing members of one's peer group die forces an individual to think about, and in some cases focus on, mortality. In a tribal society, when a warrior has been placed in such a situation, he gains maturity, which, in turn, is equated with wisdom. As a Winnebago elder remarked before the performance of a veteran's honor song during a powwow in Wisconsin, "We honor our veterans for their bravery and because by seeing death on the battlefield they truly know the greatness of life."[28]

In addition to being honored and perhaps purged of the taint of war, some Indian veterans were aided by what can only be called *a social absorption of combat-related trauma.* A brief look at the way traditional Cherokee communities function perhaps could best illustrate this process. In these communities, mature men, those 40 and over, are usually the breadwinners and political leaders. Younger men, especially those under 25, have little—if anything—to do with the economy or the running of the community. As Albert L. Wahrhaftig writes,

> Looking at Cherokee men in terms of different role expectations appropriate to different age groups of men, two things about the young are readily apparent. There is no niche for them within the institutional structure of a Cherokee settlement; and furthermore, the processes of Cherokee socialization operate to pull Cherokee men out of the settlement even as the absence of structural niche and social reward conspire to push them out.[29]

Younger men are almost expected to leave the community for a time; most often, they either find jobs in urban areas, become migrant laborers, or enter the military. When they eventually return (some never do), they are usually resocialized into the Cherokee pattern of behavior. The elders listen to the newly returned younger man's adventures and relate them "to the ancient matrix of Cherokee knowledge conveyed through myth and Indian medicine."[30] A Cherokee veteran related the following:

> After I got home, my uncles sat me down and had me tell them what it was all about. One of them had been in the service in World War II and knew what war was like. We talked about what went on over there, about the killing and the waste, and one of my uncles said that

was why God's laws are against war. They never really talked about those kind of things with me before.

This particular Cherokee was ritually cleansed and welcomed back in the community without reservation. Most important was that his experiences in Vietnam were eventually shared on an intellectual level by the community and tended to confirm the Cherokee belief that war was the ultimate evil. On a personal level, the veteran himself was never told his actions were disruptive or improper. His entrance into the service and his participation in the war were not viewed as political statements. Entering the military is just one thing that young men have to do. The Cherokee's personal bravery and service were cheered, but the war itself, simply because it was a war, was considered very bad.

CONCLUSION

It should not be concluded that all American Indian veterans of the Vietnam War have been automatically given status and ceremonies and, therefore, are purged of PTSD. Many Indian veterans now live in cities far away from their communities. Others are simply forgotten even within their own tribal groups. Some have not received ceremonies because their rituals of warfare have been lost or stripped away by government policies.

However, both ceremonialism and recognition have aided a number of Indian veterans in working through the problems associated with PTSD. In a broader context, it is possible that ceremonialism might be of benefit to non-Indian veterans. Although not seemingly viewed as such, non-Indians have several cultural features, including ceremonies, associated with warfare.

For example, Franklin Roosevelt's famous speech requesting Congress to declare war on Japan in 1941 was more ceremonial than political. The United States was already in a shooting war in the North Atlantic in 1941; the beleaguered American troops in the Pacific were not awaiting a formal declaration of hostilities to fire on the attacking Japanese. Roosevelt's speech and the subsequent declaration of war were the rituals by which American society as a whole crossed the line between war and peace. In a like manner, the formal surrenders and the homecoming parades ceremoniously brought World War II to an end. It must be remembered that one of the chief complaints of returning Vietnam veterans was that there were no ceremonies, either at the beginning or the end, to move American society into war and back to peace again.[31]

Another important part of veteran adjustment after a war such as Vietnam concerns the status a community gives its returning warriors. The recognition given to Indian Vietnam veterans in some Indian communities did not seem to involve political questions. Many Indians, in fact, thought the war was neither justified nor honorable. But political issues were not as important as the issue of service. Warriors were more important than the war. As one Sioux woman stated, "Most people here don't like the war at all but they don't like those Indian boys who are draft dodgers either."[32]

Some Indian veterans were viewed in their communities as having gained wisdom in the war. Others were seen as heroes even though the war itself was not viewed as a heroic venture. Their sacrifices were, in that sense, given meaning. Thus, the war had some positive effects on their lives. *Legacies of Vietnam,* the VA's exhaustive study of veterans, mentions this phenomenon in connection with veterans from small towns; the study notes that a minority of them felt the war was an "affirmative" experience. While it does not attempt to discover the reasons behind the positive outlooks of small-town veterans, *Legacies* does offer some theories:

> The small town Vietnam veteran may have left and returned to a community where service to one's country was considered worthy of respect, even during an unpopular war. Returning combat veterans may more frequently have been regarded as heroes in small towns. And, veteran doubts about their role may have been mitigated by the attitudes of the community and the welcome they received. Perhaps there is something about small city life that protects combat veterans from dwelling on the traumatic aspects of their combat experiences and encourages them to see military service as a part of life rather than as an inexplicable intrusion into the normal course of things.[33]

This kind of social absorption of war-related trauma apparently matches the experience of some Indian veterans. It can be concluded that culture is one of the keys to a better understanding of the problems of posttraumatic stress disorder in Vietnam veterans.

NOTES

1. John A. Fairbank et al., "A Selected Bibliography on Post Traumatic Stress Disorders in Vietnam Veterans," *Professional Psychology* 12 (1981): pp. 578–586.

2. See especially Marc Pilisuk, "The Legacy of the Vietnam Veteran," *Journal of Social Issues* 31 (1975): pp. 3–12; J. Boscarino, "Current Drug Involvement among Vietnam and Non-Vietnam Veterans," *American Journal of Drug and Alcohol Abuse* 6 (1979): pp. 301–312; Arthur Egendorf et al., *Legacies of Vietnam: Comparative Adjustment of Veterans and their Peers* (Washington, 1981); and W. E. Penk et al.,

"Adjustment Differences among Male Substance Abusers Varying in Degree of Combat Experience in Vietnam," *Journal of Consulting and Clinical Psychology* 49 (1981): pp. 426–437.

3. Tom Holm, "Indian Veterans of the Vietnam War: Restoring Harmony Through Tribal Ceremony," *Four Winds* 3 (1982): pp. 34–37.

4. *Talking Leaf* 2 (1973): p. 3.

5. *1980 Census of the Population*, vol. 1, *Characteristics of the Population*, chap. C., "General Social and Economic Characteristics." See also Francis Paul Prucha's *Demographic Map of American Indians in the United States* (January 1985). The trend toward the urbanization of American Indians was pointed out quite well in Sam Stanley and Robert K. Thomas, "Current Demographic and Social Trends Among North American Indians," *Annals of the American Academy of Political and Social Science* 436 (1978): pp. 111–120.

6. The interviews and observations took place over approximately 18 months in several Indian communities. The informants (men) were initially contacted through my own friends and relatives living in Oklahoma, Arizona, California, New Mexico, and Wisconsin. Most of the sessions were relaxed, free discussions lasting at times for as long as four hours. The informants were asked general questions about their early lives, their problems, home communities, tribal cultures, their service in Vietnam, why they entered the military, and how they have adjusted since returning from Southeast Asia. In large part, the research was conducted much like ethnological field work and seemed to have served as a catharsis for many of those interviewed.

7. Egendorf et al., *Legacies of Vietnam*, p. 52.

8. Lawrence M. Baskir and William A. Strauss, *Chance and Circumstance: The Draft, the War, and the Vietnam Generation* (New York, 1978), pp. 8–9.

9. Robin A. LaDue, "The Assessment of Post-Traumatic Stress Disorder Among Minority Vietnam Veterans" (Paper presented at the Minority Assessment Conference, Tucson, Ariz., 1983).

10. Alan L. Sorkin, "The Economic Basis of Indian Life," *Annals of the American Academy of Political and Social Science* 436 (1978): pp. 1–12.

11. Quoted in Wilcomb E. Washburn, ed., *The Indian and the White Man* (Garden City, N.Y., 1964), p. 266.

12. Harold Ickes, "Indians Have a Name for Hitler," *Collier's* 113 (1944): p. 58.

13. *Stars and Stripes*, 19 April 1984, p. 3.

14. Egendorf et al., *Legacies of Vietnam*, p. 378.

15. William T. Hagan, *American Indians* (Chicago, 1971), p. 3.

16. Harold E. Driver, *Indians of North America* (Chicago, 1975), p. 322.

17. See G. P. Horsefly, *A History of the True People: the Cherokee Indians* (Detroit, 1979).

18. Driver, *Indians of North America*, p. 317.

19. Commissioner of Indian Affairs, *Annual Report*, 1919, p. 16.

20. See especially James H. Howard, "The Dakota Indian Victory Dance, World War II," *North Dakota History* 18 (1951): pp. 31–40; and Broderick H. Johnson, ed., *Navajos and World War II* (Tsaile, Ariz., 1977).

21. Oswald G. Villard, "Wardship and the Indian," *Christian Century* 61 (1944): p. 397.

22. Johnson, *Navajos and World War II*, pp. 44, 60, 93, 112–113.

23. Tom Holm, "Fighting a White Man's War: The Extent and Legacy of American Indian Participation in World War II," *Journal of Ethnic Studies* 9 (1981): p. 75.

24. Gloria Davis, Marie McCrae, and Michael O'Sullivan, "The Veterans Administration's Responsibility: Financing Prescribed Ceremonials for Navajo Veterans." Position Paper, Veterans Administration Office, Albuquerque, N.M. 1974, p. 5.

25. Tom Holm, "Intergenerational Rapprochement among American Indians: A Study of Thirty-Five Veterans of the Vietnam War," *Journal of Political and Military Sociology* 12 (1984): pp. 161–170.

26. Tom Holm, "The 'Nativization' of the United States Military Service by Some Indian Communities" (Paper presented at Western Social Science Conference. San Diego, Calif., 1984).

27. John P. Wilson, "Conflict, Stress, and Growth: Effects of War on Psychological Development Among Vietnam Veterans, in *Strangers at Home: Vietnam Veterans Since the War*, ed. Charles R. Figley and Seymour Leventman (New York, 1980), pp. 123–165.

28. Statement made at an intertribal powwow in Waukesha, Wis., in March 1979, at which the author was present.

29. Albert L. Wahrhaftig, "More than Mere Work: The Subsistence System of Oklahoma's Cherokee Indians" (Paper presented at Southwestern Anthropological Association Conference, San Francisco, Calif., 1973) p. 4.

30. Ibid., p. 7.

31. Egendorf et al., *Legacies of Vietnam*, p. 329.

32. Quoted in Ethel Nurge, ed., *The Modern Sioux* (Lincoln, Neb., 1970), p. 242.

33. Egendorf et al., *Legacies of Vietnam*, pp. 378–379.

21

Life, Liberty, and the
Right to Protest

James Quay

19 85

I can't recall exactly when the war in Vietnam finally attracted my full attention. I remember a few snapshots from the early years: a Buddhist monk protesting against the South Vietnamese government, seated in the lotus position and burning like a torch; the overthrow and assassination of premier Ngo Dinh Diem three weeks before President Kennedy was assassinated; the alleged attack on U.S. destroyers in the Gulf of Tonkin in August 1964. But Vietnam in general and these events in particular felt remote when I arrived in Lafayette in the fall of 1964. I was supposed to register at my local selective service board when I turned 18—September 26, 1964—but I forgot. In fact, I didn't go for three weeks, but it was no big deal. I never considered not registering and they didn't think my being late meant anything. That wouldn't be true later.

My family were middle-of-the-road Republicans. I favored Nixon over Kennedy in the 1960 election and found good things to say about Barry Goldwater four years later. My junior year in high school, I applied to become a candidate to West Point, the U.S. Military Academy, and took and passed all the necessary tests. I changed my mind before the selection was made, because the only degree offered at West

James Quay is Executive Director of the California Council for the Humanities, whose offices are in San Francisco and Los Angeles. After completing his doctorate in English literature at the University of California, Berkeley, Quay held teaching positions at UC Berkeley and UC Santa Cruz. Subsequently he worked with California Public Radio before assuming his current position. During the war period, Quay exercised conscientious objector status. Since the war, he has been active in encouraging educational opportunities to learn about the war, and has written extensively on the subject. He is currently writing a book about Glendon Waters, a Vietnam War veteran who was killed in combat, whose name was arbitrarily assigned to Quay at an anti-war rally in front of the White House. The essay reproduced here was first given as an address to an undergraduate class at the University of California, Santa Barbara in February 1985, and was first published in the *Lafayette [College] Alumni Quarterly*, Fall 1985, pp. 21–26, and is reprinted here by permission.

Point was a B.A. in science and I didn't want to limit my options. I already had an inkling that West Point might be confining in other ways, but I don't remember having any moral objection to entering the military. As it was, I never had to decide: my congressman selected me only as first alternate and I went to Lafayette instead.

My father had enlisted in 1941 trusting that what his government was telling him about his war was true. That trust between the American government and its people was one of the earliest casualties of the Vietnam war. I can't take time to document all the lies here, but I remember confronting a State Department official who spoke at Lafayette in 1967 or 1968 with some of them. "Look," he told me, "I admit you've been lied to in the past, but you've simply got to believe us now." The lies continued.

Despite the difficulty in gaining an accurate picture about events occurring so far away, it became clear to me that enormous destruction was being visited upon the people of North and South Vietnam, so that finally, whether Vietnam was two countries or one, whether Ho Chi Minh was a communist aggressor or a nationalistic hero, I felt the destruction was incompatible with any proper American objective. Later, during the Tet Offensive of 1968, an American artillery officer said of the village of Ben Tre, "We had to destroy it in order to save it." That sentence crystallized what many came to feel about the war. If we were destroying South Vietnam in order to save it in the name of freedom, what and who would be left to be free?

What provoked my private reservations into public opposition was an incident in Lafayette. When an official from the South Vietnamese embassy came to speak at Marquis Hall in May 1967, a dozen people I knew stood peacefully in front of the building with signs that read "Stop the Bombing." I regret I was not one of them. For this, they were surrounded by hundreds of fraternity boys and bombarded for hours with water, ink, and verbal abuse. The campus police were strangely absent. A rally was organized to support the right of free speech: my first demonstration was for the First Amendment.

Everything I read and heard about the war violated my deepest patriotism, my pride in what this country stood for in the world, until I resolved that the American thing to do was to oppose the war. I wrote to my congressmen and received polite replies urging me to support the President. I joined The Committee Against the Crime of Silence and put my name on record at the United Nations as opposing my government's war in Vietnam. I wrote editorials for the *Lafayette* and took part in demonstrations. Today, the mention of anti-war demonstrations conjures pictures of mighty throngs of people choking the streets of major cities and chanting slogans, but at the beginning it was different. I remember joining a dozen other students and faculty members on Saturdays in the town square of Easton to stand for one hour in silent witness, protesting the war. The people who passed us were not always friendly; we were reminding them of unpleasant events far away, and many mistook our opposition to the war as opposition to the country. One Sunday I handed out leaflets at a Methodist Church and then attended the worship service, only to hear myself denounced as a "tool of the Moscow line" by the minister. It was the beginning of my education into the nature and power of governmental authority.

You see, at the beginning, I thought persuading my fellow citizens would be easy. All Americans were being lied to by their government, so all we had to do was discover the truth, reveal what was really going on in Vietnam, and the American people would rise up and demand that their government stop the war. But I came to see that the reason many Americans supported the war wasn't because they had analyzed the government's policy and approved it, but simply because they trusted whatever their government said about the war and refused to believe their government's authority should be opposed. How could the country that had saved the world from Hitler now be fighting an immoral war? In arguments repeated in homes all over the country, objections to the war were met with the reply: "The President knows more than we do. This is a democracy. We have to support the President."

Fortunately for me and for all anti-war protestors, this country was created out of resistance to governmental authority. The Declaration of Independence, after all, tells every American that the time may come when it is not only his right to rebel against his government, but his duty. The tradition of conscientious objection to war is even older, arriving with the first Quakers in 1635. James Madison, one of the architects of the U.S. Constitution, proposed making objection to war a constitutional right. It was defeated, but so were all proposals for national conscription for the first generation of this country's existence. In short, conscientious objection is as American as cherry pie.

In the spring of 1967 I told my parents that I was planning to become a conscientious objector. I remember that my parents were concerned but not opposed—mostly I think they were baffled. In a journal that I kept at the time, I noted my father's silence. I was rejecting the course of action he had taken in World War II and he could not help me. He could show me how a man does what his government asks of him: he could not show me how to oppose that government. But my father did me a very great kindness: he knew a member of the local draft board, and from that day in 1967 until the board made its decision a year later, my father made a point *not* to mention my case to his friend. Though I was making a choice he would not have made, he allowed me to make my own decision and face its consequences without angry threats or benign interference. I had friends who were not so lucky.

"I can understand the anguish of the younger generation," Henry Kissinger told an interviewer in 1969. "They lack models, they have no heroes, they see no great purposes in the world. But conscientious objection is destructive of society. . . . Conscientious objection must be reserved only for the greatest moral issues, and Vietnam is not of this magnitude." Kissinger could not be more mistaken. It was only by actively opposing the war and choosing to be a conscientious objector that I was able to find role models I could admire, to discover a new group of heroes to replace John Wayne, and to join my small individual efforts to one of the greatest purposes of this or any other time—peace.

My claim to conscientious objector status was not based on traditional religious beliefs. In fact, I had been interviewed by the Lafayette alumni magazine in an article on campus religious life and quoted as an example of an agnostic. Until 1965, you could only be released from military service if you could demonstrate that your opposition to participation in war was by reason of "religious training or belief." But in 1965 the Supreme Court had ruled that a person could not be denied C.O. status simply because he did not belong to an orthodox religious sect. It was enough, the high Court ruled, if the belief which prompted your objection occupied the same place in your life as the belief in a traditional deity occupied in the life of a believer. I have only just discovered that the Court's opinion cites several authors that I had read in a freshman religion course at Lafayette, among them, theologian Paul Tillich:

> And if the word [God] has not much meaning for you, translate it, and speak of the depths of your life, of the source of your being, of your ultimate concern, of what you take seriously without any reservation. Perhaps, in order to do so, you must forget everything traditional that you have learned about God.

I knew I objected to the war in Vietnam. What I had to discover was the ultimate source of that objection and describe it for myself and for the five ordinary Americans that comprised draft board #90 in Allentown, Pennsylvania, in the space provided on Special Form 150. That form asked: "Describe the nature of your belief which is the basis of your claim and state whether or not your belief in a Supreme Being involves duties which to you are superior to those arising from any human relation." Though I would phrase things differently today, I find I still essentially believe what I wrote 17 years ago:

> I affirm that love and justice are the essence of a Supreme Being and that every human being is divine in that he has love and justice within him to some degree. I sincerely believe that the principles of love and justice with which men have constructed their gods and their governments reside in each man. I affirm the divinity of every human being. The more a man demonstrates these two divine attributes in his daily living, the more divine he himself will become.
>
> Because I believe that from man all awareness and order comes, because I believe that each man is a divine being striving to become more divine, and because I believe that divinity manifests itself only through the love and justice of human relationships, I believe that human relationships are the highest relationships. Therefore there are no duties which to me are superior to those arising from human relations.

The Vietnam War and the draft of men to fight that war forced hundreds of thousands of young men to ask themselves what values they were willing to suffer and die for, at an age when they are just learning to think for themselves about such matters. Those who had to make that choice discovered the Authority they were willing to obey, be it the authority of family, church, public opinion, or government. To use Tillich's phrase, in choosing we learned what our ultimate concerns were, the nature of the gods we worshipped. For many, the consequences of their choices were harsh and lasting. Some of us found out that our gods were lifeless idols. Some of us found out that our gods were very much alive.

As I worked on Special Form 150 in early 1968, the government indicted Dr. Benjamin Spock and others for counseling young men to resist the draft. The USS Pueblo was seized by North Korea. The Tet Offensive brought an end to American optimism about the war. In March, peace candidate Eugene McCarthy nearly defeated Lyndon Johnson in the New Hampshire primary. Robert Kennedy announced his candidacy for president. I filed for conscientious objector status on the first day of spring, 1968. No one knew it, but old men, women, and children had just been massacred by American soldiers at My Lai. Two weeks later President Johnson announced he would not run for office. Five days after that Martin Luther King was assassinated in Memphis. Three weeks later, while students occupied the President's Office at Columbia University, at a small demonstration on my campus, a young man had his head grazed by a pellet shot from a local fraternity house. I graduated in late May. A week later, my fiancée and I went to New York City to look for an apartment. That night peace candidate Robert Kennedy was assassinated in Los Angeles.

It felt as though the country were having a nervous breakdown.

I did not know what I would do if the draft board refused my claim to C.O. status. I did know I would not enter the armed forces. I felt I was prepared to go to prison rather than flee to Canada, but fortunately I never had to find out. On June 14, Flag Day, my draft board informed me that I had been classified "1–0" (Conscientious Objector). I was further informed that they did not expect to receive any call for draftees until the fall, which meant I could sit it out and possibly not be called. Instead I volunteered for two years' alternate service as a caseworker with the New York City Department of Social Services, who assigned me a caseload of families in central Harlem. All around me, young men were going to war and to prison; I did not want to avoid service on a technicality. So I became one of 170,000 men who were granted conscientious objector status during the Vietnam War and one of 96,000 who completed the two years' alternative service.

There is a figure who haunted me then: Adolf Eichmann, a Nazi who helped coordinate the trains that carried Jews to the death camps during World War II. He fled to Argentina after the war, but in 1961 the Israeli secret police located and kidnapped him to Israel. He stood trial in Jerusalem for his role in the murder of thousands of Jews, even though, he protested, he had never personally killed a Jew. A political theorist named Hannah Arendt covered the trial for the *New Yorker* magazine and in a subsequent book, entitled *Eichmann in Jerusalem: A Report on the Banality of Evil*, explored the question of how six million human beings could be systematically killed by other human beings. What we learn is that something as abominable as the Holocaust is not accomplished by villains—there are not enough villains in the world to accomplish such horrors. No, the terrible news of that book is that crimes of this magnitude are only possible when ordinary men and women do what they're told. What Arendt found at the heart of Eichmann's deeds was—nothing. In Arendt's words, he was "thoughtless," he literally had no thoughts of his own that mattered, rather he acted in accordance with the thoughts of others.

Eichmann, like the Nazis who were tried by the Allies immediately after World War II, defended himself by saying that he was simply following orders. But at the trial in Nuremburg, the Allied judges ruled that the fact that a person acted under the orders of his government or of a superior did not relieve him of responsibility, provided a moral choice was possible. All along the chain of command that led from Hitler to the death camps were ordinary people like Eichmann who were just following orders. While I do not equate the war in Vietnam, destructive of life as it was, with the Nazi Holocaust, I came to see that Americans, too, could be content to follow orders, unmindful of the devastating impact their ordinary actions here at home had on others far away. This discovery disturbed me then; it disturbs me still.

In November 1969 my wife and I went to Washington, D.C. to join the March Against Death. In subfreezing temperatures we marched with candles from the Washington Memorial to the White House with 40,000 others, each with the name of an American killed in Vietnam around our necks. At the end of the march, each of us stood on a small wooden platform and shouted that name at the White House.

GLENDON WATERS

All I knew then about Glendon Waters was that he was from Texas. I know now that he was killed in July 1967—about the time I began protesting the war—and that his name is on the Vietnam Veterans' Memorial.

Why are those names so moving? Why do visitors to the Memorial reach up and touch the names? Why do I, after 15 years, still remember a name I spoke but once and whose owner I never knew? Because a name brings the person closer, makes it easier to remember that casualty figures contain the final news about a particular being, a lover, a son, a father, a brother, whose death brought terrible grief to his family. Often mere numbers make us numb. We must try hard not to become numb. So "Glendon Waters" is what I say instead of 59,000 dead. Glendon Waters died in Vietnam.

We have to break the cycle of men like Glendon Waters. I believe that means breaking the cycle of unquestioning obedience to authority, as I have suggested. It means fashioning a new model of manhood. And finally, it means we have to imagine more concretely and sympatheti- cally the lives of others. In the movie *Hearts and Minds,* we are shown a former Air Force pilot who sits on his porch. We have heard him describing how insulated he was in his airconditioned B-52 cockpit from the death and destruction he caused below. He tells us that he did not drop napalm but that he dropped worse: CBUs (cluster bomb units), bombs that explode sending nearly 200,000 steel balls one- quarter inch in diameter into any human beings unfortunate enough to be nearby. He tells us that he has a three-year-old son and that now, if he tries to imagine the feelings of a Vietnamese father seeing his three-year-old hit by the bombs he dropped. . . .

Well, he can't finish the sentence, he breaks down under the horror of that vision. Now that he has a son, he can imagine what it would be like. He can imagine concretely the human dimensions of the damage he inflicted so thoughtlessly before. If he had been encouraged to imagine this before he climbed into his plane, before he entered the Air Force, if 18-year-old boys were forced to consider the consequences of their actions as soldiers, if those at home were forced to imagine what we ask our soldiers to do, they might be more reluctant to leave and we more reluctant to send them off to kill.

I have a son, eight years old, named Jesse, and a daughter, three, named Jenny. I held them both within minutes of their birth. I love them more than I love my own life. I cannot imagine any cause that would justify their deaths. And I cannot imagine any cause that would justify the deaths of someone else's children. Yet that is what modern warfare means. In Vietnam, Cambodia, Laos, Biafra, Angola, Iran/ Iraq, Afghanistan, El Salvador, Nicaragua, soldiers have not just killed soldiers; willingly or unwillingly, knowingly or unknowingly, they have killed women and children. There is no cause noble enough to justify the deaths of innocent women and children. None.

Opposition to killing must begin before war begins. The crucial moment in the passage from civilian life to military life is called "induction." The word comes from the Latin meaning "to be led into." At a certain point, you are asked to take a step forward. You can't be forced to take that step and no matter how many others step forward with you, it is a step only you can take or refuse to take. Once you take that step you enter a world where you are expected to obey all lawful commands given to you, no matter what your personal objections might be. I can understand the courage that it takes to obey, especially when you consider that such obedience might ultimately cost you your life.

That is the step I refused to take. While I felt my country had the right to require service of me, I denied it the right to order me to kill other human beings. That is a step I hope that all of us might one day refuse to take.

22

What Did You Do in the Class War, Daddy?

James Fallows

Many people think that the worst scars of the war years have healed. I don't. Vietnam has left us with a heritage rich in possibilities for class warfare, and I would like to start telling about it with this story:

In the fall of 1969, I was beginning my final year in college. As the months went by, the rock on which I had unthinkingly anchored my hopes—the certainty that the war in Vietnam would be over before I could possibly fight—began to crumble. It shattered altogether on Thanksgiving weekend when, while riding back to Boston from a visit with my relatives, I heard that the draft lottery had been held and my birthdate had come up number 45. I recognized for the first time that, inflexibly, I must either be drafted or consciously find a way to prevent it.

In the atmosphere of that time, each possible choice came equipped with barbs. To answer the call was unthinkable, not only because, in my heart, I was desperately afraid of being killed, but also because, among my friends, it was axiomatic that one should not be "complicit" in the immoral war effort. Draft resistance, the course chosen by a few noble heroes of the movement, meant going to prison or leaving the country. With much the same intensity with which I wanted to stay alive, I did not want those things either. What I wanted was to go to graduate school, to get married, and to enjoy those bright prospects I had been taught that life owed me.

I learned quickly enough that there was only one way to get what I wanted. A physical deferment would restore things to the happy state I had known during four undergraduate years. The barbed alter-

James Fallows was an undergraduate student at Harvard in 1969, when he was called to report to the Draft Board in the Boston Navy Yard. This essay, describing that ordeal, was published in *The Washington Monthly*, October 1975. Subsequently Fallows worked in Washington in the Carter administration, then became an editor of *The Atlantic Monthly* as well as the author of National Defense (1981) and other books and essays.

natives would be put off. By the impartial dictates of public policy I would be free to pursue the better side of life.

Like many of my friends whose numbers had come up wrong in the lottery, I set about securing my salvation. When I was not participating in anti-war rallies, I was poring over the Army's code of physical regulations. During the winter and early spring, seminars were held in the college common rooms. There, sympathetic medical students helped us search for disqualifying conditions that we, in our many years of good health, might have overlooked. Although, on the doctors' advice, I made a half-hearted try at fainting spells, my only real possibility was beating the height and weight regulations. My normal weight was close to the cut-off point for an "underweight" disqualification, and, with a diligence born of panic, I made sure I would have a margin. I was six-feet-one-inch tall at the time. On the morning of the draft physical I weighed 120 pounds.

Before sunrise that morning I rode the subway to the Cambridge city hall, where we had been told to gather for shipment to the examination at the Boston Navy Yard. The examinations were administered on a rotating basis, one or two days each month for each of the draft boards in the area. Virtually everyone who showed up on Cambridge day at the Navy Yard was a student from Harvard or MIT.

There was no mistaking the political temperament of our group. Many of my friends wore red arm bands and stop-the-war buttons. Most chanted the familiar words, "Ho, Ho, Ho Chi Minh/NLF is Gonna Win." One of the things we had learned from the draft counselors was that disruptive behavior at the examination was a worthwhile political goal, not only because it obstructed the smooth operation of the "criminal war machine," but also because it might impress the examiners with our undesirable character traits. As we climbed into the buses and as they rolled toward the Navy Yard, about half of the young men brought the chants to a crescendo. The rest of us sat rigid and silent, clutching x-rays and letters from our doctors at home.

Inside the Navy Yard, we were first confronted by a young sergeant from Long Beach, a former surfer boy no older than the rest of us and seemingly unaware that he had an unusual situation on his hands. He started reading out instructions for the intelligence tests when he was hooted down. He went out to collect his lieutenant, who clearly had been through a Cambridge day before. "We've got all the time in the world," he said, and let the chanting go on for two or three minutes. "When we're finished with you, you can go, and not a minute before."

From that point on the disruption became more purposeful and individual, largely confined to those who deferment strategies were based on anti-authoritarian psychiatric traits. Twice I saw students walk up to young orderlies—whose hands were extended to receive the required cup of urine—and throw the vial in the orderlies' faces. The orderlies looked up, initially more astonished than angry, and went back to towel themselves off. Most of the rest of us trod quietly through the paces, waiting for the moment of confrontation when the final examiner would give his verdict. I had stepped on the scales at the very beginning of the examination. Desperate at seeing the orderly write down 122 pounds, I hopped back on and made sure that he lowered it to 120. I walked in a trance through the rest of the examination, until the final meeting with the fatherly physician who ruled on marginal cases such as mine. I stood there in socks and underwear, arms wrapped around me in the chilly building. I knew as I looked at the doctor's face that he understood exactly what I was doing.

"Have you ever contemplated suicide?" he asked after he finished looking over my chart. My eyes darted up to his. "Oh, suicide—yes, I've been feeling very unstable and unreliable recently." He looked at me, staring until I returned my eyes to the ground. He wrote "unqualified" on my folder, turned on his heel, and left. I was overcome by a wave of relief, which for the first time revealed to me how great my terror had been, and by the beginning of the sense of shame which remains with me to this day.

It was, initially, a generalized shame at having gotten away with my deception, but it came into sharper focus later in the day. Even as the last of the Cambridge contingent was throwing its urine and deliberately failing its color-blindness tests, buses from the next board began to arrive. These bore the boys from Chelsea, thick, dark-haired young men, the white proles of Boston. Most of them were younger than us, since they had just left high school, and it had clearly never occurred to them that there might be a way around the draft. They walked through the examination lines like so many cattle off to slaughter. I tried to avoid noticing, but the results were inescapable. While perhaps four out of five of my friends from Harvard were being deferred, just the opposite was happening to the Chelsea boys.

We returned to Cambridge that afternoon, not in government buses but as free individuals, liberated and victorious. The talk was high-spirited, but there was something close to the surface that none of us wanted to mention. We knew now who would be killed.

As other memories of the war years have faded, it is that day in the Navy Yard that will not leave my mind. The answers to the other grand questions about the war have become familiar as any catechism. Q. What were America's sins? A. The Arrogance of Power, the Isolation of the Presidency, the Burden of Colonialism, and the Failure of Technological Warfare. In the abstract, at least, we have learned those lessons. For better or worse, it will be years before we again cheer a president who talks about paying any price and bearing any burden to prop up some spurious overseas version of democracy.

We have not, however, learned the lesson of the day at the Navy Yard, or the thousands of similar scenes all across the country through all the years of the war. Five years later, two questions have yet to be faced, let alone answered. The first is why, when so many of the bright young college men opposed the war, so few were willing to resist the draft, rather than simply evade it. The second is why all the well-educated presumably humane young men, whether they opposed the war or were thinking fondly of A-bombs on Hanoi, so willingly took advantage of this most brutal form of class discrimination—what it signifies that we let the boys from Chelsea be sent off to die.

The "we" that I refer to are the mainly-white, mainly-well-educated children of mainly-comfortable parents, who are now mainly embarked on promising careers in law, medicine, business, academics. What makes them a class is that they all avoided the draft by taking one of the thinking-man's routes to escape. These included the physical deferment, by far the smartest and least painful of all; the long technical appeals through the legal jungles of the Selective Service System; the more disingenuous resorts to conscientious objector status; and, one degree further down the scale of personal inconvenience, joining the Reserves or the National Guard. I am not talking about those who, on the one hand, submitted to the draft and took their chances in the trenches, nor, on the other hand, those who paid the price of formal draft resistance or exile.

That there is such a class, identifiable as "we," was brought home to me by comparing the very different fates of the different sorts of people I had known in high school and college. Hundreds from my high school were drafted and nearly two dozen killed. When I look at the memorial roll of names, I find that I recognize very few, for they were mainly the anonymous Mexican-American (as they were called at the time) and poor whites I barely knew in high school and forgot altogether when I left. Several people from my high school left the country; one that I know of went to jail. By comparison, of two or three hundred acquaintances from college and afterwards, I can think of only three who actually fought in Vietnam. Another dozen or so served in safer precincts of the military, and perhaps five went through the ordeal of formal resistance. The rest escaped in one or another. . . . There are those who contend that the world has always worked this way, and perhaps that is true. The question is why, especially in the atmosphere of the late sixties, people with any presumptions to character could have let it go on.

First we should consider the conduct of those who opposed the war. Not everyone at Harvard felt that way, nor, I suspect, did even a majority of the people throughout the country who found painless ways to escape the draft. But I did, and most of the people I knew did, and so did the hordes we always ran into at the anti-war rallies. Yet most of us managed without difficulty to stay out of jail. The tonier sorts of anti-war literature contained grace-note references to Gandhi and Thoreau—no CO application would have been complete without them—but the practical model for our wartime conduct was our enemy, LBJ, who weaseled away from the front lines during World War II.

It may be worth emphasizing why our failure to resist induction is such an important issue. Five years after Cambodia and Kent State it is clear how the war could have lasted so long. Johnson and Nixon both knew that the fighting could continue only so long as the vague, hypothetical benefits of holding off Asian communism outweighed the immediate, palpable domestic pain. They knew that when the screaming grew too loud and too many sons had been killed, the game would be all over. That is why Vietnamization was such a godsend for Nixon, and it is also why our reluctance to say No helped prolong the war. The more we guaranteed that we would end up neither in uniform nor behind bars, the more we made sure that *our* class of people would be spared the real cost of the war. Not that we didn't suffer. There was, of course, the *angst*, the terrible moral malaise we liked to write about so much in the student newspapers and undergraduate novels.

The children of the bright, good parents were spared the more immediate sort of suffering that our inferiors were undergoing. And because of that, when our parents were opposed to the war, they were opposed in a bloodless, theoretical fashion, as they might be opposed to political corruption or racism in South Africa. As long as the little gold stars kept going to homes in Chelsea and the backwoods of West Virginia, the mothers of Beverly Hills and Chevy Chase and Great Neck and Belmont were not on the telephones to their congressmen, screaming *you killed my boy*, they were not writing to the President that his crazy, wrong, evil war had put their boys in prison and ruined their careers. It is clear by now that if the men of Harvard had wanted to do the very most they could to help shorten the war, they should have been drafted or imprisoned en masse.

This was not such a difficult insight, even at the time. Lyndon Johnson clearly understood it, which was the main reason why the *graduate school* deferment, that grotesque of class discrimination, lasted through the big mobilizations of the war, until the springtime

218 / Diversities of Experience

of 1968. What is interesting is how little of this whole phenomenon we at Harvard pretended to understand. On the day after the graduate school deferments were snatched away from us, a day Johnson must have dreaded because it added another set of nasty enemies to his list, the Harvard *Crimson* responded with a magnificently representative editorial entitled "The Axe Falls." A few quotes convey its gist:

"The axiom that this nation's tangled Selective Service System is bound to be unfair to somebody fell with a crash on the Harvard community yesterday. The National Security Council's draft directive put almost all college seniors and most graduate students at the head of the line for next year's draft calls. Three-fourths of the second-year law class will go off to war. . . . Yesterday's directive is a bit of careless expediency, clearly unfair to the students who would have filled the nation's graduate schools next fall."

That was it, the almost incredible level of understanding and compassion we displayed at the time—the idea that the real victims of General Hershey's villainous schemes were *the students who would have filled the nation's graduate schools next fall.* Occasionally, both in the *Crimson* and elsewhere, there were bows to the discriminatory nature of the whole 2–S deferment system and the virtues of the random lottery which Edward Kennedy, to his eternal credit, was supporting almost singlehandedly at the time. But there was no mistaking which emotions came from the heart, which principles really seemed worth fighting for.

It would be unfair to suggest that absolutely no thought was given to the long-run implications of our actions. For one thing, there were undercurrents of the sentiment that another *Crimson* writer, James Glassman, expressed in an article early in 1968. "Two years ago, Harvard students complained that the system was highly discriminatory, favoring the well off," Glassman wrote. "They called the 2–S an unfair advantage for those who could go to college." But, as the war wore on, "the altruism was forgotten. What was most important now was saving your own skin—preventing yourself from being in a position where you would have to kill a man you had no right to kill."

Moreover, a whole theoretical framework was developed to justify draft evasion. During many of the same meetings where I heard about the techniques of weight reduction, I also learned that we should think of ourselves as sand in the gears of the great war machine. During one of those counseling sessions I sat through a speech by Michael Ferber, then something of a celebrity as a codefendant in the trial of Dr. Spock. He excited us by revealing how close we were to victory. Did we realize that the draft machine was tottering towards its ultimate breakdown? That it was hardly in better condition than old General Hershey himself? That each body we withheld from its ravenous appetite brought it that much nearer the end? Our duty, therefore, was clear: as committed opponents of the war, we had a responsibility to save ourselves from the war machine.

This argument was most reassuring, for it meant that the course of action which kept us alive and out of jail was also the politically correct decision. The boys of Chelsea were not often mentioned during these sessions: when they were, regret was expressed that they had not yet understood the correct approach to the draft. We resolved to launch political-education programs, some under the auspices of the Worker-Student Alliance, to help straighten them out. In the meantime, there was the physical to prepare for.

It does not require enormous powers of analysis to see the basic fraudulence of this argument. General Hershey was never in danger of running out of bodies, and the only thing we were denying him was the chance to put *us* in uniform. With the same x-ray vision that enabled us to see, in every Pentagon sub-clerk, in every Honeywell accountant, an embryonic war criminal, we could certainly have seen that by keeping ourselves away from both frying pan and fire we were prolonging the war and consigning the Chelsea boys to danger and death. But somehow the x-rays were deflected.

There was, I believe, one genuine concern which provided the x-ray shield and made theories like Ferber's go down more easily. It was a monstrous war, not only in its horror but in the sense that it was beyond control, and to try to fight it as individuals was folly. Even as we knew that a thousand, or ten thousand, college boys going to prison might make a difference, we knew with equal certainty that the imprisonment and ruination of any one of us would mean nothing at all. The irrational war machine would grind on as if we had never existed, and our own lives would be pointlessly spoiled. From a certain perspective, it could even seem like grandstanding, an exercise in excessive piety, to go to the trouble of resisting the draft. The one moral issue that was within our control was whether we would actually participate—whether, as Glassman put it, we would be forced to kill—and we could solve that issue as easily by getting a deferment as by passing the time in jail. . . .

Lord Jim spent the rest of his days trying to expiate his moment of cowardice aboard the *Patna*. The contemporaries of Oliver Wendell Holmes felt permanent discomfort that Holmes, virtually alone among his peers, had volunteered to fight in the Civil War. I have neither of those feelings about Vietnam, so they are not the reason I feel it important to dredge up these hulks. Rather, the exercise can serve two purposes—to tell us about the past, and to tell us about the present.

The lesson of the past concerns the complexities of human motivation. Doubtless because the enemy we were fighting was so horrible in its effects, there was very little room for complexity or ambiguity in the anti-war campaigns. On the black and white spectrum by which we judged personal conduct, bureaucrats were criminals if they stayed inside the government and politicians cowards if they failed to vote for resolutions to end the war; the businessmen of Dow and Honeywell were craven merchants of death, and we, meanwhile, were nothing less than the insistent voice of morality, striving tirelessly to bring the country to its senses . . .

Of course we were right to try to stop the war. But I recall no suggestion during the sixties that it was graceless, *wrong* of us to ask the Foreign Service Officers to resign when we were not sticking our necks out at the induction center . . . If nothing else, a glance back at our own record might give us an extra grain of sympathy for the difficulties of bringing men to honor, let alone glory.

The implications for the present are less comforting and go back to the question asked several pages ago. The behavior of the upper classes in so deftly avoiding the war's pains is both a symptom and a partial cause of the class hatred now so busily brewing in the country.

The starting point for understanding this class hatred is the belief, resting just one layer beneath the pro forma comments about the unfortunate discrimination of the 2–S system, that there was an ultimate justice to our fates. You could not live through those years without knowing what was going on with the draft, and you could not retain your sanity with that knowledge unless you believed, at some dark layer of the moral substructure, that we were somehow getting what we deserved. A friend of mine, a former Rhodes scholar now embarked on a wonderful career in corporate law, put the point more bluntly than most when he said, "There are certain people who can do more good in a lifetime in politics or academics or medicine than by getting killed in a trench"; in one form or another, it was that belief which kept us all going. What is so significant about this statement is not the recognition of the difference in human abilities—for that, after all, has been one of the grand constants of the race—but the utter disdain for the abilities, hopes, complexities of those who have not scrambled onto the high road. The one-dimensional meritocracy of Aldous Huxley's *Brave New World* is not so many steps away from the fashion in which we were content to distribute the burden of the war. . . .

The "movement" of the sixties extended from the civil rights struggle through the campaign to end the war, and there was continuity as well in its view of the lower class. By the end of the sixties, when the anti-war campaign was going full steam, it exhibited contempt for the white proles in three clear ways. One was paying so little attention to the rate at which the Chelsea boys were dying; we mentioned the casualty rates, but not the fact that it wasn't our type of people being killed. The second was the bullying, supercilious tone which said that to support the war was not so much incorrect as *stupid*. (Recall how quickly arguments about the war reached the pedant's level with the question, "Have you read . . . ? It you haven't read . . . how can you presume to say anything?") And the third, rivaling even the first in ugliness, was the quick resort to the phrase "pig" for the blue-collar, lower-class people who were doing the job they thought they were supposed to do. They had been the "pigs" holding down the black people in Mississippi, the children of the pigs were being sent off to die in Vietnam, and now "pigs" were clubbing our chosen people, the demonstrators, in Chicago. We hated the pigs, and let them know it, and it was no great wonder that they hated us in return.

Now that the war is over, there is a fourth demonstration of our contempt for the proles. Among any high-brow audience, it is scarcely possible to attract a minute's attention on the subject of Vietnam veterans. Ralph Nader sponsored a study of their predicament, written by Paul Starr, but apart from that the intelligentsia has virtually willed them out of existence. The indignities they suffer rival those of any other oppressed group, but the only magazine to give sustained attention to this fact is *Penthouse*. On television the veterans are painted with extremely unflattering strokes—as war-time junkies or pathological killers who keep re-enacting the massacres they took part in—but no protests are heard about this crude stereotyping. The most frequently offered explanation for the neglect of the veteran is the *kind* of war we fought, and our eagerness to forget it. No doubt that is partly true. But our behavior is also shaped by *who* the veterans are. They are the boys from Chelsea, and if we were embarrassed to see them at the Navy Yard, when their suffering was only prospective, how much more must we shun them now?

23

A Nurse's View
Rose Sandecki

My uncle Frank had been in the Marines during World War II, an uncle that I was very close to, my mother's youngest brother. When he came back from the Marines, at age thirty-six, he went into the Franciscan Seminary to become a priest—came back from Iwo Jima a changed man. He went through a severe depression and as a result couldn't finish the seminary. He then lived in my grandmother's house and when I was a freshman in high school, my uncle took a gun and killed himself. He died because of changes in his behavior brought on by the war. I guess you could call it PTSD from World War II, and it was a classic case of it. That is probably one of the reasons I'm doing this kind of work now, because of my personal feelings about what happened in my family as a result of war.

I was feeling somewhat restless in Buffalo. I had been in nursing about seven years, having graduated from a three-year nursing school and then gone back to school to get my BS in nursing. I had a couple of job opportunities, but none of them were that exciting to me. That was in the spring of '68, and the war was really building up. I remember watching the news every night, seeing in full, glorious color the stretchers with the young guys on them, really torn up, coming off the dustoffs. I felt I had some talents as a registered nurse, a professional nurse, and probably could offer something to those young men over there.

Going into the military was not my first choice. I wanted to go over as a civilian. Checked out agencies like AID and Tom Dooley's medical organization, and every one of those was a two-year contract, and it was working strictly with Vietnamese. That was not why I wanted to go to Vietnam.

I went down to the Navy recruiter and was told I was too old (I was twenty-six or twenty-seven). The Air Force told me I would have to

Rose Sandecki served in Vietnam as an Army Nurse in the 12th Evacuation Hospital at Cu Chi and worked too in the hospital in Da Nang. After the war she became the first woman veteran to be appointed a Team Leader in a Veterans Center. Hers was the Vet Center in Concord, California. This essay is included in Keith Walker's, *A Piece of my Heart* (Novato, Calif: Presidio Press, 1985). Sandecki is an acknowledged leader among women veterans of the war, having served on the Advisory Committee of the Readjustment Counseling Program of the Veterans Administration in Washington, D.C., and a frequent lecturer on college campuses.

spend at least one year in the States before they would train me as a flight nurse, to go over to Vietnam. I said "I want to go as soon as I can, while I feel like it, while I've got the spirit that has moved me." Only the Army would guarantee that I could be over within a certain period of time. So much so that they had the recruiter on the phone from Buffalo to Washington, D.C., letting me talk to the individuals there with a guarantee that I would be in Vietnam within three months. And that did happen indeed.

I went to the 12th Evac Hospital at Cu Chi. My first job was a head nurse, surgical intensive care unit, recovery room. I was a captain—because I had seven years' experience in nursing and a bachelor's degree when I joined the Army. And in days of war they give rank out like candy. I had very little experience in recovery and no experience in surgical intensive care units. I had graduated from nursing school in 1960 when ICUs weren't around. They were just starting to be thought about. When I was told my assignment would be head nurse of this ward, I said, "No, I don't want that," because I'd never set foot in an ICU. I quickly learned you never say no in the Army; I had this job whether I wanted it or not.

I couldn't believe the numbers of people coming in, the numbers of beds and the kinds of injuries that I saw in front of me—I really wasn't prepared for that. This was in October of '68, it was what they called "post-Tet"—after the Tet offensive—but it was extremely busy. As head nurse, my job was basically to see to it that all patients were taken care of as efficiently and quickly and in the best care possible. The Medical Corps's motto was, and still is, I guess, "Preserve the fighting strength." The idea of working in a military hospital is to patch up the soldier so he can go back to the battle again. It was the whole theme of what was going on over there. It wouldn't be unusual for guys to come in with multiple frag wounds, be treated, go to surgery and have the tissue around the injury debrided, then be sent to Japan, where they would undergo a DPC (delayed primary closure) of this open wound, and then be sent back to duty. As long as an individual didn't lose a leg, arm, or an eye, as long as they were walking, they would go back to the boonies. So my job as head nurse was to make sure the patients were taken care of—always helping. I mean, I didn't sit behind a desk and order the junior nurses or corpsmen around. I was pitching in with the rest of them.

When I look back on it, I was naive when I walked through those doors. I learned a lot very quickly, seeing the types of casualties and the number of them. They were all so young. Seeing this on a daily basis twelve to fourteen hours a day, six or seven days a week, I think that I became somewhat callous and bitter. You also learned that you became almost like a commodity because you were a woman. After working twelve-hour shifts with all the blood and gore, you would change into a civilian dress to go to one of the local officers' club. We were chauffeured in helicopters, with the guns on the side, that would take six or seven of us up to an officers' club. You couldn't sit still, just have a drink and relax. There would be one guy after another coming up and more or less doing his number on you: "I haven't seen a round-eye in six months. Would you dance with me?" You'd say. "No, I'm tired. I just want to sit and put my feet up." They wouldn't take no for an answer and would play this guilt thing like, "God, you don't know how bad I'm feeling. Just one dance, that's all." So you would dance and drink until two or three in the morning, then at six go back to the blood and guts of the war again. The initial two or three months was getting used to the pace of the twelve to thirteen hours of work and then the three or four hours of play. And it was a pressure kind of play because if you didn't go to the officers' club there was something wrong with you. If you stayed back in your hooch by yourself or stayed and talked to a couple of the other nurses, you were accused of being a lesbian, or you would be accused of having an affair with one of the doctors. You know, you are damned if you do and damned if you don't. After a period of four or five months, I decided that I really didn't care what people said about me. If I choose not to go to these clubs and parties, I'm not going to do it . . . and I probably became somewhat of a recluse. So those are some of the changes that I went through personally in Vietnam.

The way of dealing with the sheer amount of patients, the long hours in the hospital, was by putting up a wall, the emotional numbing that we talk about. I think it built up over a period of time. Each day I went in and the more I saw, the thicker this wall became; it was sort of a skin protecting me from what was going on. Look at it from the point of view of a patient: how would you, as a patient, feel if you had this hysterical nurse that was crying and sobbing because there is someone in there that is badly maimed or is going to die? We had to be effective for the next people that were coming in. Nurses are trained to take care of other people, not look at their own feelings and what is going on with them. That is part of the medical profession.

A story from Cu Chi, another example of the sort of rude awakening to my military naiveté. I got a phone call on the ward from the chief nurse, saying, "You've got a patient there that is going to get an award. Make sure that the bed has clean sheets, the area is straightened up, and the ward looks good." Which really turned me off to begin with: Let's clean up the ward because we've got VIPs coming in. Well, the VIP happened to be the general of the 25th Infantry Division along with his aide and an entourage of about twelve people. And this patient, when he came through the recovery room the day before, had remembered me. This was his second visit to us. He had been there three months before with frag wounds, had been sent back to the jungle, and came back this time with both of his legs blown off—he was all of about twenty years old. When he was waking up from the anesthesia, he remembered me. He starting kidding me about how I had made him cough and deep-breathe so he wouldn't come down with pneumonia. We were kidding around, and he said, "Don't you remember me, ma'am? I said, "Oh, yeah." But I really didn't because there were just so many of them. . . . The entourage was coming to give him an award because he happened to be number twenty thousand to come through the 12th Evac Hospital. In 1968 there were twenty-four Army evac hospitals in Vietnam, and he was number *twenty thousand* through *one* of twenty-four Army hospitals. We are not talking about the Air Force hospitals, the Navy hospitals . . . but twenty thousand through one hospital. So, for this distinction, the general comes in and gives him a watch. They have this little ceremony, give him a Purple Heart and the watch. I'm standing off in the corner watching all this, and as the general handed him the watch—"From the 25th Infantry Division as a token of our appreciation"—the kid more or less flings the watch back at him and says something like, "I can't accept this, sir: it's not going to help me walk." I couldn't really see the expression on the general's face, but they all left after this little incident. I went over and just put my arms around him and hugged him . . . and if I remember correctly, I started crying . . . and I think he was crying. I really admired him for that. That was one time that I let the feelings down and let somebody see what I felt. It took a lot for him to do that, and it sort of said what this war was all about to me . . . 1968.

Our chief nurse in Vietnam was a very warm, caring colonel in the Army Nurse Corps—not too many of them around, but here was one— and when we came in-country she recommended that we work six months in a "busy" area and six months in a "nonbusy" area, for "your own psychological welfare." I think it was an excellent suggestion. The six months in Cu Chi were extremely busy, extremely hard. Then I transferred up to Da Nang, which was still busy, with critical things going on, but not as hectic as Cu Chi. It wasn't in an area that was quite as dangerous as Cu Chi was . . . and it's hard to make that comparison, because the war was all around . . . but it seemed like when we were getting mortared and shelled in Da Nang, it didn't have the same impact as when we were mortared and shelled at Cu Chi. I remember once in Cu Chi they got us all up in the middle of the night and were really not sure what to do with us because we were being overrun. . . . That one was written up in *Time* magazine. Cu Chi was full of tunnels; there were Viet Cong underneath that whole city. They had hospitals underneath the ground, firing bases. . . . It turned out our military stopped them, but they were very close. They had actually cut through the perimeter and were on the compound, the base camp. That was crazy. I've never been so scared. They gathered all of us in the kitchen of our hooch. We were told to stay there and wait for the word. . . . I remember sitting around in the kitchen in our flak jackets and helmets, just bullshitting all night long. There wasn't anything else you could do. And we just went to work the next morning at 6:30.

When I was in Da Nang the closeness of death came home to me when we heard that a nurse had been killed up in Chu Lai, Sharon Lane. I remember reading about it in the *Stars and Stripes*, and the reason it had an impact on me is that I was originally scheduled to be up at Chu Lai, and that could have been me. That was in August of 1969. I remember lying to my family when I would write home that the hospitals were real safe and not to worry.

Because I had come to Da Nang as a captain, with all this experience, they made me head nurse in the emergency room—it was called emergency and admitting and pre-op. There you would get the casualties as soon as they came off the dustoffs, the air ambulances. So you would do the lifesaving measures to be done on the wounded, and you would do triage. Nurses would have to do triage because we only had so many doctors, and most of them ended up working in the operating room. Sometimes casualties couldn't even go to x-ray; they were so bad that they would take them right into the OR. There were three or four operating rooms in Da Nang, and they were always busy. Because the docs were so busy in the OR, the nurses in the emergency room had the job of doing the triage. You had to make the decision about those people who were wounded so bad that no matter how much time you would spend on them, they wouldn't live. They were called "expectants," and you would have to put them in an area behind a screen to die—these nineteen-year-old kids . . . In triaging, there were three categories to sort out: the "expectants," the "immediates" (those that required immediate attention and surgery), then there was a third category, the "walking wounded." The doctors who worked in the emergency room were called GMOs, general medical officers, and those guys were usually interns or residents with very little experience. They were learning as they were doing, just as we were. This was an evacuation hospital, which was different than other hospitals, so I can only talk about how they functioned.

When you get down to a hundred days to go before you go home, you have a calendar that you fill in, a short-timer's calendar. And you start getting a little bit crazy, thinking about going home. Then there was also the other side of the coin, where I didn't feel that the nurse that was coming in to take my place was as qualified as I was, because it took me all this time to learn what I was doing and to do it well. Every one of us has a sense of guilt of leaving the patients behind and the nurses that we worked with, the docs, the corpsmen, all the members of the team. When a good quarterback on a football team is pulled out and a replacement comes in, it's like starting all over again. So I had this feeling that it wasn't going to work as well when I left. Also there was a combination of disillusionment versus "I did a damn good job." I felt that twelve months over there was probably one of the most rewarding nursing experiences in my life, that I'll never equal that again.

It was incredible coming back a real changed person, one who was sarcastic and bitter about what was happening in America. The news was lying about the war; Kent State was going on; the feminist movement—women were burning their bras, and I was in Vietnam saving lives. . . . It was craziness; what was going on here? So my attitude changed, but I felt that my year over there wasn't wasted. I personally felt very satisfied with what I had done. When I started to question the whole involvement in Vietnam—What were we doing over there? Why were we trying to change their attitudes?—that's when I started getting into trouble. I became immersed in my work at Fitzsimmons Army Hospital in Denver, working with psychiatric patients, but I didn't question the politics because I was still in the Army—I couldn't.

When I got out of the service I was working in a hospital in Oakland, California, in intensive care, and they wouldn't let me hang a pint of blood! They made me go through an orientation course to learn CPR. That was sort of the ultimate degradation. My intelligence and experience were not even addressed properly. It was a real insult to me. I had a real "attitude problem" working in a civilian hospital. There was this need for the recreation of the push . . . "adrenaline junkies" . . . that we are; the nurses who were in Vietnam. I really mean that. That certain rush of adrenaline, the excitement; there were all these casualties coming in that you have got to work . . . and the adrenaline starts going. So you try to perpetuate that. Nothing meant anything when I came back from Vietnam. The phrase "Don't mean nothin' " was very descriptive of the way I felt. I found it was getting in my way of jobs when I came back. Twelve to fourteen jobs in fourteen or fifteen years. You know, looking for whatever it was that I was looking for, just really unsettled, going from place to place. Never happy. Also, I refused to put down that I was in Vietnam in my applications for jobs. It didn't mean anything anyway; why bother trying to explain it to people? Vietnam was very unpopular then; you didn't want to set yourself up as being a Vietnam veteran, let alone a woman who had been there. Why cause more trouble? Learn to keep your mouth shut about it; just do your job.

After thirteen years and all those jobs in nursing, I decided to go back to school to get a master's degree in counseling. By working in counseling I'd also get a better look at myself. Just prior to that I had gone through a depression, a severe depression, so I needed to look at where I was in life, with my job and my career. Was I going to be able to maintain it? What was I doing about myself? . . . And after going through the depression and a suicide attempt, my whole life changed to do something for myself.

I had joined the Army Reserves about two years after I was discharged from the Army. One reason was financial. The pay was pretty good, and then it was one weekend a month. I also found being in the Reserves provided camaraderie with other people who had been in Vietnam, and that was important. Then, later on, especially this past couple of years, I've used the Reserve program as a way of telling people about what to expect if another crisis should occur. I try to alert them to what it is that they're going to be seeing and doing over there, which was never really told to me when I went through my officer basic training. So it's like . . . they haven't caught on to it yet. . . . I'm sure I'll get in trouble for this one of these days: telling these younger nurses that are in the units now the realities of what war and being a combat nurse is all about. It is not just wearing a pretty uniform and getting the pay for one weekend a month. There are some real serious things they have to think about. So I'm using the Reserve unit as a platform to educate those people who are part-time military.

I have about another three or four years before I retire, and I really plan to retire, but I'm also thinking that it probably won't be surprising if they ask me to leave because of the kinds of things that I am doing inside the Reserves. That is not politically correct, to be honest. "The Tightrope Walker." That could be the title of my chapter . . . and it's interesting, because I think it relates to that "adrenaline junkie" idea I was talking about. There is a certain amount of excitement, I guess, in what I am doing. I am also real excited and enthusiastic about what I am doing in the vet center and with the women vets, because my job doesn't end just being director of this vet center. My job has since become doing a lot of training across the country to other vet centers and organizations about women vets. I let them know that women are in the military, that women veterans have needs as well as men. People are starting to pick up on the fact that women were in the war and were in combat even though they didn't carry guns. So I'm an activist basically, a social activist for women in the military, especially those who were in Vietnam, because that is closest to me. And I work within the establishment, under that umbrella of the Veterans Administration and the federal government (the Army Reserves). So there is this push-pull kind of thing. The tightrope walker—I like that.

Sometimes it feels very lonely to me, the work that I am doing. I wish there were more of me. . . . I wish there were more women working within the system who are as knowledgeable or have as much experience as I do, who would be able to do this kind of work. . . . I'm responsible to the rest of my job here, and other work should go on the side: "We gave you permission to start the women's movement in the vet center system—and that's it—now go back and take care of your vet center." That's not enough for me, and again I may get into trouble because I'm not saying no to other people as far as the women's issues go. I'll do whatever needs to be done until some changes are made. That may take a long time, but I guess what I'm hoping for is that other people will become active in it and help with it. The more people who get to know about the women who were in Vietnam, the easier my job is going to be. That's why I don't hesitate when screenwriters call or somebody wants to interview me for an article in a newspaper. In one way I'm tired of being put out there and raked over the coals, but on the other hand, I know that unless I do it, it's not going to be done. The word is out, and I'm willing to talk about it if it is going to help. Not only to help women who need to come in and talk about their lives and help them to readjust from their experience, but also to make other people out there—psychologists, therapists, psychiatrists—understand that war really did a number on all of us, the women as well as the men.

24

The Role of the Press
Paul Dean

In so many respects Vietnam was a most unusual war. It was the first time in American military history that men went to war for 365 days with paid vacations in Hong Kong, Australia, Hawaii, and China Beach. Also, with the exception of the War of 1812, Vietnam was the one conflict that the American military did not win. Those at home really didn't know where Vietnam was, and those in Vietnam weren't quite sure why they were there. It was an odd war, without a front line, without a recognizable enemy. And it was fought much the way that the United States cavalry fought the American Indians. In the Dakotas the 6th Cavalry rode out of the fort on horses. In Vietnam it was the 1st Cavalry that rode out on helicopters. It was a war where that ubiquitous, clattering, vulnerable helicopter came into its own, making sure that no combat wound was more than thirty miles from surgical assistance. It also established a 74% survival rate for all wounded. Though we talk about the 58,000 who died, this translates to 200,000 American GI's who did not die.

In other respects it was a most routine war. A round from an AK47 popped a man's brain in Vietnam just as well as it did in World War II from a German Mauser. Turkey loaf and ham and lima beans remain one of the basic food groups of combat rations. In World War I it was called "shell shock." In World War II it was "combat fatigue." In

Paul Dean, a staff writer for *The Los Angeles Times*, has been a journalist for more than thirty years. He was born in London, educated in England, and served with the 2nd Tactical Air Force in Germany and Korea. Following the war, he was feature writer and foreign correspondent for the *London Daily Mirror* and *London Daily Herald* before moving to Canada in 1957, and then to the United States in 1963. He was a war correspondent in Vietnam 1965–66 and saw combat with every branch of the U.S. military. For his coverage of the war he was nominated for both a Pulitzer Prize and the Ernie Pyle Memorial Award. In addition to his work on the Vietnam War, Dean has covered the Hungarian uprising in 1956, the conflict in Belfast and Northern Ireland, and military affairs in Europe and the Middle East.

Vietnam it was "Post Traumatic Stress Disorder." But it was all basically the same. The Vietnam War was not that different. GI's were just as lonely, and as scared, and as heroic during the 1968 Tet Offensive as they were during the 8th Air Forces' daylight bombing raids over Berlin. Their generals were just as efficient and just as negligent at Choisin Reservoir and at Bull Run.

But in one area Vietnam was like no other war. It was the single campaign where the media was deflowered and served its audiences fully. While fulfilling its critical mandate like no other time in the history of the profession and of the world, the media, finally, frankly brought an end to the period wherein the media had shortchanged and carelessly misinformed its public for so long. It was a glorious era for television, radio, newspapers, magazines, wire services, reporters and cameramen, as we all lost our John Wayne naïveté.

In other words, for so long, for decades, we, the media, had believed whatever military and government told us was patriotic to believe. In Vietnam we began questioning the military decisions, the government's motives, the conduct, and even the very purpose of the war.

In World War II and again in Korea, newsmen suffered censorship without any thought of opposition on their part. They had to. They were appended to the military; they wore its uniform, and they even enjoyed privileges of rank. Correspondents ate in officers' messes, and received the priority ranking of a major when traveling on military aircraft or living in government quarters. Thus for any correspondent to deny allegiance to the military by questioning any part of his benefactors' war effort was effectively to kill any chance of closehand coverage. But in Vietnam, because of America's somewhat unique relationship as advisor to the South Vietnamese military, as guests almost at a civil war, correspondents had greater freedom to roam from ally to enemy, to travel by any means available to any destination that was reachable, to abide by military security, of course, but also to report without restriction if any official body count and claims of victory did not agree with what a correspondent in the field had actually witnessed. We the media formed largely an adversary relationship with the military; we learned to use official briefings as grist, not gospel. We paid our own way to war. We headquartered ourselves at civilian hotels in Saigon. We bought our own jungle fatigues on the black market, and we ate off the economy. It was only in forward combat areas that we did travel and eat and live with the military. But in this case there was no choice. It was also a damn sight safer.

This was a war where a more erudite breed of correspondents at the front functioned also as commentators and analysts. He and she were not satisfied with simply reporting military movements, the wins and the losses. They were only satisfied by examining the full context, by applying economic, social, and political considerations and projections. These overseas interpretations, with the enormous depth that at that time was allowed by long columns in major metropolitan newspapers and news magazines, became public opinion in Buffalo and Denver. We constructed schools of thought. We built ranks as hawks and doves. The domestic American climate at that time was of freer expression and heftier challenge to the establishment, and our dispatches from Vietnam fed and enlarged that appetite. And I think it is quite fair to say that by their detailed and sometimes costly honest reporting of the conflict, the American media bore a heavy responsibility for the conduct and, yes, even the conclusion of the Vietnam War. It has often been said that journalism is the first draft of history. In Vietnam I think it was elevated almost to the status of a final manuscript.

Now, who were these correspondents? Where did they come from? They came from around the world. Australians were fighting in Vietnam, New Zealanders were fighting in Vietnam, so the correspondents from Australia and New Zealand were there. Reporters came from France, from Germany, from England, from all over the world to witness this new American conflict. At its peak there were three hundred correspondents representing almost every major news gathering organization in the world operating out of Saigon. They fell largely into three groups. There was the "serious overview" correspondents, the J.B. Honeys and the Bernard Falls who really stayed largely with the political, economic, and social aspects of the war and the large picture of the military. That was their mandate. They wrote the Washington reviews. They wrote the Saigon reviews. They functioned at division and brigade levels. Then there were the Ernie Pyle types. They concentrated on the human drama of the war. The home state GI's, the "color side bars," the intrinsic details that are essential, and an adjunct to any major news story of war. They functioned largely at battalion level and below. And there were what I call the Tim Page types. These were the gonzo journalists, many of them freelance, all there to make a name for themselves or even as lovers of war. They got off on the thrill of combat. They got off on the freedom of drugs. They enjoyed the rush. They enjoyed the war. For them it was their glory hall. In his book, Tim Page, who was a British photo journalist, defined it best when he said that at one time he was approached by a publisher to do a book that "finally took the glamour out of war." Page said, "take the glamour out of war? How the hell can you do that? Go and take the glamour out of a Huey? Go take the glamour out of a Sheridan? Can you take the glamour out of a Cobra or getting stoned on China Beach? War is good for you. You can't take the glamour out of that. It's like taking the glamour out of sex, or trying to take the glamour out of the Rolling Stones. I mean, you know it just cannot be done." This was just one point of view, but also an essential point of view in that it reflected the view of a journalist whose mandate was to report the war for an international audience.

Above everything else, this was television's war. It was the first war Δ tV
to be brought home by television. In the American Civil War there was Matthew Brady and still photographs. In World War I there were moving pictures which sometimes took a week or months to be relayed from Europe to the United States. In World War II and even in Korea what you saw in movie theaters and eventually from Korea on television were largely movies that were actually silent. The sound of explosions and aircrafts and tanks were dubbed in the studio in the United States before they went on television. But in Vietnam, for the first time, video tape from Saigon could be flown within hours to Los Angeles, and an engagement at 10 a.m. Saigon time was part of the 6 o'clock evening news Los Angeles time. At that time, for the first time, the American public, that is, those millions of people who had never been in battle, found out what a war is like on a day-to-day basis. It was forced to acknowledge what all combat soldiers know: war is a bloody, lonely, indiscriminate, vulgar, and often fatal hell. And from this stemmed an enormous upsurge of American opinion concerning the war in Vietnam.

Not that what was happening there was any different as wars go. What was different was that now America, over its TV dinners, was seeing it while it ate. And then the public reacted. They were appalled. They turned against government. Then in turn, and sadly, they turned against the military. Questions began. Then demonstrations and campus protests. And then there was indeed massive political movements towards ending the war in Vietnam because the American public, as a result of television coverage, suddenly realized how horrible war is.

Unfortunately, as a by-product of this, the media itself found itself accused. It was accused of a conservative bias. It was accused of a liberal bias. Of course these biases existed. But what is a bias? It's simply an opinion that one doesn't agree with. But the media was blamed and an anti-media stance occurred.

In this situation, frankly, I don't think that the media should be blamed. They were nothing more than the instrument of transmission. They were not the vehicle of war. We were not part of the diplomatic or political process. Sure, there were times when we were used as such, but we didn't solicit the job. So, this bearer of bad news, the American media was beheaded, and, generally speaking, it was a bum rap. Again, I go back to the fact that the media was beheaded because this was the first time that the American public realized what war was like.

There is nothing new about war. There was very little that was new about Vietnam. We saw the My Lai massacre, and the public trial of William Calley. Was this new? Of course it wasn't. In World War I German soldiers bayoneted babies in the Beaulieu Woods. In World War II, when Dachau was relieved, SS Guards were put against the wall and shot by American soldiers, and their gold tooth fillings were removed. All of this is as horrible as anything that happened in Vietnam—but from Vietnam we saw it on television for the first time. False body counts, were they something unique to the Vietnam War? Of course they weren't. In World War II Pearl Harbor was an example of total unpreparedness on the part of the American military and almost criminal negligence on the part of Washington. It took twenty five years for that story to emerge from World War II. The American internment of Japanese in the United States was unopposed during World War II; it took almost forty years for this sin to be apologized for and for reparation to be made. The point is: these things occurred, but an alert media didn't alert you. In Vietnam the media did alert the American public.

In World War I, World War II, and in Korea, we, the American people, did not know because the press, perhaps because of its naïveté, or maybe from some sense of misplaced patriotism or some loyalty to the cause of government, allowed itself to be propagandized. It allowed itself to be censored by subtleties and even the outright edicts of field commanders. In Vietnam, we did not stand still for that. In Vietnam the American media did better than in any other war zone in the history of America at war.

I always like to end this somewhat impassioned plea for greater understanding of the media by quoting from Thomas Jefferson, who once said: "The basis of our government being the opinion of the people, the very first object should be to keep that right. Were it left to me to decide whether we should have a government without newspapers, or newspapers without government, I should not hesitate a moment to prefer the latter."

25

The Story of a
Vietnamese Refugee in America
Hien Duc Do

We left Vietnam a few days before April 30, 1975, the day the war was lost. I was 14 years old. We were among some of the more fortunate people who left Vietnam. We escaped in an American military airplane from Tan Son Nhut airport.

At that time, our family consisted of my mother, a junior high school teacher in her early forties, my older sister who was two years older than I, and my other sister who was five years younger than I. My father, a former military officer, as a result of his political and military activities was living in France with my three brothers at the time. We lived in a military housing project, in a small house on the outskirts of Saigon. Following a Vietnamese cultural practice of older parents living with their oldest son, our paternal grandparents lived with us. Finally, in addition to my grandparents, my father's younger sister and her family, as well as his youngest brother and his family, lived in the house across the street and next door respectively.

We were Catholics, which also meant that we were Vietnamese who came from the northern part of Vietnam. My grandparents became refugees in 1954 when they took their children to the south, after hearing rumors of bloodshed to Catholics if they had stayed in Hanoi, after the Geneva Accords which were supposed to have united the country. Instead, the Geneva Agreement divided the country into two parts, at the seventeenth parallel, with the northern half belonging to the Communists and the southern half being called the Republic of Vietnam.

Despite the war, our daily lives prior to the evacuation seemed

---

Hien Duc Do is currently a doctoral student in sociology at the University of California, Santa Barbara, whose major research focuses on the Americanization of Vietnamese refugees from the war in Vietnam. As a junior faculty member, Do teaches an undergraduate course on the Vietnam War, told from the perspective of Vietnamese involvement.

normal enough, at least to a 14-year-old boy. The children were students, and we went to school everyday, played with our friends the way every child does, and, occasionally, fought among ourselves. The adults went to work and carried out the affairs required by and within the adult world. The nightly reports of deaths and casualties on both sides was something that became part of our daily lives, as much as the sounds of bomb explosions and gun shots in the far distance, and sometimes in the not so distant.

However, a few months prior to April 30, 1975, there was a sense of imminent danger. The atmosphere became much more intense and chaotic. Similar to other families, our family also sensed the danger that was rapidly approaching the city as a result of the increasing numbers of television and newspaper reports which focused on the impending withdrawal of American troops and support, as well as the intensified military activities of the communists. This fear escalated as more and more displaced Vietnamese people flooded into Saigon, retreating from the advancing communist troops.

My mother originally attempted to escape through the help of her older brother who resided in Vung Tau, a coastal city south of Saigon. However, after numerous unsuccessful attempts to find space on boats going out to sea, and having exhausted all the avenues of leaving by sea, our family returned to Saigon. We were quite fortunate—had we waited a couple of days longer, we would have found all the roads back to Saigon sealed off, and no one was able to enter that city. As we returned home, the mood of the city became more and more chaotic and frantic. It wasn't long before President Thieu resigned.

Finally, on April 25, my father's younger brother, who was a member of the Diplomatic Corps of Vietnam to the Philippines, at the risk of his own life, returned to Saigon to negotiate our evacuation. He managed to obtain official documents for three families—ours, my aunt's (my father's younger sister), and her husband's older brother—to enter Tan Son Nhut Airport. We were given a couple of hours to pack our personal belongings. The instructions were to pack as little as possible, and to bring only the absolute necessities. I managed to pack a pair of pants, one or two shirts, some underwear, and, unbeknownst to everybody, my special stamp collection book.

As my uncle was desperately trying to convince my paternal grandfather to join us (my grandmother had passed away a few years earlier), my mother hurriedly went to say good-bye to her parents. We were not allowed to join her for fear of being caught for breaking the government's curfew. My uncle failed to convince my grandfather to leave for he insisted that he wanted to die and be buried in his homeland. That was the last time I saw any of my grandparents or my school friends. My paternal grandfather's wish was fulfilled—he passed away last year in his country.

As daylight neared and we began our journey to the airport, there was a sense of excitement, coupled with fear, danger, and sadness. Despite our "official" documents, we still had to negotiate with the guards, either verbally or with monetary compensation at three different locations before entering Tan Son Nhut Airport. Once inside, we managed to find a small area in what used to be the bowling lanes, which was converted to sleeping quarters for many families.

As we sat nervously and impatiently waiting in the airport, news of the withdrawal of the troops and of the advancing communist forces heightened our sense of desperation. Despite our presence in the airport, there was no guarantee that there would be space for us on any planes. The plane and seat assignments were given on a first-come, first-serve basis. Our instructions were for each family to take shifts and listen for our names to be called for boarding since the call could be given at any time. If we missed our names, there would be no second chance.

After what seemed like eternity, the names of the three families were finally called in the early morning hours. As everyone was hurriedly awakened, we ran to the designated gate and got in line for boarding. A large military plane awaited us in the runway. As we boarded the plane, I learned that it was a C–130, a military plane used for transporting equipment. We all sat on the floor, as closely packed as sardines, waiting for our journey to begin, our destination unknown.

As the plane began its flight, bombs, gun shots, and helicopters were heard in the not so far distance. After a few hours of flying, we landed at Clark·Air Force Base, an American military base in the Philippines. As we were transported to our temporary shelters, news of the loss of our country reached us. For the first time in our lives, we had no homeland. For the first time in my life, I became a refugee. For the second time in my mother's life, and those of her generation, they once again became refugees. Despite our physical safety and comfort, there was a sense of grief, as if we had just lost something that was very dear to our hearts and that could never be replaced.

There is a tremendous difference between a refugee and an immigrant. Traditionally, an immigrant is a person who has made the choice—based on his/her belief in the likelihood of finding such things as better economic opportunities, social mobility, religious freedom, and political stability elsewhere—to leave his/her native country for another one. There is a degree of voluntariness in the decision process. In short, for the immigrant, a relatively considered choice has been made to seek out a "better life."

A refugee, on the other hand, is someone who has been caught up in an emergency situation; traditionally, the refugee has had to leave his/her country in haste, for fear of immediate, extreme persecution and physical violence, stemming from his/her political, social, economic, and religious affiliations. There was very little time to prepare for the long journey that awaited us. The main concern was to leave the homeland as soon as possible, to reach safety, and obtain asylum elsewhere.

After spending three days and two nights in the Philippines, our long journey to America resumed. We boarded another plane to Wake Island, an island in the South Pacific. After processing our papers and receiving some new t-shirts, underwear, and other personal items, there wasn't much to do in Wake Island since the entire island could be covered on foot in ten to twenty minutes. In addition, Wake Island at one time served as a nuclear testing area and, consequently, we were forbidden to swim and fish. As a result, our daily routines involved waiting in lines for meals, and news of our next destination. This period was extremely difficult for the children: we were young and full of energy, but were allowed to do very little.

After a few weeks on Wake Island, our next stop was Camp Pendleton, a United States Marine Corps base in Southern California, and one of the four refugee camps opened in the United States. We arrived on a cool summer night with few warm clothes. The Marine Corps personnel immediately assigned each individual a field jacket (a long green, heavy jacket), and proceeded to assign approximately twenty persons to a tent. The canvas tents with cot beds and army blankets served as our homes for the next few weeks while we waited for the next step in this long and uncertain journey.

In order to alleviate and minimize some of the problems that might have arisen as a result of the sudden influx of Vietnamese refugees to America, the Federal government encouraged individuals, families, corporations, and church congregations to help sponsor refugees out of Camp Pendleton. Each family was matched with a sponsor who would assist the refugees in the process of entering American society. My uncle and his family as well as my aunt and her family were sponsored by a church group from Texas. As a result, after our escape together in April 1975, and through this long journey of several months, we tearfully and painfully said good-bye, and were separated.

Our family was not as fortunate in the sponsorship process. We spent a great deal more time in Camp Pendleton. It was difficult to find a sponsor for us. My mother was a single parent in her forties, with three young children, a former junior high school teacher. Her skills as a teacher were not easily transferable to those required in the

United States economy. In addition, our predicament was compounded by our inability to speak any English. As a result, after a period of a couple of months in Camp Pendleton, our family was divided into three groups and received three separate sponsors. My mother and my younger sister were to live with a family in Beverly Hills, my older sister with another family in Westwood, and I with a third family in North Hollywood. It was not until a year later that we were reunited and moved into a one-bedroom apartment in Los Angeles. Echo Park Avenue is where my life in America began. . . .

It has been almost sixteen years since we left Vietnam and resettled in the United States. Although the memories of the journey to America are still vivid in my mind, they are now invoked less often and have become only a small part of those that have been accumulated in the last sixteen years. Notwithstanding the opportunities offered in America, mainly personal freedom, liberty, higher education, occupations, and so forth, life is still hard for a Vietnamese refugee in the United States. My life has been (and will continue to be) a process of bridging between two different cultures.

Having left Vietnam at an early age, I have realized that I can never truly be a Vietnamese, and, at the same time, not having grown up in the United States, I can never fully be an American. In the final analysis, my life experience will not be that of a Vietnamese, nor that of an American, but that of a Vietnamese-American. I need to merge the world of my parents with the opportunities, experiences, and hopes that America has to offer.

26

A World Turned
Upside Down

Le Ly Hayslip

For my first twelve years of life, I was a peasant girl in Ky La, now
called Xa Hoa Qui, a small village near Danang in Central Vietnam.
My father taught me to love god, my family, our traditions, and the
people we could not see: our ancestors. He taught me that to sacrifice
one's self for freedom—like our ancient kings who fought bravely
against invaders; or in the manner of our women warriors, including
Miss Trung Nhi Trung Trac who drowned herself rather than give in
to foreign conquerors—was a very high honor. From my love of my
ancestors and my native soil, he said, I must never retreat.

From my mother I learned humility and the strength of virtue. I
learned it was no disgrace to work like an animal on our farm, provided I did not complain. "Would you be less than our ox," she asked,
"who works to feed us without grumbling?" She also taught me, when
I began to notice village boys, that there is no love beyond faithful
love, and that in my love for my future husband, my ancestors, and
my native soil, I must always remain steadfast.

For my next three years of life, I loved, labored and fought stead-
fastly for the Viet Cong against American and South Vietnamese soldiers.

Everything I knew about the war I learned as a teenaged girl from
the North Vietnamese cadre leaders in the swamps outside Ky La.

Le Ly Hayslip was born and raised in Vietnam, and was twelve years old when the
U.S. helicopters landed in her village of Ky La. She experienced all of the trauma of
the war, then, following the cessation of military hostilities, fled to the United States
with her children, resettling in the Los Angeles area. In 1986 Hayslip returned to
Vietnam to search for family members who remained there. Upon her return to the
United States, she founded a peace organization called East Meets West Foundation,
and wrote a compelling book (with Jay Wurts) about her experiences, entitled *When
Heaven and Earth Changed Places: A Vietnamese Woman's Journey from War to Peace*
(New York: Doubleday, 1989), within which the selection republished here stands as
the major portion of the *Prologue*.

During these midnight meetings, we peasants assumed everything we heard was true because what the Viet Cong said matched, in one way or another, the beliefs we already had.

The first lesson we learned about the new "American" war was why the Viet Cong was formed and why we should support it. Because this lesson came on the heels of our war with the French (which began in 1946 and lasted, on and off, for eight years), what the cadre leaders told us seemed to be self-evident.

First, we were taught that Vietnam was *con rong chau tien*—a sovereign nation which had been held in thrall by Western imperialists for over a century. That all nations had a right to determine their own destiny also seemed beyond dispute, since we farmers subsisted by our own hands and felt we owed nothing to anyone but god and our ancestors for the right to live as we saw fit. Even the Chinese, who had made their own disastrous attempt to rule Vietnam in centuries past, had learned a painful lesson about our country's zeal for independence. "Vietnam," went the saying that summarized their experience, "is nobody's lapdog."

Second, the cadres told us that the division of Vietnam into North and South in 1954 was nothing more than a ploy by the defeated French and their Western allies, mainly the United States, to preserve what influence they could in our country.

"*Chia doi dat nuoc?*" the Viet Cong asked, "Why should outsiders divide the land and tell some people to go north and others south? If Vietnam were truly for the Vietnamese, wouldn't we choose for ourselves what kind of government our people wanted? A nation cannot have *two* governments," they said, "anymore than a family can have two fathers."

Because those who favored America quickly occupied the seats of power formerly held by the French, and because the North remained pretty much on its own, the choice of which side best represented independence was, for us, a foregone conclusion. In fact, the Viet Cong usually ended our indoctrination sessions with a song that played on our worst fears:

> Americans come to kill our people,
> Follow America, and kill your relatives!
> The smart bird flies before it's caught.
> The smart person comes home before Tet.
> Follow us, and you'll always have a family.
> Follow America, and you'll always be alone!

After these initial "lessons," the cadre leaders introduced us to the two Vietnamese leaders who personified each view—the opposite poles of our tiny world. On the South pole was President Ngo Dinh Diem, America's staunch ally, who was Catholic like the French. Although he was idolized by many who said he was a great humanitarian and patriot, his religion alone was enough to make him suspicious to Buddhists on the Central Coast. The loyalty we showed him, consequently, was more duty to a landlord than love for a founding father. Here is a song the Republican schoolteachers made us learn to praise the Southern president:

> In stormy seas, Vietnam's boat rolls and pitches.
> Still we must row; our President's hand upon the helm.
> The ship of state plows through heavy seas,
> Holding fast its course to democracy.
> Our President is celebrated from Europe to Asia,
> He is the image of philanthropy and love.
> He has sacrificed himself for our happiness.
> He fights for liberty in the land of the Viet.
> Everyone loves him earnestly, and behind him we will march
> Down the street of freedom, lined with fresh flowers,
> The flag of liberty crackling above our heads!

In the North, on the other pole, was Ho Chi Minh, whom we were encouraged to call *Bac Ho*—Uncle Ho—the way we would refer to a trusted family friend. We knew nothing of his past beyond stories of his compassion and his love for our troubled country—the independence of which, we were told, he had made the mission of his life.

Given the gulf between these leaders, the choice of whom we should support again seemed obvious. The cadre leaders encouraged our natural prejudices (fear of outsiders and love of our ancestors) with stirring songs and tender stories about Uncle Ho in which the Communist leader and our ancient heroes seemed to inhabit one congenial world. Like an unbroken thread, the path from our ancestors and legends seemed to lead inevitably to the Northern leader—then past him to a future of harmony and peace.

But to achieve that independence, Ho said, we must wage total war. His cadremen cried out "We must hold together and oppose the American empire. There is nothing better than freedom, independence, and happiness!"

To us, these ideas seemed as obvious as everything else we had heard. *Freedom* meant a Vietnam free of colonial domination. *Independence* meant one Vietnamese people—not two countries, North and South—determining its own destiny. *Happiness* meant plenty of food and an end to war—the ability, we assumed, to live our lives in accordance with our ancient ways. We wondered: how can the Southerners oppose these wonderful things? The answer the Viet Cong gave us was that the Republicans prized Yankee dollars more than the blood of their brothers and sisters. We did not think to question with our hearts what our minds told us must be true.

Although most of us thought we knew what the Viet Cong meant by freedom, independence, and happiness, a few of us dared to ask what life the Northerners promised when the war was over. The answer was always the same: "Uncle Ho promises that after our victory, the Communist state will look after your rights and interests. Your highest interest, of course, is the independence of our fatherland and the freedom of our people. Our greatest right is the right to determine our own future as a state." This always brought storms of applause from the villagers because most people remembered what life was like under the French.

Nonetheless, despite our vocal support, the Viet Cong never took our loyalty for granted. They rallied and rewarded and lectured us sternly, as the situation demanded, while the Republicans assumed we would be loyal because we lived south of a line some diplomats had drawn on a map. Even when things were at their worst—when the allied forces devastated the countryside and the Viet Cong themselves resorted to terror to make us act the way they wanted—the villagers clung to the vision the Communists had drummed into us. When the Republicans put us in jail, we had the image of "Communist freedom"—freedom from war—to see us through. When the Viet Cong executed a relative, we convinced ourselves that it was necessary to bring "Communist happiness"—peace in the village—a little closer. Because the Viet Cong encouraged us to voice our basic human feelings through patriotic songs, the tortured, self-imposed silence we endured around Republicans only made us hate the government more. Even on those occasions when the Republicans tried to help us, we saw their favors as a trick or sign of weakness. Thus, even as we accepted their kindness, we despised the Republicans for it.

As the war gathered steam in the 1960s, every villager found his or her little world expanded—usually for the worse. The steady parade of troops through Ky La meant new opportunities for us to fall victim to outsiders. Catholic Republicans spurned and mistreated Buddhists for worshiping their ancestors. City boys taunted and cheated the "country bumpkins" while Vietnamese servicemen from other provinces made fun of our funny accents and strange ways. When the tactics on both sides got so rough that people were in danger no matter which side they favored, our sisters fled to the cities where they learned about liquor, drugs, adultery, materialism, and disrespect for their ancestors. More than one village father died inside when a "stranger from Saigon" returned in place of the daughter he had raised.

In contrast to this, the Viet Cong were, for the most part, our neighbors. Even though our cadre leaders had been trained in Hanoi, they had all been born on the Central Coast. They did not insult us for our manners and speech because they had been raised exactly like us. Where the Republicans came into the village overburdened with American equipment designed for a different war, the Viet Cong made do with what they had and seldom wasted their best ammunition—the goodwill of the people. The cadremen pointed out to us that where the Republicans wore medals, the Viet Cong wore rags and never gave up the fight. "Where the Republicans pillage, rape, and plunder," they said, "we preserve your houses, crops, and family"; for they knew that it was only by these resources—our food for rations, our homes for hiding, our sons and brothers for recruits—that they were able to keep the field.

Of course, the Viet Cong cadremen, like the Republicans, had no desire (or ability, most of them) to paint a fairer picture. For them, there could be no larger reason for Americans fighting the war than imperialist aggression. Because we peasants knew nothing about the United States, we could not stop to think how absurd it would be for so large and wealthy a nation to covet our poor little country for its rice fields, swamps, and pagodas. Because our only exposure to politics had been through the French colonial government (and before that, the rule of Vietnamese kings), we had no concept of democracy. For us, "Western culture" meant bars, brothels, black markets, and xa hoi van minh—bewildering machines—most of them destructive. We couldn't imagine that life in the capitalist world was anything other than a frantic, alien terror. Because, as peasants, we defined "politics" as something other people did someplace else, it had no relevance to our daily lives—except as a source of endless trouble. As a consequence, we overlooked the power that lay in our hands: our power to achieve virtually anything we wanted if only we acted together. The Viet Cong and the North, on the other hand, always recognized and respected this strength.

We children also knew that our ancestral spirits demanded we resist the outsiders. Our parents told us of the misery they had suffered from the invading Japanese ("small death," our neighbors called them) in World War II, and from the French, who returned in 1946. These soldiers destroyed our crops, killed our livestock, burned our houses, raped our women, and tortured or put to death anyone who opposed them—as well as many who did not. Now, the souls of all those people

who had been mercilessly killed had come back to haunt Ky La—
demanding revenge against the invaders. This we children believed
with all our hearts. After all, we had been taught from birth that
ghosts were simply people we could not see.

There was only one way to remove this curse. Uncle Ho had urged
the poor to take up arms so that everyone might be guaranteed a little
land on which to cultivate some rice. Because nearly everyone in
Central Vietnam was a farmer, and because farmers must have land,
almost everyone went to war: with a rifle or a hoe; with vigilance to
give the alarm; with food and shelter for our fighters; or, if one was
too little for anything else, with flowers and songs to cheer them up.
Everything we knew commanded us to fight. Our ancestors called us
to war. Our myths and legends called us to war. Our parents' teachings
called us to war. Uncle Ho's cadre called us to war. Even President
Diem had called us to fight for the very thing we now believed he was
betraying—an independent Vietnam. Should an obedient child be less
than an ox and refuse to do her duty?

And so the war began and became an insatiable dragon that roared
around Ky La. By the time I turned thirteen, that dragon had swallowed me up.

In 1986, after living for sixteen years in America and becoming a
U.S. citizen, I went back to Vietnam—to find out what had happened
to my family, my village, my people, and to the man I loved who
had given me my first son. I went with many memories and many
questions. This book is the story of what I remember and what I found.

It is dedicated to all those who fought for their country, wherever
it may be. It is dedicated, too, to those who did not fight—but suffered,
wept, raged, bled, and died just the same. We all did what we had to
do. By mingling our blood and tears on the earth, god has made us
brothers and sisters.

If you were an American GI, I ask you to read this book and look into
the heart of one you once called enemy. I have witnessed, firsthand, all
that you went through. I will try to tell you who your enemy was and
why almost everyone in the country you tried to help resented, feared,
and misunderstood you. It was not your fault. It could not have been
otherwise. Long before you arrived, my country had yielded to the
terrible logic of war. What for you was normal—a life of peace and
plenty—was for us a hazy dream known only in our legends. Because
we had to appease the allied forces by day and were terrorized by Viet
Cong at night, we slept as little as you did. We obeyed both sides and
wound up pleasing neither. We were people in the middle. We were
what the war was all about.

Your story, however, was different. You came to Vietnam, willingly or not, because your country demanded it. Most of you did not know, or fully understand, the different wars my people were fighting when you got here. For you, it was a simple thing: democracy against communism. For us, that was not our fight at all. How could it be? We knew little of democracy and even less about communism. For most of us it was a fight for independence—like the American Revolution. Many of us also fought for religious ideals, the way the Buddhists fought the Catholics. Behind the religious war came the battle between city people and country people—the rich against the poor—a war fought by those who wanted to change Vietnam and those who wanted to leave it as it had been for a thousand years. Beneath all that, too, we had vendettas: between native Vietnamese and immigrants (mostly Chinese and Khmer) who had fought for centuries over the land. Many of these wars go on today. How could you hope to end them by fighting a battle so different from our own?

The least you did—the least any of us did—was our duty. For that we must be proud. The most that any of us did—or saw—was another face of destiny or luck or god. Children and soldiers have always known it to be terrible. If you have not yet found peace at the end of your war, I hope you will find it here. We have important new roles to play.

In the war many Americans—and many more Vietnamese—lost limbs, loved ones, and that little light we see in babies' eyes which is our own hope for the future. Do not despair. As long as you are alive, that light still burns within you. If you lost someone you love, his light burns on in you—so long as you remember. Be happy every day you are alive. . . .

IV

SYMBOLIC EXPRESSIONS, RITUAL
Healing

27

Remembering the Sacrifice
Theodore H. Evans

[handwritten: 1982]

[handwritten: Dedication of VN Memorial]

They shall not grow old, as we that are left grow old.
Age shall not weary them, nor the years condemn.
At the going down of the sun, and in the morning,
We will remember them.
                    For the Fallen, st. 4 by L. Binyon

Our task here this morning is to remember and I want to count on you to help me to do that by adding your remembrances to mine; your thoughts to my thoughts; your prayers to my prayers. I want this to be *our* remembrance, not only of those who have died, our family members our friends, but also of those who are left, ourselves, those who were involved in as many ways as there were to be involved in the conflict, the struggle, the pain and sorrow of the war in Vietnam. This is a service of remembrance. Jesus said, "Take, eat, drink in remembrance of me."

About twenty years ago on this Sunday I participated in a similar service in a little church used by the Anglican-Episcopal Congregation of Saigon. We called it St. Christopher's. I know there are a few people here today who worshipped in that church. It was also a Remembrance Sunday, on the Sunday closest to November 11th. In this country (because of the difference in time between here and Europe) we are not so keenly aware of the significance of the time for this annual remembrance until we recall that the announcement of the signing of the Armistice at the end of World War I came in Europe on a Sunday morning, at the eleventh hour of the eleventh day of the eleventh month, 1918. Churches about to begin their worship that day paused to remember their dead. They have done so ever since. We did it that Sunday, which seems so long ago. We are doing it here today.

I remember feeling in that service a sense of terrible ambivalence:

The Rev. Theodore H. Evans, of Stockbridge, Massachusetts, was invited to bring the sermon message on Sunday November 14, 1982, in the National Cathedral in Washington, D.C., following the dedication of the Vietnam Veterans Memorial the day before. The "Veterans' Service" followed the reading of each of the 58,000 names that are inscribed on the black granite walls of the Memorial. Evans was selected for the task because of his reputation for excellence as a speaker, and because he is a veteran of the war. His sermon takes images of war and works to transform them into an instrument of peace.

the ambivalence of remembering the dead (especially on the anniversary of the war that was supposed to be the war to end war) at a time and in a place where another war was beginning. I remember the feeling of ambivalence in honoring people who had made sacrifices for their countries, their convictions, and their friends while wondering how it could have happened that such terrible sacrifices became necessary. And I remember wondering who it was we were supposed to be remembering. Was it only soldiers? Was it only those on "our side?" Was it everyone whose life was lost or broken or disrupted by a century of wars?

Now it is twenty years later and those questions and feelings of ambivalence remain for me and they are harder to bear because there are so many thousands more to remember; all those thousands named and thousands more un-named and the families that go with each one. I want to talk about remembering for a few minutes, to say what I think it means for us to remember, and where it may lead us.

The Bible gives us some clues. Remembering in a biblical context means more than a casual backward glance to something or someone long ago. Remembering for our religious predecessors meant bringing the past into the present. To remember even the name of a person who had died was to remember his very being, and to bring that person into the present with reality, substance, and power. To remember means what the word itself suggests; to re-member, to put together again, to reconstruct. It is that kind of remembering that we have been doing in this city in the past few days, not passing thoughts, but a bringing of the past into the present with power and emotion and caring and love. We have been overcome by our memories, of a time and a place, but mostly memories of people. That is what comes through to me in so many conversations, not the memories of hardships and battles, but of all the people we knew and with whom we shared deep relationships.

Remembering is hard work. It means reliving the pain, the alienation, the debate. It means recalling the dehumanization that is always, tragically, a part of war; when enemies turn each other into something less than human so that they can be treated as less than human. Remembering Vietnam means something similar to what it may mean for a person who has had some terrible childhood experience that restricts his or her growth. It has to be remembered if she or he is to be whole. For us at this time in our history it means that we have to pull a painful memory from the recesses of our collective memories, look at it, understand it, and begin to reconcile it as an important and tragic part of our national life, but one with power to heal and make us whole again.

That kind of remembering has always been a part of our religious life too. That is why we read the Bible, to remember the old stories, to relive them in our own ways, to recognize ourselves in them, and to discover in ourselves that mixture of good and evil, that we know ourselves to be; people with moments of glory and heroism, and people with moments of horrendous cruelty and stupidity. But in all the stories there is an affirmation that while we remember, there is also a God who remembers us, who loves us, who takes and judges our worst and brings it to life. Part of that strange Gospel you heard this morning when Jesus is talking about a terrible time to come, when all hell would break loose, is saying just that, that even in the darkness God is already there, involved, picking up the pieces, re-membering, putting us and our lives and our shattered communities back together. The consistent testimony of Scripture and our own experience is that God is always found where the wounds are, where the agonies are, even where the defeats are. Surely the Vietnam experience, no matter what our opinion about it or part in it, was a kind of apocalyptic, shaking moment, and also one that had, and still has, the potential to be that place where God re-members us; where we discover that God has already joined us with the living and the dead, the wounded and the hurt, and made us whole.

Of course, to discover God in the middle of chaos is no guarantee that we will live happily ever after. The author of the Epistle to the Hebrews reminds us, "It is a fearful thing to fall into the hands of the living God." It means that we are often called to take extraordinary risks, risks that make us terribly vulnerable. I want to hold up for you on this occasion, the incredible risks that the organizers of this memorial time and of the events of these last days have themselves taken: the risk of doing something that everyone else had shied away from, the risk of criticism and humiliation in daring to expose old wounds and old memories, the risk of just being able to say, "That is what we must do to reconcile our people, our nation, our veterans."

Perhaps their risk-taking which has had such a wonderful result can move us to take the next steps: to make certain that the real needs of veterans are met; that their families and survivors, the injured and the wounded are cared for as they should be cared for. It is inconceivable that a nation that is calling to spend nearly a quarter of a trillion dollars on its defense cannot also care for its people, and especially those who gave themselves in such tremendous ways.

And perhaps we can also take the steps needed to heal the wounds of racial tensions and injustices, and finish the unfinished business from which war and reparation for war have diverted us. Then we will have ensured that all people enjoy the benefits as well as the responsibilities of our society.

Isn't it also possible in our remembering of so many sacrifices and so many losses of our most precious resources, the youth of our nation, that we will find other ways of solving problems and resolving differences instead of war? As we discover the power of God's reconciling love in Christ's sacrifice can we take the first steps toward making sure there will never need to be another war? Can we reach out first in acts of reconciliation in a divided nation and a divided world? Can we discover again out of darkness and tragedy a new vision, a new perspective that sees the world as one: one people, one fellowship, joined in God's love for us?

Somewhere over our heads there are some men in a tiny spacecraft. They can see the earth as a lovely, glowing jewel in the vastness and darkness of space; life in all its infinite variety as we have been privileged to know it. They see it whole, its national boundaries erased, its conflicts forgotten. They see it with a new perspective. Our remembering can help us to have that kind of perspective. We can be renewed by the sacrifices of those who have given their lives in wars, and we can be renewed by Christ's sacrifice which once looked like defeat. We can become instruments of God's peace. Pray that in our remembering we may become a living memorial, bound in love with the living and the dead as ministers of peace.

Let us pray using a prayer attributed to St. Francis:

> Lord, make us instruments of your peace. Where there is hatred, let us sow love; where there is injury, pardon; where there is discord, union; where there is doubt, faith; where there is despair, hope; where there is darkness, light; where there is sadness, joy. Grant that we may not so much seek to be consoled as to console; to be understood as to understand; to be loved as to love. For it is in giving that we receive; it is in pardoning that we are pardoned; and it is in dying that we are born to eternal life. Amen.

28

Pilgrimage to the Wall
John K. Simmons

It was not thoughts of pilgrimage or sacred shrines that swirled about in my mind as our group rode up the long escalator from the Foggy Bottom metro station to the streets of Washington, D.C. No, it was just simple amazement at the changes that life brings that preoccupied me. Thirteen years ago, I was a conscientious objector to the Vietnam war. Living and working across the Potomac River in Arlington, Virginia, I served the nation for the required two years as an instructor in a program for mentally retarded adults. Declaring conscientious objection had not been an easy decision. After all, I was the son of a World War II Navy pilot and had been brought up to accept my obligation to serve my country—especially in time of war.

But it was clear to me by 1970 that the Vietnam war was a grave mistake. My conscience would not allow me to enter the military, yet I could not just wait out the war, hiding behind my student deferment. The Selective Service system itself was unjust, scooping up the poor and underprivileged to fight and die in Vietnam, while those more fortunate feasted on a veritable cornucopia of deferments. Alternate service seemed like a morally acceptable compromise, so I left family and college friends for the suburbs of northern Virginia.

Professor John Simmons is on the faculty of Western Illinois University where he has won several awards for distinguished teaching. Simmons was a conscientious objector during the war, and did alternative service in mental institutions in the Washington, D.C. area. He became a Teaching Assistant in an undergraduate class at UC Santa Barbara as he was doing his doctoral work, and was instrumental in encouraging and organizing the class's first annual field trip to the Vietnam Veterans Memorial in Washington. This essay reflects Simmons's experience in returning to the city of his alternative service, but, this time, in company with several Vietnam veterans who made the journey to pay tribute to friends and family members who had been killed in Vietnam. From this vantage point, the reconciliation to which Simmons refers near the end of the essay identifies a specific ritual act. The essay first appeared in *Christian Century*, November 6, 1985, pp. 998–1002.

254 / Symbolic Expressions, Ritual Healing

Weather permitting, I usually spent part of the weekends during those two years in the shadow of the Lincoln Memorial. I always found solace in the expansive lawns and wooded areas near the shrine. Perhaps the sturdy, marble columns surrounding the almost spiritual, guiding presence of the seated Lincoln offered a sense of security and continuity to a country that was now being torn apart by war.

Thirteen years ago, like today, the lawns were the setting for picnics and Frisbee games. People would climb the marble steps of the Lincoln Memorial to read that tribute to the soldiers who gave their lives at Gettysburg: " . . . from these honored dead we take increased devotion to that cause for which they gave the last full measure of devotion that we here highly resolve that these dead shall not have died in vain."

But 13 years ago, when the tourists turned to walk back down the memorial steps, they would not have looked out over a dark granite V cut into the green grass of the mall—a wall bearing the names of more than 58,000 American men and women who gave their lives so that "government of the people, by the people, for the people, shall not perish from this earth."

Walking with me down 17th Street from the Foggy Bottom station toward the mall were 18 students from the University of California, Santa Barbara, plus three highly decorated Vietnam combat veterans from the Santa Barbara community. As a teaching assistant for a class offered by the religious studies department at UCSB, "Religion and the Impact of the Vietnam War," I had organized a weekend excursion across the country to the Vietnam Veterans Memorial—a kind of pilgrimage to the wall.

At first it seemed like an improbable journey. Would students be willing to spend $400 for a weekend that didn't include skiing, a Prince concert, or a down payment on a BMW? Why would 20-year-olds, who weren't even born when the war started, be interested in Vietnam? And why would these veterans want to share such a profound personal experience with a conscientious objector and a group of students practically young enough to be their children?

That such a diverse group of people would make this journey is comprehensible only in light of Religious Studies 155. Founded in 1979 by Walter H. Capps as a course through which students could come to grips with the impact of the Vietnam war on American culture, the class has grown from its original 60 students to become the largest class in the university's history. Out of an undergraduate population of 15,000, 900 students regularly attend the course—easily outdrawing the perennial favorite, "Human Sexuality."

More than just an academic class, RS 155 has become a rite of

passage for UCSB students as well as a national forum for reconciliation and healing. Vietnam veterans—who were fighting in Vietnam
when they were the age of these students—come to the class to describe the highs and horrors of war. The vets have clearly been hurt
by the stigma of a "lost war," and by a nation that literally "spat in
their faces" when they returned home. Their heroism and sacrifice are
only just now being recognized. The students sense this pain and reach
out to them. Perhaps for the first time in 15 or 16 years, a veteran
hears those healing words, "Welcome home!" And a life that was
shattered by blood and bullets when it was 19 years old can begin
anew.

Nebraska governor Bob Kerry, who won a Congressional Medal of
Honor during the Vietnam war, has spoken to the class about the
positive lessons of the war. On another occasion James Quay, a conscientious objector during the war and currently administrative head of
the California Council for the Humanities, passionately reminded
students of the alternatives to military service. At the end of Quay's
lecture one of the veterans who regularly participates in the class
stood up and welcomed the conscientious objector home. Nine hundred students leapt to their feet applauding. Tears were shed. Beneath
the sometimes overwhelming emotions that often permeate the room,
however, students discover new dimensions of compassion and caring
within themselves.

Another visitor, John Wheeler, planted the seed that inspired the
trip to Washington. Wheeler, a West Point graduate and Vietnam
veteran, was a chairman of the Vietnam Veterans Memorial Fund. As
one of several Vietnam vets who raised the money, selected the design,
and supervised the construction of the memorial, Wheeler spoke eloquently and openly of the presence of the sacred that surrounds it.
The wall is not just a sign that healing is taking place in the nation,
he said. It is the center of that healing—a power spot where Americans
can come to renew a sense of national unity and belonging. To confront
the wall, he said, is to confront the collective pain and suffering left
from the war. I knew I had to go there. Others in the class felt as
strongly.

When I announced the possible adventure to the class, there was,
of course, immediate excitement. Many were called, but few could
rationalize the expenditure. Then one student suggested that the entire class could go symbolically by taking up a collection so that Mario
could go. Mario, who was dying of Agent-Orange poisoning, was the
last living member of his company. A single firefight in Vietnam took
the lives of 123 of his buddies. Of the five survivors who returned to
the States, four had committed suicide. Mario wanted to pay his

respects to his fallen comrades while he still could. Several hats were passed among the 900 students. Mario was able to join fellow veterans Paul and Wilson, 18 students and myself on our pilgrimage to the memorial. Everyone but Mario paid his or her own way.

We were a jovial, excited group, practically strutting down 17th Street. There is something warm and reassuring about embarking on an adventure surrounded by the friendship of fellow travelers. But the banter stopped once we crossed Constitution Avenue and approached the wall. Reaching the monument, the veterans, understandably, asked for some time to themselves.

Maybe our silence was the first sign of the sacred. People seem instinctively to become quiet and introspective in the presence of the monument.

At first I was hit with a looming sense of disappointment. The vets knew what they were doing, but what about the students? Would they get their money's worth? Something was wrong. It just didn't look like an appropriate setting for a sacred experience. The bright sunshine seemed to have brought the entire population of a winter-weary Washington out onto the mall. A constant stream of people flowed past the wall and the statue of the Vietnam soldiers. I guess I was expecting "clouds, blustery winds, and solitude"—nature's requiem for the dead.

My consternation quickly dissipated when we found John Wheeler and Jan Scruggs, who had agreed to meet us. Scruggs, a vet and a Washington attorney, initiated the Vietnam Veterans Memorial Fund and served as its president from the first dollar to the memorial's dedication on November 13, 1982. As we stood in a ragged, silent circle between the statue and the wall, Scruggs began to tell the story of the wall in hushed, even tones. It was a story of a dream, of struggle, of suffering, and of final accomplishment and reward—a classic "religious" narrative in the sense of the passing on of the myth of creation to new initiates. We were spellbound, frozen in that moment of our lives.

When Scruggs finished, Wheeler and the three veterans, without a word, marched briskly toward the statute of the three Vietnam veterans. The line of tourists filing past the bronze soldiers—at least 100 yards long—instinctively parted to let the four men through. Wheeler brought the vets to attention, and they saluted first the statue, then the wall. Holding a folded American flag, the three living Vietnam veterans raised their hands toward their immortalized comrades. Hands of flesh touched hands of bronze with the flag, empowering the sculpted warriors to act as sentries to guard the names of the honored dead that grace the wall.

Though 300 people had witnessed the rite, only the wind and a few muffled sobs were audible. Our small group grew by several who felt compelled to join us. Some stared at the wall, others at the statute. The long silence was finally broken when a young woman suggested that we form a circle and offer a prayer. John Wheeler, looking up to the sky, spontaneously prayed: "Lord, make us instruments of healing. Let this nation be healed." Then, friend and stranger alike embraced.

As we flew back across the country at 37,000 feet, we reflected on the monument's healing power and the sense of the sacred which we all felt. Something very vital and very real had come upon us, binding us together in an electrified communion. Toward the back of the 727, Mario and several students were busily organizing the rubbings they had taken from the wall—charcoal and paper impressions of the names of Mario's fallen comrades. He had promised to bring the souvenirs to friends and relatives in southern California. Each name was an invitation to a reunion, and the students stood transfixed as Mario wove stories that filled the plane with the memory of another generation "born in the U.S.A."

In the midst of our light-headed conversation in the front of the plane, Wilson and Paul had become increasingly subdued. Suddenly, Wilson held up his hand to break my enthusiastic chatter and said simply, "The real is not always a high."

Paul then elaborated. Vietnam had changed him forever. Feeling the life pass out of a mortally wounded compatriot, seeing starving Vietnamese children fighting over a handful of rice, smelling the stench of death that hung over a napalmed village—all the horrors of war had made the world searingly real for him. For the 17 years since he left Vietnam, it had been practically impossible to adjust to life in the United States. He had stared into the face of death; the American dream was just another nightmare dressed up in a three-piece suit and carrying a gold credit card.

Yet at the wall, Paul had experienced a genuine release from his long-term burden. After the spontaneous ceremony, he had gone off by himself and, sitting under a nearby tree, had cried for hours. There were tears for fallen friends, but, much to Paul's amazement, there were also tears of joy. He had encountered a realness bursting, for once, with hope. In the presence of the wall—a tombstone commemorating the dead—life, paradoxically, seemed not only possible but promising.

John Beyer, a student, understood. He had found his own name on the wall: a John Beyer had given his life in Vietnam at age 20—this student's own age. When he read the name and saw his reflection in the black marble, he was overcome with a sense of his own mortality—as well as the ultimate sacrifice that war demands. His interconnection with this John Beyer, a generation his senior, seemed to extend beyond the sharing of the same name.

But a moment later, despair had yielded to new awareness. The John Beyer on the wall could come alive in the John Beyer who understood the fragility and preciousness of peace and who had touched death and pulled back his hand. Once again, out of death springs new life and purpose.

Wilson's eyes were on fire. "Of course! That's how the wall heals," he said, pounding a fist on the arm rest. "We are all Vietnam veterans— soldiers, conscientious objectors, politicians, protestors—everyone whose life was torn apart by the war. But those whose names are crucified on the wall made the supreme sacrifice. And they are in charge of our resurrection into the real." He continued: "When we stand before the wall, all triviality vanishes. When we complete the circle, the dead on the wall become so much alive, reaching out to the living with this lesson: We all belong to life!"

I felt atonement in Wilson's burning gaze, and absolution in his message. Vietnam veterans are more than just teachers; they are high priests in a society that is struggling to break through years of repressed frustration and guilt. No human beings are better equipped to lift the veil of triviality from our lives than the men and women who endured the struggle that was Vietnam.

And just as there are no answers to the mystery and paradox of the sacred, the Vietnam Veterans Memorial engenders only questions. But they are the right questions, because out of death comes resurrection and out of emptiness comes compassion, wisdom, and life. We do not need to know the secrets of the sacred or how the wall heals. We need only to learn to live with the mystery. That in itself is a step toward the real.

29

The Father I Hardly Knew
Roger Worthington

The single most important event in my development as a human being, and certainly as a man, was the death of my father in Vietnam. Nothing else one could know about me could explain as much about who I am today as this one event.

On January 11, 1969, just weeks before my sixth birthday, Laurence David Worthington was killed in action while flying a helicopter in Vietnam. How did it change my life? Well, when I was a child, I never got a chance to explore or express my anger, rage, grief, or sadness. Why? At the time I hardly knew it was happening. As an adult I attribute this to the fact that, during the time, everyone in the nation was deeply affected by the war. Everybody had some reason to have an intense amount of emotion about the war. When they were confronted with me, my experience got lost in the intensity of the emotions that surfaced in them. The effect that had on me? I learned that other people couldn't understand my experience. Oftentimes adults told me how I *should* feel, how I *must* feel, rather than finding how I actually *did* feel. Eventually I began to tailor my descriptions of my feelings to what I thought each person expected me to feel. Most often this was related to whether they were a hawk or a dove, a hippie or a member of the establishment. To this day I still have difficulty saying how I feel.

What happened was that I vacillated between extreme pride and patriotism over having my father die for something he believed our country was founded upon and resentment toward the government for killing my father.

When I was about eleven years old, I was home sick one day, watching game shows on television, when a newscaster interrupted the program I was watching. The coverage was of a jet landing in Wash-

Roger Worthington is a doctoral candidate in educational psychology in the University of California, Santa Barbara. He journeyed to Washington, D.C., to pay respects to his father's name on the Vietnam Veterans Memorial in February, 1990.

ington, D.C. full of returning POW's. As the first man came through the doorway to exit the plane, I examined his face closely . . . Maybe, just maybe. No, it wasn't him. Then the next man appeared, and I scooted closer to the set. No, that wasn't him either. Yes, I told myself. It might be possible that there had been a mistake . . . some horrible mistake and my father would be the next person to step off the plane. But as the plane emptied, my heart began to sink. My anger began to surface, and suddenly I was crying desperately, beating my fists on the ground, asking the never-ending question, Why?!!! Why me?!!!

I think this was probably the beginning of a very destructive period in my life. I began to get into fights, mostly at school or after school, usually with kids who were bigger and older, and I almost always won. You see I had an advantage. I had the channeled energy of hatred and rage I had carried with me for a long time inside. I also started smoking cigarettes, and abusing substances regularly by the time I was thirteen. My grades dropped from straight A's in grade school to mostly D's and F's in junior high and high school, with an occasional A or B when a teacher connected with me or inspired me.

After dropping out of high school at the end of my junior year, I went back to begin my senior year at a new school in a new district. My old school refused my senior preference; they were glad to be rid of me, and didn't want me back if they didn't have to take me. I was in this sophomore English class; we had a substitute that day. And his lesson plan was to do what substitute teachers do best, that is, talk about current events. In the news that day was the re-establishment of the Selective Service, the Iran hostage situation, the presidential election of 1980, and the turmoil in Nicaragua. It wasn't long before the discussion turned into a heated debate between me and another guy about sending troops into Nicaragua. You'll never guess what side I was on. . . . I was hawk that day. I said "Send 200,000 men in against their 10,000, and it will all be over in a matter of days. We don't want no more Vietnams." The other guy stood up, glared at me, and said, "I lost two uncles in Vietnam!" *I lost my father in Vietnam*!! As if the loss of his two uncles could ever compare to the loss of my father. If he were here today, though, I would apologize to him.

Later my best friend from high school became my best friend. I told him what had happened, and, more than anything else, he wanted to know what it was like for me, what it was like for *me* to have lost my father in the war. It wasn't out of morbid curiosity or intense feelings from inside himself; it was about compassion. I spent hours, for the first time telling anybody, what I had been feeling all those years. All it took was for somebody—a seventeen-year-old kid—to listen.

Today I am the godfather to his first son.

Not too long after that he and I were supposed to meet after school at the house of one of his friends who was only an acquaintance of mine. I won't mention why we were going over there, but it was illegal. He was already there when I arrived. The door was open, and just before I knocked on the screen door I could hear them talking inside. "Man, I don't want that guy coming into my house." "Why, what do you have against Roger?" "Nothing, man, I just don't trust him, man. He's kinda weird." "Man, there ain't nothin' wrong with Roger. Give the guy a break, man. His dad was killed in Vietnam." "Who cares, that was ten years ago, man." My reaction? I knocked on the door and never said a word about what I had heard. Needless to say, we took care of our business and left immediately.

From that day on I started to look at my life in terms of how being a Vietnam War Orphan affected the way I behaved. The fighting, the drugs, the conflict with my mother and my brother, the lack of intimate relationships. . . . Had all that unexpressed emotion made me weird? Yes. Luckily I haven't recovered from it yet.

Suddenly I became a pacifist and joined the anti-nuke movement. I did a presentation in a college history class about Vietnam Veterans, covering much of what was said in this class and in the movie *Platoon.* I started researching the war through movies, books, and music. I created a homemade video of Hollywood's representation of the war. I explored my deepening feelings in support groups as part of my training to become a psychologist. And then about three years ago the energy I was putting into stuffing all those emotions had been released.

It wasn't until the birth of my son, and my entry into fatherhood, that I suddenly became aware of new aspects of the situation I had never considered. *Dreams.* Then one day, January 12, 1990, almost twenty-one years to the day after my father was killed in action in Vietnam, I was given a document that read as follows:

> By Direction of the President, the Distinguished Flying Cross (Posthumously) is Presented to Warrant Officer Laurence D. Worthington, United States Army, for heroism while participating in aerial flight evidence by voluntary actions above and beyond the call of duty: Warrant Officer Worthington distinguished himself by exceptionally valorous actions as pilot of an armed helicopter covering extraction of friendly soldiers from a command post. When the extracting aircraft came under enemy fire, he fearlessly flew his aircraft at low level, drawing fire from the enemy in order to locate their positions. He sighted an enemy unit advancing toward the command post and immediately halted their advance by placing devastating machine gun fire into their positions, until he was fatally wounded by an enemy round. Warrant Officer Worthington's courageous perfor-

mance permitted the friendly forces to be extracted without casualties. His actions were in keeping with the highest traditions of the military service and reflect great credit upon himself, his unit, and the United States Army.

To that day, I had never known that my father was a hero.

Later I went to the Wall in Washington, D.C. with my brother Ken. Before going to the Wall, in the hotel room, we read aloud a letter our mother had written to both of us. She said she was proud of us, and that she wished she could have been there with us. She said she wished things could have been different, that we could have known our father, and that he would be most proud of us now.

At the Wall we read aloud another letter from our mother to our father. She said that she was sorry things hadn't worked out in their marriage before he left. She said things had been hard for all of us without him in our lives. She said how proud he would be of his sons. She was the first to tell him that he was a grandparent, that I had a beautiful son he would love . . . that he would be proud of the father I had become. We also read a Psalm and a poem sent along with us by our grandparents. We cried and hugged each other, and tried to shut out the tourists who were now beginning to watch us in our personal moments—taking pictures.

As we laid the letters and the poems at the base of the Wall in front of his name, hugged, and turned to leave, a group of four teenage girls walked up, grabbed the letters, and began to read them out loud, unaware that my brother and I, who were only a few feet away from them, had just left them there. We watched them for a moment without saying a word. One said, "Put it back. These don't belong to you." The other responded, "she told us to read the letters. She said they would make us cry. I want to see if this makes us cry." We didn't stay around to find out.

When we came back to the Wall the next day, the letter was gone, but the poem and the Psalm were still there—neatly tucked into a crevice between the panels of the Wall. We circled and passed once before reapproaching the panel with my father's name. I went up to the Wall and touched my father's name, pointing it out to a friend. I bent down into a crouch and my brother joined me as we began to scratch out an etching with a pencil and a piece of paper. The silence was deafening for a moment before I heard a sniffle from behind me, and then a hushed expression of sadness.

The first step away from the Wall was very difficult. I felt almost guilty that on this day I was showing no outward sign of emotion. I felt a little as if we were on display. It was difficult to look into the eyes of those around us.

We were introduced to Wanda Ruffin and her daughter, Wende. Wende had lost her father in the war. We talked politely, briefly, about how Wende had met a man at the Wall who knew her dad during the war. Chills ran up and down my spine. I couldn't imagine what that would be like, but I wanted to find out. Wende's mother happened to be the projects coordinator of In Touch, the program that puts families and friends of the men whose names are on the Wall in touch with the veterans who served with them. She provided us with the paperwork to join the program.

We also talked with Eleanor Wimbish, briefly, exchanging addresses for correspondence. Eleanor understood what we were experiencing, for she had lost her son Billy in the war.

Later that night I went back to the Wall. I had to leave two more pieces of paper with my own words written on them. I stopped at my father's name, touched it, said a silent prayer and neatly tucked the poems into the crevice at the bottom of the Wall so they wouldn't blow away. As we walked away, suddenly the wind died, and we stopped in our tracks, standing very still for just a moment before we again began to walk, and the wind came again. These are the words of one of the poems:

VIETNAM
Vietnam
Vietnam
Vietnam
Oh how that word haunts me
Vietnam
The word rings in my head
And oh how I wish that you weren't dead
I think you may have left your soul
In Vietnam
I don't know
What may have been different
Had you never gone
Volunteered to give your life
In that bloodstained strip of land
Called Vietnam
Maybe you would have taught me things
About peace and freedom and liberty?
Or maybe wine, women, and song?
I don't know
All I really wanted was to know you
What you believed
The things you stood for
Or just to hear those words once more

"I love you, son."
Maybe you don't know
Just who you left behind
Or how much your image torments my mind
The child within me
Yearning for your touch
   to climb into your lap
   feel your arms around me
   as they squeeze me tight
   telling me, quietly,
   "It's all right."
And all the years
Running, running, running away
Looking, hoping, searching
Wondering if ever I might find
What it takes to fill the void
The one you left behind
When you volunteered to die
In that bloodstained strip of land
The one they call
Vietnam.

When I got back home, it took some time to put it all in perspective. Finally, twenty one years after Laurence David Worthington was killed in action in Vietnam, I have found a voice for the emotions that lived so violently beneath the silence of a child—one that I can live with. One that tells me not to live a life that has put this war "behind me." One that tells me that I never have to "get over it." One that tells me I don't have to pretend "it didn't really matter because I never really knew him." One that tells me that what is important in life sleeps quietly at night in the bedroom next to mine—my son. One that tells me that I am responsible to help create a world where he does not fear the kind of war his grandfather died in. And I have hope.

I hope we can turn to one another in efforts to heal the wounds an entire generation suffered to one degree or another. I hope we can continue to learn how to comfort the lives of the men who had to suffer through it—only to return home to silence and hatred. I hope we can put our best medical technology to work for those who came home torn, and burned, and diseased. My hope is that it will someday represent something that made my father's life worth giving—the war that taught our nation how to escape the tragedy of another war. For me this war will never end—not until we have healed the wounds of all of us who suffered from it, and we begin to learn how to build a world without war.

30

In Tribute to Bill
Eleanor Wimbish

Dear Bill,

Today is February 13, 1984. I came to this black wall again to see and touch your name and as I do I wonder if anyone ever stops to realize that next to your name, on this black wall, is your mother's heart. A heart broken 15 years ago today, when you lost your life in Vietnam.

And as I look at your name, William R. Stocks, *I think of how many, many times I used to wonder how scared and homesick you must have been in that strange country called Vietnam. And if and how it might have changed you, for you were the most happy-go-lucky kid in the world, hardly ever sad or unhappy. And until the day I die I will see you as you laughed at me, even when I was very mad at you, and the next thing I knew we were laughing together.*

But on this past New Year's Day I had my answer. I talked by phone to a friend of yours, from Michigan, who spent your last Christmas and the last four months of your life with you. Jim told me how you died, for he was there and saw the helicopter crash. He told me how you had flown your quota and had not been scheduled to fly that day. How the regular pilot was unable

---

Eleanor Wimbish first became known to persons outside her family and community after she left letters to her son, William R. Stocks, attached to his name on the wall of the Vietnam Veterans Memorial in Washington, D.C. She lives in Glen Burnie, Maryland, and, on Christmas Day, each year, brings a Christmas tree, together with gifts and food, to the Memorial in Washington, recognizing that on this "the loneliest of all holidays" a number of Vietnam War veterans will gather there. Mrs. Wimbish's letters have been published in Laura Palmer's *Shrapnel in the Heart*. The two letters and one statement included here were sent to the editor directly by Eleanor Wimbish, in her own hand, with permission to reproduce them in the hope that others will join the peace effort, a. .d bring to an end the devastation that brings such thorough grief to mothers of those who were killed in battle.

to fly that day and had been replaced by someone with less experience. How they did not know the exact cause of the crash. How it was either hit by enemy fire or they hit a pole or something unknown. How the blades went through the chopper and hit you. How you lived about a half hour, but were unconscious and therefore did not suffer.

He said that your jobs were like sitting ducks. They would send you men out to draw the enemy into the open and that they would send in the big guns and planes to take over. Meantime, death came to so many of you.

He told me how, after a while over there, instead of a yellow streak, the men got a mean streak down their backs. Each day the streak got bigger and the men became meaner. Everyone but you, Bill. He said how you stayed the same, happy-go-lucky guy that you were when you arrived in Vietnam. How your warmth and friendliness drew the guys to you. How your Lt. Romeriz gave you the nickname of Spanky and soon your group, Jim included, were all known as Spanky's gang. How when you died it made it so much harder on them for you were their moral support. And he said how you, of all people, should never have been the one to die.

Oh, God, how it hurts to write this. But I must face it and then put it to rest. I know that after Jim talked to me, he must have re-lived it all over again and suffered so. Before I hung up the phone I told Jim I loved him. Loved him for just being your close friend and for sharing the last days of your life with you and for being there with you when you died. How lucky you were to have him for a friend, and how lucky he was to have had you.

Later that same day I received a phone call from a mother in Billings, Montana. She had lost her daughter, her only child, a year ago. She needed someone to talk to for no one would let her talk about the tragedy. She said she had seen me on CNN-TV on New Year's Eve, after the Christmas letter I wrote to you and left at this Memorial had drawn newspaper and television attention. She said she had been thinking about me all day and just had to talk to me. She talked to me of her pain, and seemingly needed me to help her with it. I cried for this heart-broken mother, and after I hung up the phone I laid my head down and cried so hard for her. Here was a mother calling me for help with her pain over the loss of her child, a grown daughter. And as I sobbed I thought, how can I help her with her pain when I have never completely been able to cope with my own?

They tell me the letters I write to you and leave here at this Memorial are waking others up to the fact that there is still much pain left, after all these years, from the Vietnam War.

But this I know: I would rather to have had you for 21 years and all the pain that goes with losing you than never to have had you at all.

Mom

Dear Bill,

Today is February 13, 1985. I sit here writing to you with the tears falling quietly down my face while outside the rain is hitting on the window as if to tell me the whole world is crying with me because it, too, feels my pain. This time of the year is so hard for me because I can never forget the exact moment when I heard of your death. And the pain as my heart broke in that never to be forgotten day. Even today I have a hard time really believing my big young son is no longer here. Each year I wish I could sleep this day through. But this is your father's birthday and you also have a nephew, Bryan, who was born on this day, twelve years after you died.

And with two very special people in my life, celebrating their birthday today, I have to try not to give in to my emotions and, for your father's sake, must try to be happy with him on his special day.

So instead of a long letter to you today, Bill, I am adding a story, of sorts, of my never ending pain of losing you and the pain the 2,482 P.O.W./M.I.A.'s and their families are still living with each and every day. And my hopes that those who read this will do what they can to help end this terrible tragedy for these men and their loved ones and bring them home.

I wish every day that things were different and you were still with us, but that's not the way it is. So I'll close for now, but not before telling you how much we still love and miss you.

There have been many changes in our lives as the years went by, but the love we all have for you, my son, my Billy, will never change.

Mom

In our family, in our home, and in our lives, the Vietnam War will never end. There is no enemy that you can see. There are no weapons, no fighting, no hardships. Only an emptiness because a loved one is missing, and the never ending questions of Why?

For, you see, this loved one of ours went to that war, that Vietnam War. He took his laughter, his jokes, and his love for life, and went to that far-away country. Flying away, late one night, from the ones who loved him. Away to unknown dangers and unknown lands.

Where did he go, this young son of mine, who was so full of life and had this gift of laughter, this gift of always giving love and happiness to others?

Where did he go, this brother, who gave so much to his younger brother and three sisters, as any brother ever has?

Where did he go, this friend, who left an emptiness in the lives of so many?

And where is he now? Now, he is just a memory. Now he is a name on a black wall in Washington, D.C., surrounded by 58,011 other names. I come to this Memorial often to see his name, WILLIAM R. STOCKS, and to rub each letter as I once again feel the pain of losing him, for you see I am his Mom.

I'm the one who rocked him as a baby. I'm the one who kissed away the hurts. I'm the one who taught him right from wrong. I'm the one who cried when Uncle Sam said, "I want you." I'm the one who hugged and kissed him for the last time and watched him fly away from me to war. I'm the one who prayed each night, "Dear God, please keep him safe." And I'm the goofy Mom who sent a Christmas tree to him in Vietnam. I'm also the one whose heart broke when told this big young Son of mine had died in that far away country called Vietnam. And I'm the one who still cries because of all the memories I have of him that will never die.

So Vietnam, Vietnam, what did you take from me? You took my son Bill. You took part of my hopes and dreams. You broke my heart! You took something from me that most people do not even realize they have until they lose it, and that is a feeling of security. These things and more you took from me when you took my son Bill. You absolutely changed my life, and from then on, nothing was ever the same.

Vietnam was a tragedy for so many. But how many people know the tragedy of that war still goes on for the 2,482 American men who are still being held in Vietnam? What is being done to get these men back where they belong? What is being done to end the suffering for these men and their families?

Think about the word *Freedom*. If we live in the land of the brave and the free, then why are our brave young men who went to Vietnam to fight for that freedom, why are *they* not free? These men are listed as P.O.W./M.I.A.s but they are more than that. They are human beings. They are *husbands, sons, fathers, brothers,* and much, much more. Please help to get these men home and end this suffering for them and their loved ones. (Written by a mother who lost her son in Vietnam, but still cares about the ones who are still there.)

31

Reunion
Wilson Hubbell

We had been in DC for several days and were scheduled to leave for home in the afternoon of a day when some of us made one last visit to The Wall. I was helping students take rubbings of names for fellow classmembers, and noticed a man about my age who was watching us work. After some time he came over to where we were and approached me. He looked into my face and asked, "Were you with an Army helicopter unit dear Qui Nhon in 1968?"

I just stared at him in stunned silence for a few seconds. He had just described my old unit and the very year I served in it. "Yes," I said.

"Yeah, I remember you," he responded. For a moment I stared even deeper into his eyes, searching for something that would remind me of one young soldier long ago, somebody I flew with: a pilot, a crew chief, a door gunner, a mechanic. But it wasn't there.

"I was with the 173rd Airborne," he said. "You used to carry us in and out of LZs all over II Corps."

I couldn't believe it. I just kept staring at the guy. He had been an infantryman we had hauled around periodically and had remembered my face twenty years later!

We talked the old soldiers' talk of good times and bad. He knew I hadn't recognized him, and he knew why. "You saw the whole world come and go from the back of that helicopter," he said. "All I knew was that you were the last face I would see when you dropped us in on a mission and the first I would see when you came back to pick us up. I will never forget your face, man."

Wilson Hubbell is a Santa Barbara Vietnam War Veteran who has been a frequent participant in the UC Santa Barbara class. In 1988 he traveled with members of the class to Washington, D.C. on the annual field-trip to the Vietnam Veterans Memorial. The "reunion" event is described in Hubbell's words, as it was written specifically for this anthology.

We talked some more. He was living in Florida, and doing odd jobs. He had managed to get bus fare together for a trip to Washington and was bound and determined to come to the Memorial.

Looking back now it seems ironic. I had to leave him to catch the plane back to California. For days afterward I kept feeling that I should have brought him with me.

32

The Memorial as Symbol and Agent of Healing

Lisa M. Capps

War creates wounds—figuratively as well as literally. It generates separations among citizens. It produces impassioned differences of opinion and cements opposing ideologies. These wounds are acknowledged as the war is discussed and clarified, and as we work toward understanding individual losses, personal tragedies in the light of positive national significance. Healing occurs as we bestow meaning upon the war experience. War memorials both signify and promote this process. Thus, any commemoration of the Vietnam experience had to be an integral part of our nation's healing. The problem that architect Maya Lin had to solve was that of designing a healing monument for a war with no generally agreed upon meaning.

The existence of a traditional monument is a symbol of the fact that we, as a nation, have reached a consensus about the meaning of the experience, and that we stand united behind it. Its design embodies the meaning of the experience that we have chosen to adopt. Thus, the design which is agreed upon constitutes a concrete object according to which healing can continue. William James captured the function of traditional commemorations to wars and warriors in a speech he gave at the unveiling of the Robert Gould Shaw Memorial in Boston on May 31, 1897. The monument told him that the Civil War would not take its place amongst all other "old, unhappy, far-off things and battles long ago."[2] It was a sign of our commitment to remember, honor, and redress unhappiness. It identified all lives lost in the war, those "commemorated solely in the hearts of mourning mothers, wid-

Lisa M. Capps is currently enrolled in the doctoral program in clinical psychology at UCLA. The essay included in this anthology is a portion of an honor's thesis that was completed in 1987 while she was a student in Stanford University. Her contention that "the wall's symbolic capacity has its roots not in a system of signs, but in the emotional texture of the Vietnam experience itself" was developed during the course of hundreds of interviews of persons (vets, family members, citizens, tourists) who came to visit the Memorial during the summer of 1985.

owed brides, or friends" with that of Robert Shaw, and lauded and praised selfless service. It spoke to James of lessons learned, conflicts resolved, the nobility of sacrifice, and reestablished national unity. The monument granted the experience "but one meaning in the eye of history." That meaning was symbolized, through the memorial to Shaw, in the virtues of the first Negro regiment, a regiment that "moved together, a single resolution kindled in their eyes [as they] marched, warm-blooded champions of a better day for man."[3] As James himself conceded, "the bronze that makes their memory eternal betrays the very soul and secret of those awful years."[4]

The bronze that makes their memory eternal, symbolizes their experiences, provided James with a model for both thought and action. It portrayed the miserable legacies of the war, the less-than-secret awful years, as a testimony to the fact that "Americans of all complexions and conditions can go forth like brothers, and meet death cheerfully if need be, in order [to preserve] the religion of our native land," which James defined as "faith that a man requires to master to take care of him, and that common people can work out their salvation well enough together if left to try . . ."[5] Through the monument, James explained, American citizens were able to link themselves with "a nation blest above all nations," they found solace in the notion that the civic virtues of the people saved the State in time. It instilled faith that their adoption of such virtue would ward off boundless evil, and united all in this continued battle against the powers of darkness. Thus, the traditional war memorial was revealed as both a symptom and agent of healing.

The traditional pattern of healing could not be followed in the case of Vietnam. There was, is not now, and may never be a consensus about the meaning of America's involvement in Vietnam. America was "torn apart for nearly a decade [by] the inability of three presidents to persuade enough Americans that freedom was at issue in Indochina,"[6] at least to a degree that warranted an exhaustive, expensive, destructive American intervention—the price of which was paid with 58,000 American lives. Vietnam, America's most unpopular, most divisive, and longest war, "created its own San Andreas Fault between and within the hearts and minds of Americans."[7] The cracks and fissures continued to spread and divide. Divisions were so deep that some are still unclear and unrecognized. Bill Mahedy, a former chaplain who has worked with troubled veterans, called Vietnam an "undigested lump of life. It simply won't go down."[8] "The war" is still debated in bars and boardrooms, in homes and colleges. We struggle with the meaning of what we did, with the propriety of America's involvement in Vietnam. We question whether Western values and interests were so threatened as to "warrant the war that was fought ostensibly on the [behalf of the South Vietnamese], and the destruction wrought in their name."[9] We question the validity of the "convincing evidence" which indicated that American military had the power, or knew how, to halt or defeat the Vietcong. We continue to debate the nature of our loss—whether it was a "failure of the will to win," or whether, given time and assistance, we would have, and should have, won. We question the extent to which the United States supported its soldiers, the reason we allowed so many lives to be lost. We discuss the role of those who resisted and demonstrated against the draft. But instead of resolution, frustration, finger-pointing, and contradictory lessons bred by a decade of television images are all embedded in our nation's psyche. Thus, it seems that the losses in Vietnam cannot be soothed by deeming it "a war to end wars," or to save freedom, or to make the world safe for democracy. For this war, there is no easily achieved consensus according to which individual losses and wounds can be given unambiguous positive national meaning.

If a memorial is viewed as a symbol and agent of healing—an embodiment of nationally ordained meaning which accelerates the healing process—the lack of accepted meaning with respect to the war in Vietnam presents a problem for those who wish to memorialize the experience; to address sustained losses through traditional symbol systems. In light of this, a memorial to the Vietnam War seems to present a paradox. The situation in which Lin's design was selected, and the "message" it conveys, evince the absence of established meaning, and in so doing, seem to reinforce the sense of its paradoxical nature. However, analysis reveals that the wall is a symbol and agent of healing, but functions in a way that is radically different from the traditional mode.

The Vietnam Veterans Memorial was not conceived as an effort to create a structure which reflects and promulgates agreement regarding the meaning of the war. It was not a result of the adoption of a particular consensus of opinion which might resolve the Vietnam experience. But rather, it was preceded by Jan Scruggs' (who was the first to conceive of a national memorial) *desire* to begin the healing process. He regarded memorialization as a vital part of this process, and sought the support of others who shared both his belief in the need and his desire to heal. The wall, then, began not as a symbol of healing, but, rather as a symbol of the *desire to heal.*

The traditional sequence of healing through memorialization moves from agreement upon meaning, to the selection of a design which conveys sculpturally or architecturally the meaning that has been agreed upon. However, with respect to the situation in America following Vietnam, Scruggs acknowledged not agreement, but its absence. The multitude of Americans who shared his desire for healing similarly acknowledged the lack of consensus with regard to meaning. Thus, neither Scruggs nor the wider community had a sense of the shape that a memorial would take. All were open to suggestions—crying out for suggestions—and were united only in their cries. Their selection of Lin's abstract design reflected general agreement that no consensus had been reached, as well as the fact that those creating a memorial were not attempting to designate or promote one view in particular. They did not select a concrete embodiment of a clear-cut message. It is indeterminate. In short, it is a symbol of their desire to promote healing, and a crucial part of the effort to do so.

In addition to its symbolic function, the wall serves as an agent. Insofar as it symbolizes the desire to heal, it instigates this desire in those who reflect upon it. The wall makes way for healing by attacking the barriers which obstruct the traditional flow of healing inherent in the Vietnam experience—barriers of discord and silence. Disagreement regarding the events of the war and the propriety of our nation's involvement was ferocious, widespread, and continuous. The discord is well documented. But as important, and perhaps more distinctly true of the Vietnam experience, was the silence which prevailed among significant numbers of Americans in the postwar period. It was a frustrating silence that took three general forms: the silence of denial; the silence of inarticulate emotions in need of a vehicle of expression; and the silence of those so alienated from the experience that they were unable, or refused, to engage their feelings.

For many Americans, including those in the media and government, the war once over was treated as a dead subject.[10] Vietnam veterans returned to a nation which neither celebrated nor affirmed their service, but rather refused to legitimize it, ignored it. John Wheeler wrote in *Touched With Fire*, "The shock and [the hurt] for a lot of us coming home was the gradual realization over the first few hours, then days, that there was a social taboo against our experience."[11] "Friends and family only wanted you to quietly and happily join their sanitized, safe lives."[12] The war and its soldiers were disassociated from other wars in which our nation has been engaged. Postwar America largely denied the service of those who fought on her behalf with lingering, subtle, and reproachful disregard.

However, silence and denial did not remove Vietnam from its powerful place in our nation's psyche. Rather, the events and circumstances that characterize the Vietnam War years created an array of divisions which were not dissipated, but consolidated, by silence. A decade after he ceased his activities, Sam Brown, a leader of the antiwar movement said, "My feelings toward members of my generation are different. We remain split from within and from the generations before and behind us. I feel a sense of separateness . . ."[13]

Widespread personal and national efforts to deny the reality of the war in the postwar period caused the multitude of wounds which stemmed from these divisions to continue to fester. They did not alleviate pain, but prolonged feelings of separation and loneliness, and suspended grief, anger, and guilt. The silence in the form of denial, with which America bound its wounds, proved instead to breed and aggravate them. As John Wheeler wrote:

> [The] man who wore the uniform is separated from [those] who did not . . . woman is separated from man . . . Finally, self has been separated from self as most of us suppress recognition of the memories and consequences of our choices made in the 1960's and 1970's. These separations . . . leave many of us harboring unnecessary hurts.[14]

Because the war held different meanings for different people, "putting it back in the closet"[15] required burying a variety of wounds. This process spawned an insidious lingering silence, masking heartfelt emotion and stifling expression.

According to Wheeler, silence hid, and continues to hide, a vast array of wounds born by veterans. He wrote that "Those who came back were made to keep [their] sense of loss and grief inside . . ."[16] While debate and demonstrations raged at home, our soldiers underwent challenges equal to or greater than those faced in earlier wars. For the soldier, intense guerilla warfare meant isolation and months of unrelieved combat with an unseen enemy.[17] There were no definite fronts and objectives were vague.[18] Distinctions between ally and enemy were unclear. The farmer by day was the soldier by night; the smiling "mamasan" was often a Viet Cong sympathizer. Soldiers were subjected to unimaginable pressures. Exposure to fighting was the rule, not the exception, and combat paranoia was endemic.[19] For many veterans nervousness—and confusion, horror, bitterness, boredom, fear, and exhaustion—were accompanied by depression stemming from the feeling that their efforts were wasted in a war they could not win.[20]

> The "unpopular war," the "dirty little war," also produced intense feelings of guilt. According to Phil Caputo, author of *A Rumor Of War*, Vietnam created a triple burden of guilt. . . . There is the guilt all soldiers feel for having broken the taboo against killing, a guilt as

old as war itself. Add to this the soldier's sense of shame for having
fought in actions that resulted, indirectly or directly, in the deaths
of civilians. Then pile on top of that an attitude of social opprobrium,
an attitude that made the fighting men feel personally morally responsible for the war, and you get the proverbial walking time
bomb.[21]

"Those at home" also "harbor hurts" amidst the lingering silence.
For non-fighting men, wounds stemming from the war years touched
nerves connected to loyalty, power, and masculinity. Christopher
Buckley wrote of the wounds of those who did not go:

> I didn't suffer with them. I didn't watch my buddies getting wiped
> out next to me. And although I'm relieved, at the same time I feel as
> though part of my reflex action is not complete. . . . I haven't served
> my country. I've never faced life or death. I walk by the Memorial
> and look at the names and think, "There but for the grace of God.
> . . ." The dean once told me, "You know, the one thing your generation
> has done is [to have] made martyrdom painless. . . ." [My wound] is
> guilt at not having participated. At not having done anything. I blew
> up neither physics labs in Ann Arbor nor Vietcong installations. I just
> vacillated in the middle . . . I know I should have gone, if only to bear
> witness.[22]

There were gaps between generations in which silent pain fed on
itself. Some years later, Buckley confessed his anxiety in knowing that
if he has a son who asks him what he did in the Vietnam War, he'll have
to tell him that his own war experience, unlike that of his grandfather,
consisted of a hemorrhoid check.[23] The events in Vietnam transformed
patriotism into a barrier of pain which stood between World War Two
veterans and their sons and daughters. Fathers who remembered a
time of simpler choices, a time when one went to war without question, experienced shame, heartbreak, and anger over sons who chose
not to go to Vietnam. They felt betrayed, they felt that their own
service to America had been tainted, that their selfless dedication to
a noble cause had been made less meaningful—defiled. These private
battles constitute a significant class of the wounds of war. They are,
however, battles waged in silence.

Silence covered guilt felt by women because they were not obliged
to go to war. Suzanne Woolsey, who served as the associate director
of the Office of Management Budget in the Carter administration,
traced seeds of anger and pain implanted by the Vietnam experience.

> [I had] a feeling I suspect most women have, of guilt. Of being safe. We
> went through that generation never having to worry about student

deferments. We had to worry about our men. We never had to worry about our physical safety . . . it was all so very nice I wasn't about to give it up. But it made me feel guilty . . .[24]

In the preoccupations of the movements, amid the chaos and confusion, all of those in love with men serving in Vietnam suffered a great deal of pain. Lynda Siegel Zengerle, wife of a veteran, elaborated:

> While Joe was in Vietnam . . . I was trying to stop the war. I was a woman alone in Washington . . . I had no friends or family . . . I just sort of met people. I was often invited to cocktail parties and dinner parties where people would ask, "Well, where is your husband?" Back in the sixties that's how you were identified. I would answer, "He's in Vietnam." Talk about a conversation killer! I was left alone so quickly. I would look around and, all of a sudden nobody would be talking to me. They didn't want to know about it . . . I was a pariah, and it was not just Joe that was an outcast—I was an outcast. There was nobody I could talk to in 1968 except other Army wives, and I was not living on a military base. I was not affiliated in any way . . . When Joe came back, one of the first things I said to him was that he was not the only one out there who was being touched by all of this. As worried as I was about him, I was angry about the way people were treating me . . .[25]

The wounds which surfaced from beneath Lynda's silence indicate unexpressed emotions. She was like many members of the Vietnam generation who were "out of touch" with parts of themselves because they simply could not express what they felt.[26] Much of the Vietnam experience, then, remains undigested. In the place of concrete, clarified expression, silence manifests the "separation of self from self."[27]

John Wheeler recalled that "for five years of [his] life, [he] followed society's rule that part of life—[his] life—was to be excised."[28] And as Christopher Buckley wrote:

> I think, there was in almost all the people at least a modicum of this feeling that they were doing their duty too, and the problem now is that, because there were also these other elements which most of them look back on with some chagrin, with some shame, that most people have not been able to honestly sort out the things they should be proud about and advertise as values to their children, to other people, and the things they should honestly regret. And so it was the unspoken and unanalyzed [which caused] the hurt . . .[29]

Unspoken wounds were indistinct and blurred. The pain was only vaguely identified, yet nonetheless powerful.

The presence of the wall was in effect a direct attack on the denial that prevailed in America. It brought the Vietnam War back into public consciousness. Its excruciating display of 58,000 names of those whose lives it took made denial impossible. The presence of the wall contradicted "orders" which insisted that Vietnam belongs "in the closet." Furthermore, it provided for "honest reflection" such that

> no matter how you look at it, you always saw yourself reflected back among the names. No matter who you were, you could no longer deny that you shared responsibility. You realized that you had to learn from this war, that you could not escape its pain.[30]

Its location on the Mall also caused us to acknowledge Vietnam as a part of American history. As a national memorial to those who served, the wall was a retraction of messages—those blatantly hostile as well as silently insidious—conveyed to veterans which negate the nobility of their sacrifice, and suggest that they do the same. It pledges that "at the going down of the sun and in the morning we shall remember them."[31] To hear the names being read, to read the names, is to remember.

The wall brought people together, and in so doing redressed the situation of denial. It gathered those with opposing viewpoints— the silenced, confused, angry, resentful, and proud—simultaneously housing assortments of visitors which include Vietnam veterans, veterans from previous wars, mothers, wives, sons, people adorned with anti-war paraphernalia.[32] This helped to decrease separations between people and to reduce the reluctance to divulge and to share, thus allowing the Vietnam experience to surface. As Jan Scruggs wrote, time spent at the wall is

> a time for decompression. For remembering youth and innocence. For talking and thinking. For telling the story of the guy who walked point instead of you and died. For seeing a familiar face and shouting, "Is that you! Is that really you?" For saying what you were so afraid your wife would leave you. For finally breaking down. For finding that piece of yourself that had been missing.[33]

As Scruggs's statement indicates, the wall redresses efforts to "overcome" through denial. It breaks the silence masking unexpressed emotions.

Although Lin did not seek to shape a particular response, or convey a single message, her effort was not devoid of intent. As we saw, she sought to stimulate reflection, to create a place for the emotional catharsis that was frustrated through the repression of the war experience.[34] The wall's design reflects the complex diversity of wounds which yearn for a vehicle of expression. In its open-endedness it houses a limitless array of feelings.

The wall serves as a much needed focal point for expression. As the friend of a Vietnam veteran wrote in a letter of gratitude to Scruggs, the Memorial "provides visitors with the opportunity to express the grief, to relieve the pain and the tears . . ."[35] Following a visit to the wall journalist Philip Boffey described what he saw as "a catharsis for openly moved spectators and for veterans who have long felt themselves a neglected, discarded army . . ."[36] One vet who stood before the wall spoke for many in expressing, for the first time since Vietnam, the desire to grieve.[37] The Memorial facilitates long-awaited expressions of grief. Art McGovern wrote in *The Congressional Record*, "Our moments at the Memorial constituted the most intense mourning of our lives."[38]

Others, like nurse Sarah Lee McGoran, said, with tears in her eyes, that before viewing the wall she was "unable to get together with people and talk out the bottled up pain." For her, the real release came when she was able to "ask these guys how they felt about what the nurses did over there . . . I've been waiting fourteen years to work up the nerve to ask for the thanks I need"[39]. The wall inspired her to articulate unexpressed emotions, and gave her the place to do so.

While at the base of the wall, I witnessed another sign of the wall's capacity to elicit expression of previously silenced emotion. Vietnam veterans continue to wear their jungle fatigues, indicating that they had not yet resolved their grief into national honor[40]. For some, staying in fatigues is also a way to express their feelings of alienation in their new America, the America which treated them with scorn and reproach. It is a way to say that, somewhere in their hearts, they remain in Vietnam. One veteran I observed broke down as he touched the names. He said that he found solace and camaraderie among surrounding veterans, and that he finally felt "at home." I saw him later that day. He had shed his fatigues, and wore the clothes of "an average citizen." He had found words for his feelings as he faced the wall.

As Lin said of the wall, "It's not meant to be cheerful or happy, but to bring out in people the realization of loss and a cathartic healing process"[41]. Lin's psychological design demands that its observers realize and dress their own wounds, by acknowledging their pain and identifying pieces of self which were isolated or denied as they located the emotional roots of their experience. The wall helps to dissolve internal divisions, to link "separate selves," selves which have been excised by silence. A former "grunt" explained that

> "there just wasn't the emotional time in Nam to know what happened . . . If I can touch the name of my friends who died, maybe I will finally have time to react. Maybe I will end up swearing, maybe crying, maybe smiling, remembering a funny incident. Whatever it is, I will have time and the focal point to do it now . . ."[42]

It is not surprising, then, that many veterans and non-veterans who thought that the war had no lasting effect on them unexpectedly discovered rage and pain, guilt and sorrow while viewing the wall. The wall taught them what they felt, brought "the missing piece" to the surface, and provided a place for its experience and expression. Thus, the desire to heal led to the attempt to create a memorial which would pierce the barrier of silence that frustrated the healing process. It was designed to reveal the wounds of war, and thus to acknowledge the need, the desire, for healing.

Lin's open-ended—metonymical, theatrical—strategy, then, has worked. As she herself said, her design is a circle. One part is the two arms of the wall. The final segment of the circle is the living person who visits, and through his or her presence fills in part of the circle that has been omitted. She sought to complete the wall with the person, and the person with the wall; to give closure to the experience through completion of the circle.

However, closure was not fully achieved with the wall. Although it dismantled barriers to healing for the silent, the wall did not meet the demands of the vociferous. There was discord among the non-silent as they engaged in discussion about the war. Furthermore, those with already settled opinions had strong feelings about the direction which our nation's healing should take, and about the Memorial, as an integral part of the healing process. Many wanted a more traditional memorial—one which would shape meaning in an unambiguous way. They were not satisfied with the healing metaphor Lin's design offered, one she eloquently described as "cutting the earth open with a knife, and letting the grass grow over it to heal the wounds." They were not among those for whom the wall tapped the strength of the quiet garden of peace in which it lives, and like the grass, soothed and dissolved wounds. They were not among those who, by touching the wall, seemed to regain a sense of life; or come to peaceful terms with death.

While those opposed to Lin's design did not suggest that we attempt, through a memorial, to engage in revisionism, to say that Vietnam had been glorious, the sculptor Frederick Hart and other like-minded people believed that a Vietnam Veterans Memorial had an obligation to affirm that, "in an age of doubt and selfishness, millions of Americans found their country worth fighting—and dying—for."[43] They saw in the simple granite walls not merely a means of honoring the dead, but a way of declaring that the Vietnam War was different from past wars, from wars whose veterans could be honored in a powerfully positive memorial such as the Iwo Jima monument to World War II.[44]

Novelist James Webb said it plainly: "[We must] allow all those who served in Vietnam to feel that they are honored when they visit the site."[45] Jack Smith, an ex-marine and psychologist explained

> In past wars, symbolically . . . society shared the blame and responsibility by saying, "We sent you off to do this for us." Victory banners, medals, and parades were ways of recognizing the tasks they did in the country's name. Vietnam was not "in our name." . . .[46]

A number of veterans needed to feel that it was "in our name," to feel as if we would truly "share the blame." They claimed that Lin's design did not enable all of them to do so. They argued that healing would take place if guided by an appropriate, patriotic symbol, not a "black gash of shame and dishonor." These veterans wanted a national remembrance which was clearly in *their* honor, one which would counteract myths of the war that suggest that all Vietnam veterans are pitiful loners. They wanted a national monument. They wanted to heal and unify through an emotional transfusion, to dissolve pain and guilt through national pride.

The fight over the design of the Memorial echoed the political struggle over the war itself in its intensity and acrimony, and in revealing elemental divisions.[47] There was, however, a significant difference in results. A consensus was reached. Furthermore, the process through which the dispute over the design was resolved is a model for the healing of the agony of the Vietnam experience which continues to plague America. And, in addition, it is a model for the dialogue between wall and the statue which was to come: a dialogue founded on principles of reconciliation.

However, following the initial consensus in favor of Lin's design, Scruggs's success in erecting a memorial seemed threatened. Opposition grew strong. A divisive battle escalated between fellow veterans. Congressmen became involved. The Vietnam Veterans Memorial Fund needed a way to unite dissidents. They asked Senator John

Warner to invite supporters and opponents of Lin's memorial design to a private meeting in an effort to resolve differences amid shared feelings of patriotism. The meeting was scheduled for January 27, 1982, just eleven months away from the planned dedication.[48]

After much discussion and debate, the group agreed to add a statue and flag to the design, and improve the inscription.[49] As might have been expected, Maya Lin resented the fact that the work was being tampered with. But she realized that the addition was politically necessary if construction was to begin, and honored the veterans' requests.[50]

In a newspaper article, Milt Copulos commented on the sequence of events through which they arrived at a decision:

> Something remarkable happened. Veterans split over the issue real-ized that the project was in jeopardy, and chose to set aside their preconceptions and come together in an effort to develop a consensus. ... Some might argue that these changes are mere symbols, and hardly worth the pain and anguish they caused. But soldiers fight for symbols, symbols that embody the principles in which they believe. ... Pain, is often a necessary part of healing, and in a very real sense, the healing process for the wounds of Vietnam began. ... The wall of the memorial could have been a wall between us. Instead it became a bridge.[51]

On March 4, 1982, the National Capital Planning Commission and Fine Arts Commission approved the flag and statue in concept. Soon thereafter, Secretary of the Interior James Watt issued the construc-tion permit. The wall would be built. Following an emotional cere-mony, groundbreaking took place on March 26, 1982.

The same reconciliatory principles operated in selecting the statue. The Vietnam Veterans Memorial Fund drafted a charter for the sculp-tor panel. The panel's assignment was to recommend a sculptor, a statue design, and to suggest a location for the flag and statue. In forming the panel, the fund followed the same strategy that they had employed under the leadership of Senator Warner. The panel consisted of James Webb and Milt Copulos—opponents of Lin's de-sign; and Art Mosley and Bill Jayne—loyal supporters of the proposed wall.[52] There could be no majority. They had to come to an agreement together, to bridge the gaps which distanced them. The panel agreed to award the design commission to sculptor Frederick Hart, who envisioned a realistic statue that would "neither obscure nor compete with Lin's design"[53].

Hart displayed a model of the statue on September 20, 1982. The actual statue was to be a life size representation of three fighting men. Hart used Caucasian, Black, and Hispanic models to represent the diversity of the combatants. The sculpture is realistic—from open flak jackets to dog tags. In gesture and facial expression, it captures the feelings and texture of combat.

The unveiling of the statue generated more controversy. Lin found the statue a threat to the integrity of her design. She stated her complaints in an article in the *Washington Post* entitled "Lin's Angry Objections" and in so doing launched what journalists soon labeled an "art war."[54] Heavy firepower soon assembled on the other side. Hart's statue was called "breathtaking," "a work of genius."[55]

On October 13, 1982, the National Capital Planning Commission met to decide whether or not to authorize the statue. The meeting involved impassioned testimony in which Webb pleaded with the Commission to "allow all those who served in Vietnam to feel that they are honored when they visit the site,"[56] and an onslaught of anti-statue statements, the most powerful made by Lin herself:

> I [appeal] to the Commission to protect the integrity of the original design. What is realistic? Is any one man's interpretation better able to convey an ideal than any other's? Should it not be left to the observer? The original design gives each individual the freedom to reflect upon the heroism and sacrifice of those who served . . .[57]

The Fine Arts Commission was faced with a difficult task. However, the Chairman, James Carter Brown, walked safely through this political and artistic minefield. He announced that by unanimous vote the Commission found the statue acceptable, but that location of both statue and flag would be subject to further study.[58] The approval of the statue and flag appeased once angry veterans, and made it impossible for Watt to delay dedication. And by refusing to place the statue at the apex of the wall, he sapped the strength of Lin's outrage, avoided the contempt of her allies in the arts community.

The government formally accepted the Memorial on November 9, 1984, thus allowing America to acknowledge the war experience through an object belonging to everyone.[59]

The wall and statue are now together. The statue and fifty foot flagpole are beautifully located in a grove of trees seventy feet from the Southwest edge of the wall. Neither offends the other. Even Lin admits that the sculpture and flag "do not destroy the quiet and simplicity of the original design."[60] The combination of the group of soldiers and the wall creates interplay, a resonance that echoes from one element to another. "Standing in the hollow next to those great black walls you see these three figures . . . there is something in their stance that makes the space between you and them come alive."[61]

Not only do they coexist in harmony, neither could exist without the other. Their temporal relationship, as well as the way the two function together, help to heal a wounded nation. Although, as we have seen, the wall would not have been built without approval of the statue, it was necessary that the acceptance of Lin's design come first. It was necessary in the way that the desire to heal must precede healing itself. More specifically, it was necessary to break the self-perpetuating silence before traditional, less ambiguous images could be proposed and constructed.

Furthermore, for many, the more positive process could not begin without assurance that it was not an effort to hinder accurate portrayal of the Vietnam years. As *New York Times* critic Paul Goldberger wrote "to try to represent a period of anguish and complexity in our history with a simple statue of armed soldiers is to misunderstand all that has happened, and to suggest that no lessons have been learned."[62] Had statue preceded wall, it would have met this response. Lin's open-ended design is a means of guarding against symbols that distort the truth in order to inspire the living. The abstract wall is capable of functioning in a ways that the less ambiguous, more representative statue cannot. It is a call to remember, an opportunity to express. Without this call, the Memorial would have perpetuated the denial, emotional frustration, and alienation which accompanied the war. It would have contributed to the forces of silence. Instead, the combination of wall and statue accelerates healing through acknowledgment, determination of meaning, and acceptance—all of which stem from a desire to heal that is genuine and heartfelt. Together, wall and statue enable each other to function in ways that neither could function alone. They enter into a kind of dialectic of healing with each other.

The dialogue between them provides the opportunity for observers to assimilate the war experience in a positive way, while sustaining the complexity and intensity of the situation. The statue depicts the dedicated service of our nation's warriors, and portrays the heroism of their endurance. It speaks of commitment, of brotherly love generated in the name of a country worth fighting and dying for. But it does not speak without the wall. In its ambiguity and open-endedness, the wall is a testimony to the complexity of the situation, to the multitude of meanings which can be drawn from the experience. The wall gives those who would have viewed the statue as an oversimplification or distortion of the truth access—symbolically as well as functionally— to its affirmative power. The wall is a symbol of our commitment to break the silence, to formulate individual and collective experiences honestly and openly, and thus alleviates fear of national deception. In addition, because the wall provides a place for reflection, it initiates the healing process which is most appropriate for each individual. This process, once started, can progress in the direction indicated by the statue.

Dialogue between wall and statue also facilitates assimilation of the war experience by fostering self-conscious acknowledgment of the collective desire to heal, of the fact that we have united as a nation in order to provide each other with an appropriate model for healing. In light of the reconciliatory principles through which they came to be, the ambiguous wall and controversial statue speak of our desire to integrate, to alienate no one. The Memorial is both a symbol and agent of our unified attempt to, as is stated in Lincoln's Second Inaugural Address, "bind up the nation's wounds; to care for him who shall have borne the battle," both in Vietnam and at home: to care for each other, to be healed.

Thus, when one visits the Memorial, he or she becomes caught up in the dialogue between statue and wall. It is a dialogue that addresses silence and non-silence, the individual and the collective. It is a dialogue which flows between questions and answers; desire and healing. It is a dialogue involving distinction and assimilation; confrontation and comprehension. It is a one which moves from complexity to simplicity; from reflection to assertion; and from catharsis to calm. It is a dialogue which facilitates honest location and expression of the meaning of often painful, often stifled wartime experiences. It is a dialogue, then, which provides the conditions for promoting national healing. And it is a dialogue which moves us hopefully from silence to serenity.

NOTES

1. Jan Scruggs, *To Heal A Nation* (New York: Harper and Row Publishers, 1985) 113.

2. William James, *Memories and Studies* (New York: Longmans, Green, and Co., 1911) 56.

3. James, 40.

4. James, 40.

5. James, 43.

6. Tom Wicker, "The Reason Why," *New York Times* 12 Nov. 1982: A27.

7. Myra Mac Pherson, *Long Time Passing* (New York: Doubleday and Company, Inc., 1984) 13.

8. Mac Pherson, 13.

9. Wicker, A27.

10. John Wheeler, *Touched With Fire* (New York: Avon Books, 1984) 93.

11. Wheeler, 95.

12. Scruggs, 11.

13. Horne, A. D., ed. *The Wounded Generation: America After Vietnam* (Englewood Cliffs: Prentice-Hall, 1981).

14. Wheeler, 7.

15. Wheeler, 134.

16. Wheeler, 93.

17. Mac Pherson, 738.

18. Mac Pherson, 61.

19. Mac Pherson, 58.

20. Mac Pherson, 6.

21. Mac Pherson, 57.

22. Mac Pherson wrote of "a theme encountered in every veteran I have ever met is searing anger at their homecoming—both at being shunned and of having to becomes "closet" vets (Mac Pherson 6). Veterans were embittered by the viciousness and silent-treatment they received upon coming home. They were not deemed soldiers, but baby killers. They both spawned and nurtured penetrating wounds. Mac Phearson told the story of Fred Downs, who lost an arm in Vietnam. He was walking across campus when a student noticed his hook. "Get that in Vietnam?" he asked. Downs replied, "Yes." The student sneered. "Serves you right."

23. Wheeler, 124.

24. Wheeler, 125.

25. Wheeler, 144.

26. Wheeler, 87.

27. Vietnam was a war plagued by isolation and alienation. It was a loner's war; and a loner's return. Unlike other wars, Vietnam veterans came home not on troop ships where they could wind down, decompress and be together. "From firefight to front porch in thirty-six hours" (Mac Pherson 64). In light of the untraditional nature of the war—the multi-dimensional uncertainty, the isolation, the intense and relentless warfare—few had had the opportunity to process the experience in Vietnam. The jet flight back to civilization made it impossible for veterans, as well as those to whom they returned, to create a personal formula for summarization, to process and express their emotions and experiences. The Vietnam veteran was not permitted to grieve, and America did not let herself grieve either.

28. Wheeler, 153.

29. Wheeler, 155.

30. Wheeler, 155.

31. Wheeler, 154.

32. This is quoted from the Tomb of the Unknown Soldier in Edinburgh Scotland: "They shall not grow old as we that are left grow old. Age shall not worry them, nor years condemn. At the going down of the sun and in the morning we shall remember them."

33. The need to work together, to engage all in the name of the desire to heal, is best portrayed through scenes that occurred at the dedication in November of 1982— a dedication made possible through the combination of wall and statue: veterans

hugged veterans, mothers and fathers of the men whose names flank the wall spoke with veterans who had fought in units, husbands and wives shared hidden fears with their sons.

34. Scruggs, 144.

35. The book *Strangers at Home* concludes "with the war experience suppressed, the emotional catharsis of homecoming was nullified." This conclusion is rooted in a statistically based survey which runs throughout the book.

36. Scruggs, 126.

37. Phillip Boffey, "Vietnam Vets Parade: A belated welcome home," *New York Times* 14 Nov. 1982: A1.

38. Mary Battiata, "Remembrance on a Train," *Washington Post* Nov. 10 1984: A7.

39. Art Mc Govern, "Veterans' Reflection on the Dedication," *The Congressional Record* 11 Nov. 1982: 154.

40. "Voices from a War," *Washington Post* 13 Nov. 1982: A1.

41. Wheeler noted that occasional wearing of a hat or other small items is a sign of pride, like the tactical service issue watchband made of olive-drab nylon. Living in jungle fatigues is something else (Wheeler 108).

42. Scruggs, 147.

43. Scruggs, 125.

44. Scruggs, 44.

45. Paul Goldberger, "Vietnam Memorial: Questions of Architecture," *New York Times* 7 Oct. 1982: sec. 3: 25.

46. Scruggs, 132.

47. Mac Pherson, 56.

48. Benjamin Forgey, "A Mood is Built," *Washington Post* 13 Nov. 1982: C1.

49. Christopher Buckley, "The Wall," *Esquire* Sept. 1985: 66. Texas billionaire Ross Perot, who before the selection of Lin's design had been the fund's single largest contributor, and his band of distinguished allies were unexpected guests. Those against the design outnumbered advocates by four to one. They repeated a list of demands made familiar by James Webb and Tom Cathcart: the memorial had to be white, it had to be above ground; it had to include a flag and an appropriate inscription.

50. Scruggs, 101.

51. Scruggs, 105. On March 4, 1982, the National Capital Planning Commission and Fine Art's Commission approved the flag and statue in concept. The NCPC indicated that it would have preferred no additions to Lin's design, but that it was responding to a political situation. Its approval was contingent upon the stipulation that the additions be located and designed so as not to compromise or diminish the basic design of the memorial as previously approved. The Fine Arts Commission similarly approved the statue and flag, in principle. But Watt continued to ignore the Fund's request for the construction permit which would enable them to begin work on the wall. It seemed that opponents of Lins' design had convinced him to refuse to grant a construction permit until they were guaranteed that a flag and statue would be added.

52. Scruggs, 106–108. Two points in particular illustrate the principles of reconcilia-

tion in operation, the "remarkable sequence of events" to which Copulos referred. Maya Lin stood silently in the back of the room filled with veterans whose passions seemed to verge on violence. At one point, Senator Warner asked her what she thought of the ideas on placement. She could have said it was a ridiculous idea. She could have battled them. Instead she advised, "If you're going to do this, it should be done in an integrated, harmonious way." At another point during the discussion, someone made a motion to throw out Lin's design and start over, Perot silently shook his head no, and the motion was defeated.

53. Scruggs, 115.

54. Scruggs, 115.

55. Rick Horowitz, "Maya Lin's Angry Objections," *Washington Post* 7 July 1982: F7. Lin claimed "This farce has gone on long enough . . . I have to clear my own conscience . . ." Her views on Fredrick Hart were painfully clear: "I can't see how anyone of integrity can go around drawing mustaches on other people's portraits." She cited Robert Lawrence, president of the American Institute of Architects, who called the addition of Hart's statue "ill conceived," a "breach of faith," and "a dangerous precedent." Lin retained a law firm of national repute to protect her interests.

56. Scruggs, 132.

57. Scruggs, 132.

58. Scruggs, 133.

59. John Dreyfuss, "Vietnam Memorial Launched," *Los Angeles Times* 26 March 1982: sec. 5: 1.

60. Arthur Brisbane, "President Leads Tribute to Vietnam Veterans," *Washington Post* 12 Nov. 1984: A1.

61. "The Vietnam War Memorial," *Art News* 12 Jan. 1983: 12.

62. Benjamin Forgey, "The Statue and the Wall," *Washington Post* 10 Nov. 1984: A1.

63. Scruggs, 129.

33

The Road to Hill 10
William Broyles, Jr.

When I came to Da Nang in 1969, the airport was one of the busiest in the world. Fighters and transport planes competed with airliners on the runways, and in the sky helicopters of every description buzzed like swarms of dragonflies. The noise was deafening. The airport itself was crammed with American soldiers and Marines. The waiting rooms were jammed with Americans waiting for flights, sleeping on their duffle bags. The parking lots and surrounding roads were choked with traffic. In the background from time to time we could hear the sounds of shelling. On this trip, when I landed, there was only a strange, pre-modern silence.

During the war Da Nang had been a mini-Saigon—loud, raucous, and teeming with refugees, mutilated beggars, hustlers. Now it was obviously less crowded; it was, in fact, back to a population of 350,000, its size before the refugees swelled it to more than a million people in 1970. We drove north from the city, with "Gloria" playing on the driver's stereo. We crossed the Nam O Bridge and began the climb up to Hai Van Pass. High up on a switchback I asked the driver to stop. I got out, the wet sea air in my face, and looked back on Da Nang. I could see almost the entire area of my unit, the 1st Marine Division—from Elephant Valley out Route 37 in the north, stretching south past Ba Na Mountain, Charlie Ridge, and the Arizona Territory, and down the coast past Marble Mountain and beyond the Que Son Mountains, visible only as a dim smudge on the southern horizon. Beyond the narrow stretch of coastal plain, where the Tuy Loan and other rivers flowed out in a wide delta, were the mountains, hidden in clouds. On the mountain behind me waterfalls coursed down through tropical

This selection is taken from Broyles's article in *The Atlantic Monthly*, April 1985, pp. 90–118. The journey Broyles describes is the subject for more comprehensive treatment in his book *Brothers in Arms* (New York: Alfred A. Knopf, 1986).

foliage; hundreds of feet below me gentle swells broke on deserted beaches scalloped from the rocks. It was one of the most beautiful places I had ever seen. It seemed unthinkable that so much war had been here.

From the car the only clue to the presence of an old American base was a sudden increase in scrap metal for sale in the houses along the road. We passed Phu Bai, the first American base built between the DMZ and Da Nang. All that remained was some rubble, a lonely, abandoned watchtower, and a few strands of rusty barbed wire. And so it was with all the trappings of what had been a vast American civilization in Vietnam: Red Beach, Marble Mountain airfield, Camp Eagle—all gone. The huge staging areas, the movie theaters, the ice-cream parlors, the officers' clubs—built to last forever—have all vanished. At none of the old bases does anything grow; the bare red dirt lies on the earth like a scar.

We drove north from Hue toward the DMZ, into some of the most fiercely contested areas of the war. Among veterans of the war this is the heart of the beast, where names that have now faded into obscurity then told of the war's most brutal fighting: Hill 881, Con Thien, the Rockpile, Dong Ha, Quang Tri, the A Shau Valley, Hamburger Hill, Lang Vei, Firebase Ripcord, Khe Sanh. Stacks of old shell casings were everywhere, to be recycled into tools. Along the road and fields were stands of newly planted eucalyptus and falao pine. Throughout the war virtually the entire region had been a free-fire zone. The people had been evacuated, the fields abandoned, and the trees and houses blasted into the mud. Even Quang Tri, the one town of any size, had been obliterated in 1972, during the 138 days the Communists had held it against some of the heaviest bombing of the war. Now the people are back, and rice is being harvested and brought in from the fields.

Long before we should have arrived at the DMZ—my mind being attuned to the old travel times in military vehicles along less than secure roads—we were there. Some sampans floated idly in the Ben Hai River, for twenty-one years the boundary between the two Vietnams and for more than ten years a fearsome no-man's-land of bitter fighting. Without ceremony we crossed the bridge to *their* side. On the south side—our side—were rice paddies, a few houses, a boy on a water buffalo. Three women were wading slowly in the river, gathering water potatoes and oysters. An old Dodge van, converted to a bus, lumbered across the bridge from the south and stopped by our car. Five or six children poured out and ran off down a narrow trail, chattering and carrying their satchels from school. The wind made patterns in the yellowing rice. The mountains were gray in the distance. From the sea, clouds were blowing in. There was simply nothing to do but get in the car and go back.

After dinner we went for a drive around the darkened streets of Hue. A mass was in progress at the Hue cathedral, rebuilt as a strikingly modern structure grafted onto the Gothic architecture of the Hue seminary. In a field behind the church, during the Tet offensive, the Communists executed a young USIA employee named Stephen Miller. I am sure they did this as brutally and as matter-of-factly as General Loan executed the Viet Cong terrorist in the streets of Saigon. That execution, so dramatically caught on film—the captive being led up, the pistol being raised to his head and fired, the man falling over, blood spurting on the pavement—became a visual metaphor for the brutality of the whole war. Stephen Miller died no less brutally, but his death wasn't theater, and therefore in the practical terms of politics it might as well never have happened. While my guides smoked in the car, I stood in the field and bore him silent witness.

That night a hurricane blew in from the South China Sea. The wind beat against the windows of my room, the power, of course, went out, and the Perfume River rose steadily, churning with debris. The next day I had lunch with Nguyen Minh Ky, the vice-president of the province's People's Committee. Ky has the wavy hair and the good looks of a movie star. It was impossible for me to imagine that he had spent fifteen years living in the jungle. The Viet Cong whom we captured or who defected to us were tough, dedicated people, but they had the look of peasants who had just come from the fields. Ky looked as if he had just come from discussing a movie deal.

We ate lunch—the most lavish meal of my trip—on the roof of the hotel, overlooking the river, which by now was roiled and angry. The old city was barely visible through the storm, but I could see sampans balanced precariously against the howling winds in the center of the flood, the children on board searching for anything of value in the debris being swept past them. A young waitress in a yellow *ao dai* laid out giant prawns.

I asked Ky if he had been in Hue during the Tet offensive. He beamed. "Oh, yes. I was here for twenty-four days and nights. I was in the Citadel; I was everywhere in the city. The Americans and the puppets bombed us with everything they had, but we made them fight for every street. It was very fierce. The people had been living under oppression for fourteen years. Many of our fighters had not seen their families since 1954. They hugged each other and cried. It was glorious."

Ky asked me if I had seen the PBS program *Vietnam: A Television*

History. "Everyone here saw it," he said. "I remember watching American troops throwing grenades into shelters. I thought of so many places I had seen such crimes. Those poor people were just peasants and laborers—they only wanted to plant rice, and they were killed. I could have cried."

As he talked, my own memories came back. In 1970 I had spent several weeks teaching English at night in Da Nang. One of my students told me this story: "My parents were living in Hue in 1968, when the Viet Cong took the city. They were schoolteachers. The Viet Cong came to the door and took them away. They told my grandmother they had to ask them some questions. My parents never came back. They found their bodies near the imperial tombs. They had been tied up and strangled."

And I remembered a Viet Cong attack in 1970 on a hamlet south of Da Nang called Thanh My. The Viet Cong had gone from bunker to bunker, throwing in satchel charges. Anyone who tried to flee was shot—old men, women, young children. When I got there the next morning, the mangled bunkers were still smoldering, the bodies were laid out in long rows, and a few survivors with blank faces were poking in the rubble. They were "just peasants and laborers— they only wanted to plant rice." And I could have cried too, and did.

"I remember two things about Hue," I said. "I remember your flag flying from the Citadel, and I remember the bodies of all the innocent people the Viet Cong killed."

A shadow crossed Ky's face, a fleeting moment of hardness that made me glad I was his guest and not his prisoner. Then the smile returned. "That was a total fabrication," he said. "It was completely to the contrary. We *were* the people. How could we kill ourselves?"

Having proved to his own satisfaction that such a massacre was, in metaphysical terms at least, impossible, he went on: "Since 1959 the puppets had brought the guillotine to every corner of our country. They tied us up and rubbed chili pepper into our mouths, noses, and eyes." He warmed to his theme. "They ran electric current into women's private parts. They nailed your fingers down and then tore out the fingernails. They put out your eyes and cut off your ears and wore them around their necks—for publicity. They ripped open your belly and tore out your heart and liver. They cut open the womb and yanked out the baby inside, then stomped it into the dust." He paused. "Now, *that* was terrible. If they could do that, they could make up any lie about us."

I asked him if he meant to say that his forces had not executed any civilians.

"That is correct," he replied, reaching across the table for some more prawns.

"Then where did all those bodies come from?"

He looked at me with sympathy. "It was a very chaotic time. A few criminals may have been spontaneously eliminated by the people, like stepping on a snake. But most of these bodies—if there were any— were probably patriots who helped us and were murdered by the puppets after we left."

He put down his napkin. "You know," he said, "I often came into Hue during the war. I pretended I was a fisherman, or a student, or a peasant coming to market. The Americans would come right up to me. They'd pat me on the back and offer me cigarettes."

"And what did you do?" I asked him, as the table was being cleared and the coffee brought.

He looked at me with a sly smile. "I just said, 'GI, GI, number one.' " With that he pushed back his chair and said good-bye. The flood was rising, and the rice harvest was in danger. In today's Vietnam, where the people barely have enough rice to survive, nothing is more serious. Outside, the storm had abated. The trees that had blown over had already been cut up and carried away for firewood.

Milan Kundera writes about a Czech leader whose usefulness to the state had ended. For the leader to remain in official photographs of the period raised too many questions; it was inconvenient. So he was simply airbrushed out: he no longer existed. The massacre of civilians at Hue, the massacres at places like Thanh My, are now inconvenient, so they have been airbrushed out of history: they no longer exist. The Vietnamese stand in the flood of history and pluck from the water only what is useful; the rest flows out to sea. History is like the toppled trees of Hue, to be cut up and used to heat and light the present.

The next day we drove south to Duy Xuyen district, a once bitterly contested area about twelve miles south of Da Nang. The district headquarters was in a low stucco building; I had been there before, during the war. I was greeted by a delegation of officials and offered tea, beer, and fruit. I began to talk to Nguyen ruong Nai, the vice-president of the People's Committee. He had been part of the Viet Cong local forces during the war. He had joined the guerrillas in 1964, when he was seventeen. During the long years of the war he had been wounded eight times. He began to show me his scars—"This one, on my arm, was in 1967. This one, on my leg, was in 1972. This one, my hand and my head, was in 1969, this one. . . ." His body was like a history of the war, written with M-16 bullets, artillery shrapnel, rockets, and bomb pellets from B-52s.

The worst year was 1969, he said, confirming what General Tuan had told me in Hanoi. "The situation was terrible. This whole district was a no-man's-land. There were thousands of Americans, Koreans, and puppet troops in the area, but there were only four of us left out of all the total guerrilla forces. Only four. We were hungry. There was nothing to eat. I was the commander. We all gave serious thought to surrender. But each time, we talked about our traditions, about our country, and we kept on fighting."

Two young men from the rice cooperative who had been fighting the flood arrived. One of the men seemed young, too young to have been in the war. But he had been fighting since 1969, when he was nine. "I went to school during the day and helped the guerrillas at night. We were scouts. We watched the Americans, sold them cigarettes and talked to them, and then reported back." He went on and almost idly pulled off a bit of the veil of kitsch that surrounds Vietnamese accounts of the war. "Part of my job was to identify the leaders of the strategic hamlets." I asked what happened then. "I helped work out ways to kill them," he said, smiling pleasantly, as if he were discussing the school fund-raising auction. When history is on your side, killing a village official, even if he has been your neighbor all your life, is simply not a matter of much consequence.

"The tasks facing us after the war were enormous," said one of the officials. "The land had lain fallow for many years. We had to organize cooperatives, clear the fields of mines and bombs, develop irrigation and electric projects, plow and plant and begin to harvest. We had to plant trees and build houses and schools and clinics. And it was hard at first. All our lives we had been guerrillas. War is simple; our problems now are more complicated. We had, in truth, to start over. And we are far from finished."

I had been in Duy Xuyen during the war. Part of it had been known as Go Noi Island, which by 1970 had been cleared of all signs of life, like an apple peeled of its skin. There was nothing, literally nothing, there. No trees, no cemeteries, no houses, no fields, no people. It was the archetypal free-fire zone. In 1970 we began resettlement work. Land was set aside for villages, and some of the old residents were brought back and lodged in rows of houses with tin roofs set beneath the blazing sun. It was not a bad effort, and it flowed from some of our best motives. But we were taking a terrible situation and trying to heal it with Band-Aids. We were trying to rebuild the land we had destroyed, in the name of the Vietnamese people, and wanting them to love us for it.

During the war I had flown over this area in a helicopter day after day. I had been struck by the thought of how beautiful it must have been, a fertile green blanket between the mountains and the sea, before it had been pockmarked by bombs and cleared of people. Now the people were back. Trees by the thousands had been planted. The free-fire zones of Go Noi and the Arizona Territory were again rice paddies, as they had been for centuries. Children on their way to school walked giggling down trails where Marine patrols had been ambushed, and rice dried on roads where tanks and halftracks had churned up dust.

Two miles southeast of Da Nang had been the Marble Mountain airfield, a large recreational area called China Beach, and the head-quarters of the 1st Marine Regiment, an area notorious for its booby traps. We drove out to China Beach. Where once Red Cross doughnut dollies and Army nurses in bathing suits had drawn the hungry stares of thousands of lonely men, there was only one old woman, gathering seaweed. Driving along the beach, we passed some shacks. Inside one of them two men were playing chess. They were fishermen, uninvolved in politics. The older man, Phung Tha, was thirty. "We were all in the Viet Cong," he said. "All the boys and girls I knew fought the Americans here." An old woman, whose teeth were stained with betel, cackled. "All of us fought. Some of us, like me, fought with our mouths." I mentioned that she seemed a bit old for that sort of thing. "I am fifty-two," she said—she looked at least seventy—"and I fought for my country and for my husband." She gestured at a photograph that stood in the place of honor on a handmade shelf, the only piece of furniture in the house besides a bed and the table. "He was killed by the Americans." I asked them whether, after all that, ordinary life wasn't empty. They laughed. "We are fishermen. All we have ever wanted to do is fish. Now we do. So we are happy."

When I was here during the war, the Marines in this area had been commanded by Colonel P. X. Kelley, an intelligent, aggressive officer with a subtle grasp of politics, a dedication to excellence, and even a sense of humor. When I had left Vietnam, he had given me an eight-by-ten picture of himself, signed "Semper Fi, P. X. Kelley." He is now the commandant of the Marine Corps. On the days when he and the other colonels, the really good ones, were up at division headquarters, I would think that there was nothing we couldn't do. But today the area where we did our best for him, ourselves, and our country is the domain of fishermen and old women with stained teeth who gather seaweed on the beach.

Just inland from China Beach five mountains of solid marble tower up out of the dunes like the snouts of whales breaching out of the ocean. Pagodas and Buddhist monasteries are hidden away on the largest mountain, and around the base are hamlets of marble cutters who patiently carve Buddhas, bracelets, and little statues of roaring lions and dragons. On weekends during the war Marines would occasionally go there to visit a pagoda and buy some marble souvenirs. But there were several caves and pagodas on the mountain that were off limits. We supposed that the religious sensibilities of the Vietnamese would be deeply offended if we were to go there.

I had always been curious about the mountain; it had loomed over our area like a brooding shrine, honeycombed with caves and mysteries. Minh and I climbed up steep steps to the first pagoda. We then made our way along a narrow path, past gardens kept by monks, and came upon a grotto. We entered, and saw that it opened into a huge cave, seventy-five feet high, dimly lit through a hole in the ceiling. Statues of Buddhas, some twenty feet tall, had been carved out of the rock. Incense burned at several altars. There were other, smaller statues of soldiers and guards painted in dramatic reds, blues, and yellows. In one corner was a small shrine and next to it a plaque, which seemed oddly official in what was so clearly a religious place.

I asked Minh to translate it, and then I knew why it had been inappropriate for Americans to visit here, even though the cave was only three miles from the center of Da Nang and was square in the middle of one of the largest concentrations of American troops in Vietnam. The plaque said that this cave had been a field hospital for the Viet Cong. Now it was empty and the only sound was that of water dripping from the hole in the roof. I walked out of the cave, and a few steps away I could look directly down on the main road that had led to the 1st Marine Regiment's headquarters. We had driven right by here on our way to China Beach. The Viet Cong in the hospital must have heard our trucks, and the helicopters from the airfield, every day. No doubt they could listen to the parties at the airfield or China Beach—the Filipino bands singing "Proud Mary" and "We Gotta Get Out of This Place."

How little we knew. And our enemy had been so certain of our ignorance, so confident that we would learn nothing, that he had hidden his hospital in plain sight, like Poe's purloined letter. To have been defeated was bad enough. To have been treated with such contempt seemed far worse.

LOOSE ENDS

We were leaving Marble Mountain when I saw her. She was a girl in her early teens, working at one of the small stands selling marble bracelets, carved Buddhas, busts of Ho Chi Minh, and other souvenirs. For a moment I didn't know why she had caught my eye, but there was something about her, about the way she stood, about her features, something different . . . And then Minh, who didn't miss much, noticed my stare. "So you've seen the Amerasian girl?" he said.

She was the first Amerasian I had seen on the trip. I hadn't been prepared for how powerful the experience would be. I had become conditioned to Vietnam as it was, and she was a living link to the past I had lived here. We Americans were all gone, but we had left behind a new generation neither American nor Vietnamese—outsiders, wearing history on their faces—as if the power of sexuality had proved stronger than all our armies, all our weapons, all our technology. She had been raised a Vietnamese, had spent all her life in a hamlet, but still I felt a bond with her. I felt guilty when I saw her, guilt and fascination.

Her name was Huynh Thi Dien. She was fourteen years old, a student in the seventh grade. That afternoon she had been at a meeting of the Good Nieces and Nephews of Uncle Ho. We were sitting at the table inside her house, which was behind the souvenir stand. There was only one room. Her mother sat on the bed; her grandfather, an old man with a wispy beard, dressed in white cotton, slowly moved about the room, preparing tea, and then sat down in a corner and smoked the cigarette I had given him.

Her mother began to talk about Dien's father. "I remember his name but not his address," she said. "He was in the military police. He returned to the U.S. in 1971; he wanted us to come with him, but my mother was sick and we couldn't go. I had a letter in 1974, but I haven't heard from him since."

She had applied for a visa for herself and her daughter to go to America; they were waiting for it to come through. I asked Dien if she wanted to go to the United States. She looked at the marble bracelet on her arm and said nothing. Tears began to flow down her face. The house had gradually filled up with villagers. More than forty people had crowded into all the available spaces, pressing around us. It was suffocating, claustrophobic. No one made a sound.

I asked her if she was crying because she wanted to go or because she wanted to stay.

"Both," she said. "I have a father . . ." She began to cry again. "And I have my native land . . ." She paused. Her mother watched her from the bed. The room was quiet. Her dilemma was public; I had unwittingly asked her to choose between the country of a father who had abandoned her, which and whom she had never seen, and Vietnam, the people around her, the only world she had ever known—and to do so in full view of the whole hamlet. "But I don't know my father," she said, and then she began to sob, her shoulders shaking. I squeezed her hand, told her that she would like America, that it would be different but that she would like it. Minh translated as the girl cried. The villagers listened in silence.

On the way back to Da Nang I told Minh that I blamed the father, that he had behaved as irresponsibly with the mother as we had with our Vietnamese allies. Minh didn't agree. "You can't blame the father," he said. "He was a soldier, far from home. I'm sure he didn't intend to create such a sad situation." No, he probably didn't intend to, any more than we intended to make a whole people dependent upon us and then abandon them. But he had done it, and so had we; he had walked away from it, and so had we. . . .

As we approached Hill 10, we came upon a ditch cut through the road. Beyond the ditch, where the base had been, was only a red scar on the hilltop. I got out and walked up to it. I could remember perfectly how it had been: where everyone had lived and worked, where everything in that little world had happened. I walked over to where the command post had been, where the Filipino bands had sung, where the PX and the enlisted-men's club had stood, where the showers and the mess hall had greeted us when we came in from the bush. This hill had been a little piece of America, our connection to the world, to reality. Now there were only the paddies, the mountains beyond, and the silence.

Hien, the former Viet Cong company commander, my old enemy, the man we had built all the Hill 10s in Vietnam to kill, walked quietly up to me and stood at my side as I stared toward the mountains. With a stick he drew diagrams in the dirt of how his company could have attacked Hill 10. I watched with interest, but there was really nothing left to say. In the end he didn't have to attack it; all he had to do was survive until we left, and then the country was his.

Four months before my trip to Vietnam, Americans of another generation revisited their battlefields on the beaches of Normandy. President Reagan spoke, his voice quavering. The veterans and their relatives cried. The American flag flew over a cemetery where crosses stretched as far as the eye could see. It was a powerful, patriotic moment. I thought of that moment as I stood on Hill 10. I did not feel patriotic; I simply felt sad.

"It is easier to start a war," the North Vietnamese general had told me, "than to end one." A valuable lesson, seldom learned. The cost of that lesson is beyond calculation: the long black wall in Washington, with all its names of young Americans who died so far from home; the cemetery just down the road, with its headstones bearing the word *hero;* the grief of the woman whose husband I might have killed, the grief of every family who had lost someone here. There are times when such costs must be paid: we had to fight the Nazis. We did not have to fight here.

I looked around this deserted hill for one last time. I could imagine a line of Marines making their way across the paddies, bound for the hill. The images were from a dream I still have, fifteen years later. My old platoon is returning to Hill 10 from the mountains. In the shadow of the base we are ambushed. No one comes to help us. We are cut to pieces. . . . But this time there was no ambush. The men just kept coming, headed for home, together.

As I turned to go, I noticed an old empty sandbag lying buried in the dirt. I picked it up and took it back, as a souvenir. When I returned to New York, I washed the sandbag over and over, but I could never get it to come clean.

34

Marching Along
Together at Last
William P. Mahedy

It is difficult to write for readers of another culture, readers whose language and modes of expression are very different from one's own. As a member of an American delegation invited to visit the Soviet Union by the Foundation for Social Invention at Komsomolskaya Pravda and as a writer asked to submit an article for this journal I can only begin with a phrase which is found in all languages and all culture: "Thank you very much." Thank you for this opportunity to visit your land and to meet your people in their homes. This is a most ancient and honored form of hospitality that has never lost its meaning.

Though visits by Americans to the Soviet Union have become more common recently, this visit by our delegation has a unique significance. For we have come to discuss with you a momentous issue, one which is much more familiar to you than it is to us. That issue is war. You have suffered the terrible ravages of war in your own country far more recently than have we Americans. Your heroic battles against the Nazi threat to civilization were fought on your own soil. All the horrors of modern war were inflicted upon your civilian population. Your soldiers fought to protect their homeland. Millions of your people still living remember these terrible times.

With us it is different. Though millions of our soldiers fought as your allies during that war, their battles were not in our own homeland. We have not been devastated by a war at home since the end of our Civil War in 1865. Even then we were not invaded by an outside aggressor, but we fought among ourselves. So our national memories of war are

William P. Mahedy, already identified in this volume, was one of the leaders of a delegation of American veterans of the Vietnam War who traveled to the Soviet Union to meet their counterparts from the war in Afghanistan. This essay was originally published in *XX Century and Peace*, a Soviet journal in peace-studies, in January/ February 1989.

302 / Symbolic Expressions, Ritual Healing

different. Yours are far more recent and more sharply etched than ours.

The Foundation for Social Invention extended the invitation to the members of our delegation because each of us has some expertise in the rehabilitation of returning war veterans. Much of this expertise has been gained from a rather recent American experience, the war in Vietnam. We have among us experts in the construction and use of prosthetic devices, people who are knowledgeable in the techniques and tools of physical rehabilitation and in the construction and use of wheelchairs. Others of us are skilled in healing the psychological and spiritual wounds of war. We have come to share with you what we know and to learn from you as well.

It is well known that our veterans of the war in Vietnam (I am one myself) did not re-enter American society easily. At first there were difficulties in obtaining benefits comparable to those granted to older veterans. There were problems in finding jobs. Medical treatment was sometimes shoddy. Psychological services offered by the Veterans Administration were initially very poor. We found also that cynicism, nihilism and loss of meaning are as much the fruits of war as are death, destruction and maiming. Tragically many of our vets were overcome by despair before they found healing. Great numbers, perhaps as many as were killed in combat, took their own lives by suicide.

When the news of our forthcoming visit began to circulate among Vietnam vets, the response was frequently: "I wish I could go." When they learned that we would meet face to face with Soviet veterans of the Afghan war, many of our vets were deeply touched, for they feel a sense of comradeship with Soviet veterans, men, who like themselves, have recently returned from a war on foreign soil. Quite a few of these Americans, fearing that their Soviet counterparts might be facing the stress of re-entry from a foreign war, asked us to convey a message. "Tell them (the Afghan vets) there's hope." There is healing for the scars of war. There is a successful re-entry back into one's own culture. It is possible to leave behind the bleakest regions of the soul and to walk once more in the sunshine of life.

We have come to share with you our experience of more than fifteen years in rehabilitating veterans who have fought a war beyond their own borders. It is our fondest hope that you will be able to avoid our mistakes and shorten the road to healing. Because America did not attend soon enough to the problems of its veterans, many were lost along the way. Our wish beyond all others is that you will be spared this tragedy.

For all veterans, war is the decisive experience of a lifetime. Combat memories intrude upon consciousness throughout one's life, shaping attitudes and feelings, influencing decisions and conditioning behavior in many ways. But *war's prism is set according to certain mental contours; it is located within a certain philosophical (moral) religious context.* For veterans of different wars within the same culture and for veterans of different cultures this inner landscape is vastly different. What we share with you, our Soviet brothers and sisters, is the common experience of war. The difference lies in our angle of vision, the *context in which we interpret war's meaning.*

We recognize, of course, our differences of language and culture as well as differences between our wars. Some of what we share with you will not transfer from the American to the Soviet experience; but much of it will because there is a commonality to the tragedy of war. We have come also in order to learn much from your experiences. Having learned from you, we will then be able in turn to enrich our own people. It is no small thing to share together the haunting and tragic memories of war, for in this way their burden is somehow lifted from us all.

We will tell you of the long period of readjustment after our return from Vietnam. During this time many vets battled alone and without any help the symptoms of what is now called "delayed stress": depression, rage, anger, guilt, sleep disorders, psychic numbing, flashbacks, suicidal and homicidal impulses, alienation—the list is long. Psychiatrists, trained in traditional modes of treatment, were of no use. Only a few American psychiatrists in the early 1970's had any notion of how to treat the psychic scars of war. Those few who did became our greatest allies and their influence was important in changing attitudes among the medical professions. Now even psychiatrists understand that during combat one suppresses all feelings in order to survive, but that these feelings must emerge later on and then they must be faced.

The war raised questions for the young soldiers for which there were no easy answers. What about the killing of civilians—or the killing of any other human person? How can one be absolved from guilt? Most Americans attempt to live by moral and religious standards and so there can be no final healing until these questions are resolved. As time passes, more veterans learn to deal with these most troubling issues.

The Veterans Administration, the government agency legally charged with providing medical and psychological treatment for veterans and for distributing monetary benefits, only slowly and reluctantly came to fulfill its obligations to younger veterans. Eventually this agency set up a system of outreach centers all across the United States where Vietnam veterans could obtain treatment for combat stress. These places were called "Vet Centers," and much of the treatment was non-traditional, including such things as veteran "rap groups."

It is important to remember that, even though Vietnam veterans faced significant difficulties upon their re-entry, they remained loyal and patriotic Americans. Consciousness that one has sacrificed much for one's country provides the motivation to surmount obstacles and forge deeper bonds with one's own people. I am sure that is also the case in the Soviet Union.

The Vietnam war was fought on foreign soil. Clearly, neither Vietnam nor its army was ever a real threat to the United States, so questions about why we were there—killing and being killed—arose from the very beginning. These questions continue to trouble us. Men returned home and no one cared where they had been or what had happened to them. Many returning veterans agreed with the protest against the war. Some even threw down their medals in a public display of disgust right in the nation's capital. For the first time in American history, veterans turned against a war they had fought. This angered many older veterans and a vast gulf arose between the veterans of World War II and Vietnam veterans. Only recently has this gulf begun to narrow.

As the nation itself gradually turned against the war, much of the blame for it was thrust upon the returning soldiers. People who had no understanding of war, who had never been there themselves secure in their own smug self-righteousness, called us "baby-killers" and spit upon us. The generational split here was not between older and younger, but within a generation itself. Many vets found solace in drugs and alcohol.

The scars of Vietnam were burned deeply within the soul of an entire generation that came of age during the longest of America's wars. Some young men chose to go and fight, some were drafted and went reluctantly. Others protested and went to jail for refusing to serve. Some left the country. Others "dodged the draft" through college deferments. Some obtained letters from doctors stating they were physically unfit to serve. Still others joined the National Guard, performing six months of military service while knowing they would never go overseas. Romances and marriages broke up. America's Vietnam generation was turned upon itself.

Now we understand the need for a "circle of treatment," a term first used by Shad Meshad, one of the members of this delegation, more than fifteen years ago. By it he meant that intrapsychic healing isn't enough. For veterans there must be jobs, acceptance in the community, further education: all the things that make for a good life. But now we are learning that the circle must include much more than this. We must also make peace with former enemies or somehow the war remains within our hearts. A few vets have already returned to visit Vietnam in peace. These infrequent visits must blossom into a full reconciliation between our countries. Between our two nations we must account for the missing, discover the effects of defoliants upon the countryside, care for the children of Vietnamese mothers and American fathers. Where before there was mutual destruction there must now be mutual efforts toward rebuilding and restoration.

As we meet together in a mutual effort to ease the burdens of war upon our veterans, we must be very honest about a painful historical reality. Our peoples have been enemies for more than seventy years— with a brief and uneasy interlude between 1941 and 1945. Not since 1921 have Soviet and American soldiers faced each other directly, but for years we have been choosing surrogates in third world countries to do our fighting for us. In Korea and again in Vietnam, American servicemen fought, killed, and died in a war against an enemy which was a close ally of and a surrogate for the Soviet Union. The AK47 rifle used by the North Vietnamese army in Vietnam with such deadly effect is a Russian-made weapon. There was never any question who the "real" enemy was. For your soldiers in Afghanistan the converse was true. Your "real" enemy was the United States. We supported and armed the people who killed your men.

Surely neither of us ever really feared the Vietnamese or the Afghans. Since the end of World War II, both nations have had only one real enemy: each other.

Now for the first time, the soldiers of the two hostile superpowers who have actually tasted each others' steel come together face to face. We come together, not only in peace, but in mutual effort to heal the wounds of war. To call this occasion historically significant is not to exaggerate.

If the "circle of treatment" ends only in peace, then ultimately this must be peace between us. Someday we must become reconciled with Vietnam as you must with Afghanistan, but even peace at this level is deficient unless we extend to each other the hand of friendship. If we fail to do this, then history's final verdict upon us will be harsh. Only if we, Soviets and Americans, succeed together in peace and friendship can any true meaning emerge from our painful past.

Steve Mason, a Vietnam veteran poet, believes that there is one last mission awaiting each soldier in every war:

"One last commitment worthy of a lifetime—to fight for peace in each of our hearts against the fierce enemies of our darkest natures. And to march in lock-step with veterans of all wars from all nations for human dignity."

Now, at last, we meet face to face. Let us commit ourselves to embark together upon our final and most important mission. And as we march along together for peace let us enlist the warriors of other nations to journey with us: friends and foes alike, our allies and our enemies.

"Then," as Mason writes, "shall we pass in review and each will hear mankind whisper to the gods, 'There, then, goes one of ours.' "

35

Vietnam:
My Enemy, My Brother
Frederick Downs, Jr.

Twenty years ago this past January, in Tam Ky, Vietnam, I stepped on a land mine. It was a type we called a "Bouncing Betty," because when you stepped on it, it bounded into the air and exploded waist-high, so it would do maximum damage. My left arm was blown off; grievous damage was also done to my right arm, both buttocks, both legs and both feet. Five of the men in my platoon were wounded along with me.

Within a four-week period after that, my platoon—already reduced from 40 men to 27—was destroyed. All but seven of those remaining 27 were killed or wounded, and the platoon, Delta 1-6, my family and my responsibility, ceased to exist as a fighting unit. I had given my all to Vietnam. I was proud to have been an infantryman. I was proud of my men. I wept when South Vietnam fell.

So I had good reason to be carrying a lot of hate when I returned to Vietnam for the first time in August 1987, as part of a team sent by President Ronald Reagan to explore greater cooperation with Vietnam on a range of humanitarian issues. The leader of our group was retired Gen John W. Vessey Jr., a former chairman of the Joint Chiefs of Staff. I was included because I am head of prosthetic services for the Veterans Administration. My job was to study the needs of disabled Vietnamese and see how we could help, particularly in the area of prosthetics. It was a trip that changed the way I think about Vietnam—and maybe about America, too.

We let down through a clear, sunny sky. Hanoi was off to the left. As we descended, we could see "Uncle Sam's Duck Ponds," our slang for bomb craters, scattered across the landscape. I was surprised at

---

Presently the director of the Prosthetic and Sensory Aids Service of the Veterans Administration, Frederick Downs, Jr. is author of *The Killing Zone* (New York: W.W. Norton, 1978) and *Aftermath: A Soldier's Return from Vietnam* (New York: W. W. Norton, 1984). This essay was originally published in *The Retired Officer*, November 1988.

the large number and by the fact that they hadn't been filled in all this time. Some were spaced haphazardly, others in neat rows spread from the American aircraft that had dropped the bombs 15 or more years ago.

CONFUSING EXPERIENCE

Flying into Hanoi was a confusing experience for me. When I first got off the airplane and stood on the tarmac, I was surprised and slightly embarrassed to realize that my knees were weak and my hands were trembling. The adrenaline was pumping through my body, and I felt the way I had long ago as I waited for the helicopters to take us into battle.

I could not suppress the feeling that I was in enemy territory. I was surrounded by North Vietnamese. The shock of this after two decades was strange and unexpected. "What the hell am I doing here?" I asked myself. I had lost my arm fighting against Hanoi! In the years since, I had stayed angry at the Hanoi government for a number of reasons: their mistreatment of the South Vietnamese, their meanness on the POW/MIA issue, their arrogance and intractability on everything to do with America and the simple fact that they had won the war.

And yet, driving from the airport into Hanoi, that hard edge of hatred seemed to soften. So little had changed in this land in 20 years. The women wore the same black pajamas and conical hats; bicycles still clogged the roads; water buffalos toiled in the rice paddies; fish traps stood at every drainage point in the fields and ditches; children played alongside the roads; adults squatted in the doorways of their dwellings.

Here and there along the road, I could see cemeteries, graveyards for the soldiers who died in the war with America, each tombstone bearing a large red star.

IMPOVERISHED CITY

We crossed the Red River on the bridge next to the one so frequently bombed during the war. It had taken 20 years, but we were finally in the city limits of Hanoi. The city looked poor but reasonably neat. It could be called shabby. Streets, curbs, sidewalks, and buildings were in need of repair. None of the buildings were taller than the trees. In the tropical heat and humidity, the entire city looked faded. But it takes money to keep paint looking good, and this is a desperately poor country. According to the United Nations, Vietnam ranks 162nd out of 164 countries in the world in per-capita income.

What I saw over the next few days turned my thinking about Vietnam upside down. We checked into the government guest house and were allowed to go where we wanted in the city. What happened to me, to put it in the simplest terms, was that I began to see the Vietnamese as a people.

My impressions of Hanoi were of an impoverished city, one drained of all resources by 50 years of war. A city too poor even to generate much trash. The North Vietnamese had finally won their war, but at the expense of consuming practically everything they had. A true Pyrrhic victory! Their problems were compounded by an economic policy that for the last 15 years was, by their own admission, a dismal failure.

The signs of poverty were everywhere. Women stood in line to buy a single smear of lipstick; street vendors used hypodermic needles to refill ballpoint pens; fixing flats was a constant activity on the streets. There was very little soap in the country, which perhaps accounts for the gray drabness of the clothing. Cigarettes were sold one at a time. Practically no one had a watch, so they all seemed to depend on the big clock on the main post office for telling time. What a sound it made. Not a bell but a gong.

We often walked in the park observing the people and in turn being observed by them. The kids were fascinated by my hook. They gathered around us, their faces full of curiosity and wonderment. They followed along for a short distance until their parents called. I was fascinated by the number of fathers who had their children on outings or spins around the lake. I did not expect to see this from hard-core Vietnamese. Maybe I hadn't imagined that these men I had hated for so long could love their children. That is what war does to us: It prevents us from seeing our enemies as human beings. But there was a great deal of love and pride evident in the faces of these Vietnamese fathers.

COMMON AFFLICTIONS

I walked over to the lake to see what the water looked like. I had watched a father squat by the edge and cool himself and his child with water he scooped up in his hands, and I was curious whether the water was clean. It was filthy—cloudy with the look of sewage and runoff from the gutters. I learned later that malaria and other infectious diseases are rampant throughout Vietnam. And I thought: The Vietnamese, my old enemies, suffer the afflictions that plague so much of the world—polio, typhoid, diarrhea—the whole host of microorganisms that afflict mankind.

Because the Vietnamese are so poor, they lack the medicine to combat disease and infection. In one operating room, we observed a 7-year-old girl with polio being prepared for surgery. There was no disinfectant on her skin or in the operating room, and there were no antibiotics. The infection rate in the operating rooms was more than 50 percent, we were told. To put this in perspective, the international standard that countries try to achieve is 3 percent. And I thought: This Vietnamese girl's mother and father don't love their child any less than I love my own two daughters.

VIETNAMESE VETS

One night I walked into a cafe with Bill Bell, a colleague who speaks Vietnamese and has been coming to Vietnam since 1973 as part of the official team that has been trying to recover POWs and MIAs. A group of about 15 older men were sitting around a couple of tables. They stopped talking immediately when we entered and watched us suspiciously as we walked to the bar. "Old cadre," remarked Bill, as we leaned against the teak bar.

Bill told me about one old veteran he had met a few years ago who related his travels along the Ho Chi Minh trail. During one trip, while driving a truck full of supplies, he had been strafed by American planes three times. Each time the bullets punctured his tires. He did not have any patching material, so he improvised by hunting around the jungle and killing frogs. He skinned the frogs and used the hide to patch the tires.

Bill also told me stories of editorials in the Hanoi newspapers raising hell with the government for not living up to the promises made to its veterans. The Vietnamese vets were complaining that they were not getting prosthetic limbs to replace the real arms and legs they had lost while fighting for their country. And younger veterans were complaining that the older veterans had all the good jobs.

I knew exactly what those Vietnamese vets were talking about. Certain problems are universal in nature, and veterans of any country voice much the same type of complaints. And I realized that I was beginning to feel a sense of kinship for their problems.

The odd thing was, the people I met seemed to genuinely like us, too. When we were out walking, they usually assumed we were Russian, since there are plenty of Russians around, and they seemed wary of us. But when they learned that we were Americans, their coldness turned to friendliness and curiosity. Maybe it's that we all shared the same horrific experience of the Vietnam War.

This sense of kinship bothered me, to be honest. I had spent 20 years thinking of the North Vietnamese as the murderous ghouls who degraded our dead soldiers by holding them as ransom. Like my fellow Vietnam vets, I believed that they received some perverse pleasure from torturing the unfortunate families of gallant American men lost in battle. I hated the Vietnamese and believed they hated Americans just as much.

But here I was in the middle of Hanoi relating to these people as human beings, discovering that I did not hate them as people. What was even more unsettling was that these people did not seem to hate us. As I walked around the lake in the evening or in the hot, humid noonday sun, watching the busy streets full of Vietnamese, I felt a sense of freedom. Not politically but spiritually. I was actually enjoying myself for the most bizarre of reasons: I was taking a walk in Vietnam, and I wasn't on guard for my life.

As a soldier in Vietnam 20 years ago, I had always wanted to be able to take a walk, to go for a stroll and look around without having to worry about getting shot or blown up by the Vietnamese. Now, here I was in the middle of Hanoi, among friendly people, having a good time. I could relax. The war was over.

NEW RESPECT

One evening, the Vietnamese delegation hosted a dinner for us. At the dinner, I spoke to a Vietnamese official. He represented to me the quintessential North Vietnamese. He had been a prisoner of war under the Japanese, had been shot in the stomach in 1952 while he was a Vietminh fighting the French and was in charge of "Clandestine Affairs in Urban Areas" in the fight against the Americans. His brother was killed in a B–52 raid in 1972. Surely this man would hate me.

As we relaxed and conversed in comfortable surroundings, I thought to myself that my dinner companion was no pilgrim. He was a hardcore soldier who had been fighting for his country's freedom from foreign domination all his life. Whether I agreed with his political philosophy or his definition of freedom or not, I respected the man for his determination and sacrifice. He had fought hard, because he had wanted his countrymen to have a better life.

So I began to ask myself: Who will help these people achieve the goals they fought for so long and hard? Certainly not the Soviets. We saw nothing—in any area of civilian life—that the Russians have done to help the people of Vietnam achieve that better life. The North Vietnamese know they need help from someone. What country is rich enough to help them? And what country, in their eyes, owes them that help?

For years I have been reading about Vietnamese claims that we owe them war damages for what we did to them. I thought they had it backwards; my concern had been with the damage Vietnam had inflicted on America—the dead and wounded, the POWs and MIAs and the psychological damage inflicted on literally millions of other Americans. I didn't pay much attention to their demands for help.

Americans are a generous people. When we finish our wars, we usually try to help the other side back on its feet, no matter how many casualties we suffered or how hateful our adversaries. We helped create the modern economic miracles of Japan and Germany. But for Vietnam, we have done nothing. And if we're honest, we know why. It is because they won the war. . . .

When we left Vietnam, our delegation recommended that humanitarian aid be provided to Vietnam by non-governmental organizations. As medical experts, we knew this was the right thing to do, because the medical needs are enormous. We did not like the politics of Vietnam, but we liked the people. I came to believe that they deserved the assistance of the people of America. There will always be differences between our two countries, but there is a lot of common ground to work with.

Let me put it another way: Twenty years ago, when I lost my arm in Tam Key, I thought that I was fighting for the people of Vietnam. Today, although the government in Hanoi is not what I would like, the people still need our help. The North Vietnamese we fought and the South Vietnamese who were our allies are all under one government now. There are hundreds of thousands of our former friends and enemies who were left disabled by that war. They all share a common plight now. Do we leave these people handicapped with no hope for rehabilitation, no hope of recovering either physically or economically? Or should we try to help them?

Any soldier who has been in combat knows that there comes a time after the battle, when the smoke has blown away and the dust has settled, when you must lean down and give your foe a hand. For in that moment of generosity, the war is truly over. .

36

On Remembering the
Vietnam War

J. Robert Kerrey

Around the farm, there is an activity that no one likes to do. Yet it is sometimes necessary. When a cat gives birth to kittens that aren't needed, the kittens must be destroyed. And there is a moment when you are holding the kitten under the water when you know that if you bring that kitten back above the water it will live, and if you don't bring it back above in that instant the kitten will be dead. This, for me, is a perfect metaphor for those dreadful moments in war when you do not quite do what you previously thought you would do. I do not choose to recount such moments here now, because I find myself unable and unwilling. However, this is an experience that is not mine alone, but is faced by everyone, whether in war or in peace time: one has a moment in which one makes a decision, and afterwards one feels as if one has fallen from grace. One receives not only one's own judgment, but the judgment of other human beings, and, in the end, the judgment of Almighty God.

I have learned since that time that the fall that occurred with me in Vietnam was not the first time that I fell. I had done so long before this. In fact in Vietnam, what I was able to do in a rather curious and fortunate way was to go to a hospital, where, as a result of having an explosive device go off close to me during a firefight, I had to have a leg amputated from these injuries. Suddenly, for the first time in my life, I was different. I was unable to change it. I was unable to disguise it. I was unable to pretend that it was not so. So now I walk with a limp that I cannot disguise no matter how hard I try. I had to learn—

J. Robert Kerrey is currently junior United States Senator, from the State of Nebraska. Prior to being elected Senator, he was Governor of Nebraska from 1982 to 1986. He is a Veteran of the War in Vietnam, serving with distinction with the Navy Seals, for which valor he was awarded the Congressional Medal of Honor. In 1987 he co-taught a class on the Vietnam War at the University of California, Santa Barbara, and has lectured regularly in the class in succeeding years.

and it was a wonderful thing to learn—that being different is good, and that being different from other people is a good thing. Very closely connected with this recognition was the awareness that I had to attempt to do the most difficult thing of all: to work with my conscience in connecting my own actions and my own behavior with me, Bob Kerrey—not with my parents, my friends, my government, not with anybody else but my own self—and accept the responsibilities of those decisions. I had to accept gratefully the consequences of the decisions that I would make, even when those consequences were not all that I had wanted them to be.

It is a terrifying and yet liberating moment, when instead of feeling the guilt that is attached when you do not live up to somebody else's expectations, you now feel the remorse of conscience for not having done what your own conscience tells you you ought to be doing. A remorse of conscience for me is a liberating feeling, whereas the guilt that is based upon what your expectations (or someone else's expectations) are is a prison. In this prison, under the weight of guilt, I find myself unable to do anything, whereas I find myself being able to do everything in the moment of remorse.

I would also say that I learned in the hospital that I am not unique. I was not the only one to experience pain. Now one of the marvelous functions of the human body is that one forgets pain, otherwise I suspect a woman would not have more than one child. I suspect most of us would not do repetitively what we know we must do because we are afraid and do not wish to experience pain. But we learn, or I have learned, that a little bit of pain can keep me awake.

I have also learned that when you cross the line and have too much pain, it is impossible for you to do anything. Then it is impossible for you to do what, to me, is fundamentally the most human thing of all, and this is to consider the feelings of other people around you. When I am really hurting physically, it is impossible for me to look out and give you much individual consideration at all. I might be able to consider you in the abstract. I might be able to talk about people in the hypothetical. But it is impossible, or extremely difficult, to give much consideration to another person in that moment.

As a consequence of this, I find myself with a political urgency to do something about the homeless. I find myself with a political urgency to do something about health care. Yes, I saw the film *Born On the Fourth of July*, and, yes, the South Bronx VA Hospital is a terrible hospital. But there are hospitals in New York City, in Los Angeles, and in Chicago that are exactly like the hospital Ron Kovic faced in 1968. The pain felt by veterans in the late 1960s, and felt by veterans today, is not a pain that is unique. What I have found myself able to do is to remember. The memory that I carry with me most of all from the pain of the hospital is that the pain is still there for others.

I also carry from the war a belief that place is important. I think we need to have a reverence for place. My friend Gary Parrott, who did three tours in Vietnam, then went back over to work with the CIA in Laos for a couple of years, has good eyes and ears for a culture and for the people around him. He commented that if there is reincarnation, he wanted to come back as a Vietnamese. Parrott had acquired a reverence for the culture and for the Vietnamese people, because he believed that they had a reverence for place. Parrott believes, as I believe, that reverence for place enables us to make good decisions—decisions about how we treat the place we call home, and decisions about how we treat the place that others call home. Panama, for example, is not just the focus of a political decision, but the people who live there: it's a place they call home. El Salvador, Nicaragua, Hungary, Czechoslovakia, Poland, East Germany—all of these nations that we consider as political issues are places and homes for people. Thus, before we intrude with conclusions that we've reached as a consequence of being Democrats or Republicans, or from a desire to please our audiences by impressing them with our knowledge and intelligence, it seems to me that we must have a respect for the place that people identify as home.

In Vietnam, I believe, we did not have the requisite amount of respect for the place that the Vietnamese called home. Yes, it was difficult for many of us to be separated from our families, and to be shipped thousands of miles away to fight a war that in the end very few people supported. But imagine how difficult it must have been to have been a Vietnamese. Think of what it would have been like to be fighting with your family all around you, fighting without being able to leave your home or your family safe thousands of miles behind you—fighting while watching your own homes being burned to the ground, watching your own families being relocated to camps, watching as your homeland was being shattered and changed beyond recognition. It seems to me that we did not have a proper amount of respect for the place the Vietnamese called home. Instead we created too much of an environment at home where Americans had the luxury of being able to decide simply whether we were "for" or "against" the war in Southeast Asia. If you ask me, it was a self-indulgent action, permitting Americans the luxury of sitting in coffee shops, sitting in their living rooms, or talking (as politicians do), sometimes grandly from a lectern, about a belief about what is "right" and "wrong" and is best for all concerned. Such pontificating displays little regard for the sense of place.

In the end, I find myself saying (and being able to say) that the experiences of the war have been decidedly good for me. Yes, I would have preferred to have gotten this experience in some other way. I would rather have acquired the knowledge in some less painful, traumatic fashion. And yet, in the end, I feel fortunate to have been able to go to Vietnam. I feel fortunate to have learned, in the way that I did, that, ultimately unless someone loves you and you love them back, it's not likely that you're ever going to be able to make much progress. In the end, unless you do it with other people, it is not likely that you, all by yourself, are going to be able to become all that you were meant to be. I come away feeling fortunate to have survived, painfully aware that dead men tell no tales, painfully aware too that I have an obligation sometimes to say what I think, what I believe, and occasionally how I feel.

Postscript

Between the time this anthology was completed and the time it was ready for publication there has been another war. We refer, of course, to United States military involvement in the Persian Gulf for purposes of reversing Saddam Hussein's illegitimate seizure of Kuwait. Since our book was already in press, there was no way to provide adequate acknowledgement of these more recent events within its pages, and certainly no way to provide an in-depth assessment of relationships between the two wars.

But the connections are there. When President Bush explained the intention of Desert Storm, he pledged that the nation would avoid the recurrence of the Vietnam War. In sanctioning the President's action, the Congress gave only grudging encouragement, for its members too were acting out of an acutely painful memory. In designing the military action, Generals Norman Schwarzkopf and Colin Powell, both of whom had experienced Vietnam first hand, deliberately protected themselves against involvement in a debilitating episode a second time. And the troops that were sent to the region were promised that they would receive a well-deserved "Welcome Home" at war's end, and would have the nearly unqualified support of the citizenry while they were away from home.

The memory of Vietnam was invoked so that the new war would be conceived and understood as the exact opposite of the previous one. But, as we have noted in this volume, the most compelling interpretations of the Vietnam War work by contrast, opposition, and inversion too. That is, Vietnam is a war that can only be explained by inverting the interpretive categories that apply to wars of rightful expectation.

Thus, since the Vietnam War was not a war of rightful expectation, the Persian Gulf War, by contrast, has become so. The new war succeeded the way American wars are supposed to succeed. It functioned to confirm our best hopes about ourselves, the primacy of the moral cause by which our actions are motivated, and the supremacy of our

317

place within the international community. This makes the new war a "feel good war" like World War II, for it was prompted by the same combination of elements: a diabolical enemy, a menacing global situation, a manifest just cause, and a compelling plea for assistance on the part of a nation that had been invaded.

By being judged as antithesis to a war that was also understood as antithesis, the Persian Gulf War became what the Vietnam War could not be. Would the new war have been necessary had it not also become desirable to take advantage of a situation within which rightful expectation might prevail? We may not know the confident answer to this question for some time. But it is already quite apparent that the new war stands as a dramatic chapter in a continuing and unfinished story about a previous war. Because it finally came out right, from the point of view of intrinsic American interests, the Persian Gulf War will, in the end, turn out to be more about Vietnam than it is about the Middle East.

But subsequent American military successes will not prove to be adequate substitutes for the necessary constructive and reconstructive work that must be undertaken and accomplished "in country." From this vantage point, Vietnam is still with us, less now as a bone stuck in our throats, difficult to swallow, than as a matchless opportunity to manifest and exercise our compassion and good will.

Santa Barbara, California
May 5, 1991